Universal Jurisdiction in Modern International Law: Expansion of National Jurisdiction for Prosecuting Serious Crimes under International Law

SCHOOL OF HUMAN RIGHTS RESEARCH SERIES, Volume 19

The titles published in this series are listed at the end of this volume.

Universal Jurisdiction in Modern International Law: Expansion of National Jurisdiction for Prosecuting Serious Crimes under International Law

Mitsue Inazumi

INTERSENTIA
Antwerpen – Oxford

This Volume is an adapted version of a dissertation defended at Utrecht University on 27 October 2004.

Mitsue Inazumi
Universal Jurisdiction in Modern International Law: Expansion of National Jurisdiction for Prosecuting Serious Crimes under International Law

CRC prepared by: G.J. Wiarda Institute, Utrecht University Institute for Legal Studies, Boothstraat 6, 3512 BW Utrecht

ISBN 90-5095-366-2
D/2005/7849/19
NUR 828

ACKNOWLEDGEMENT

This research forms the basis of my doctoral dissertation submitted to the Faculty of Law at Utrecht University (the Netherlands). I am greatly indebted to my supervisors Prof. G.J.H. van Hoof and Prof. Cees Flinterman, who generously provided me with the opportunity to work on my doctoral thesis and who inspired me with their valuable comments. I would also like to thank the members of the review committee and my 'highly esteemed opponents' (interlocutors) at the defence of my thesis which took place on 27 October 2004: Prof. Menno Kamminga, Prof. Andre Klip, Prof. Geert Jan Knoops, Prof. Peter Baehr, Dr. Annemarieke Beijer, Prof. Chrisje Brants, Prof. Bas de Gaay Fortman, Prof. Constantijn Kelk, Prof. Titia Loenen, Prof. Sacha Prechal, Dr. Goran Sluiter and Prof. J. Vervaele, for their challenging questions and stirring comments, and am especially grateful to the chairman, Dr. Alfred H.A. Soons, in this regard. I am grateful to my friends Ms. Chiseche Mibenge and Mrs. Maria Nybondas for assisting me and providing encouragement throughout my defence.

During the process of writing this thesis, I also benefited from the encouragement and highly intellectual advice of my friend, Dr. Goran Sluiter. I would also like to express my gratitude to my former colleagues at the Netherlands Institute of Human Rights (SIM) at Utrecht University for welcoming me like their family and offering me a great academic environment, making my stay in the Netherlands comfortable. I also very much appreciate the many efforts of my colleagues at Kanazawa University in Japan, especially my former colleague Prof. Masahiro Igarashi for giving me the time to conduct my research in the Netherlands. Special thanks are extended to the Wiarda Institute of Utrecht University:, Mr. Peter Morris, Mrs. Titia Kloos, and Mrs. Willemien Vreekamp for efficiently assisting me in finalizing my text for the book. Finally, I could never have completed my thesis without the warm support and unconditional love of my mother Kiseko and my family.

Mitsue Inazumi
Kanazawa, Ishikawa, Japan
January 2005

TABLE OF CONTENTS

Chapter I
Introduction

1 Theme of the Study

The twentieth century is often referred to as the bloodiest century in human history. Modern international law was developed as a result of the strong condemnation of the brutal atrocities committed during the Second World War, placing emphasis on the maintenance of peace and the protection of human rights. As one means of preventing the recurrence of similar atrocities, international law has categorized and condemned certain acts such as genocide and crimes against humanity, and promulgated that their prevention and punishment are within the concern of the international community. Yet up until today, we have continued to witness crimes amounting to systematic and massive violations of human rights. Observing how the international community has failed to deter such crimes, scholars and activists have long searched for ways to prevent and punish them, and have submitted various proposals to enhance the exercise of jurisdiction by States or by international organs over these crimes. But it has taken further bloodshed to provide the necessary momentum to substantially advance the formation of a more extensive jurisdictional regime to that end. The large-scale genocide and other heinous crimes in Yugoslavia and Rwanda in the 1990s shocked the international community, inducing it to reaffirm its commitment to punish and prevent such crimes and to end the adverse effect of the prevalence of impunity.[1] Impunity arises from 'a failure by States to meet their obligations to investigate violations, to take appropriate measures in respect of the perpetrators, particularly in the area of justice, by ensuring that they are prosecuted, tried and duly punished, to provide victims with effective remedies and reparation for the injuries suffered, and to take steps to prevent any recurrence of such violations.'[2] The international community has become less tolerant of such failures.

In order to end impunity, the international community established international criminal courts, namely, the International Criminal Tribunal for the Former Yugoslavia

---

1 Impunity is defined as 'the impossibility, *de jure* or de facto, of bringing the perpetrators of human rights violations to account – whether in criminal, civil, administrative or disciplinary proceedings – since they are not subject to any inquiry that might lead to their being accused, arrested, tried and, if found guilty, sentenced to appropriate penalties, and to make reparation to their victims.' 'Set of Principles for the Protection and Promotion of Human Rights Through Action to Combat Impunity', Annex to the Question of the Impunity of Perpetrators of Human Rights Violations (civil and political), revised final report prepared by Mr. Joinet, UN Doc. E/CN.4/Sub.2/1997/20/Rev.1.

2 *Ibid.*, Principle 18.

(ICTY),[3] the International Criminal Tribunal for Rwanda (ICTR),[4] and the International Criminal Court (ICC).[5] Furthermore, it also urged States to exercise their jurisdiction to prosecute and punish individuals responsible for committing such crimes.[6] Under this campaign to end impunity, States have started to take a more active role in prosecution. For instance, the Pinochet Case[7] was most notorious for Spain's innovative effort to seek the extradition of a former head of State. This case attracted attention to and prompted intensive discussions about the prosecution of serious crimes, opening the door for other States to follow and take an active role in enforcing international law.

Recognising that the prosecution of individuals responsible for such acts promotes the better realisation of human rights and the prevention of crimes in the future, as well as institutionalising the rule of law,[8] this study is devoted to an examination of the jurisdictional regime under international law for the prosecution of individuals for criminal responsibility for gross and serious violations of human rights.

Throughout this study, the term jurisdictional 'regime' or 'system' is used to refer to the general structure in which various national and international jurisdictions function. However, as I will demonstrate in this writing, the current state of affairs is less than a systematically institutionalised framework constructed in accordance with clear rules and principles of international law. This ambiguity underlies a primary

3 The International Tribunal for the Prosecution of Persons Responsible for Serious Violations of International Humanitarian Law Committed in the territory of the Former Yugoslavia Since 1991. For the Statute of the ICTY, see UN Doc. S/25704, annex (1993), reprinted in 32 *International Legal Materials* 1192 (1993).

4 The International Criminal Tribunal for the Prosecution of Persons Responsible for Genocide and Other Serious Violations of International Humanitarian Law Committed in the Territory of Rwanda and Rwandan Citizens Responsible for Genocide and Other Such Violations Committed in the Territory of Neighbouring States. For the Statute of ICTR, see Security Council Resolution 955, annex, reprinted in 33 *International Legal Materials* 1602 (1994).

5 International Criminal Court. See Rome Statute of the International Criminal Court, UN Doc. A/CONF.183/9, reprinted in 37 *International Legal Materials* 999 (1998).

6 The Secretary-General recommended that the Security Council should, '[p]ending the establishment of the International Criminal Court, encourage the development of judicial and investigative mechanisms with national and international components, which may be used when the prosecution of those responsible for genocide, crimes against humanity and war crimes in either national or international tribunals appears unlikely given the unwillingness or inability of the parties involved.' 'Report of the Secretary-General to the Security Council on the Protection of Civilians in Armed Conflict', UN Doc. S/1999/957, p. 10, Recommendation B5.

7 For the detail of the Pinochet Case, see Chapter III of this study.

8 'The rule of law, sometimes called "the supremacy of law", provides that decisions should be made by the application of known principles or laws without the intervention of discretion in their application.' Henry Campbell Black, *Black's Law Dictionary* 6th ed. (West Publishing Co., 1990), p. 1332. On the other hand, when invoked in the context of international law, it refers to 'an international order based on compliance with international law ... as opposed to an order determined by power or expediency.' See Bruce Broomhall, *International Justice and the International Criminal Court: Between Sovereignty and the Rule of Law* (Oxford University Press, 2003), p. 53. In this study, 'the rule of law' is used in both the international and domestic connotations explained above depending on the context.

objective of this study to structure and describe the current situation and to delineate some rules on the jurisdictional matter under international law.

2 Central Question of the Study

This study originates from an inquiry into how to end the impunity of individuals responsible for gross and serious violations of human rights. This study is based on the following questions: *Which jurisdiction can and should be exercised for the prosecution of individuals responsible for gross and serious violations of human rights? And especially, in this regard, what is the role of universal jurisdiction?*

One should bear in mind that the possible answers to these questions may differ as time passes. For instance, under the classical jurisdictional regime, the answer generally given to the first question would be territorial jurisdiction. Therefore, in investigating international law in search of an answer to this question, it is important to examine law at the time of and in the circumstances pertaining to the society in which the law is functioning. In addition, rather than adhering to the *lex lata*, we should inquire into how the law has changed and what has caused the change in order to gain a broader perspective, which will help to indicate the development of the law in the future.

I recognise that the above question includes two different aspects: the legality of jurisdiction (including whether or not there is an obligation to exercise jurisdiction), and the appropriateness thereof. I also recognise that these two aspects are different in nature. The first is concerned with the legality and recognition of a basis for jurisdiction under international law, while the second relates to the behaviour in exercising such jurisdiction. Yet, these two are argued interrelatedly in scholarly discussions, as well as in practice. For instance, the status of jurisdiction is evaluated based on an assessment of the ability of a particular State in being effective, efficient, and rendering justice in a fair and impartial manner. By analysing both aspects, this study intends to show how international law is changing towards taking the appropriateness of this exercise in addition to its legality into consideration.

The search for an answer to the legality of jurisdiction requires an exploration of the definition and legal status of each basis of national jurisdiction in conventional and customary international law. How is the jurisdictional regime structured under international law? What are the norms regulating the jurisdictional regime? The question of norms entails a consideration of the relationship between various bases of jurisdiction, any rules on priority, and other rules and principles that States must respect in exercising jurisdiction. In addition, the significance of these rules also needs to be considered within the historical development of international criminal law.

Apart from describing *lex lata*, this study endeavours to present certain propositions. The proposition that links the fairness and impartiality of a court with the primacy over other competing claims of jurisdiction will be examined. The inferences deduced from contemplating the above questions are expected to shed some light on the relations between jurisdictional bases, together with some future prospects for the exercise of national jurisdiction over individuals responsible for gross and serious violations of human rights.

3 Aim of the Study

The aim of this study is to clarify the overall structure of the present-day jurisdictional regime. Whereas today's jurisdictional regime in an international context is formulated in the form of the concurrency of both national and international jurisdictions, the present study focuses on national jurisdiction in order to define the role of States in the enforcement of international criminal, humanitarian, and human rights law.

In explaining the modern jurisdictional regime, this study illuminates the phenomenon referred to here as the *'expansion'* of jurisdiction – theoretical and practical enhancement in the recognition, acceptance as well as the application of various bases of jurisdiction. I consider this phenomenon to be the major change that has instigated the modern jurisdictional regime to depart from some traditional principles that dominated the classical jurisdictional regime. In order to exemplify the change from the classical to the modern jurisdictional regime, and also to illuminate the tension between different bases of jurisdiction, this study adopts a special categorization to distinguish territorial jurisdiction and other bases of national jurisdiction. In this study, bases of States' jurisdiction other than territorial jurisdiction are referred to as '*non-territorial jurisdiction*'. As this study explains in detail later, various bases of national jurisdiction have been expanded considerably under conventional international law since the 1970s, through the attempt to overcome the failure of territorial jurisdiction in ending impunity.

Amongst the various non-territorial bases of jurisdiction acknowledged under international law, this study conducts in-depth research particularly into universal jurisdiction – a form of national jurisdiction based on the custody or presence of suspects or, instead, according to some, based exclusively on the assumption that the serious nature and gravity of certain crimes allows any State to exercise jurisdiction.[9] An analysis of universal jurisdiction constitutes the core of this study because it is the most prominent jurisdictional basis for its innovative nature in international law and, as this study indicates, forms a vital basis for distinguishing the jurisdictional regime of today from the classical jurisdictional regime.[10] However, at the same time it is strongly disputed both at the theoretical and practical level. In this respect, this study aims to build on earlier academic research into universal jurisdiction such as the

9 A more extensive consideration of the definition of universal jurisdiction is to be found in Chapter IV of the present study.

10 In order to illuminate the changes, a distinction is made throughout this study between law before and after the Second World War. See the explanation on the time frame of this study later in this chapter.

Princeton Principles,[11] the Cairo-Arusha Principles,[12] and Kamminga's report on behalf of the International Law Association.[13] Furthermore, this study adds to the said research by not only studying the phenomenon of universal jurisdiction, but also its legal status and propriety within the jurisdictional regime.

After analysing the historical formation as well as the components of the modern jurisdictional regime, this study addresses one of the problems which is persistent in the concurrency of jurisdictions – the problem of jurisdictional conflicts. Jurisdictional conflicts are noted in the form of a *negative conflict* – when there is no State or other entity willing to prosecute a case – or a *positive conflict* – when there is more than one State or entity willing to prosecute the same case. To begin with, the modern jurisdictional regime has chosen concurrency of jurisdiction in order to prevent negative conflicts. However, norms are not yet sufficiently clear and developed to prevent and solve negative conflicts, and even more so for positive conflicts. In the current state of the modern jurisdictional regime, which is characterised by the concurrency of various jurisdictions, many questions are waiting to be answered. What will happen if a State claims that the exercise of jurisdiction by another State is illegal? What will happen if two or more States wish to exercise jurisdiction simultaneously? Conversely, what if there is no State willing to exercise jurisdiction? The first two problems are more visible than the latter, since they may manifest themselves as an international dispute. In fact, in recent years we have seen many conflicts between States concerning jurisdiction.[14] Many conflicts have the potential of aggravating serious adversarial relations between States, as well as threatening the maintenance of peace and security amongst States. In order to safeguard international security, it is therefore imperative to clarify the regulations concerning jurisdiction.

This study intends to go further than identifying the problem of jurisdictional conflicts. It takes an in-depth approach in tentatively setting forth some guiding rules to be taken into consideration in solving jurisdictional conflicts. The proclamation of the guiding rules is a new attempt, but it cannot be dismissed as a mere suggestion, since the criteria presented are extracted from norms established and evidence found under international law. This study especially takes cognisance of criteria that stipulate the exercise of national jurisdiction in a fair and impartial manner, and also promote due regard of human rights.

Also, this study presents the following hypothetical and somewhat extreme question in order to elucidate the needs of 'non-territorial jurisdiction'. Bearing in mind

---

11 Princeton Project on Universal Jurisdiction, *The Princeton Principles on Universal Jurisdiction* (Program in Law and Public Affairs, Princeton University, 2001).

12 Africa Legal Aid (AFLA), the Cairo-Arusha Principle on Universal Jurisdiction in Respect of Gross Human Rights Offences: An African Perspectives, adopted at the Follow-up Expert Meeting held at Arusha, 18-20 October 2002, http://www.afla.unimaas.nl/en/act/index.html.

13 International Law Association (Committee on International Human Rights Law and Practice), Final Report on the Exercise of Universal Jurisdiction in respect of Gross Human Rights Offences, 2000.

14 The examples and problems of jurisdictional conflicts are elaborated in Chapter V.

that the establishment of international criminal courts and the expansion of non-territorial jurisdiction (including universal jurisdiction) was instigated due to the failure of territorial jurisdiction to be exercised promptly and effectively in a fair and impartial manner, then if we could improve the system to diminish that failure, would we still need international criminal courts or non-territorial jurisdiction?

The present study intends to examine the jurisdictional regime for the following reasons. To begin with, there is a need to systematically recapture the structure and dynamics of the existing jurisdictional regime. As the complexity of law increases, many scholarly works closely follow individual phenomena revealing complex findings, but some fail to place them in a larger perspective. It is important to understand and place such findings within a context in order to appreciate them fully. We should not only look at the exercise of each national jurisdiction, but also try to recognize a system, a framework in which it functions. Even for studies on international criminal jurisdiction (such as that of the ICTY, ICTR or ICC), it is imperative to bear in mind the role of national courts and the existing jurisdictional regime.

Furthermore, there is a substantial ambiguity in law concerning the exercise of national jurisdiction which needs to be clarified in order to prevent and solve jurisdictional conflicts. This ambiguity derives from the substantial realm left to the discretion of States, as well as the uncertainty of law caused by the rapid and radical development of international criminal and humanitarian law. For instance, although widely observed in conventional international law, to what extent the expansion of national jurisdictions has become a part of customary international law remains uncertain. In addition, although the modern jurisdictional regime has promoted the concurrency of jurisdictions to foster a great increase in the possibility of actual prosecution, it has not explicitly shown to States a clear norm allocating the competence and obligation to adjudicate. Consequently, impunity may still prevail as the result of jurisdictional conflicts and uncertainty as to which State can/should exercise its jurisdiction.

In sum, this study is intended to contribute to clarifying the extent to which the content and legal status of the substantive norms of the jurisdictional regime are sufficiently clear and precise, together with lessening the existing perplexity and ambiguities arising from *lex lata* norms governing States' exercise of their criminal jurisdiction. Furthermore, this study presents some propositions for realizing effective and impartial trials, and for solving jurisdictional conflicts.

4 Scope of the Study

4.1 Jurisdiction over which Crimes?

The crimes and cases that are the subject of this study are limited to those human rights violations prohibited by international law and of such criminal gravity as to fall within the scope of the exercise of universal jurisdiction. Therefore, less grave crimes characterised as 'ordinary crimes', which fall within the ambit of a domestic legal regime will be excluded from consideration.

This study addresses jurisdiction over crimes undermining the most fundamental human rights, such as the right to life or to human dignity, committed in a systematic or massive manner, irrespective of whether they were committed in an international or non-international conflict, or in an armed conflict or not.

Gross and serious human rights violations may also become the subject of prohibition and punishment under international humanitarian law, since they are often committed during armed conflicts. It is not surprising that there is an overlap between international human rights law and international humanitarian law, since the development of the latter was promoted by respect for human rights.[15] Consequently, many war crimes and crimes against humanity also fall within the scope of this study. However, the crimes examined in this study cannot be encompassed entirely by the category of 'crimes against humanity', since they also include crimes committed during unarmed conflict or internal disturbances.

Even in a non-international conflict or internal disturbance, the commission of grave crimes is not justified as they violate the most basic human rights that cannot be derogated from in any circumstances. Article 4(1) of the United Nations Covenant on Civil and Political Rights (1966) provides that State Parties may derogate from obligations under the Covenant during times of emergency if such emergency is on such a scale that it 'threatens the life of the nation'. However, Article 4(2) makes it clear that for some fundamental human rights such as the right to life (Article 6), to be free from torture, inhuman and degrading treatment (Article 7), and from slavery (Article 8), States may not derogate therefrom under any circumstances. Thus, those violations will not be justified even in a state of emergency in a State. In addition, as to the crime of genocide and similar crimes, their prohibition particular is acknowledged to be an obligation *erga omnes*.[16] In particular, serious and gross crimes of war and crimes against humanity, genocide, torture, and slavery fall within the subject of this study.

4.2 The Time Frame of the Subject of the Study

Throughout this study a distinction is made between law before and after the Second World War. General international law of the former period is described as 'classic' or 'traditional' international law, while the latter is referred to as 'modern' or 'contemporary' international law. And, accordingly, this study refers to the jurisdictional system in the former period as the '*classical jurisdictional regime*' while that in the latter period as the '*modern jurisdictional regime*'. Although this study analyses the classical

15 See Theodor Meron 'The Humanization of Humanitarian Law' *American Journal of International Law* Vol. 94 No. 2 (April, 2000).

16 See the Case concerning Barcelona Traction, Light and Power Company, Limited (*Belgium* v. *Spain*), *ICJ Reports 1970*, p. 32. The notion of *erga omnes* and its effect on the expansion of national jurisdiction is illustrated in Chapter III, and its relation with universal jurisdiction is discussed in chapter IV.

jurisdictional regime as well, this is done in order to highlight the change in, and the characteristics of the modern jurisdictional regime.

In discussing the development of a jurisdictional regime to punish individuals responsible for gross and serious human rights violations from an international law perspective, we must bear in mind that it was only after the Second World War and since the establishment of the United Nations (UN) that the respect for human rights and accountability for serious crimes have been widely recognised to be of international concern. Under classical international law, what we now call human rights was generally treated as a domestic matter, not as an international concern. Consequently, international law did not intervene in the human rights practices of States except in limited situations, such as for the protection of the rights of foreigners or of minorities. It was only after the horrific tragedies of gross human rights violations committed during the Second World War that the world came to realize the need to obligate States to respect human rights and to develop systems to enforce such prohibitions. As the notion of human rights developed and as the international community began to increasingly appreciate its value, the subject of human rights became an important part of international law.[17]

In order to illuminate how and why international law concerning jurisdiction has developed, this study divides time into four periods. *The first period* covers the time before the Second World War, which is within classical international law, in which the classical jurisdictional regime existed. The time span of *the second period* is from the aftermath of the Second World War to the end of the 1960s. *The third period* is the 1970s and the 1980s. Finally, *the fourth period* dates from the 1990s to the present. This division of time into four periods, each marked by events having an impact on the law, serves to clarify more explicitly the changes of political and ethical situations and concerns of the international community that has inspired changes in the law.

4.3 Other Enforcement Mechanisms for Accountability

This study concentrates on jurisdiction to prosecute and punish individuals for serious violations of human rights. I recognize that there are many other mechanisms established under international law to respond to such violations, some within the U.N. and others established by multilateral treaties. As to the measures involving accountability for crimes, there are fact-finding measures such as an investigatory commission or a truth commission which could also be established based on the national law. A State may choose to pursue the accountability of individuals responsible for violations in combination with an acknowledgment of the truth through some commission of

17 Apart from the appreciation of their value in the minds of the members of the international community, a political motive is also noted as the key factor. What induced human rights to be one of the fundamental values in international law was the political motive of powerful States, which justified the war against the Axis States as the fight for freedom and human rights.

inquiry. Ratner and Abrams include the following consideration as one of the general principles which is relevant in choosing the means of pursuing justice:

> 'Any mechanism can only work with the support of the people of the particular state. Although the crimes concern all mankind, it is ultimately the people of a state – past, present, and future – who remain most affected. If they have a democratically elected government, it must be their primary voice on this question. If that government rejects accountability in favour of a compromise with former abusers, amnesty, or other forms of impunity, or seeks to use accountability as a weapon against political enemies, almost any effort at accountability seems crippled, if not stillborn.'[18]

It is my belief that territorial States generally have a duty to address violations. They should confront the criminality of such violations and express some form of accusation for future deterrence. This can be done by appointing a truth commission or seeking the judicial prosecution of individuals, or by other means. In any case, such violations should not be ignored or tolerated. This study concentrates on the legal proceedings in pursuit of individual criminal responsibility.

4.4 Entity Responsible for Crimes

The present study focuses on criminal justice proceedings against natural persons. This study is based on the recognition of the importance of pursuing individual criminal responsibility in enforcing international human rights law. However, an act by an individual may be attributed to a State in certain situations. For example, when an individual has acted as an agent or on behalf of the State. The present study is without prejudice towards the issue of State responsibility. However, because of the scale and gravity of the crimes considered in this study, these acts are mostly committed by persons acting as members of the government or the military, or a group with particular political intent, such as a liberation group or ethnic group, etc. The possible involvement of the State in acts of individuals and its effect on the exercise of jurisdiction are addressed later. The main subject of this study, however, concentrates on the individual responsibility of persons committing such acts, not on the collective responsibility of the group behind the perpetration of such atrocities.

18 Steven R. Ratner and Jason S. Abrams, *Accountability for Human Rights Atrocities in International Law: Beyond the Nuremberg Legacy* (Oxford University Press, 2001), p. 343.

4.5 Which Kinds of Jurisdiction?

This study considers the jurisdiction[19] to prosecute individuals for serious violations of human rights. Jurisdiction in civil cases is excluded.[20]

This study examines national jurisdiction for prosecuting and punishing individuals, therefore mainly the jurisdiction exercised by courts. In addition to the trial in the courts, this study examines the pre-trial exercise of jurisdiction. Therefore it includes the claiming of jurisdiction by a State over a case such as the issuing of an arrest warrant, and requesting the extradition of a suspect from abroad. These State actions for exercising jurisdiction are valuable in determining the legal status of each jurisdictional basis under international law. This is because such actions are expected to originate from at least one valid jurisdictional base, and they symbolise the fact that a State is formally claiming its entitlement to prosecute a suspect to another States.

In dealing with the competence of States to prosecute and punish international crimes, this study analyses the various basis of jurisdiction. It deals with related problems, such as the abduction of suspects, only to the extent that they have influence on the assertion of basis for jurisdiction.

4.6 National or International Jurisdiction?

Among the various jurisdictions recognized in today's concurrent jurisdictional regime, the subject matter of this study is national jurisdiction, particularly universal jurisdiction exercised by States. International criminal jurisdiction – the jurisdiction exercised by international criminal courts such as the ICTY, ICTR, and ICC – is not an independent subject for thorough research in the present study. The focus here is on national jurisdiction because: 1) domestic courts are the primary forum for prosecuting individuals for crimes; and 2) rules and regulations which the international criminal courts must obey are legislated in written form, thus they are sufficiently clearer under conventional international law while, on the other hand, rules which States must respect in exercising their national jurisdiction are often not formulated in a written, clear form in international law; and 3) the above-mentioned ambiguity of rules may cause impunity and injustice and, moreover, a dangerous dispute among States over conflicts relating to jurisdiction. In addition, there are many contemporary academic studies on international criminal courts, but there are few on national jurisdiction that comprehensively examine the jurisdictional regime as a whole.

---

19 Jurisdiction is defined as 'powers exercised by a State over persons, property, or events.' P. Malanczuk, *Akehurst's Modern Introduction to International Law*, 7th ed. (1997), p. 109.

20 There are civil proceedings providing an opportunity for victims of certain international crimes to seek monetary compensation for damages against perpetrators, such as the Alien Tort Claim Act in the United States. However, they deal with civil cases, and do not adjudicate criminal responsibility, therefore they will not be studied in this research. The question of jurisdiction over civil cases is generally within the sphere of private international law and the law of conflict.

4.7 International Criminal, Humanitarian, Human rights Law in Correlation

Notwithstanding the existence of some rules and practice involving criminal matters or human rights in classic international law, it is only in modern international law that the branches of *international criminal law* and *international human rights law* have come to be widely recognized. 'International human rights law' has only fully developed after the establishment of the UN system. As for the branch of international criminal law, it is possible to trace it back to the rules under a classical jurisdictional regime concerning criminal matters, which were composed mainly by rules on inter-State actions against transnational crime, such as the extradition of ordinary criminals. However, its ascent to, and its importance as a field of international law became more commonly acknowledged after the international community underscored the fact that international law imposes criminal responsibility upon individuals for serious crimes. Therefore, international human rights law and criminal law are fairly new in being crystallized into a legal field of norms. On the other hand, *international humanitarian law* has its roots in laws of war which have a long history well back in classic international law. Yet it is only under modern international law that the heading of 'international humanitarian law' has started to be utilised, placing emphasis on the humanitarian concern for and the human rights of war victims rather than military necessity. Although these three disciplines of law are different, there are substantial overlaps as well as interdependency between them. Therefore, they should be studied in correlation.

5 Method of the Study

5.1 Theoretical Approach

This study examines various international instruments and the practice of States in order to ascertain rules on jurisdiction. It employs a theoretical approach in determining the role of States in enforcing international law, and the definition and nature of the basis of national jurisdiction. The analysis is conducted bearing in mind the four fundamental objectives that international law has in regulating jurisdiction.[21] The four objectives are described as follows. The first is to establish limits of jurisdiction that protect the independence and sovereign equality of States by balancing each State's interest in exercising jurisdiction. The second is to recognize the interdependence of States by ensuring that effective jurisdiction exists to achieve certain common objectives of States. The third is to harmonize the rights of two or more States when they have concurrent jurisdiction. And, lastly, the fourth is to protect individuals from unreasonable exercises of jurisdiction by States.

---

21 See Bernard H. Oxman 'Jurisdiction of States', in Rudolf Bernhardt (ed.), *Encyclopedia of Public International Law* Vol. 3 (Elsevier Science, 1997), p. 56.

With these objectives in mind, this study illuminates the tension and balance between various notions, namely, between the classical and modern jurisdictional regime, territorial and non-territorial jurisdiction, and State sovereignty and the interest of the international community as a whole as well as the interests of individuals.

5.2 Perspective of Law in Transition

All law reflects the society that it regulates, and is transformed as society changes. This changing character suggests that law should not be recognised only in *status quo*, but in the context of society and of the whole process of legal transition. By following this premise, we can perceive the significance of a specific law from a wider perspective. Accordingly, a historical approach is taken in investigating the formation of the current jurisdictional system and rules on jurisdiction. It thereby enables this study to capture these developments in their broader historical context.

Retaining a historical approach should not be understood to mean that this study restricts itself to a description of events and anecdotes. As explained earlier, this study divides time into four periods in order to highlight the transition of law, and it further analyses how rules of international law were/are perceived by States and scholars in each period. This is done through examining the domestic law of States, treaties and conventions, and both domestic and international cases, as well as the legal literature. Among various scholarly bodies of research, the drafts of conventions prepared by the Harvard Law School are especially noteworthy and valuable in understanding the classical jurisdictional regime since the research was based on a careful and detailed compilation of numerous domestic laws and practices of States as well as works of scholars during the first period (the time of classic international law). Hence this study takes note of and evaluates the draft of the convention on 'Jurisdiction with Respect to Crime' (hereafter referred to as the Harvard Research) and the draft of the convention on 'Extradition' under the auspices of the Harvard Law School in relevant chapters below. Another work by scholars that is often referred to by various courts and scholars as an authentic annotation of international law concerning jurisdiction is the Restatement of the Law of Foreign Relations Law of the United States, which is published by the American Law Institute. The Restatement is a compilation of pieces of domestic and international law that is applicable to the United States with comments. It is not a law as such, but rather an interpretation by a group of scholars, and therefore it is not legally binding. Nevertheless, it has a great influence as an authoritative prominent interpretation and is cited by many scholars and courts throughout the world. This study especially examines the third version of the Restatement published in 1987 (hereafter referred to as the Third Restatement) to explain the transition of the nature of universal jurisdiction from the second to the third period.

The main objective in adopting a historical approach is to evaluate the changes as a part of the whole development of international law within its social context and in conjunction with the changes in the international community. My analysis of the system of concurrent jurisdiction is not only descriptive, but examines the conflicts with traditional principles and, furthermore, offers an insight into the future through searching for means to assure effective functioning of that system. Assessments bearing in mind the transitional character of law enable this study to foresee the promises and problems of the emerging system and norms under the modern jurisdictional regime. This is particularly important because international norms on the jurisdictional regime seem to be still undergoing rapid development. An evaluation of the norms and regime should be made with the recognition that they are social institutions in a society changing over time.

6 Structure of the Study

The structure of this study is as follows. First, in the next chapter, I will briefly sketch the development of the current jurisdictional regime, and explain how States are expected to play a greater role in international law enforcement. After summarizing the classical jurisdictional regime, this study explains how and why the most basic jurisdiction – territorial jurisdiction – was not effectively exercised against gross human rights violations. Then I will illustrate how the shortcomings of territorial jurisdiction stimulated the phenomenon of the 'expansion' of national jurisdictions since the 1970s – the phenomenon in which non-territorial jurisdiction is specifically incorporated into the provisions of treaties and conventions. In addition, this chapter describes how this phenomenon has instigated conflicts with some traditional rules and principles of international law.

Next, Chapter III addresses the most prominent and controversial development of national jurisdiction – the development of universal jurisdiction. This chapter examines the history of its development. This study intentionally conducts examination of the history of universal jurisdiction before its theoretical examination because the history shows how its notion has changed over the years.

Based on the examination in Chapter III, Chapter IV conducts a theoretical analysis of the notion of universal jurisdiction. There is great uncertainty and dispute concerning the definition and nature of universal jurisdiction. What is the definition of universal jurisdiction? Can it be claimed by a State not having the presence of suspects within its territory? Is it a right or an obligation? Is exhausting the effort to extradite suspects to other States a prerequisite? This study clarifies the definition and characteristics of universal jurisdiction through an analysis of its expansion observed in State practice and in academic literature, which is elaborated in Chapter III. Although many scholars make an analogy between the universal jurisdiction of States and the jurisdiction of the international criminal courts, I elucidate the theoretical and practical differences between them.

After illustrating the phenomenon of the expansion of national jurisdiction that has formed today's jurisdictional regime in the above chapters, I recapture the state of the current jurisdictional system and observe the problem of jurisdictional conflicts in Chapter V. It illustrates the flaws of the jurisdictional regime and the current state of uncertainty in rules on jurisdiction. Furthermore, this chapter considers some guiding rules for solving jurisdictional conflicts. It examines criteria to be taken into consideration in deciding the venue of a trial. The criteria include the appropriateness of national jurisdiction in the light of their ability to conduct proceedings in a fair and impartial manner, respecting fundamental rights of the accused and due process. I examine the argument that no entity has the power to try individuals responsible for gross human rights violations unless proceedings are effective, efficient, and capable of rendering justice in a fair and impartial manner.

Chapter VI tentatively applies these guiding rules in order to determine the appropriateness of non-territorial jurisdiction, including universal jurisdiction. This chapter concludes that non-territorial jurisdictions, including universal jurisdiction, are not *per se* inappropriate. Although the preference for territorial jurisdiction remains to some extent in the modern jurisdictional regime, non-territorial jurisdiction is considered to be desirable in certain situations. It depends on the circumstance of each individual case, and the guiding rules should be taken into consideration in each case.

Finally, Chapter VII recaptures the observations made in this study. This study recognises that non-territorial jurisdiction – especially universal jurisdiction – is attracting growing expectations from many scholars and activists that it will play a greater role in the future. But, at the same time, this study takes note the reluctant or sometimes repulsive attitude from States toward its exercise. This concluding chapter presents some propositions concerning the prosecution and punishment of individuals responsible for gross and serious violations of human rights. The observations and propositions presented in this chapter aims to illustrate the essence and the role of territorial jurisdiction and non-territorial jurisdiction under the modern jurisdictional regime.

CHAPTER II
OVERVIEW OF THE MODERN JURISDICTIONAL REGIME

1 INTRODUCTION

The objective of this chapter is to illustrate the overall picture of the modern jurisdictional regime. At the outset, it is important to reiterate some basic principles related to the issue of jurisdiction in order to understand the premises of and the background to the current jurisdictional system under international law. After a brief explanation of each principle, I shall introduce the historical development of the current jurisdictional regime.

2 RELEVANT BASIC NORMS

2.1 Principle of State Sovereignty

State sovereignty is a principle forming a basic pillar in international law. Brownlie states that the principal corollaries of the sovereignty and equality of States are '(1) a jurisdiction, prima facie exclusive, over a territory and the permanent population living there; (2) a duty of non-intervention in the area of exclusive jurisdiction of other states; and (3) the dependence of obligations arising from customary law and treaties on the consent of the obligor.'[1]
The relation between international law and States is explained by the Permanent Court of International Justice (PCIJ) as follows:

> 'International law governs relations between independent States. The rules of law binding upon States therefore emanate from their own free will as expressed in conventions or by usages generally accepted as expressing principles of law and established in order to regulate the relations between these co-existing communities or with a view to the achievement of common aims. Restrictions upon independence of States cannot therefore be presumed.'[2]

Ramifications of the entrenchment of the concept of State sovereignty in relation to international criminal law are described as follows: No interference in the domestic affairs of another sovereign State, leading to the doctrine of sovereign or State immu-

---

1 Brownlie, *Principles of Public International Law*, 4th ed. (Oxford University Press, 1990), p. 285.

2 The Case of the SS. Lotus (*France* v. *Turkey*), PCIJ Judgement of 7 September 1927, PCIJ Rep., Series A, No. 10, pp. 18-19.

nity and the act of State doctrine; and territorial jurisdiction as the primary basis for criminal jurisdiction.[3]

In general, enforcement of criminal law has been a power enjoyed almost exclusively by States. Legislation and enforcement of criminal law are one of the principal attributors of State sovereignty, thus they are regarded as being within the scope of domestic matters. Each individual State may freely legislate and apply its domestic criminal law, and enforce it through its authorities such as the police and the court system. When a crime has been committed, the power to try suspects and to decide on their punishment belongs to States. Consequently, other States or international law cannot intervene according to the principle which respects State sovereignty. Especially because traditional international law was based on the principle of absolute State sovereignty, it is understandable that international law generally did not have extensive and decisive rules and principles concerning national jurisdiction. Whenever international law starts to impose or merely imply some form of intervention in the exercise of jurisdiction by States, or to obligate States to exercise it in one way or another, States may fervently object by arguing that it is the interest of the State which is at stake.

Likewise, intervention on the part of other States receives even more vigorous criticism. It is still a general rule today that the administration of justice in a State is free from other States' intervention.[4] The tension between the notion of State sovereignty and a judicial action or even an attempt to do so by an international entity or foreign State in pursuit of individual responsibility is relatively apparent, since jurisdiction is a manifestation of State sovereignty.[5] Because applying the law and prosecuting individuals is one of the most basic and fundamental powers of a State, it is not surprising that States are generally reluctant to accept interference from international law or other entities (including international organizations) in this sacrosanct domain of sovereignty.

The exercise of jurisdiction over serious crimes involves the question of State sovereignty, together with the tension between national and international concerns – the benefit and interest of an individual State on the one hand, and the international community as a whole on the other. While the international community acknowledges the need to establish a system to supervise, prevent, and sanction breaches of international human rights obligations, especially those amounting to serious crimes, some States are reluctant to depart from the traditional attitude – that human rights are

3 Kriangsak Kittichaisaree, *International Criminal Law* (Oxford University Press, 2001), p. 6.

4 States have the right to freely determine without external interference their political status, and to pursue their economic, social and cultural development. See the 1970 Declaration on Principles of International Law concerning Friendly Relations and Co-operation among States, General Assembly Resolution 2625 (XXV) of 1970, UN Doc. A/8082, reprinted in *American Journal of International Law* Vol. 65 (1971), p. 243.

5 D.W. Bowett 'Jurisdiction: Changing Patterns of Authority over Activities and Resources' *British Year Book of International Law* Vol. 53 (1982), p.1. R.Y. Jennings 'The Limits of State Jurisdiction' *Nordisk Tidsskrift for International ret og Jus Gentium* Vol. 32 (1962), p. 209.

domestic matters, and that the power to prosecute individuals belongs exclusively to States, and also that such a power lies generally in the hands of the State of the territory where the crime was committed. For example, especially in the early days of modern international law, many States were not eager to establish an international criminal court. States invoked the principle of non-intervention[6] and State sovereignty to block any restriction on their discretion in exercising their jurisdiction over individuals.[7] Consequently, even in the age of modern international law, despite a considerable improvement in the international legislation prohibiting gross human rights violations, the measure to prosecute individuals responsible for crimes – one of the actual enforcement mechanisms of the prohibition – very much remained under the influence of traditional principles and the attitudes of States adhering to them.

2.2 The Applicability of International Law to Issues of Jurisdiction

States possess the power to prosecute individuals, as the Permanent Court of International Justice (PCIJ) confirmed that jurisdiction is a sovereign power.[8] Nevertheless, this does not imply that States can exercise jurisdiction without any respect for international law. The PCIJ also declared that States can exercise their jurisdiction within the general framework provided under international law.[9] It explained that a State has to respect the limits 'which international law places upon its jurisdiction' and 'within these limits, its right to exercise jurisdiction rests in its sovereignty'.[10] It is true that States have substantial discretion concerning their jurisdiction under the principle of State sovereignty, but it must be reiterated that the principle of State sovereignty itself is a principle within the framework of international law. In the Barcelona Traction Case, Judge Fitzmaurice confirmed the existence of limitations on jurisdiction as follows:

---

6 See Article 2(7) of the Charter of the UN.

7 For example, see the attitude of the Soviet Union against the idea of an international criminal tribunal in the discussion during the legislation of the Genocide Convention, E/794, p. 11, footnote 19. See also, statement made by the delegate of the Soviet Union in UN General Assembly Official Records, 3rd Session, C.6, 98th meeting, p. 379. Also the UN Doc. A/766, and UN General Assembly Official Records, 3rd Session, 178th plenary meeting, pp. 814-815. For the same reasons, the Soviet Union opposed General Assembly Resolution 260B(III), which requested the International Law Commission to consider the possibility of establishing an international institution to prosecute individuals responsible for genocide and other crimes.

8 Jurisdiction 'is one of the most obvious forms of the exercise of sovereign power.' Legal Status of Eastern Greenland Case, *PCIJ Series* A-B (1933), p. 48.

9 The PCIJ declared that 'jurisdiction, which, in principle, belongs solely to the State, is limited by rules of international law'. Case of Nationality Decrees in Tunis and Morocco (1921), *PCIJ Series* B. No. 4, pp. 23-24. It is considered that 'the existence of the State's right to exercise jurisdiction is exclusively determined by public international law.' F. A. Mann 'The Doctrine of Jurisdiction in International Law' *Recueil des Cours* Tome 111 (1964-I), pp. 10-11.

10 The Case of the SS. Lotus (*France* v. *Turkey*), *supra* note (2), p. 19.

> 'It is true that under present conditions international law does not impose hard and fast rules on States delimiting spheres of national jurisdiction in such matters ... but leaves to States a wide discretion in the matter. It does, however, (a) postulate the *existence* of limits – though in any given case it may be for the tribunal to indicate what these are for the purposes of that case; and (b) involve for every State an obligation to exercise moderation and restraint as to the extent of the jurisdiction assumed by the courts in cases having a foreign element, and to avoid undue encroachment on a jurisdiction more properly appertaining to, or more appropriately exercisable by, another State.'[11]

Therefore, not only is international law applicable, but it should regulate the exercise of jurisdiction. As noted in Chapter I, it is recognised that international law has four fundamental objectives in regulating jurisdiction, namely: balancing States' interests, achieving certain common State objectives, regulating concurrent jurisdiction, and protecting individuals from the unreasonable exercise of jurisdiction,[12] and to achieve these objectives, international law should regulate the exercise of jurisdiction by States.

2.3 Interests Involved

Interests concerning the prohibition and prosecution of certain acts can be categorised into three levels in the light of the public order affected by the commission of such an act: the interest of individual States, the common interest of two or more States, and the interest of the international community as a whole. The first such interest involves the maintenance of domestic or municipal public order, while the common interest of States is identified when a crime is within the interest shared by two or more States. The interest of the international community as a whole involves crimes that threaten the public order of the international community as a whole. The latter two are sometimes treated as one, constituting matters of international concern. The distinctions between the three interests do not solely depend on the number of States involved, but also on the gravity of the crimes and the perception of the international community as to which level of public order is affected by a certain category of crimes. Therefore, a crime once thought to be within the common interest of States may later fall within the scope of the interest of the international community as a whole as this category of crime is increasingly acknowledged by States to be a vital international concern.

Classic international law was largely based on respect for the interests of each State. Under classic international law, the interests of States were generally protected under the principle of absolute State sovereignty; the exercise of jurisdiction was thereby within the sphere of domestic matters, which was left to the discretion of States

11 Separate Opinion of Sir Gerald Fitzmaurice, Case Concerning the Barcelona Traction, Light and Power Company, Limited (Belgium v. Spain), *ICJ Reports 1970*, para. 70. This citation concerns the Spanish authority to conduct bankruptcy proceedings in respect of Barcelona Traction, a Canadian company.

12 See Bernard H. Oxman 'Jurisdiction of States', in Rudolf Bernhardt (ed.), *Encyclopedia of Public International Law* Vol. 3 (Elsevier Science, 1997), p. 56.

under the principle of non-intervention.[13] However, as the interaction and interdependency of States increased, some transboundary measures were required in order to protect the individual and common interests of States. In addition, as more matters are recognised as falling within the interest of the international community, modern international law has started to construct a different regime of jurisdiction for heinous crimes.

The UN was established due to the bitter lesson learned from the disaster of the Second World War. Its very foundation being the recognition of the importance of individual human dignity, the UN has worked to establish an international systems to promote and protect human rights more effectively. Gross violations of human rights do not fall within domestic matters, and the concept of sovereignty is no longer an excuse for the international community to ignore such violations. Witnessing the mass exterminations and gross violations of human rights in the Second World War, there was a wide consensus among States as to the criminality of such acts. Gross violations of human rights became crimes of international concern since they are breaches of fundamental values and threaten the maintenance of peace and security of the international community. Their exceptional gravity and impact on the integrity of humanity and order, as the UN General Assembly declared in a resolution condemning the crime of genocide, 'shocks the conscience of mankind'.[14] It is recognised that gross and serious human rights violations have become a matter of international concern. Therefore, the prevention and punishment of such crimes are within the interest of the international community as a whole.[15]

In addition, the interest in accountability is explained from the perspective of the right of victims to obtain legal redress. Joyner interprets Article 8 of the Universal Declaration of Human Rights as purporting that everyone has 'the right to effective remedy by the competent national tribunal for acts violating the fundamental rights granted him by the constitution or by law', and concludes that in the event of the violation of fundamental human rights, the victims have an undeniable right to

---

13 No State has the right to intervene, directly or indirectly, for any reason whatsoever, in the internal or external affairs of any other State. See the 1970 Declaration on Principles of International Law concerning Friendly Relations and Co-operation among States, General Assembly Resolution 2625 (XXV) of 1970, UN Doc. A/8082, reprinted in the *American Journal of International Law* Vol. 65 (1971).

14 General Assembly Resolution 96(I), adopted on 11 December 1946. Furthermore, this resolution expressed the view that genocide 'is a denial of the right of existence of entire human groups, as homicide is the denial of the right to live of individual human beings ... and is contrary to moral law and to the spirit and aims of the United Nations. ... The punishment of the crime of genocide is a matter of international concern.'

15 Broomhall notes that the establishment of the direct international responsibility of individuals for core crimes is justified by fundamental international interests, more specifically, 'international peace and security' and 'conscience of humanity'. See Bruce Broomhall, *International Justice and the International Criminal Court: Between Sovereignty and the Rule of Law* (Oxford University Press, 2003), pp. 44-51.

justice.[16] He deduces that States are obliged to investigate those violations, to take appropriate measures against the perpetrators, to ensure that they are prosecuted, and to furnish the victims with effective remedies.[17]

2.4 Principle of Individual Criminal Responsibility

Being deeply conscious of the heinous crimes committed during the Second World War, the international community made a firm determination to establish some measures for international accountability. Hence, in the aftermath of the Second World War, the punishment of individuals for war crimes and crimes against humanity was attained at the Nuremberg and Tokyo Tribunals.[18] As the Nuremberg Tribunal declared in its judgement, 'Crimes against international law are committed by men, not by abstract entities, and only by punishing individuals who commit such crimes can the provisions of international law be enforced.'[19]

Also, after the War, efforts were made to create substantive laws and systems with binding international legal obligations upon States to protect the individual from gross and serious violations of human rights. Together with the prohibition of violations thereof, measures to pursue individual responsibility were discussed immediately after the establishment of the UN. An example of such efforts in the very early stages of the UN was the adoption of the Convention on the Prevention and Punishment of the Crime of Genocide (hereinafter referred to as the Genocide Convention) in 1948. It was based on the commitment never again to allow such gross human rights violations anywhere in the world.[20] In the Genocide Convention, the act of genocide is condemned, and any individual who commits such a crime will be subject to punishment. Article 6 of the Genocide Convention prescribes that those suspected of having committed genocide will be prosecuted by the State in which the crime was committed, or by an international tribunal. As a result, not only States, but also individuals became the bearers of international responsibility for any commission of such a crime.

---

16 See Christopher C. Joyner 'Redressing Impunity for Human Rights Violations: The Universal Declaration and the Search for Accountability' *Denver Journal of International Law and Policy* Vol. 26 (Summer, 1998), pp. 591-592.

17 *Ibid.* Similarly, the UN Sub-Commission on Prevention of Discrimination and Protection of Minorities has given due attention to the victims' right to know, right to justice, and right to reparations, in formulating the set of principles for ending the impunity of perpetrators of civil and political human rights violations. See the Revised Final Report Prepared by Mr. Joinet on the Question of the Impunity of Perpetrators of Human Rights Violations (Civil and Political), UN. Doc. E/CN.4/Sub.2/1997/20/Rev.1.

18 See Article 6 of the Agreement for the Prosecution and Punishment of the Major War Criminals of the European Axis, and Establishing the Charter of the International Military Tribunal (hereinafter Nuremberg Charter), London (8 August 1945), reprinted in the *American Journal of International Law* Supplement Vol. 39 (1945). Charter of the International Military Tribunal for the trial of the major war criminals in the Far East, proclaimed at Tokyo on 19 January 1946.

19 *Nazi Conspiracy and Aggression: Opinion and Judgement* (U.S. Government Printing Office 1947), p. 223.

20 See General Assembly Resolution 96(I), and the Preamble of the Genocide Convention.

The international community has shown more and more intolerance for the impunity of those individuals who commit crimes such as genocide and crimes against humanity, particularly since the 1990s. Through the establishment of the ICTY, the ICTR, and the ICC, the international community has expressed its commitment to abolish impunity for these crimes. It is considered that pursuing individual accountability contributes not only to comforting victims, but also to reconciliation and the restoration of peace, as well as deterrence and the prevention of future crimes.[21]

As a result of the interrelated developments in international humanitarian, criminal and human rights law, the principle of individual responsibility for serious crimes has become one of the norms under international law.[22] Yet, how firmly and how far States must pursue individual responsibility remains vague. Does the principle of State sovereignty or immunity preclude the pursuit of individual criminal responsibility?[23] Do States have the rights and obligations to prevent and punish crimes beyond their territorial border? Many legal questions are still waiting to be answered.

3 Bases of Jurisdiction Recognised under International Law

Despite the lack of detailed regulations on the limitation of national jurisdiction, international law has recognised some bases for national jurisdiction. The five bases specifically acknowledged under international law are territorial jurisdiction, nationality jurisdiction, passive personality jurisdiction, protective jurisdiction, and universal jurisdiction.[24] I will introduce each basis briefly below, especially noting how they were perceived under the classical jurisdictional regime, in order to highlight the later changes in the modern jurisdictional regime which we will observe later in this chapter. Special attention will be devoted to universal jurisdiction.

---

21 For the preventive effects of prosecution in international criminal courts, see Payam Akhavan 'Beyond Impunity: Can International Criminal Justice Prevent Future Atrocities?' *American Journal of International Law* Vol. 95 No. 1 (January 2001).

22 As to how the principle of individual responsibility is formulated in laws of war and international human rights law, see Lyan S. Sunga, *Individual Responsibility in International Law for Serious Human Rights Violations* (Martinus Nijhoff Publishers, 1992).

23 For example, the conflict between the effort to establish individual responsibility and the principle of immunity was dealt with at the ICJ. The ICJ ruled that an incumbent Foreign Minister suspected of having committed crimes against humanity enjoys full immunity against the exercise of national jurisdiction by a foreign State. See the Case Concerning the Arrest Warrant of 11 April 2000 (Democratic Republic of the Congo v. Belgium), ICJ Judgment of 14 February 2002.

24 Research in International Law (Under the Auspices of the Faculty of the Harvard Law School), 'Drafts of Conventions Prepared for the Codification of International Law: Jurisdiction with Respect to Crime' (hereinafter referred to as Harvard Research), Supplement to the *American Journal of International Law* Vol. 29 No. 3 (1935), Introductory Comment.

3.1 Territorial Jurisdiction

Territorial jurisdiction is exercised by the State where the crime was committed.[25] A State is an international entity based on a particular territory, governing a population within its territory. A State has 'exclusive competence in regard to its own territory',[26] and it has the power to legislate and enforce its domestic law through various domestic mechanisms. Under the principle of State sovereignty, it is respected as the highest authority within its territory. Accordingly, territorial jurisdiction, which is exercised by a State of the territory where a crime is alleged to have been committed, is recognised to be the most basic jurisdiction under customary international law. The PCIJ declared in the Lotus case that 'in all systems of law the principle of the territorial character of criminal law is fundamental.'[27] Furthermore, the PCIJ held that 'the exclusively territorial character of law relating to this domain constitutes a principle which, except as otherwise expressly provided, would, *ipso facto*, prevent States from extending the criminal jurisdiction of their courts beyond their frontiers'.[28] The jurisdiction of a State is considered to have effect generally within the territory of that State, as evidenced by the practice of States and the principles of territorial sovereignty and non-intervention. It is interpreted that the UN Charter itself implicitly endorses this territorial principle by proclaiming the sovereign equality of States.

The notion of territorial jurisdiction has been somewhat widened, for instance, to include jurisdiction over a crime that is only partly committed in its territory. The subjective territorial jurisdiction allows the jurisdiction of a State where a crime was commenced,[29] while objective territorial jurisdiction acknowledges the jurisdiction of a State where a crime was completed or had effect.[30] Also, the effects doctrine, according to which a State can claim jurisdiction over acts committed abroad that produce harmful effects within its territory, is sometimes included under the heading of territorial jurisdiction.

To sum up, national jurisdiction is an integral part of State sovereignty and is often claimed to be an exclusive power belonging to States, and to be within the discretion of States as a domestic matter. International law prohibits States from intervening in the domestic matters of another State, thus a State generally enjoys exclusive power within its territorial boundaries under the principle of State sovereignty. As a consequence, territoriality has been strongly emphasised as a basis for national jurisdiction. The State exercising jurisdiction is almost always the State where the crime was

25 'A State has jurisdiction with respect to any crime committed in whole or in part within its territory.' Harvard Research, Article 3.

26 Island of Palmas case, Award of 4 April 1928, *United Nations Reports of International Arbitral Awards (RIAA)*, Vol. II, p. 838.

27 The Case of the SS. Lotus (France v. Turkey), *supra* note (2), p. 20.

28 *Ibid.*

29 See Harvard Research, pp. 484-487.

30 See Harvard Research, pp. 487-494.

committed.[31] Of course, international law can place some limitations on national jurisdiction, and territorial jurisdiction must be exercised within the general framework provided under international law. Having said this, however, international law has not been actively setting limitations on territorial jurisdiction.

3.2 Non-Territorial Jurisdiction

There can be no doubt that the principle of territorial jurisdiction is the strongest basis for national jurisdiction. However, it does not preclude other bases of jurisdiction *ipso facto*.
The PCIJ in the Lotus Case upheld:

> '...[J]urisdiction is certainly territorial; it cannot be exercised by a State outside its territory except by virtue of a permissive rule derived from international custom or from a convention. It does not, however, follow that international law prohibits a State from exercising jurisdiction in its own territory, in respect of any case which relates to acts which have taken place abroad, and in which it cannot rely on some permissive rule of international law. ... Far from laying down a general prohibition to the effect that States may not extend the application of their laws and the jurisdiction of their courts to persons, property and acts outside their territory, it [international law] leaves them in this respect a wide measure of discretion which is only limited in certain cases by prohibitive rules...'[32]

Even under the classical jurisdictional regime in which territorial jurisdiction has been dominant, the existence of other bases of jurisdiction has been recognised. It was observed that States exercise their jurisdiction based on some nexus (linkage) to the crime concerned, and diverse bases of jurisdiction based on different nexuses were acknowledged under international law. They are namely: nationality jurisdiction, passive nationality jurisdiction, protective jurisdiction and universal jurisdiction.

In this study, jurisdiction other than territorial jurisdiction is referred to as '*non-territorial jurisdiction*'. I have adopted this term to illustrate and highlight the tension between territorial jurisdiction and other bases of jurisdiction. I have intentionally avoided using the more common phrase of '*extraterritorial jurisdiction*' for the following reason. It is important to bear in mind the difference between extraterritorial jurisdiction and extra-territorial measures of enforcement. The phrase 'extraterritorial jurisdiction' is often used to refer to any national jurisdiction of States other than the territorial State where a crime has been committed.[33] The exercise of adjudicating power by States through their domestic courts, which is the subject of this study, thus

31 For an in-depth study on the principle of territorial jurisdiction, see Durmus Tezcan, *Territorialité et Conflits de Juridictions en Droit Pénal International* (L'Univesité D'Ankara, 1983).

32 The Case of the SS. Lotus (*France* v. *Turkey*), *supra* note (2), pp. 18-19.

33 See Rosalyn Higgins, *Problems and Process: International law and How We Use It* (Clarendon Press, 1994), p. 73.

takes place within the territory of each respective State. Therefore, it is not 'extraterritorial' in actual practice. This is different from extraterritorial enforcement measures, in which a State takes measures on the territory of another State in order to enforce international or national laws. A State's direct exercise of its power inside another State's territory, such as abducting suspects abroad, is a different question from the 'extraterritorial jurisdiction' discussed in this study.

3.2.1 Nationality Jurisdiction

Nationality or *active personality jurisdiction* is asserted by a State whose national is a suspect.[34] It includes jurisdiction asserted by a State based on the domicile or residence of a suspect. Nationality jurisdiction is understood to be 'universally conceded'.[35] It is noted that under the classical jurisdictional regime, nationality jurisdiction has been commonly circumscribed by many conditions and safeguards by the domestic law of many States, and the Harvard Research observes that this widespread inclusion of limitations 'tends to confirm the opinion that jurisdiction based on nationality is properly regarded as subsidiary to the territorial jurisdiction of the State where the crime was committed.'[36] Yet, the Harvard Research did not expressly attribute a subsidiary character to nationality jurisdiction in its draft provision after noting that these are 'matters which each State is free to determine for itself'.[37]

3.2.2 Passive Personality Jurisdiction

Passive personality jurisdiction is asserted by a State whose national is the victim of a crime. Under the classical jurisdictional regime, passive personality jurisdiction has been observed to be 'asserted in some form by a considerable number of States and contested by others' and is 'admittedly auxiliary in character'.[38]

---

34 Article 5 of the Harvard Research prescribes in its draft convention as follows: 'A State has jurisdiction with respect to any crime committed outside its territory,
(a) By a natural person who was a national of that State when the crime was committed or who is a national of that State when prosecuted or punished; or
(b) By a corporation or other juristic person which had the national character of that State when the crime was committed.'

35 The Harvard Research, p. 519.

36 The Harvard Research, p. 531.

37 *Ibid.*

38 The Harvard Research, Introductory Comment, p. 445. The Harvard Research did not prescribe a separate provision for passive personality jurisdiction since it saw no need for this as it is adequately provided for within other bases of jurisdiction.

3.2.3 Protective Jurisdiction

Under *protective* or *security jurisdiction*, a State claims jurisdiction over crimes that are injurious to its national security. Hence, the nexus for this base of jurisdiction is the nature of the interest which is harmed. This jurisdiction allows a State to claim jurisdiction over offences directed against its security or vital interests, or other offences threatening the integrity of governmental functions that are generally recognised as crimes, e.g., plans to overthrow its government or counterfeiting its currency.[39] Under the classical jurisdictional regime, protective jurisdiction is understood to be 'claimed by most States, regarded with misgiving in a few, and generally ranked as the basis of an auxiliary competence.'[40]

3.2.4 Universal Jurisdiction

3.2.4.1 The Definition of Universal Jurisdiction

What is universal jurisdiction? There are some differences in its definition depending on who is using the term. What is common in their understanding is that universal jurisdiction is exercised by States having no relation to territorial or nationality aspects.[41] The Final Report on the Exercise of Universal Jurisdiction in Respect of Gross Human Rights Offences presented to the International Law Association (hereafter, ILA Report) describes the concept as follows:

> 'Under the principle of universal jurisdiction, a state is entitled, or even required to bring proceedings in respect of certain serious crimes, irrespective of the location of the crime, and irrespective of the nationality of the perpetrator or the victim.'[42]

The ILA Report also specifically notes that '[t]he only connection between the crime and the prosecuting state that may be required is the physical presence of the alleged offender within the jurisdiction of that state'.[43] Accordingly, universal jurisdiction is

---

39 Article 7 of the Harvard Research explains as follows:
'A State has jurisdiction with respect to any crime committed outside its territory by an alien against the security, territorial integrity or political independence of that State, provided that the act or omission which constitutes the crime was not committed in exercise of a liberty guaranteed that alien by the law of the place where it was committed'.

40 The Harvard Research, Introductory Comment, p. 445.

41 Meron stated, 'Indeed, the true meaning of universal jurisdiction is that international law permits any state to apply its laws to certain offenses even in the absence of territorial, nationality or other accepted contacts with the offender or the victim.' Theodor Meron 'International Criminalization of Internal Atrocities' *American Journal of International Law* Vol. 89 (1995), p. 554, 570.

42 International Law Association, 'Final Report on the Exercise of Universal Jurisdiction in Respect of Gross Human Rights Offences', Committee on International Human Rights Law and Practice, London Conference, 2000, p. 2.

43 *Ibid.*

generally claimed as a jurisdictional basis allowing the State which has custody of a suspect to prosecute and punish that suspect irrespective of the place where the crime was committed or the nationality of the suspects or victims.[44]

3.2.4.2 Universal Jurisdiction *in absentia*

In general, universal jurisdiction is associated with the presence of a suspect in the executing State, whereas some interpret universal jurisdiction as allowing *all* States to exercise jurisdiction.[45] Some suggest that a State can assert universal jurisdiction even without the presence of a suspect within its territory. For example, the Princeton Principles on Universal Jurisdiction[46] state as follows:

> 'Principle 1 – Fundamentals of Universal Jurisdiction
> 1. For purposes of these Principles, universal jurisdiction is criminal jurisdiction based solely on the nature of the crime, without regard to where the crime was committed, the nationality of the alleged or convicted perpetrator, the nationality of the victim, or any other connection to the state exercising such jurisdiction.
> 2. Universal jurisdiction may be exercised by a competent and ordinary judicial body of any state in order to try a person duly accused of committing serious crimes under international law as specified in Principle 2(1), provided the person is present before such judicial body.
> 3. A state may rely on universal jurisdiction as a basis for seeking the extradition of a person accused or convicted of committing a serious crime under international law as specified in Principle 2(1), provided that it has established a prima facie case of the person's guilt and that the person sought to be extradited will be tried or the punishment carried out in accordance with international norms and standards on the protection of human rights in the context of criminal proceedings.
> ....'

Princeton Principle 1(3) suggests that a State can seek the extradition of a suspect based on universal jurisdiction. This means, according to the Princeton Principle, that the presence of a suspect is not a prerequisite for a State in claiming its universal jurisdiction against another State. Note that the Princeton Principle denotes that the absence of a suspect is only allowed in pre-trial proceedings, such as when commencing an investigation and issuing an arrest warrant. Therefore, the actual conduct of a court trial in the absence of a suspect (trial *in absentia*) is a different question entailing a possible violation of the human rights of a suspect, and Principle 1(2) admits that the

44 See, for example, Christopher C. Joyner 'Arresting Impunity: The Case for Universal Jurisdiction in Bringing War Criminals to Accountability' *Law and Contemporary Problems* Vol. 59 No. 4 (Autumn 1996), p. 165.

45 See D. W. Bowett, *supra* note (5), p. 11. See also, Christopher C. Joyner, *ibid.*, p. 165.

46 *The Princeton Principles on Universal Jurisdiction* (Princeton University Press, 2001).

actual exercise of the universal jurisdiction to adjudicate can only take place after the suspect is in custody.

On the other hand, there are some criticisms to include such a notion within ordinary universal jurisdiction. Cassese holds that 'universality may be asserted subject to the condition that the alleged offender be on the territory of the prosecuting state.' Furthermore, he notes as follows:

> 'It would seem contrary to the logic of current state relations to authorize any state of the world to institute criminal proceedings (commence investigations, collect evidence, and lay out charges) against any foreigner or foreign state official allegedly culpable of serious international crimes.'[47]

Whether or not the presence of a suspect within the territory is secured at the time of instigating a claim of jurisdiction over a case is an important factor that may drastically change the nature and characteristic of 'universal jurisdiction'. The act of requesting the extradition of a suspect denotes that the requesting State is formally claiming its entitlement to prosecute that suspect, which is usually done based on the jurisdictional basis recognised under international law. Considering that the concept of universal jurisdiction has long been understood in association with the presence of a suspect, the validity and appropriateness of the interpretation adopted by Princeton Principle may require further examination. Therefore, we should make a distinction between these two different interpretations.

In this study, such a jurisdictional base which allows a State to assert its jurisdiction without any nexus to the case in question, even without the presence of a suspect within its territory as 'universal jurisdiction *in absentia*' in this study. This term 'universal jurisdiction *in absentia*' is also used by the International Court of Justice (ICJ) in the Case Concerning the Arrest Warrant of 11 April 2000, however, without indicating a definition.[48] Although no clear definition is given by the ICJ, it is clear from the context that the term is employed by the ICJ in order to refer to the jurisdiction asserted by Belgium based on its domestic law which authorises its courts to exercise jurisdiction regardless of the nationality of the suspect or that of the victims 'even if the accused (Belgian or foreign) is not found in Belgium.'[49]

The differences between ordinary universal jurisdiction and universal jurisdiction *in absentia* become apparent when considering the State which has such jurisdiction.

---

47 Antonio Cassese 'Is the Bell Tolling for Universality? A Plea for a Sensible Notion of Universal Jurisdiction' *Journal of International Criminal Justice* Vol. 1 No. 3 (December 2003), p. 592.

48 See Case Concerning the Arrest Warrant of 11 April 2000 (Democratic Republic of the *Congo* v. *Belgium*), *supra* note (23), para. 41. On the other hand, in making the same distinction, Amnesty International calls the former 'custodial universal jurisdiction'. See Amnesty International 'Universal Jurisdiction: The Duty of States to Enact And Implement Legislations' (Sept. 2001), AI Index IOR53/003/2001, p. 15.

49 See Separate Opinion of President Guillaume, Case Concerning the Arrest Warrant of 11 April 2000 (Democratic Republic of the *Congo* v. *Belgium*), *ibid.*, para. 3.

Ordinary universal jurisdiction is considered to be enjoyed by a State where a suspect is present; while universal jurisdiction *in absentia* is attributed to all States constituting the international community.

Also, one may say that there is no need to distinguish universal jurisdiction and universal jurisdiction *in absentia* because it is simply a temporal difference, precisely at which stage the presence of a suspect must be obtained. Then the key question would be, 'At which stage does the presence of a suspect becomes imperative under international law?' In my opinion, this is more than a temporal difference. We should not ignore that ordinary universal jurisdiction and universal jurisdiction *in absentia* have different rationales and status under conventional and customary international law. Therefore this study analyses them separately.

3.2.4.3 Two Aspects Differentiating Understandings of Universal Jurisdiction

Many people often neglect the differences in the nature of the perceived universal jurisdiction. One has to be careful in comparing their opinions since the content of their arguments varies according to the kind of 'universal jurisdiction' they have in mind. Therefore, in order to avoid any misunderstanding, whenever universal jurisdiction is discussed, two aspects of its nature must be distinguished: First, is it a right or an obligation? Second, is it supplemental or primary?

Since the first aspect (a right or an obligation?) is sufficiently clear, let me briefly explain the second aspect (supplemental or primary?). The question of whether a given universal jurisdiction is supplemental or primary is important in relation with other bases of jurisdiction. To be more specific, this relates to the option between the exercise of universal jurisdiction and extradition to other States when one or more extradition request has been made. Universal jurisdiction may entail a supplementary character when the extradition of suspects is given preference over its exercise. On the other hand, universal jurisdiction may become primary jurisdiction when a requested State demonstrates no preference on extradition notwithstanding the existence of an extradition request made by other State.

Attempting to answer the above questions according to two aspects may produce different combinations. For instance, universal jurisdiction could be considered to be both a right and having supplementary character, or it may be viewed as obligatory and primary. The four possible combinations are explained below. This categorisation is made in order to clarify the differences and also to help to clarify the historical expansion of universal jurisdiction. The details of each will be clarified through my examination of the history of the development of universal jurisdiction, so I will only identify them briefly here.

Figure 1: Nature of Universal Jurisdiction

	Supplemental	*Primary*
Permissive	**Supplemental Permissive Universal Jurisdiction** • No obligation to exercise. It is a *right.* • Priority on extradition. Can be exercised only after the exhaustion of the effort to extradite to other State or entity when there is any extradition request.	**Primary Permissive Universal Jurisdiction** • No obligation to exercise. It is a *right.* • Can be exercised even when there is any other State or entity that has jurisdiction, to which the suspect can be extradited.
Obligatory	**Supplemental Obligatory Universal Jurisdiction** • There is an obligation, usually either to exercise jurisdiction or to extradite. • Priority on extradition. Can be exercised only after the exhaustion of the effort to extradite to other State or entity when there is any extradition request.	**Primary Obligatory Universal Jurisdiction** • There is an obligation, usually either to exercise jurisdiction or to extradite. • Can be exercised even when there is any other State or entity that has jurisdiction, to which the suspect can be extradited.

The first category is *supplemental permissive universal jurisdiction.* This is the most classic understanding. It is a right, therefore a State has the discretion to decide whether or not to exercise jurisdiction. This category is based on the understanding of universal jurisdiction in the classical jurisdictional regime. Since it regards universal jurisdiction as an auxiliary right supplementing other national jurisdictions, especially territorial jurisdiction, if there are any extradition requests from other States, they must be respected and given priority.

The second category is *primary permissive universal jurisdiction.* It is universal jurisdiction that has overcome the supplementary characteristic. It is no longer supplemental to other jurisdictions. Therefore, a requested State does not have to give priority to extradition requests from other States, and can exercise its jurisdiction freely. An example of this is the universal jurisdiction over piracy which has been recognised under customary international law for centuries. It considers universal jurisdiction to be a right, not an obligation.

The third category is *supplemental obligatory universal jurisdiction.* It obligates States to exercise universal jurisdiction whenever the effort to extradite suspects has failed. Notice that States should first to extradite suspects to other requesting States;

therefore, the obligation to exercise universal jurisdiction is rather passive. Even though extradition is preferred, it is remarkable that the principle of *aut dedere aut judicare* is adopted, attaching a selective yet obligatory nature to universal jurisdiction. Because it signifies an obligation not a right, thereby requiring active action from States instead of passive allowance, it is more likely to invite opposition from States.

The fourth category is *primary obligatory universal jurisdiction*. It also obligates States to extradite or prosecute suspects. The difference between this and the third category is that the exhaustion of the effort to extradite is not a prerequisite in exercising universal jurisdiction.

In order to understand fully what universal jurisdiction exactly is, one must carefully reflect on conventional and customary international law. In the following section, I will illustrate the historical development of today's jurisdictional regime, while universal jurisdiction is specifically examined in depth in the next chapter.

4 History and Analysis of the Formation of the Jurisdictional Regime

Today, gross violations of human rights can be prosecuted in national or international criminal courts having jurisdiction over such crimes. In addition to territorial jurisdiction, which is the most traditional basis, several bases of non-territorial jurisdiction are recognised under international law. The situation in which there exist multiple jurisdictions can be described as a system of concurrent jurisdiction.

Before studying the formation and structure of the current system, let us briefly observe the classical jurisdictional regime. Comprehending the classical system is useful because many of the problems still apparent in present jurisdictional regimes are caused by the influence of traditional rules and principles. As I will explain later in this section, the factors that have induced the development of the concurrent jurisdictional regime of today include the failure of the human rights mechanism and shortcomings on that part of the traditional jurisdictional regime. It is the continuous struggle in search of an effective measure to overcome such shortcomings that promoted concurrency. In this section, the history is illustrated in line with the four periods outlined in Chapter I.

4.1 The First Period: The Classical Jurisdictional Regime[50]

4.1.1 The Laissez-faire Attitude of International Law

Since the power to investigate, prosecute, and punish individuals is an essential part of State sovereignty, adjudicating jurisdiction generally falls within the discretion of

50 As explained in Chapter I, the term 'classical jurisdictional regime' is used in this study in order to highlight the development of the current jurisdictional regime. The use of this phrase does not purport that there ever existed a systematised regime for prosecuting individuals for gross and serious violations of human rights under classic international law.

individual States, and States can hence choose which type of jurisdiction to uphold. Therefore, international law did not originally interfere in the way in which a State exercised its sovereign power as long as exercising that power did not affect other States, since international law primarily governs relations between sovereign States. International law duly respected the sovereignty of States and prohibited States or any other entity from intervening in the domestic matters of a State. As the PCIJ upheld in the Lotus Case, States were free to legislate and exercise any form of jurisdiction they liked,[51] as long as it did not undermine the territorial integrity of other States or interfere with the domestic matters of other States. Consequently, classic international law did not intervene in order to lay down strict rules of jurisdiction.

4.1.2 The Dominance of Territorial Jurisdiction

Apart from the recognition of territorial jurisdiction as the most basic principle,[52] the scope and extent of the acceptance of other forms of jurisdiction among States were unclear under classic international law. At least bases of non-territorial jurisdiction were not expressly prohibited, so it can be said that there was concurrency of jurisdiction to some extent in the classical jurisdictional regime as well. The emergence of custom on universal jurisdiction over piracy marked an important development, but this development was possible largely because the crime of piracy was committed on the high seas, beyond the territorial control of any State. It developed from an effort to fill the lacuna as regards jurisdiction, rather than overriding territorial or any other jurisdiction. In my opinion, the extent and scope of the recognition of concurrency was narrow and overshadowed by the prevalence of territorial jurisdiction.

Evidence of the dominance of territorial jurisdiction can be observed in the expansion of the scope of 'territorial jurisdiction' itself. There are some variations in the notion of 'territorial jurisdiction' widening the territorial nexus to include subjective and objective territorial jurisdiction as well as the effect principle. They originated from attempts to justify the exercise of jurisdiction under the territorial nexus. It can be observed that States preferred to utilise territorial jurisdiction instead of justifying it as protective jurisdiction or with any other bases, even if it involved widening the notion of territorial jurisdiction.

51 'Far from laying down a general prohibition to the effect that States may not extend the application of their laws and the jurisdiction of their courts to persons, property and acts outside their territory, [international law] leaves them in this respect a wide measure of discretion which is only limited in certain cases by prohibitive rules; as regards other cases, every State remains free to adopt the principles which it regards as best and most suitable.' The Case of SS. Lotus (*France* v. *Turkey*), *supra* note (2), p. 19.

52 Even in continental countries, which relied on nationality jurisdiction more than common law countries did, prosecutions based on territorial jurisdiction were more frequent than those based on nationality jurisdiction. See Donnedieu de Vabres, *Les Principes Modernes du Droit Pénal International* (1928), p. 68.

4.1.3 Uncertainty Tolerated under International Law

As described above, classic international law did not lay down extensive norms concerning jurisdiction. The uncertainty of rules concerning jurisdiction did not cause much of a substantial problem when there were few interactions between States. However, even in the era of classic international law, as the technologies of transportation and communication developed, States began to be aware of their interest and needs in punishing fugitives who had escaped from their territory or who had committed crimes in a foreign territory.[53] Adhering to the system in which the effect of a State's actions is limited by territoriality could not fulfil these interests and this need. Consequently, the emergence of crimes having effect beyond a State's boundary led to the development of inter-State co-operation.

As a result, international law emerged concerning inter-State co-operation such as extradition and co-operation in judicial aid. Yet this law and practice were considerably limited by traditional principles, namely the principles of State sovereignty and reciprocity. For instance, extradition was generally based on international comity, and even if it was prescribed as an obligation by treaties, it only had effect between the States that had ratified the agreement in question and only in a reciprocal manner. Judicial aid was generally a bilateral reciprocal co-operation as well. Therefore, inter-State co-operation was 'international' in the sense that it contained some aspects beyond the territorial boundary of a State, but it was mainly bilateral co-operation, and not a subject regulated by general international law to be applied worldwide. There was an attempt to establish international criminal jurisdiction over terrorism under the League of Nations, but the relevant convention did not attain sufficient ratifications to come into effect. Under the era of classic international law, it was difficult to establish an institution or system that could encroach into the sacrosanct sovereignty of States to prosecute and punish crimes. It should be remembered that promoting the protection of human rights through individual criminal accountability was not a common idea under classic international law.

In sum, the classical jurisdictional regime was significantly based on territoriality, reciprocity and international comity. It mainly encompassed crimes damaging a domestic order, rarely crimes of international concern such as piracy. Even for those crimes that touched upon the common interest of States, there was neither a comprehensive system of co-operation nor extensive rules concerning jurisdiction under international law.

---

53 See Research in International Law (Under the Auspices of the Faculty of the Harvard Law School), 'Drafts of Conventions Prepared for the Codification of International Law: Draft Convention on Extradition', Supplement to the *American Journal of International Law* Vol. 29 No. 3(1935), Introductory Comment.

4.2 The Second Period: After the Second World War up to the End of the 1960s

4.2.1 Prosecution of Crimes Committed during the World Wars

In dealing with the crimes committed during the World Wars, the international community came to realise the need to overcome the flaws of the traditional jurisdictional system and, consequently, to adjudicate certain crimes at the international level. After the unsuccessful attempt to prosecute Kaiser Wilhelm for acts of aggression in the First World War, the idea of establishing an international criminal judicial organ was put into practice in the form of the Nuremberg and Tokyo Tribunals for crimes committed during the Second World War.[54] In addition to crimes against the peace and war crimes, Article 6(c) of the Charter included the following human rights violations in particular as 'crimes against humanity' which fell within the jurisdiction of the Nuremberg Tribunal:

> '(c) Crimes against Humanity: Namely, murder, extermination, enslavement, deportation, and other inhumane acts committed against any civilian population before or during the war, or persecutions on political, racial or religious grounds in execution of or in connection with any crime within the jurisdiction of the Tribunal, whether or not in violation of the domestic law of the country where perpetrated.'

Apart from acknowledging the importance of human rights to protect individuals, a political motive was also noted as a key factor. What induced human rights to be one of the fundamental values in the aftermath of the Second World War was the political motive of the powerful States among the Allies, which justified the war against the Axis States as the fight for freedom and human rights. The experience of prosecuting individuals for serious war-related crimes at the Nuremberg and Tokyo Tribunals resulted in the formulation of the Nuremberg principles.[55] Also, the prosecution of crimes committed during the Second World War was pursued in the national courts of many States as well.

4.2.2 Becoming Aware of the Shortcomings of the Classical Jurisdictional Regime

The classical jurisdictional regime was mainly based on territorial jurisdiction in a dispersed environment where individual national jurisdictions were working alone and co-operating only occasionally in a reciprocal manner. However, the world became

---

54 See the Agreement for the Prosecution and Punishment of the Major War Criminals of the European Axis, and Establishing the Charter of the International Military Tribunal, London (8 August 1945), reprinted in *American Journal of International Law* Supplement Vol. 39 (1945).

55 Principles of International Law Recognised in the Charter of the Nuremberg Tribunal and in the Judgement of the Tribunal, Yearbook of the International Law Commission 1950, Vol. II, 374, and UN General Assembly Resolution 95(I) adopted on 11 December 1946. The General Assembly resolution did not specify the content of the principles.

aware of the difficulty in prosecuting crimes against international law. Some shortcomings of the traditional jurisdiction system became apparent.

It was feared that the shortcomings of territorial jurisdiction would result in the virtual impunity of individuals responsible for serious crimes. Virtual impunity may be facilitated by the active or passive involvement of a government in the commission of a crime. Gross violations of human rights are often perpetrated by State authorities, be they military or police agents.[56] The power and influence of such forces often result in the impunity of such criminals. In this respect, impunity does not directly derive from norms, but from the political and social situation of society.[57] Even when the government of a territorial State does not support or defend the perpetrator, it is often powerless or reluctant to prosecute such crimes. Because many gross and serious violations of human rights are committed by a powerful group or authorities with some political intent, the territorial State has difficulty in conducting a trial. It is not surprising that if the government or ruling group of the territorial State is actively involved in such violations, the possibility of a trial within its territory is considered to be very low. On the other hand, if a crime has been committed by a foreign government, most likely during an armed conflict between States, prosecution may influence relations between the States involved. If the territorial State tries to prosecute individuals who have acted as agents of other States or superiors who ordered such perpetration, it will be tantamount to adjudicating the legality of another State's action. It is likely to provoke opposition from that State together with pressure to circumvent the commencement of judicial proceedings in the territorial State.

If the suspects and victims of a crime are within the territory of a State where the crime was committed, then there is less need to worry about aggravating relations with other States. However, a territorial State may be reluctant to conduct a trial for different reasons. A territorial State may find that prosecution will trigger more violence and instability and that it will not contribute to regaining and maintaining peace. The territorial State might also fear for the safety of victims, prosecutors, judges or anyone involved in proceedings in a place close to the hostilities. In extreme cases, the situation can be so devastating that there is no authority capable of exercising jurisdiction, owing to the total collapse of all national systems, as was the case in Rwanda in 1994. The fairness and effectiveness of proceedings are also questioned.

Some States were aware of such shortcomings in territorial jurisdiction from the early days of the UN. Being aware that territorial jurisdiction could not be exercised

---

56 See Alex P. Schmid, *Research on Gross Human Rights Violations* (2nd enlarged ed.), (Center for the Study of Social Conflicts: C.O.M.T., 1989), pp. 106-107.

57 Therefore, the cause of impunity is analysed as being more factual than normative, such as the political and social influence of a power in a State. See Theo van Boven 'Accountability for International Crimes: The Victim's Perspective' in 'Reining in Impunity for International Crimes and Serious Violations of Fundamental Human Rights' *Nouvelles Études Penales* Vol. 14 (1998), p. 349. See also, Madeline H. Morris 'International Guidelines Against Impunity: Facilitating Accountability', *ibid.*, p. 359. Also, Christopher C. Joyner, *supra* note (16), pp. 616-617.

effectively against grave crimes as evidenced by past experience, they proposed to incorporate universal jurisdiction and international criminal jurisdiction in the provisions of the Genocide Convention. While the idea of universal jurisdiction was rejected during the drafting stage, the idea of an international criminal court managed to be laid down in a provision, but it remained virtually meaningless (until recently) as the work on the establishment of an international criminal court had been frozen since the early 1950s. It was difficult to effectuate a substantial change in the jurisdictional regime at that time.

4.2.3 *Failure to Establish an Effective Jurisdictional Regime After the Nuremberg and Tokyo Tribunals*

The Nuremberg and Tokyo Tribunals could have opened door for international action to establish a new system of accountability for future crimes. However, the international community failed to do so. In an effort to overcome limitations on the traditional jurisdiction system, the idea of establishing an international criminal court and expanding the principle of universality were proposed both within and outside the UN. The idea of an international criminal court could have overcome the flaws of the classical jurisdictional regime. However, the effort in the UN to establish an international criminal court became lost in a deadlock caused by political and ideological conflicts between East and West. Therefore, the prosecution and punishment of individuals for serious crimes were left in the hands of individual States. Nonetheless, bringing about a change in national jurisdiction for a more effective prosecution of future crimes faced difficulty as well. Even though serious and systematic violations of human rights became matters of international concern instead of only domestic matters for the States in question, States were nevertheless reluctant to accept measures that might limit their discretion as to whether or not to exercise their jurisdiction in a particular case. Consequently, although the horrors of the Second World War provided momentum for the establishment of a more extensive jurisdictional regime, the traditional jurisdictional regime was generally retained for crimes unrelated to the war, leaving the active prosecution of war crimes more or less an exception.

An example of the influence of the classical jurisdictional regime can be observed in the Genocide Convention, one of the first human rights instruments drafted by the UN. As national jurisdiction to pursue individual responsibility for the crime of genocide, the Genocide Convention provides only territorial jurisdiction, failing to expressly authorise other bases of jurisdiction in its provisions. In that sense, the Genocide Convention was still subject to the influence of the classical jurisdictional regime, adhering to the principle of territoriality.[58] Theoretically, even though '[t]he

58 The initial draft of the Genocide Convention provided for universal jurisdiction and the jurisdiction of international criminal tribunal, but did not include territorial jurisdiction. See 'Draft Convention on the Crime of Genocide', *UN Economic and Social Council Official records*, 4th Session, UN Doc. E/447, Articles 7-10. However, the subsequent draft provided for territorial jurisdiction instead of universal

punishment of the crime of genocide is a matter of international concern',[59] the enforcement and prosecution measures against individuals were virtually left within the ambit of domestic affairs. This was due to the reluctance of States to depart from the traditional principle of State sovereignty. The backbone of this reluctance was a fear by a State that other States or an international institution might interfere in its internal affairs. The conflicts between the West and the East had already started both within and outside the UN, and there was an anxiety that human rights ideology would be used to justify an intervention into matters categorised as domestic matters in classic international law. In sum, the ideological and political conflicts among States made them adhere to territorial jurisdiction and stubbornly defend the principles of State sovereignty and non-intervention.

Subsequently, in spite of the commitment to prevent and punish gross and serious violations of human rights, the international community repeatedly witnessed the ineffectiveness of the UN system and the jurisdictional regime in responding to serious violations of human rights. For example, since the legislation of the Genocide Convention, numerous massacres alleged to constitute the crime of genocide were committed,[60] but only a few were prosecuted before the 1990s. Moreover, actions to prosecute genocide were observed to be causing further disputes which endangered international peace. When Bangladesh decided to establish a special domestic court to prosecute genocide and other war crimes committed in the armed conflicts leading to its independence in 1971,[61] it caused an international dispute among States involved in those armed conflicts. Pakistan opposed the exercise of jurisdiction by Bangladesh, causing further confrontation between Bangladesh, Pakistan, and India. In order to prevent Pakistani prisoners of war and civilians held captive in India from being

---

jurisdiction. This modification was in accordance with the attitude of the Soviet Union and others. The Soviet Union emphasised that the establishment of the Nuremberg and Tokyo Tribunals was only possible due to exceptional circumstances, and that only territorial jurisdiction is compatible with State sovereignty. See UN Economic and Social Council Official Records, 6th Session, Ad Hoc Committee on Genocide, UN Doc. E/AC.25/SR.7, pp. 4-5. How the proposals for universal jurisdiction were voted down during the legislative discussion of the Genocide Convention is explained in the next chapter. Although the Genocide Convention denied universal jurisdiction in its drafting stage and prescribed only territorial jurisdiction as national jurisdiction, this does not deny the innovative characteristics of Article 6 of the Genocide Convention which provides adjudication in the territorial States as an obligation rather than a right of State Parties, and also prescribes the jurisdiction of an international tribunal.

59 General Assembly Resolution 96(I), 11 December 1946.

60 See generally, Samuel Totten and others eds., *Genocide in the Twentieth Century* (Garland Publishing, 1995). Also see, Kurt Johassohn and Karin Solveig Bjornson, *Genocide and Gross Human Rights Violations: In Comparative Perspective* (Transaction Publishers, 1998), pp. 256-258. See also, 'Revised and Updated Report on the Question of the Prevention and Punishment of the Crime of Genocide', UN Doc. E/CN.4/Sub.2/1985/6, 9-10.

61 The International Crimes (Tribunals) Act 1973. See, 'International Crimes Tribunals in Bangladesh' *The Review* (International Commission of Jurists) No. 11 (December 1973), pp. 29-34. For an analysis of the crimes committed in this armed conflict, see, East Pakistan Staff Study 'International Penal Law' *The Review* (International Commission of Jurists) No. 8 (June 1972), pp. 26-41.

extradited to Bangladesh, Pakistan instituted proceedings against India at the ICJ.[62] Although the dispute was resolved by negotiation, Pakistan did not keep its promise to punish those returned to Pakistan, arguing that the prosecution would endanger the restoration of democracy in Pakistan.[63]

Unfortunately, in reality the impunity of individuals responsible for such violations was the rule rather than the exception. This virtual impunity of criminals nullified any deterrent effect expected from effective punishment. Moreover, it completed the seemingly infinite cycle of the further negligence of international human rights law.

In sum, in the period after the Second World War, modern international law developed a new emphasis on peace and the protection of human rights. In condemning the serious crimes committed during the Second World War, the international *ad hoc* tribunals were established and, at the same time, States exercised their national jurisdiction over these crimes. However, such an innovative and active exercise of international and national jurisdictions remained the exception rather than becoming a general jurisdictional regime applicable to future crimes. Therefore, the jurisdictional regime for prosecuting future crimes was still left under the immense influence of the rules of the classical jurisdictional regime.

4.3 The Third Period: Expansion of National Jurisdictions in the 1970s and the 1980s

Since the 1970s, we have been able to observe the 'expansion' of national jurisdiction, which has led to the formation of concurrency of jurisdiction that characterises the modern jurisdictional regime of today.

4.3.1 Factors that Promoted the Expansion of National Jurisdiction

The substantial modification of the jurisdictional system came about after international crimes such as terrorism increased dramatically after the end of the 1960s. An increase in terrorist activities, especially criminal acts directed against aircraft since the late 1960s, have posed a serious threat to life and to the viability of international civil aviation. However, there was some confusion over which State has legal jurisdiction over crimes with a transnational character. It sparked the attention of the international community and, as a result, led to new conventions to prohibit such acts, enhancing international co-operation between States. The Tokyo Convention on Offences and Certain Other Acts Committed on Board Aircraft (hereafter, Tokyo Convention), which was adopted in 1963, did not fully enunciate the expansion of national jurisdic-

62 Case Concerning Trial of Pakistani Prisoners of War (*Pakistan* v. *India*), Order of 13 July 1973, *ICJ Reports 1973*.

63 See Antonio Cassese, *Human Rights in a Changing World* (Temple University Press, 1990), p. 83, note 21 on p. 215.

tion, because it only allowed for the multiplicity of jurisdiction as an exception.[64] It was in the 1970s that the phenomenon of the expansion of national jurisdiction could be observed. The Hague Convention for the Suppression of Unlawful Seizure of Aircraft (hereafter, Hague Hijacking Convention) in 1970, which was followed by the Montreal Convention for the Suppression of Unlawful Acts against the Safety of Civil Aviation in 1971, opened the door for the substantial modification which was vital for the formation of today's jurisdictional regime.

Not only crimes related to aircraft, but other criminal acts and human rights violations were also prohibited by separate conventions.[65] This increase in international legislation was due to the failure of the classical jurisdictional regime to effectively prosecute and punish crimes. The development of international transport has made it easier for criminals to flee abroad and to seek a safe haven. This was especially evident in the case of terrorists hijacking an aircraft, who would have the means of transport under their control, and were thereby able to greatly distance themselves from the place of the initial commission of the crime and thereby to move from one State to another. In such a case, relying solely on territorial jurisdiction was highly unlikely to prompt effective prosecution. In addition, the system (or, rather, the lack thereof) of inter-State cooperation and judicial aids needed to be re-examined. For instance, the extradition system based on the principle of reciprocity under the classical jurisdictional regime proved to be hindering the effective administration of justice.

In sum, there were a number of reasons why the international community started to adopt many conventions: (1) the increase in international crimes; (2) their significant threat to international peace; and (3) the ineffectiveness of the classical jurisdictional

64 Art. 4 of the Tokyo Convention reads as follows:
'A Contracting State which is not the State of registration may not interfere with an aircraft in flight in order to exercise its criminal jurisdiction over an offence committed on board except in the following cases:
(a) the offence has effect on the territory of such State;
(b) the offence has been committed by or against a national or permanent resident of such State;
(c) the offence is against the security of such State;
(d) the offence consists of a breach of any rules or regulations relating to the flight or manoeuvre of aircraft in force in such State;
(e) the exercise of jurisdiction is necessary to ensure the observance of any obligation of such State under a multilateral international agreement.'
The acknowledgement of various bases of jurisdiction in the Tokyo Convention may be interpreted as predicting the expansion of national jurisdiction, but the Tokyo Convention itself does not fully encompass the expansion of national jurisdiction by only partly departing from the classical jurisdictional regime, for instance by not including universal jurisdiction, compared to the jurisdictional provisions in the Hague Hijacking Convention.

65 For example, The New York Convention on the Prevention and Punishment of Crimes against Internationally Protected Persons, including Diplomatic Agents (1973); the New York Convention Against the Taking of Hostages (1979); the New York Convention Against Torture and Other Cruel, Inhuman or Degrading Treatment or Punishment (1984); the Montreal Protocol of 24 February 1988 concerning acts of violence at airports; the Vienna Convention Against Illicit Traffic in Narcotic Drugs and Psychotropic Substances (1988).

regime which was mainly based on territorial jurisdiction and which provided limited international co-operation among States under the principle of reciprocity. Because of these factors, States gathered together to act upon the need to take effective measures against such crimes, and to form a jurisdictional system that was different from the classical jurisdictional regime.

This legal development triggered by the increase in international crimes affected the enforcement measures of international human rights law as well. A similar expansion of jurisdiction was incorporated in various human rights treaties and conventions. It can be said that the development of international criminal law and human rights law interacted with each other, promoting a more extensive jurisdictional regime. As the international community became increasingly aware of human rights as a fundamental norm under international law, it gradually became convinced that it should consider the prosecution and punishment of gross violations of human rights as an important measure for enforcing international human rights law. At the same time, globalisation in many fields caused States to be aware of the international community as a whole. Consequently, interests beyond the individual national interest became more apparent to States. Gradually, the notion of the obligation of a State towards the international community, and the interest of the international community as a whole, was beginning to settle in the minds of member States of the international community and reflected in State practice. It was in 1970 that the ICJ acknowledged the obligation *erga omnes*. In the Barcelona Traction Case, the ICJ stated:

> '[A]n essential distinction should be drawn between the obligations of a State towards the international community as a whole, and those arising *vis-à-vis* another State in the field of diplomatic protection. By their very nature the former are the concern of all States. In view of the importance of the rights involved, all States can be held to have a legal interest in their protection; they are obligation *erga omnes*.'[66]

The ICJ further noted:

> 'Such obligations derive, for example, in contemporary international law, from the outlawing of acts of aggression, and of genocide, as also from the principles and rules concerning the basic rights of the human person, including protection from slavery and racial discrimination. Some of the corresponding rights of protection have entered into the body of general international law (*Reservations to the Convention and Punishment of the Crime of Genocide, Advisory Opinion, ICJ Reports 1951*, p. 23); others are conferred by international instruments of a universal or quasi-universal character.'[67]

Another factor that facilitated the expansion of national jurisdiction was the absence of international criminal jurisdiction. There was no *ad hoc* or permanent international

66 Case Concerning the Barcelona Traction, Light and Power Company, Limited (*Belgium* v. *Spain*), Judgment of 5 February 1970, *ICJ Reports 1970*, p. 32.

67 *Ibid.*

criminal court during this period. Witnessing how an attempt within the UN failed to establish international criminal jurisdiction in the early 1950s, there was scepticism concerning the realisation of an international criminal court. On the other hand, there was a growing need to respond to crimes with international concerns. To meet this need, there was not much choice but to rely on the national courts of States to prosecute and punish these crimes.

In conclusion, the social situation as well as the development and increased acceptance of some normative ideas promoted the modification of the jurisdictional regime in order to achieve a more effective prosecution and punishment of such crimes.

4.3.2 Expansion of National Jurisdiction

With the aim of ensuring the accountability of individuals responsible for international crimes and serious violations of human rights, many treaties and conventions prohibiting such crimes were enacted in a multilateral manner. They encouraged comprehensive multilateral and international systems to be set up in order to institutionalise international co-operation not limited by the principle of reciprocity. They expressly prescribed multiple national jurisdictions (most notably, including non-territorial jurisdiction), sometimes even as an obligation on the part of States – a phenomenon that I will call the 'expansion' of national jurisdiction in conventional international law.

The modifications made to conventions can be generalised into the following factors: 1) the explicit recognition of various bases of national jurisdiction, often accompanied by the obligation of States to exercise jurisdiction or to enact domestic law to that end; 2) the incorporation of provisions allowing for universal jurisdiction;[68] 3) the inclusion of express provisions for the *aut dedere aut judicare* principle;[69] and 4) the addition of a special provision facilitating the extradition of suspects between State Parties.

Let us observe these four factors taking the United Nations Convention Against Torture and Other Cruel, Inhuman or Degrading Treatment or Punishment (hereinafter referred to as the Torture Convention) as an example.[70] The example of the first factor is Article 5 of the Torture Convention.[71] It obligates each State Party to establish its

---

68 The nature of universal jurisdiction prescribed in multilateral conventions and its effect are explained in the next chapter.

69 The difference and relationship between the *aut dedere aut judicare* principle and universal jurisdiction is explained in Chapter IV.

70 For a detailed analysis of the jurisdictional provisions of the Torture Convention, see Ahcene Boulesbaa, *The U.N. Convention on Torture and the Prospects for Enforcement* (Martinus Nijhoff Publishers, 1999), pp. 175-235.

71 Article 5 of the Torture Convention reads as follows:
'1. Each State Party shall take such measures as may be necessary to establish its jurisdiction over the offences referred to in article 4 in the following cases:

jurisdiction based not only on territorial jurisdiction, but also on nationality and passive nationality jurisdiction. Unlike the classical jurisdictional regime, which was mainly based on territorial jurisdiction as a right of States, this provision obligates States to establish other bases of national jurisdiction too. Additionally, the third paragraph of the article further permits any criminal jurisdiction allowed by domestic law. The second paragraph of the article allows States to establish universal jurisdiction. This provision in the Torture Convention well illustrates the trend in conventional international law, which allows wider possibilities for national jurisdiction. The third factor is represented in Article 7.[72] According to this article, if a suspect is found in the territory of a State Party and is not extradited to another State, the former State has an obligation to submit the suspect to its prosecuting authorities. Lastly, Article 8 makes the crime of torture an extraditable offence, and offers itself as the legal basis for extradition.[73] This provision allows States to depart from the traditional principle of

---

(a) When the offences are committed in any territory under its jurisdiction or on board a ship or aircraft registered in that State;
(b) When the alleged offender is a national of that State;
(c) When the victim is a national of that State if that State considers it appropriate.
2. Each State Party shall likewise take such measures as may be necessary to establish its jurisdiction over such offences in cases where the alleged offender is present in any territory under its jurisdiction and it does not extradite him pursuant to article 8 to any of the States mentioned in paragraph 1 of this article.
3. This Convention does not exclude any criminal jurisdiction exercised in accordance with internal law.'

72 Article 7 of the Torture Convention prescribes as follows:
'1. The State Party in the territory under whose jurisdiction a person alleged to have committed any offence referred to in Article 4 is found shall in the cases contemplated in Article 5, if it does not extradite him, submit the case to its competent authorities for the purpose of prosecution.
2. These authorities shall take their decision in the same manner as in the case of any ordinary offence of a serious nature under the law of that State. In the cases referred to in Article 5, paragraph 2, the standards of evidence required for prosecution and conviction shall in no way be less stringent than those which apply in the cases referred to in Article 5, paragraph 1.
3. Any person regarding whom proceedings are brought in connection with any of the offences referred to in Article 4 shall be guaranteed fair treatment at all stages of the proceedings.'

73 Article 8 of the Torture Convention prescribes as follows:
'1. The offences referred to in Article 4 shall be deemed to be included as extraditable offences in any extradition treaty existing between States Parties. States Parties undertake to include such offences as extraditable offences in every extradition treaty to be concluded between them.
2. If a State Party which makes extradition conditional on the existence of a treaty receives a request for extradition from another State Party with which it has no extradition treaty, it may consider this Convention as the legal basis for extradition in respect of such offences. Extradition shall be subject to the other conditions provided by the law of the requested State.
3. States Parties which do not make extradition conditional on the existence of a treaty shall recognize such offences as extraditable offences between themselves subject to the conditions provided by the law of the requested State.
4. Such offences shall be treated, for the purpose of extradition between States Parties, as if they had been committed not only in the place in which they occurred but also in the territories of the States required to establish their jurisdiction in accordance with Article 5, paragraph 1.'

reciprocity. Comparing the above jurisdictional provisions with that of the Genocide Convention of 1948, which does not have such provisions, the changes are indeed significant.

All these provisions on jurisdiction followed the model of the 1970 Hague Convention for the Suppression of Unlawful Seizure of Aircraft and of the 1971 Montreal Convention for the Suppression of Unlawful Acts Against the Safety of Civil Aviation. There was a general trend in conventional international law to allow the wider jurisdictional bases shown above. The underlying intention is to authorise a wide jurisdiction to be asserted over criminals in order to end impunity by spreading the web of jurisdiction to fill any lacunae, so as to leave no safe haven for criminals. As expressed by Higgins, Kooijmans and Buergenthal in the ICJ, 'a gradual movement towards base of jurisdiction other than territoriality can be discerned. This slow but steady shifting to a more extensive application of extraterritorial jurisdiction by states reflects the emergence of values that enjoy an ever-increasing recognition in international society. One such value is the importance of the punishment of the perpetrators of international crimes.'[74]

In sum, in the absence of an international criminal court, the effort to put an end to impunity required the exercise of national jurisdiction. The movement to expand the recognition of various bases for national jurisdiction can be witnessed, particularly after the increase of international crimes in the 1960s, in many new conventions prohibiting such crimes. As a result, various jurisdictional bases gained greater acceptance and recognition than under classic international law.

Yet, this expansion of national jurisdiction in conventional international law did not quite bring about the actual prosecution of all the crimes prohibited. This is due to the fact that most of the conventions neither provided for the further obligation of States to exercise their adjudicating jurisdiction, nor did they lay down a mechanism to ensure the actual exercise of jurisdiction by States. For instance, compared to the Genocide Convention, which explicitly asserts duties by prescribing that the offenders 'shall be punished' and 'shall be tried', the Torture Convention only requires State Parties to 'submit' cases to their competent authorities. Consequently, Joyner concludes that 'the anti-torture instrument fails explicitly to mandate that prosecution must occur for all alleged cases of torture, or to stipulate that, without exception, severe penalties will be handed down for persons found guilty of a torture offense.'[75]

Furthermore, the norms regulating a jurisdictional system for many of the crimes under customary international law were still unclear. In addition, the fairness of the proceedings in States was questioned.

---

74 Joint Separate Opinion of Judges Higgins, Kooijmans and Buergenthal, the Case Concerning the Arrest Warrant of 11 April 2000 (Democratic Republic of the *Congo* v. *Belgium*), *supra* note (23), para. 73.

75 Christopher C. Joyner, *supra* note (16), p. 606.

4.4 The Fourth Period: From the 1990s to the Present

In the 1990s, the jurisdictional system underwent a great transition as a result of the substantial development of international criminal and humanitarian law. Many factors contributed to this development. Of course, the increased international attention devoted to measures to cope with international crimes as observed in the third period continued to influence the development of international criminal law. Also, the change in the international political situation, especially the end of the Cold War between the East and the West that had halted the discussions on an international criminal court in the 1950s, had a notable influence. Judicial and normative discussions triggered by the Lockerbie Case and the work of the International Law Commission on the Draft Code of Crimes Against Peace and Security of Mankind[76] prompted States to become more interested in ending impunity. However, there is no doubt that the greatest impetus was the establishment of the *ad hoc* international tribunals. The large-scale massacres in Yugoslavia and Rwanda in the early 1990s shocked the conscience of the international community.

4.4.1 International Criminal Jurisdiction in Action

In 1993, the UN Security Council established the ICTY to prosecute those responsible for serious crimes committed in the former Yugoslavia. In the following year, the ICTR was established to prosecute serious violations of international humanitarian law, to establish law and order, and thereby to contribute to the restoration and maintenance of peace and national reconciliation in Rwanda.[77] It was deplored that a culture of impunity had developed within Rwanda, because no punishment was possible within that country in spite of recurring massacres since 1959,[78] and the international community, at the request of Rwanda itself, stepped in to end impunity and promote accountability. Therefore, the ICTY and the ICTR were created as a result of the inability of national jurisdiction – or, more specifically, the territorial jurisdiction of the States in the former Yugoslavia region and Rwanda – to be effectively

---

76 Draft Code of Crimes Against the Peace and Security of Mankind, Report of the International Law Commission on the Work of its Forty-Eighth Session, UN Doc. A/51/10.

77 See UN Security Council Resolution 955 (1994), UN Doc. S/RES/955 (1994).

78 The Rwandan delegate to the UN stated that 'it is impossible to build a state of law and arrive at true national reconciliation if we do not eradicate the culture of impunity which has characterized our society.' Statement of the Rwandan Ambassador at the UN Security Council, 'The Situation Concerning Rwanda: Establishment of an International Tribunal for the Prosecution of Persons Responsible for Serious Violations of International Humanitarian Law Committed in the Territory of Rwanda and Rwandan Citizens Responsible for Such Violations Committed in the Territory of Neighbouring States', UN Doc. S/PV. 3453 (1994). See also Christina M. Carroll 'An Assessment of the Role and Effectiveness of the International Criminal Tribunal for Rwanda and the Rwandan National Justice System in Dealing with the Mass Atrocities of 1994' *Boston University International Law Journal* Vol. 18 No. 2 (Fall 2000), p. 171.

exercised. In addition, the ICC has recently started to function after the entry into force of the convention including its Statute on 1 July 2002.

Several other conditions were recognised as prompting the establishment of the international tribunals. These include: the lack of a stable judicial system within the territorial State due to the collapse of national systems; the political nature of crimes committed during the power struggle; and the possibility of hatred between opposing groups or ethnic groups affecting the procedures within the territorial State and undermining justice and peace.[79]

These international criminal courts contribute to: 1) spreading the web of jurisdiction to fill any lacunae, diminishing safe havens for criminals; and 2) ensuring the fairness and impartiality of proceedings in prosecuting and punishing individuals. It is considered that justice cannot be achieved unless proceedings are conducted in a fair and impartial manner, and fully respecting due process and the rights of suspects. Therefore, the impartiality of proceedings is greatly emphasised in the international criminal courts. If 'the national court proceedings were not impartial or independent, were designed to shield the accused from international criminal responsibility, or the case was not diligently prosecuted',[80] this would not bar the ICTY from taking over the case. The ICTR and ICC have similar provisions. This suggests that States are under the surveillance of the international community with regard to the way in which they perform and pursue their rights and duties regarding criminal proceedings.

4.4.2 Encouraging the Active Exercise of National Jurisdiction

The establishment of the international criminal courts, national jurisdictions, especially universal jurisdiction, have been re-evaluated and the expectation for their role in effectively enforcing international law has grown. As is evident from the respective statutes of the international criminal courts, the existence of international judicial organs does not preclude national courts from pursuing an active role in punishing

79 The Commission of Experts reported the need to establish the ICTR, stating the danger of conducting trials in domestic courts as one reason. It was argued that to prosecute such highly emotional and political crimes in the Rwandan domestic courts had the danger of becoming a retaliation without a guarantee of fair trial, and even if the trials were conducted while respecting the rights of suspects, there was a great possibility that such trials would not be regarded as fair. See Preliminary Report of the Independent Commission of Experts established in accordance with Security Council Resolution 935 (1994), UN Doc. S/1994/1125, para. 136. Others argue that the Rwandan domestic courts were actually incapable of conducting trials in an independent and fair manner, therefore the new Rwandan government had to build a new judicial system rather than reconstruct the former. See Catherine Cissé 'The End of a Culture of Impunity in Rwanda? Prosecution of Genocide and War Crimes before Rwandan Courts and the International Criminal Tribunal for Rwanda' *Yearbook of International Humanitarian Law* Vol. 1 (1998), p. 176. See also, Robert F. Van Lierop 'Report on the International Criminal Tribunal for Rwanda' *Hofstra Law and Policy Symposium* Vol. 3 (1999), pp. 205-207, 211-221.

80 Article 10.2(b) of the Statute of ICTY.

individuals responsible for serious crimes. On the contrary, national courts have been encouraged to do so.

The ICTY Appeals Chamber declared that the 'national jurisdictions of the States of ex-Yugoslavia, as those of all States, were required by customary law to judge or to extradite those persons presumed responsible for grave violations of international humanitarian law.'[81] In response to this expectation, many States have enacted domestic law to co-operate with the international tribunals as well as to exercise their national jurisdiction against serious crimes, and several trials based on universal jurisdiction have been conducted in the domestic courts of third States against alleged offenders from the former Yugoslavia and Rwanda.[82]

Whereas the international criminal courts greatly contribute to globalising the campaign to end impunity, they cannot bear the entire burden of upholding individual accountability. Despite the existence or the future existence of international judicial organs in this matter, the main forums for trying individuals will always be domestic courts. The role of national jurisdiction in the international campaign to end impunity should not be disregarded.

Not every serious violation of human rights may trigger the establishment of an international judicial institution. On the contrary, the establishment of such an international institution is exceptional, usually contemplated after the occurrence of atrocities, thus requiring some time before it can start to function. The more readily functioning forum is the ordinary national courts of each State. With proper domestic legislation or through the direct application of international law, national courts are the most easily available forums to act promptly in prosecuting individuals responsible for such crimes.

Also, it is obvious that the international criminal courts cannot and do not in fact try all cases single-handedly. The ICTY and ICTR are *ad hoc* in nature, only having jurisdiction limited in time, in territory, and/or in terms of people with a particular nationality. Furthermore, the ICC operates under the principle of complementarity,[83] which means that as a point of departure national prosecution has priority, and, therefore, the principal forums remain the domestic courts. Not only in normative terms, but also practically speaking, the international criminal courts cannot try all cases of serious crimes. Therefore, notwithstanding the existence of the international criminal courts, the domestic courts of States are still urged by the international community to exercise their jurisdiction over those serious crimes. In fact, domestic

81 The Blaskic Case at the ICTY, 29 October 1997, case IT-95-14-AR, para. 29.

82 See the Annex of the 'Final Report on the Exercise of Universal Jurisdiction in Respect of Gross Human Rights Offences', *supra* note (42). See also Brigitte Stern 'La compétence universelle in France: le cas des crimes commis en ex-Yougoslavie et au Rwanda' 40 *German Yearbook of International Law* 280 (1997). See also, Andreas Ziegler 'International Decisions: In re G.' 92 *American Journal of International Law* Vol. 92 (1998), and Christoph J. M. Safferling 'International Decisions: *Public Prosecutor* v. *Djajic*' *American Journal of International Law* Vol. 92 (1998).

83 See the Preamble to and Article 17 of the ICC Statute.

courts are expected to take an active role in the international campaign to end impunity. Today, the role of the domestic courts is being reappraised.

As a result of the expansion of national jurisdiction since the 1970s and the establishment of international criminal courts, the modern jurisdictional regime of today is composed of multiple international and national jurisdictions. These jurisdictions are generally formulated in the form of concurrency, rather than excluding each other.

5 Conclusion

In this chapter, I have explained basic principles which are relevant to this study and five bases of national jurisdiction recognised under international law. The notion of universal jurisdiction requires a thorough study as it is used with different connotations by many people. This study specifically distinguishes between universal jurisdiction and universal jurisdiction *in absentia*. In addition, in order to illustrate the nature of universal jurisdiction in different contexts, I have presented two aspects to be used in categorising universal jurisdiction: whether it is a right or an obligation, and supplemental or primary. This categorisation helps to illuminate how the notion of universal jurisdiction has developed, as I will explain in the next chapter.

In the latter half of this chapter, I have illustrated and analysed the development of the jurisdictional regime from classic international law to the present. In sum, the development of the concurrent jurisdictional system of today has been achieved through many efforts in previous decades to overcome the shortcomings of the classical jurisdictional regime – one of the main shortcomings being that of territorial jurisdiction. Although the international criminal courts were established to prosecute serious crimes, the primary burden of achieving justice today still rests upon States. In the next chapter, we will look at the most controversial basis of national jurisdiction which has significantly evolved during the era of the modern jurisdictional regime – universal jurisdiction.

CHAPTER III
HISTORICAL DEVELOPMENT OF UNIVERSAL JURISDICTION

1 INTRODUCTION

1.1 Aim of this Chapter

This chapter will illustrate how universal jurisdiction has expanded considerably in theory and practice over the years. The gradual acceptance of universal jurisdiction both in conventional and customary international law will be sketched, special attention being devoted to the historical background of and factors that became an impetus for its development. I believe it is important to understand the history of the development of universal jurisdiction in order to achieve a proper perception of universal jurisdiction at the theoretical and practical levels, which is analysed in the next chapter. In addition, the role and status of universal jurisdiction within today's jurisdictional regime are not independent from the background of how universal jurisdiction came into being and how it was accepted. Therefore, the inquiry in this chapter acts as a prerequisite to a thorough analysis of the notion of universal jurisdiction which is conducted in the next chapter.

This chapter introduces the historical development of universal jurisdiction, especially the universal jurisdiction against genocide. Focus is placed on the crime of genocide since it is widely recognized as being one of the most grave human rights violations. Due to its seriousness, even the reluctant States are likely to accept a more liberal form of jurisdiction than for other categories of crimes. It is interesting from the perspective of the development of international law to determine how far the jurisdiction over genocide has expanded.

In examining the historical development of universal jurisdiction, this chapter observes how universal jurisdiction has gained expectation and support in a situation where States, especially territorial States, were unable or reluctant to effectively exercise jurisdiction and where no international criminal court was available. On the other hand, the history also illustrates that discussions on universal jurisdiction at various times have entailed a conflict between classical principles and a newly spreading perception: principles of State sovereignty and territorial jurisdiction which were dominant in the classical jurisdictional regime on the one hand, and the interest of the international community which has encouraged the expansion of universal jurisdiction on the other. The examination of various discussions in the UN and in academic literature over the years reveals that, partially due to the influence of principles in the classical jurisdictional regime and largely due to the lack of incentives among States, universal jurisdiction has been greatly disputed as regards the precise scope of its acceptance within customary international law.

1.2 A Reminder of the Different Definitions and the Nature of Universal Jurisdiction

First, it is imperative to acknowledge the diversity of theoretical understandings concerning universal jurisdiction. As I explained in Chapter II, 'universal jurisdiction' has been referred to in various instruments and writings with different definitions and a divergent nature in mind. In this study, *universal jurisdiction* is a form of national jurisdiction exercised by a State where a suspect is present. It is distinguished from international criminal jurisdiction that is exercised by international tribunals or courts. Furthermore, this study distinguishes universal jurisdiction and universal jurisdiction *in absentia*. The latter is a national jurisdiction asserted by a State with no nexus to the crime in question, even without the presence of a suspect on its territory when making its claim of jurisdiction.

In facilitating the illustration of the nature of universal jurisdiction as conceived during different periods of history, it must be reiterated that this study describes the nature of universal jurisdiction with two aspects: permissive or obligatory, and supplemental or primary. The first aspect asks whether universal jurisdiction is recognized as a right or obligation. The second aspect entails relations with other bases of jurisdiction, and asks whether universal jurisdiction is perceived to be supplemental (secondary) to another jurisdiction or whether it can be exercised irrespective of the jurisdiction of other States.

1.3 Overview of the Development of Universal Jurisdiction

The historical examination in this chapter is undertaken as chronologically as possible, from traditional international law to modern international law, which has gradually accomplished the acceptance of universal jurisdiction for various gross human rights violations. A detailed introduction to the individual historical and recent cases of universal jurisdiction can be found in many writings by scholars and NGOs.[1] Therefore, I concentrate on presenting my view of the historical development of universal jurisdiction rather than describing all the cases.

---

1 See, for example, M.C. Bassiouni 'Universal Jurisdiction for International Crimes: Historical Perspectives and Contemporary Practice' *Virginia Journal of International Law* Vol. 42 (2001). For an example of NGO papers, Amnesty International 'Universal Jurisdiction: The Duty of States to Enact and Implement Legislation', September 2001, AI Index IOR 53/2001. For an introduction to cases of universal jurisdiction in Europe since the 1990s, see the paper prepared by Fiona McKay for REDRESS 'Universal Jurisdiction in Europe: Criminal prosecutions in Europe since 1990 for war crimes, crimes against humanity, torture and genocide', obtainable at http://www.redress.org/unijeur.html.

I divide and describe the history of universal jurisdiction in the four periods mentioned in Chapter I: the first period falls coincides with traditional international law; the second period is after the Second World War until the end of the 1960s; the third period dates from the 1970s to the time before the establishment of *ad hoc* tribunals; and the fourth period is from the 1990s to the present. Utilizing this time-frame facilitates an understanding of the gradual development of universal jurisdiction in conjunction with the changes in the global political realities and in the thinking of the international community and scholars during each period.

2 The First Period: Universal Jurisdiction in Classical International Law

2.1 The Emergence of Universal Jurisdiction: Jurisdiction Against Piracy

As explained in Chapter II, the most traditional jurisdictional basis is territorial jurisdiction. All jurisdictional bases have their justification based on some nexus between a State and a particular crime. Then, how did the notion of universal jurisdiction, which seems to be lacking a firm nexus, develop? To put the answer in a simple phrase, it has developed in relation to the recognition of common interests among States.

It is commonly asserted that the idea of universal jurisdiction was expressed in the writings of classical scholars from centuries past. President Guillaume in the ICJ descried the thinking of the classical scholars as follows:

> 'Some writers, like Covarruvias and Grotius, pointed out that the presence on the territory of a State of a foreign criminal peacefully enjoying the fruits of his crimes was intolerable. They therefore maintained that it should be possible to prosecute perpetrators of certain particulary serious crimes not only in the State on whose territory the crime was committed but also in the country where they sought refuge.'[2]

However, it became most apparent in State practice with regard to the crime of piracy.[3] The crime of piracy is the longest recognized crime to be subject to universal jurisdic-

2 See the Separate Opinion of President Guillaume to the Judgment of 14 February 2002, in the ICJ Case Concerning the Arrest Warrant of 11 April 2000 (Democratic Republic of the *Congo* v. *Belgium*), para. 4. For the reference to the classical works, see also, M. Cherif Bassiouni, *ibid.*, pp. 96-101.

3 Condemnation of piracy was mostly under customary international law. In conventional international law, the Geneva Convention on the High Seas (1958) outlawed piracy. Also the recent codification of the law of the sea outlaws piracy and allows States which have conducted a seizure to exercise universal jurisdiction over piracy. See Arts. 103-107 of the 1982 United Nations Convention on the Law of the Sea, December 10, 1982, UN Doc. A/CONF. 62/L2 (entered into force November 16, 1994). Art. 105 provides that 'every State may seize a pirate ship or aircraft, or a ship or aircraft taken by piracy and under the control of pirates, and arrest the persons and seize the property on board. The courts of the State which carried out the seizure may decide upon the penalties to be imposed.'

tion with centuries of history.[4] The jurisdiction of any State that has custody of suspects of piracy was widely recognized, without controversy, to be in conformity with international law.[5]

There are two rationales as to why universal jurisdiction was recognized for piracy under international law. The first was the gravity of the crime, amounting to '*hostis humani generis*', inciting States to recognize that the punishment of piracy served not only the interest of the individual State, but also the interests of the States constituting the international community.[6]

The second rationale was the lack of eligible or effective jurisdiction, or the uncertainty as to which State had jurisdiction over a case.[7] Because acts of piracy are committed on the high seas – the high seas belonging to no State – more often than not no State possessed jurisdiction to punish such acts, and States including the flag State were unable to prosecute effectively. For this reason, it was held that any State that

---

4 Cowles says piracy was subject to universal jurisdiction at least from the sixteenth century deriving from the treatment of brigards. See Willard B. Cowles 'Universality of Jurisdiction over War Crimes' *California Law Review* 33 (1945), pp. 181-194.

5 The draft for the codification of international law concerning piracy, prepared by Bingham, made the *lawful* custody of a suspect a prerequisite. It proposed as follows:
'Article 14
1. A state which has lawful custody of a person suspected of piracy may prosecute and punish that person.
2. Subject to the provisions of this convention, the law of the state which exercises such jurisdiction defines the crime, governs the procedure and prescribes the penalty.
3. The law of the state must, however, assure protection to accused aliens as follows:
(a) The accused person must be given a fair trial before an impartial tribunal without unreasonable delay.
(b) The accused person must be given humane treatment during his confinement pending trial.
(c) No cruel and unusual punishment may be inflicted.
(d) No discrimination may be made against the nationals of any state.
4. A state may intercede diplomatically to assure this protection to one of its nationals who is accused in another state.'
Joseph W. Bingham 'Research in International Law IV: Piracy (Draft of Convention Prepared for the Codification of International Law)' *Supplement to American Journal of International Law* Vol. 26 (1932).

6 'The attacks of pirates are directed against the interests of maritime trade throughout the world, and pirates are therefore justiciable in every civilized country. The State which seizes the pirate vessel and arrests the crew is the obvious judge of the validity of the capture and the guilt of the parties concerned. It should by preference be accorded the right to investigate and to pass judgment in the case, unless the internal law or some international convention otherwise decides ...' Report of the Sub-Committee of the League of Nations Committee of Experts for the Progressive Codification of International Law, cited in Joseph W. Bingham, *ibid.*, p. 854.

7 The existence of this second rationale is ignored or denied by some. See, for example, Kenneth C. Randall 'Universal Jurisdiction Under International Law' Texas Law Review 66 (March 1998). Randall explains the rationale solely on the fundamental nature of the crime of piracy. On the other hand, Cowles emphasizes that piracy occurs only where there is a 'lack of governmental control' in the pirate's area of operation. He contends that this fact, not the physical location of the pirate on the high seas, provide the justification for jurisdiction under the universality principle. Cowles, *supra* note (4), p. 193.

was capable of capturing suspects and of prosecuting and punishing them effectively could take that opportunity. Otherwise, it would be very difficult to combat the crime of piracy.

In short, because of the gravity of the crime, the prosecution of piracy was recognized as a common interest among States. Also due to the lack of eligible or effective jurisdiction, it was necessary to allow all States that had the opportunity to capture suspects to actually exercise jurisdiction. As a consequence, universal jurisdiction for the crime of piracy was established under customary international law.

Some States enacted domestic legislation allowing universal jurisdiction for crimes other than piracy. However, these domestic legislation did not necessarily create a customary norm under international law comparable to that of piracy. Since universal jurisdiction over the crime of piracy had become established under international law, some States began to assert universal jurisdiction over crimes related to slave trading, although the Slavery Convention of 1926 does not expressly provide for universal jurisdiction.[8] In addition to the crime of trading in slaves, trafficking of women and children, counterfeiting, and drug trafficking were argued to be subject to universal jurisdiction.[9] In claiming the applicability of universal jurisdiction over certain categories of crimes other than piracy, discussions were often based on the nature of the crimes. It was argued that because they were similar in gravity to the crime of piracy, they should be susceptible to the exercise of universal jurisdiction as well.

---

8 Article 2 of the Slavery Convention which entered into force on 9 March 1927 provides as follows: 'The High Contracting Parties undertake, each in respect of the territories placed under its sovereignty, jurisdiction, protection, suzerainty or tutelage, so far as they have not already taken the necessary steps:
(a) To prevent and suppress the slave trade;
(b) To bring about, progressively and as soon as possible, the complete abolition of slavery in all its forms.'
As cited above, Article 2 does not expressly prescribe universal jurisdiction, compared to Article 3 which clearly prescribes territorial jurisdiction as follows: 'The High Contracting Parties undertake to adopt all appropriate measures with a view to preventing and suppressing the embarkation, disembarkation and transport of slaves in their territorial waters and upon all vessels flying their respective flags.' One may argue that capturing a ship registered to a foreign State that is carrying slaves constitutes the exercise of universal jurisdiction, but the definition of slavery and prohibited acts relating to slavery includes acts of trading, therefore, capturing a ship within its territorial waters constitutes territorial jurisdiction. It is categorized as the exercise of universal jurisdiction when the ship is captured in non-territorial waters. Article 1 defines the acts as follows:
'(1) Slavery is the status or condition of a person over whom any or all of the powers attaching to the right of ownership are exercised.
(2) The slave trade includes all acts involved in the capture, acquisition or disposal of a person with intent to reduce him to slavery; all acts involved in the acquisition of a slave with a view to selling or exchanging him; all acts of disposal by sale or exchange of a slave acquired with a view to being sold or exchanged, and, in general, every act of trade or transport in slaves.'

9 Research in International Law (Under the Auspices of the Faculty of the Harvard Law School), 'Drafts of Conventions Prepared for the Codification of International Law: Jurisdiction with Respect to Crime' (referred in this study as Harvard Research), *Supplement to the American Journal of International Law* Vol. 29 (1935), pp. 569-572.

However, a common understanding as to which offences fell within *hostic humani generis* or *delicta juris gentium* that could be prosecuted and punished on the same basis as piracy seemed to be lacking during the first period.[10] In addition, for crimes other than piracy, universal jurisdiction was construed to be supplemental to other jurisdictions. In other words, for crimes other than piracy, a State could choose to exercise universal jurisdiction if the States involved were not themselves prepared to put the suspect on trial. Furthermore, some were of the opinion that a State had to be recognized as having a sufficient interest in the prosecution under a convention or custom before exercising universal jurisdiction. It seems that universal jurisdiction became a customary rule only for the crime of piracy, and not for other crimes.

The difference in customary status can be explained through the possible conflict with the rules and principles in the classical jurisdictional regime. It is important to note that the lack of conflict with territorial jurisdiction was a major reason that enabled the development of universal jurisdiction against piracy. Because the crime of piracy was committed on the high seas, a conflict with territorial jurisdiction was not a matter of concerns. The Harvard Research – a draft convention concerning jurisdiction prepared by the Harvard Law School – explains that universal jurisdiction over piracy was justified 'upon the ground that the punishable acts are committed upon the sea where all have an interest in the safety of commerce and where no state has territorial jurisdiction.'[11] Therefore, the formation of custom concerning universal jurisdiction over piracy did not alter the dominance of territorial jurisdiction under the classical jurisdictional regime.

Considering how universal jurisdiction over piracy was formed, the two rationales – the gravity of the crime which signifies the common interest of the international community,[12] and the absence or uncertainty of effective jurisdiction – are equally important. In my opinion, these two rationales for universal jurisdiction are still relevant today in determining the role, the necessity, and the appropriateness of universal jurisdiction, as I will explain in Chapter VI.

2.2 The Nature of Universal Jurisdiction in Classical International Law

Exercising of jurisdiction was generally a right under the classical jurisdictional regime unless otherwise expressly provided in a treaty or convention. Naturally, universal

10 Harvard Research, *ibid.*, p. 569.

11 Harvard Research, p. 566.

12 Although acts of piracy are still being committed in modern times, the gravity attached to the crime may be perceived to be less than that of genocide or other serious crimes acknowledged today. In this respect, piracy is characterized as a crime which damages the common interest of the members of the international community, rather than the interest of the international community as a whole. For an explanation of the difference between the common interest of States and the interest of the international community as a whole, see Chapter II.

jurisdiction was also understood as a right (rather than an obligation) of States. Therefore, universal jurisdiction was ordinarily perceived to be *permissive* jurisdiction.

Next, let us consider whether universal jurisdiction during the first period is considered as primary or supplemental jurisdiction. During the first period, universal jurisdiction for ordinary crimes could be found in the domestic law of some States. However, except for the crime of piracy, universal jurisdiction was associated with a *supplemental* characteristic under the classical jurisdictional regime. In other words, universal jurisdiction was only practised when there was no extradition request or if there was any, when extradition to requesting States had failed. This supplemental nature of universal jurisdiction is explicitly stated in the Harvard Research.[13] The Harvard Research distinguished between universal jurisdiction for the crime of piracy which was fairly well-established and universal jurisdiction for other crimes which was observed to be rarely invoked, and it stated that the latter universal jurisdiction was recognised only as an auxiliary competence.[14] Its research into the domestic laws of States during this period showed that, except for the Penal Code of Norway, all the codes and the projects for codes which it had studied prescribed universal jurisdiction as an alternative to extradition.[15] Also, Article 10 of the Harvard Research recognised the superiority of territorial jurisdiction and nationality jurisdiction, and emphasised that extradition to a territorial or nationality State was the ordinary procedure.[16] Only when extradition was not accepted could the custodial State exercise universal jurisdic-

13 Harvard Research.
14 Harvard Research, *ibid.*, pp. 569-571.
15 Harvard Research, p. 583.
16 The article demonstrates that significant respect was given to other bases of jurisdiction, especially territorial jurisdiction. Article 10 of the Harvard Research prescribes as follows:
Article 10. Universality: Other Crimes
'A State has jurisdiction with respect to any crime committed outside its territory by an alien, other than the crimes mentioned in Articles 6, 7, 8, and 9, as follows:
(a) When committed in a place not subject to its authority but subject to the authority of another State, if the act or omission which constitutes the crime is also an offence by the law of the place where it was committed, if surrender of the alien for prosecution has been offered to such other State or States and the offer remains unaccepted, and if prosecution is not barred by lapse of time under the law of the place where the crime was committed. The penalty imposed shall in no case be more severe than the penalty prescribed for the same act or omission by the law of the place where the crime was committed.
(b) When committed in a place not subject to the authority of any State, if the act or omission which constitutes the crime is also an offence by the law of a State of which the alien is a national, if surrender of the alien for prosecution has been offered to the State or States of which he is a national and the offer remains unaccepted, and if prosecution is not barred by lapse of time under the law of a State of which the alien is a national. The penalty imposed shall in no case be more severe than the penalty prescribed for the same act or omission by the law of a State of which the alien is a national.
(c) When committed in a place not subject to the authority of any State, if the crime was committed to the injury of the State assuming jurisdiction, or of one of its nationals, or of a corporation or juristic person having its national character.
(d) When committed in a place not subject to the authority of any State and the alien is not a national of any State.'

tion instead of extradition. This view on the supplemental nature of universal jurisdiction was shared by many, *e.g.*, in the work of Donnedieu de Vabres and by a resolution adopted by the Third International Congress of Penal Law held in 1933.[17]

It is concluded that universal jurisdiction was thus characterized as being inferior to other jurisdictional bases, especially territorial jurisdiction. Therefore, it could be exercised only when other jurisdictions were not exercised. In this sense, universal jurisdiction was not a primary, but a *supplemental* (secondary) jurisdiction which was exercised only after other jurisdictions had failed.

This supplemental characteristic of universal jurisdiction is in conformity with the principles that governed the classical jurisdictional regime. It is consistent with the almost absolute respect given to the principles of State sovereignty and territoriality. By giving priority to extradition requests, it avoided undermining the supremacy of territorial jurisdiction within the classical jurisdictional regime. At the same time, it respected the freedom of a State where a suspect is present by allowing it to exercise jurisdiction whenever extradition had failed. This was also in accordance with the general freedom given to a State as long as it does not interfere with the interests of another State. In addition, it respects the nexus rule. Because universal jurisdiction had a considerably weak standing as against other bases of jurisdiction with a stronger nexus, universal jurisdiction was allowed only after efforts to extradite had been exhausted.

One reason why universal jurisdiction did abide by the above principles was the lack of consensus among States on the question of which crimes, other than the crime of piracy, violate the common interest or the interest of the international community. Universal jurisdiction relates to the common interest or the interest of the whole international community, but besides the crime of piracy, it was difficult to find the unity of opinion among States concerning the severity of the crime in question amounting to be a violation of the common interest of the international community. Since States lacked the incentive to create a special jurisdiction setting aside the rules of the classical jurisdictional regime, it is not surprising that universal jurisdiction remained to be generally characterised as supplemental in nature.

If certain principles in classic international law induced universal jurisdiction to be supplemental in character, then why should the crime of piracy fall under *primary* universal jurisdiction? One reason could be that the crime of piracy directly and substantially damaged the national security and commercial interests of powerful States, so much so that it provoked an active and rigorous response on the part of States to prosecute and punish, and thereby formed a custom and *opinio juris* to this end.

To sum up, for the crime of piracy, universal jurisdiction was recognized as being a primary permissive universal jurisdiction. But for other crimes, it was only recognized as a supplemental jurisdiction. It should also be remembered that universal

---

17 See Harvard Research, p. 572.

jurisdiction was generally understood as a right of States which had custody over suspects. Therefore, universal jurisdiction was a jurisdiction which was exercisable by a State where a suspect was present, and universal jurisdiction *in absentia* was not a common notion under the classical jurisdictional regime.[18]

2.3 Concluding Observations on the First Period

I have illustrated above the understanding of universal jurisdiction under classic international law. Within the classical jurisdictional regime, territorial jurisdiction was the dominant rule. Under such dominance, universal jurisdiction was an exception, and was therefore considerably limited. It was construed that universal jurisdiction would only be allowed when the effort to extradite suspects to other States had become exhausted. In this respect, universal jurisdiction was supplemental to other jurisdictions. On the other hand, universal jurisdiction over piracy was admitted as being primary jurisdiction. This was due to the seriousness of the crime and the lack of effective jurisdiction thereover. In addition, there was great interest in the safety of navigation since it was directly linked to personal safety and national security as well as trading profits for States. Moreover, prosecuting and punishing piracy committed on the high seas were unlikely to undermine the territorial jurisdiction of States, therefore a primary permissive universal jurisdiction over piracy was accepted even within the classical jurisdictional regime. However, for other categories of crimes there was not enough consensus and incentives among States to compel classic international law to develop a jurisdiction setting aside the dominance of territorial jurisdiction.

3 The Second Period: After the Second World War Up to the End of the 1960s

3.1 Universal Jurisdiction Concerning War Crimes

3.1.1 Post-WWII Trials

Let us now examine universal jurisdiction in modern international law. In the aftermath of the Second World War, trials involving major war crimes were conducted in the international military tribunals at Nuremberg and Tokyo. The Nuremberg and Tokyo Tribunals were international institutions established under multilateral treaties, but many crimes were also prosecuted and punished by the national courts of the Allied States under Control Council Law No. 10 (December 20, 1945). These trials (in military or other forms of domestic courts) were different from the Nuremberg and Tokyo

18 The Harvard Research clearly states that universal jurisdiction 'may be invoked only if the alien is present in a place subject to the authority of the State assuming jurisdiction', and the 'presence of the accused provides the basis for jurisdiction'. Harvard Research, p. 582.

Tribunals, in that they were not directly established under international law and were mainly based on the exercise of national jurisdiction which was primarily the discretion of each State. The question is, on which basis of jurisdiction did the above domestic courts operate?

Some authors are of the opinion that the prosecution of crimes committed during the Second World War demonstrated the exercise of universal jurisdiction,[19] and conclude that universal jurisdiction became customary international law immediately after the War. They are also of the opinion that the trials of Nazis were the exercise of universal jurisdiction since the Allied States were neither the States in which the crimes had been committed nor the States of which the suspects were nationals. Moreover, they conclude that the supplemental characteristic of universal jurisdiction was overcome after observing the manner in which jurisdiction was exercised by the Allied States.

Rather, however, those trials were based on territorial jurisdiction and/or passive personality jurisdiction (jurisdiction based on the nationality of the victims). It was observed that the military tribunals located in Germany, Italy, and the Netherlands usually tried offences committed against the country's own nationals.[20] Carnegie noted that even the prosecutor in the Nuremberg Tribunal explained its jurisdiction as being based on territorial jurisdiction.[21] 'It is just theoretically conceivable that the principles of territorial jurisdiction and nationality jurisdiction could justify all trials of German accused anywhere, and of defendants of any nationality for offences committed in Germany, by one of the four occupying Powers in Germany.'[22] In addition, taking into consideration the trials held in States other than the four occupying Powers, Carnegie concluded that the passive personality principle was also applied.[23] Similarly, another commentator clarified this as follows:

> '[T]he jurisdiction of war crimes tribunal is ... normally confined to offences committed on the soil of prosecuting state or against its nationals and residents. Special occupation courts therefore become necessary in order to deal with those war crimes which are within the jurisdiction of the prosecuting state only *qua* military occupant. In the absence of these bases of jurisdiction, the state employing municipal law is powerless ... to deal with other offences committed even by the same accused, despite the fact that war

---

19 See *Demjanjuk* v. *Petrovsky*, 776 F. 2d 571, 582 (6th Cir. 1985), *cert. denied*, 475 U. S. 1016 (1986). For an examination of cases referring to universal jurisdiction, see Kenneth C. Randall, *supra* note (7), pp. 804-810.

20 See Willard B. Cowles 'Trials of War Criminals (Non-Nuremberg)' *American Journal of International Law* Vol. 42 (1948), p. 299. See also A.R. Carnegie 'Jurisdiction over Violations of the Laws and Customs of War' *British Yearbook of International Law* 39 (1963), pp. 402, 422-423.

21 See A.R. Carnegie, *ibid.*, p. 414.

22 A.R. Carnegie, *ibid.*, p. 418.

23 Carnegie preferred to regard the *Hostages* trial and the *Justice* trial as being based on territorial jurisdiction or active or passive nationality jurisdiction, rather than on universal jurisdiction. See, *ibid.*, p. 422.

criminals have often been guilty of a course of conduct which does violence to nationals or interests of a number of states.'[24]

In addition, considering the interests of Allied States, it can be interpreted that jurisdiction was based on protective jurisdiction – jurisdiction based on the interest of a State infringed by that crime.

Even if the trials could be regarded as precedents for universal jurisdiction, there is great opposition to generalizing the practices that have taken place immediately after the Second World War. This is because they were conducted under an extraordinary situation where the Allied States were the victorious States, having total control and occupying the territory of the defeated. It is difficult to presume the peculiar practices of that period to be proof of a general custom in customary international law. In sum, in order to conclude that universal jurisdiction became customary international law, more evidence is required in addition to the prosecution of war crimes conducted in the domestic courts of the Allied States.

3.1.2 The 1949 Geneva Conventions

Next, I will examine the provisions of the Geneva Convention for the Amelioration of the Condition of the Wounded and Sick in Armed Forces in the Field (Geneva Convention I); the Geneva Convention for the Amelioration of the Condition of Wounded, Sick and Shipwrecked Members of Armed Forces at Sea (Geneva Convention II); the Geneva Convention Relative to the Treatment of Prisoners of War (Geneva Convention III); and the Geneva Convention Relative to the Protection of Civilian Persons in Time of War (Geneva Convention IV) (hereinafter, all referred to as the 1949 Geneva Conventions). The 1949 Geneva Conventions provide as follows:

> 'Each High Contracting Party shall be under the obligation to search for persons alleged to have committed, or to have ordered to be committed, such grave breaches, and shall bring such persons, regardless of their nationality, before its own courts. It may also, if it prefers, and in accordance with the provisions of its own legislation, hand such persons over for trial to another High Contracting Party concerned, provided such High Contracting Party has made out a *prima facie* case.'[25]

The above provisions found in all four conventions oblige State Parties to search for and try suspects in their own courts. The majority view this as a prescription of universal jurisdiction.[26] But there are opposing views by other commentators. They assert that since universal jurisdiction is not mentioned explicitly, it is not prescribed.

---

24 R.R. Baxter 'The Municipal and International Law Basis of Jurisdiction Over War Crimes' *British Yearbook of International Law* 28 (1951), p. 387.

25 Art. 49, Art. 50, Art. 129, and Art. 146 of the 1949 Geneva Convention I, II, III, IV, respectively.

26 For example, see Lauterpacht, *British Yearbook of International Law* 29 (1952), p. 362; Yingling and Ginnane, *American Journal of International Law* 46 (1952), pp. 393, 426.

However, although the provision may be interpreted as lacking reference to universal jurisdiction, it may be deduced by the same reasoning that it leaves room for interpretation in favour of universal jurisdiction since it does not expressly forbid it. Cowles justified universal jurisdiction over war crimes by saying that war crimes were to be regarded as offences against the conscience of the civilized world and that every nation therefore had an interest in their punishment.[27] Van Elst explains that universal jurisdiction was included in the Geneva Conventions to end the *de facto* impunity that existed with regard to violations of humanitarian law prior to WWII.[28]

There is another view arguing that jurisdiction under the Geneva Conventions is not universal jurisdiction, but a jurisdiction which is traditionally attributed to belligerents. It was also argued that, even if the Geneva Conventions provided universal jurisdiction, only belligerent States had the right to exercise universal jurisdiction and not all States.[29] Bowett noted that '[w]ar crimes are certainly crimes against international law, but it is by no means clear that they are subject to universal jurisdiction. The jurisdiction has been traditionally that of a belligerent Power'.[30] By limiting jurisdiction to belligerents, Röling denied universal jurisdiction and contended that it is a protective jurisdiction, exercised on the basis of the national interest of those belligerents.[31]

However, this view is criticized as contradicting the intention of the drafters. During the drafting of the Geneva Conventions, a proposal from the Italian delegate to limit the obligation to the parties to the conflict was withdrawn.[32] Instead of 'Parties to the Conflict' as the Italian delegate proposed, the final provision prescribed that 'Each High Contracting Party' would be subject to this obligation.

Acknowledging that the scope of the provisions in the Geneva Conventions can entail universal jurisdiction, what is more extraordinary is that it inferred universal jurisdiction of a different nature from the one perceived under the classic jurisdictional regime. Let us further examine this special nature in line with the two aspects distinguishing the nature of universal jurisdiction: permissive or obligatory, and primary or supplemental jurisdiction. First and most important, the universal jurisdiction implied

27 Willard B. Cowles, *supra* note (4), pp. 177-218.

28 Richard van Elst 'Implementing Universal Jurisdiction Over Grave Breaches of the Geneva Conventions' *Leiden Journal of International Law* Vol. 13 No. 4 (2000), pp. 823-825.

29 See B.V.A. Röling 'Aspects of the Criminal Responsibility for Violations of the Laws of War' in Cassesse, *The New Humanitarian Law of Armed Conflict* (1979), pp. 200-203. Bowett took the same view. See, D.W. Bowett 'Jurisdiction: Changing Patterns of Authority Over Activities and Resources' *British Yearbook of International Law* 53 (1982), p. 12.

30 D.W. Bowett, *ibid.*, p. 12.

31 See B.V.A. Röling 'The Law of War and the National Jurisdiction Since 1945' *Recueil des Cours* Tome 100 (1960-II), pp. 359-363. Röling contended that 'apart from specific provisions applicable to neutrals, the Conventions obtain only between belligerents. And between belligerents the principle of universality can be recognized, but then, it signifies nothing more than the principle of extended protection.' *Ibid.*

32 See, A.R. Carnegie, *supra* note (20), p. 408. See also, Richard van Elst, *supra* note (28), pp. 821-822.

under the Geneva Conventions is an *obligation*. The ICTY stated that 'the Conventions create universal mandatory criminal jurisdiction among Contracting States'.[33] Second, from the wording of the provisions, prosecution is emphasized over and above the extradition of suspects, thus implying *primary* universal jurisdiction rather than supplemental universal jurisdiction. It is noteworthy that the provisions of the Geneva Conventions emphasize the obligation to prosecute rather than to extradite suspects.

On the other hand, there are some limitations to universal jurisdiction inferred in the Geneva Conventions. First, it cannot be stated that universal jurisdiction became an obligation for all war-related crimes. The provisions in the Geneva Conventions mentioned above apply only to 'grave breaches' of the Geneva Conventions. For lesser crimes and for other war-related crimes, there was no indication under international law that these were subject to the same universal jurisdiction during this period of time. Secondly, note that the obligation of universal jurisdiction over grave breaches of the Geneva Conventions was only for those breaches committed during an international armed conflict. Dealing with non-international armed conflict in the conventional form of a protocol came much later in the 1970s.

3.2 Universal Jurisdiction and the Genocide Convention

Under the principles of the prohibition of interference in the internal affairs of a State and of the sovereign equality of States, States had been free to treat their nationals as they saw fit. However, as a means of placing limits on such State freedom and in order to forbid cruel treatment of nationals, an initiative was taken to draft legislation to prevent and punish the crime of genocide. The UN General Assembly unanimously adopted Resolution 96(I) which declared that the punishment of the crime of genocide is a matter of international concern, and affirmed that 'genocide is a crime under international law which the civilized world condemns'. Driven by the bitter memory of the gross violations of human rights committed during the Second World War, the Genocide Convention was drafted and was expected to lay down a powerful enforcement mechanism in order to never allow such atrocities in the future.

Nevertheless, the 1948 Genocide Convention does not provide for universal jurisdiction.[34] However, during the drafting of the Genocide Convention, universal

33 *Prosecutor* v. *Tadic*, Case IT-94-1-T, Decision on Jurisdiction, 2 October 1995, para. 79.

34 Article 6 of the Genocide Convention laid down territorial jurisdiction and the jurisdiction of an international criminal tribunal.
'Article VI
Persons charged with genocide or any of the other acts enumerated in article V shall be tried by a competent tribunal of the State in the territory of which the act was committed, or by such international penal tribunal as may have jurisdiction with respect to those Contracting Parties which shall have accepted its jurisdiction.'

jurisdiction was proposed on a few occasions.[35] It was incorporated in the draft prepared by the UN Secretary-General,[36] which served as the starting point for the drafting of the actual articles. It was also proposed by Iran in its amendment proposal submitted to the Sixth Committee.[37]

It is remarkable that Article 7 of the draft prepared by the UN Secretary-General prescribed universal jurisdiction as the obligatory jurisdictional basis under this treaty, while at the same time not excluding other bases of jurisdiction as well.[38] The draft Article 7 seemed to provide for a *primary obligatory universal jurisdiction*. The comment on the draft explained that it prescribed universal jurisdiction because UN General Assembly Resolution 96(I) (which admitted that the punishment of genocide was an international concern) seemed to intend this, because genocide is a crime under international law and because the convention would fail in its goal if it ignored this point.[39] This draft proposed the concurrent jurisdiction of universal jurisdiction of States and an international criminal court.[40] Its aim was to have serious cases that involve powerful persons or authorities tried in an international criminal court, while other cases were to be handled by national courts.[41]

The universal jurisdiction proposed by Iran was somewhat different in nature from the draft proposed by the UN Secretary-General.[42] First, in the Iranian proposal,

35 For details of the discussion concerning universal jurisdiction during the drafting of the Genocide Convention, see my article 'Criminal Jurisdiction in Article 6 of the Genocide Convention: Arguments During the Drafting Procedure' *Journal of Law and Politics of Nagoya University* No. 168 (March 1997) and No. 170 (September 1997) [in Japanese]. See also, William A. Schabas, *Genocide in International Law* (Cambridge University Press, 2000), pp. 355-360.

36 UN Doc. E/447.

37 UN Doc. A/C.6/218.

38 Because draft Article 8 allowed for extradition, it implied that universal jurisdiction is not an exclusive basis. The draft Articles 7 and 8 provided as follows.
Article VII 'The High Contracting Parties pledge themselves to punish any offender under this Convention within any territory under their jurisdiction, irrespective of the nationality of the offender or of the place where the offence has been committed.'
Article VIII 'The High Contracting Parties declare that genocide shall not be considered as a political crime and therefore shall be grounds for extradition.
The High Contracting Parties pledge themselves to grant extradition in case of genocide.'

39 See, UN Doc. E/447, p. 18.

40 Draft Art. 9 read as follows.
'The High Contracting Parties pledge themselves to commit all persons guilty of genocide under this Convention for trial to an international court in the following cases:
1. When they are unwilling to try such offenders themselves under Article VII or to grant their extradition under Article VIII.
2. If the acts of genocide have been committed by individuals acting as organs of the State or with the support or toleration of the State.' See UN Doc. E/447.

41 See UN Doc. E/447, pp. 19, 41.

42 Iran proposed to delete the reference to an international criminal court, and in its place, to add the following sentence: 'They may also be tried by tribunals other than those of the States in the territories of which the act was committed, if they have been arrested by the authorities of such States, and provided no request has been made for their extradition.' See, UN Doc. A/C.6/218.

universal jurisdiction was proposed in lieu of an international criminal court. Unlike the UN Secretary-General, Iran planned to have only national jurisdiction prescribed in the treaty, and it wanted to remove the idea of an international criminal court. Secondly, Iran proposed universal jurisdiction as a right, not as an obligation. And, lastly, Iran made it clear that the primary jurisdiction should be territorial jurisdiction, and that universal jurisdiction should be a 'subsidiary' one,[43] complementing territorial jurisdiction. Therefore, universal jurisdiction as foreseen in the Iranian proposal was a *supplemental permissive universal jurisdiction*. It can be said that the Iranian proposal was based more on the traditional notion of universal jurisdiction typical to the classical jurisdictional regime for crimes other than piracy.

The above two proposals illustrate that the idea of universal jurisdiction was proposed by both the supporters of an international criminal court and of territorial jurisdiction. The draft by the UN Secretary-General, which had supported the establishment of an international criminal court, proposed universal jurisdiction. On the other hand, the Iranian proposal, which was centred on the supremacy of territorial jurisdiction, also intended to allow universal jurisdiction. Therefore, it was proposed by both the proponents of a liberal conception of the jurisdictional system and by the proponents of traditional rules.

Unfortunately, both the proposals for universal jurisdiction were rejected. States involved in the drafting of the Genocide Convention were reluctant to prescribe universal jurisdiction. This reluctant attitude toward universal jurisdiction can also be noticed by the fact that universal jurisdiction was not included in the special explanatory note attached to Article 6, which specified that nationality jurisdiction is nevertheless allowed to be exercised.[44]

It is interesting to note that there were many divisions in supporting and objecting to the idea of universal jurisdiction among States. Those who favoured the idea of an international criminal court were aware that relying on territorial jurisdiction might not result in the prosecution or punishment of genocide since territorial States themselves may be involved in the commission of the crime. Therefore, they supported universal jurisdiction, hoping that universal jurisdiction would enhance the possibility of actual prosecution and punishment. Also, considering that universal jurisdiction could be exercised by States that already have suspects in custody, there would be no need to seek extradition or other measures to secure custody in order to commence proceedings, hence less procedural difficulties. However, France, which strongly supported the establishment of an international criminal court, voted against universal jurisdiction, claiming that an international criminal court would be of greater importance than

43 See the statement made by the delegation of Iran, *UN General Assembly Official Records*, 3rd Session, C. 6, 100th mtg., pp. 394-396.

44 The comment on the provision stated as follows:
'The first part of article VI contemplates the obligation of the State in whose territory acts of genocide have been committed. Thus, in particular, it does not effect the right of any State to bring to trial before its own tribunals any of its nationals for acts committed outside the State.'

universal jurisdiction. Moreover, it was argued that universal jurisdiction could lead to dangerous tensions in international relations by allowing States with different political ideologies to try leaders of other States which would consequently result in non-impartial or unfair trials.[45] The danger of politically-manoeuvred trials being held by the domestic courts of States was raised by many delegates during the drafting procedures.

On the other hand, those who strongly supported territorial jurisdiction found universal jurisdiction to be more attractive than the idea of an international criminal court since universal jurisdiction is a national jurisdiction exercised by the domestic courts of States. Therefore, universal jurisdiction appeared to be more contingent with the notion of State sovereignty. However, at the same time, the proponents of the classical jurisdictional regime thought that universal jurisdiction might interfere with the domestic matters of States. The Soviet Union was of the opinion that universal jurisdiction violated State sovereignty and the principle of State equality, and universal jurisdiction therefore remained generally unaccepted.[46] Allowing States which have nothing to do with a crime to prosecute and adjudicate, solely because it has suspects in custody, means that the State may freely determine the existence of genocide in another State. It might even end up suffering repercussions for taking on this role, such as accusations of domestic intervention and intrusion in State sovereignty. The Soviet Union believed that universal jurisdiction invades State sovereignty just as an international criminal court might.

As a result, universal jurisdiction was ironically both proposed and opposed by those with traditional as well as liberal conceptions of the jurisdictional system. What was shared among those delegates taking different positions was the deep-rooted mistrust of the judicial systems and proceedings within other States. As a result of this, universal jurisdiction was not prescribed in Article 6 of the Genocide Convention.

One can conclude that the rejection of the proposed universal jurisdiction for the Genocide Convention was the result of UN Member States attributing greater importance to 'peace' rather than 'justice'.[47] It is true that one of the reasons why universal jurisdiction was rejected was the fear of causing more international conflicts among States, entailing new threats to peace. Yet, it should not be forgotten that there were other reasons, such as the concern for, and doubts as to the impartiality and fairness which would be achievable with the exercise of universal jurisdiction – in other words, the distrust of 'justice' determined by other States. The significance of the discussions in the drafting of the Genocide Convention will be evaluated in the next chapter.

---

45 See the statement by the delegation of France, E/AC.25/SR.8, pp. 6-7, 10-11. For the opposition to the Iranian proposal, see the statements by the delegations of Egypt, the United States, and the Dominican Republic, *UN General Assembly Official Records*, 3rd Session, C. 6,100th mtg., pp. 398, 399, 401.

46 See the statement by the delegate of the Soviet Union, E/AC. 25/SR.7, p. 4.

47 B.V.A. Röling, *The Tokyo Trial and Beyond: Reflections of A Peacemonger* (Polity Press, 1993), p. 95.

3.3 The Eichmann Trial

The Eichmann Trial[48] is considered to be the most prominent precedent for universal jurisdiction over genocide. The Eichmann Trial involved the prosecution of Adolf Eichmann who was suspected of ordering the mass murder of Jews during the War. He was abducted by the Israeli secret police in 1960 from Argentina where he was hiding and indicted by an Israeli domestic court in accordance with Israeli law – the 'Nazis and Nazi Collaborators (Punishment) Law of 1950'.[49] This domestic law was modelled on the Genocide Convention, and was intended to prosecute such crimes committed against the Jews. What was extraordinary was that Israel exercised its jurisdiction over Eichmann, who was not an Israeli national or resident, for crimes committed outside its territory *before* the existence of the State of Israel. Eichmann appealed against his conviction by the District Court of Jerusalem in 1961, but was unsuccessful. After the Supreme Court upheld the judgment of the lower court in 1962, he received the death penalty.

Before the courts, Eichmann did not contest the basic facts; instead he strongly challenged the jurisdiction of the Israeli domestic courts. For instance, the defence denied the jurisdiction of the Israeli national courts based on the illegality of Eichmann's arrest and abduction. However, the courts admitted that although the method of bringing the suspect to Israel might be disputed as being a violation of international law between two States on the international plane, that dispute would be solved between those States and would not affect the proceedings of his prosecution.[50] Eichmann made other objections against jurisdiction including the problem of the retroactive application of the law, but both the District Court and the Supreme Court rejected those objections and approved jurisdiction over the case. As the basis of the Israeli jurisdiction, the courts recognized three jurisdictions: passive personality jurisdiction, protective jurisdiction, and universal jurisdiction.

First, let us examine the passive personality jurisdiction and protective jurisdiction. As explained in Chapter II, States having some kind of nexus to a crime generally

---

48 The Eichmann Trial consists of two decisions. One is the decision by the District Court of Jerusalem, and the other is the decision by the Supreme Court of Israel. '*Attorney-General of the Government of Israel* v. *Adolf Eichmann*', District Court of Jerusalem, Israel (December 12, 1961), and Supreme Court (May 29, 1962), English translation by E. Lauterpacht(ed.), *International Law Reports* Vol. 36, (Butterworths, 1968). For details on the background and proceedings, see, Hannah Arendt, *Eichmann in Jerusalem: A Report on the Banality of Evil* (The Viking Press, 1963).

49 The abduction of Eichmann by the Israeli authorities provoked a dispute concerning the question of the infringement of Argentina's State sovereignty. See, UN Security Council Resolution 138 (23 June 1960), UN Doc. S/4349 (1960). However, the courts concluded that the illegality of the manner of apprehending a suspect does not affect the judicial jurisdiction of a State. Likewise, the present study is on the issue of judicial jurisdiction, and therefore we will not dwell on the issue of the abduction. For a discussion on the arrest procedure in the Eichmann Trial, see, Helen Silving 'In Re Eichmann: A Dilemma of Law and Morality' *American Journal of International Law* Vol. 55 No. 2 (April 1961).

50 The District Court Judgment, para. 41.

exercise their jurisdiction. In this trial, the District Court reasoned that because Israel was a nation of Jews, it had a nexus to the crime committed against Jews by Eichmann based on passive personality jurisdiction[51] as well as protective jurisdiction.[52] On the other hand, Eichmann had argued that since the State of Israel did not exist at the time of committing the crime, it could not claim that its interests had been infringed by that crime. However, the court found that the interest protected under the protective jurisdiction for this case was the Israeli interest which existed at the time of drafting the domestic Nazis and Nazi Collaborators (Punishment) Law.[53] The Supreme Court upheld the decision of the District Court with the same reasoning and stated that Israel had jurisdiction based on protective jurisdiction and passive personality jurisdiction.[54]

How did both courts rule on universal jurisdiction? The District Court ruled that the crimes defined in the Nazis and Nazi Collaborators (Punishment) Law were not only crimes under the domestic law of Israel, but also represented a violation of international law.[55] In the absence of an international criminal court, international law does not restrict or deny the authority of a judicial organ of each State to try these crimes. On the contrary, it requires the organs of each State to try suspects because the jurisdiction to adjudicate crimes against international law is universal.[56] As reaffirmed by the UN General Assembly resolution adopting the Genocide Convention, as well as by the Advisory Opinion of the ICJ in 1951 concerning the question of reservations to the Genocide Convention, there is no doubt that genocide is a crime under international law. As a result, according to the principles of international law, the jurisdiction to prosecute such crimes is universal.[57] The District Court interpreted Article 6 as not excluding other bases of jurisdiction.[58] The court also made it clear that universal jurisdiction was based neither on Israeli domestic law nor on Article 6 of the Genocide Convention, but rather on the nature of genocide as the most serious crime under international law.[59]

Next, the Supreme Court held that, in this case, it was sufficiently justifiable to apply universal jurisdiction because the characteristic of the crime dealt with in this case was undoubtedly a crime against humanity. For example, the primary reason why international law allows States to exercise such jurisdiction over piracy is the existence of the important interest of the international community. Consequently, States prosecuting piracy acted simply as organs of the international community. The Court concluded that the same arguments justifying universal jurisdiction over piracy justified the Israeli jurisdiction over the present case. The application of universal

51 The District Court Judgment, para. 34.
52 The District Court Judgment, paras. 30, 35.
53 The District Court Judgment, para. 36.
54 The Supreme Court Judgment, para. 13.
55 The District Court Judgment, para. 16.
56 *Ibid.*, para. 12.
57 *Ibid.*, para. 19.
58 *Ibid.*, para. 23.
59 *Ibid.*, para. 25.

jurisdiction went beyond the crime of piracy to now include war crimes.[60] In response to the opposing claim that universal jurisdiction could not be exercised before efforts had been made to extradite the suspect to the territorial State or the State of which the suspect was a national, the court pointed to the fact that Germany had not requested the extradition of Eichmann. Moreover, the court explained that the requirement of extradition to territorial States was based on the practical reasoning that the territorial State was the most reasonable place for a trial since witnesses and items of evidence were present and could be more readily obtained. It is interesting that the court stated these practical advantages as the reason, rather than basing its reasoning on the protection of territorial sovereignty. Finally, the court concluded that Israel was the most appropriate forum for a trial since most of the witness and evidence were in Israel.[61]

As summarised above, both the District Court and the Supreme Court upheld Israeli universal jurisdiction. Consequently, many people cite the judgements as an indication of universal jurisdiction over genocide becoming customary international law.

However, some scholars question the value of the Eichmann Trial as a pure case of universal jurisdiction.[62] In addition to the unusual situation under which this case was brought, it is noted that passive personality jurisdiction and protective jurisdiction were also mentioned as the basis of jurisdiction.

Justifications for the judgments were based on the seriousness of genocide and its recognition as a crime under international law. The Israeli courts found that since the crime in question constituted a crime under international law, universal jurisdiction was therefore justified. But there is opposition to this simple assumption as explained earlier. Furthermore, the judgments were also criticized for too readily drawing an analogy between piracy and genocide.

Emphasizing the Eichmann Trial as a prosecution of war crimes, Bowett highlighted three reasons for doubting the reasoning of the courts. First, a neutral State does not possess the same interests in trying war crimes as it does for piracy. Second, unlike piracy, criminal evidence is likely to be found within the belligerent States or a territorial State rather than in the States which have the suspects in custody. Finally, there is a real danger of political influence being thrust upon a trial in the case of war crimes. Bowett concluded that the Eichmann Trial was an extraordinary case, and, moreover, there was no basis for universal jurisdiction.[63]

60 The Supreme Court Judgment, para. 13(c).

61 *Ibid.*, para. 13(d).

62 Some authors consider the Eichmann Trial to be a dangerous precedent, doubting that the judges could have decided the case without prejudice. See, J.E.S. Fawcett 'The Eichmann Case' *British Year Book of International Law* Vol.38 (1962), p. 215. See also, John W. Bridge 'The Case for an International Court of Criminal Justice and the Formulation of International Criminal Law' *The International and Comparative Law Quarterly* Vol.13 Part 4 (October 1964), pp. 1255, 1270.

63 See, D.W. Bowett, *supra* note (29), p. 12. Bowett held that universal jurisdiction is not provided in the 1949 Geneva Conventions and the Genocide Convention. He opposed the extension of national jurisdiction based on universal jurisdiction. *Ibid.*, p. 14.

Moreover, because Israel did not yet exist as a nation at the time when the alleged crime was committed, it was argued that Israel could not be bestowed with jurisdiction.[64] Some oppose this argument by saying that the time of the establishment of Israel as a State has no effect on the exercise of universal jurisdiction by Israel. There is no doubt that when the crime was committed, there was no such State as Israel, therefore the subject of the crime was not Israeli or against the interests of Israel. It may have been beyond the scope of the relevant rules of jurisdiction for Israel to claim passive personality jurisdiction and protective jurisdiction over the case. However, the contention of universal jurisdiction is that all States have an interest in punishing crimes that are of international concern. Therefore, States allowed to exercise universal jurisdiction are not limited to States that existed when the crime took place.[65] However, it is noted that Israel's exercise of jurisdiction over this case was derived from its political intention to establish national identity as a Jewish State, rather than from an intention to serve and protect the interest of the international community.

As illustrated above, there has been some criticism of the jurisdiction in the Eichmann Trial. In reality, however, his prosecution in Israel met little opposition both in and out of the courts. Although the propriety of the Israeli jurisdiction over this case was doubted by some, it did not halt the proceedings. This is much due to the fact that Germany and Argentina (which were the States which had a more common jurisdiction over Eichmann) did not claim jurisdiction over the case. Therefore it can be said that the universal jurisdiction recognized for the Eichmann Trial was only a supplemental permissive universal jurisdiction. Yet the Eichmann trial has greatly influenced the subsequent claims of universal jurisdiction as being customary international law.

3.4 Concluding Observations on the Second Period

During the time-span studied under this second period, modern international law developed but the notion of universal jurisdiction was still subject to the immense influence of the rules of the classical jurisdictional regime. In conventional international law, the 1949 Geneva Conventions innovatively opened the door for the exercise of universal jurisdiction. But, at that time, there were strong opposing views asserting that universal jurisdiction over war crimes could be only exercised by belligerents, or that the 1949 Geneva Conventions did not incorporate universal jurisdiction to begin with. As to its customary status, some asserted that universal jurisdiction over war crimes had become a customary norm. The mixed feelings of expectations concerning universal jurisdiction and uncertainty as to the law can be ascertained in the Carnegie's observations from 1963:

64 For an analysis of the issue of retroactivity in this case, see L.C. Green 'The Maxim *Nullum Crimen Sine Lege* and the Eichmann Trial' *British Yearbook of International Law* 38 (1962).

65 See, Kenneth C. Randall, *supra* note (7), pp. 813-814.

> 'It would seem ... that in the developing process of international law major war crimes may be well on their way to becoming crimes of universal jurisdiction. The evidence for the exercise of this kind of jurisdiction in State practice is not as clear as that for the exercise of passive personality jurisdiction, but the weight of authority in favour of the applicability is so considerable that this might be sufficient to decide the issue in any future dispute. Furthermore, now that so many major war crimes are crimes of universal jurisdiction by agreement among States, the principle seems likely to be adopted by customary international law on this account alone.'[66]

On the other hand, in denying universal jurisdiction, Röling contended that '[t]o authorize nations to try every war crime committed somewhere in this world in a completely foreign war has great disadvantages. Prosecution in such cases may be regarded as meddling and intervening in other's affairs.'[67]

To put it succinctly, there are some difficulties in affirming universal jurisdiction over war crimes as falling within the scope of customary international law. First, the various trials held in the aftermath of the Second World War could be, and were generally thought to be, based on jurisdictions other than universal jurisdiction. Second, there was insufficient evidence of the practice of universal jurisdiction during this second period. On the contrary, it seemed that States were hesitant to exercise universal jurisdiction over war crimes. This reluctant attitude became evident in the absence of practice, custom and *opinio juris* on universal jurisdiction. Finally, during the second period, there were some convincing views which adhered to the traditional rule that only belligerents had jurisdiction over war crimes.

Opposition to universal jurisdiction was manifested in the drafting of the Genocide Convention. Although the 1948 Genocide Convention was innovative in providing for the jurisdiction of an international criminal court in addition to obliging territorial jurisdiction, it failed to prescribe other bases of national jurisdiction. Of course, Article 6 went further than the traditional sense by providing territorial jurisdiction as an obligation rather than a right, but lacked any mention of other bases of jurisdiction – thus the sole burden of prosecuting individuals rested on territorial States. This is ironic since the concern that a territorial State might not respond to highly political crimes was one of the driving forces behind the drafting of the Genocide Convention in the first place. This contradiction between the initial motivation and the final provision articulates how strongly the dominance of territorial jurisdiction in the classical jurisdictional regime influenced the discussion during the drafting procedure. Although it was possible to include a mention of the international criminal court in the article, it was not possible to establish the court. Following the adoption of the Genocide Convention, the UN started to discuss the possibility of establishing an international criminal court, but this effort reached a deadlock in the 1950s.

---

66 A.R. Carnegie, *supra* note (20), p. 423.

67 B.V.A. Röling 'The Law of War and National Jurisdiction since 1945' *Recueil des Cours* Tome 100 (1960-Part II), p. 329.

As a result of the failure to prescribe universal jurisdiction and to establish an international criminal judicial body, the crime of genocide was left under the traditional system based on territorial jurisdiction of States. Article 6 of the Genocide Convention does *obligate* State Parties to exercise territorial jurisdiction, yet, as feared by many, it did not contribute to actual prosecution and punishment. The Genocide Convention neither prescribed nor implied universal jurisdiction. In fact, considering the discussions which took place during its drafting and the novelty of the crime of 'genocide', it is difficult to conceive universal jurisdiction over genocide as being customary international law at that time. Therefore, the Genocide Convention left a vacuum of legal enforcement and judicial organs capable or willing to prosecute the crime of genocide. In an effort to fill this jurisdictional vacuum, scholars and activists encouraged the establishment of an international criminal court. At the same time, they also encouraged States to exercise other forms of national jurisdiction. It was in this environment that the Eichmann Trial took place.

Whether or not the Eichmann Trial can be interpreted as a precedent for universal jurisdiction over the crime of genocide remains a point of contention, but there is no doubt that it was a case where a national jurisdiction not provided in Article 6 of the Genocide Convention – more specifically, non-territorial jurisdiction – was exercised.

In sum, universal jurisdiction was observed to be much more vulnerable during the second period – in early contemporary international law. Its status in both conventional and customary international law was disputed. The existence of all these opposing views and criticism shows how significant the difficulty was in obtaining the acceptance of universal jurisdiction during this period. Although there was overall agreement in recognizing war crimes and genocide as heinous crimes which should be condemned by the international community, States were hesitant to accept and implement universal jurisdiction even for those crimes. As a result, universal jurisdiction remained much the same as it had been in the classical jurisdictional regime. It was only a supplemental permissive universal jurisdiction.

As the Cold War halted the work on establishing an international criminal court and prevented the adoption of some human rights treaties, enforcement measures in responding to human rights violations were slow to develop. Although there was unanimous consent among States as to their desire to condemn atrocities committed during the Second World War, the same States were somewhat hesitant when it came to the application of prevention and prosecution measures for future acts. The United States and the Soviet Union both opposed provisions that might be used to condemn their conduct in the period coinciding with the drafting of the Genocide Convention. During the discussions, States were manipulative in drafting in order to avoid their own acts falling within the scope of the provision, and, at the same time manipulating the provisions so as to criticize acts of other States as 'genocide'. The ideological and political polarisation of the West and East impelled each to completely distrust the other. Later, the confrontation between North and South added to the distrust of proceedings in foreign States. Hence the consensus on the interest of the international community as a whole was difficult to ascertain in a divided world where States or blocs of States were vehemently confronting each other. Both sides were involved in armed conflicts during that period, sensitive to any accusation against them and any interference in what they perceived to be domestic affairs. Decolonization and liberation movements, and armed struggles for independence and other forms of disputes were taking place all over the world. International peace and security were fragile. It could have been dangerous to expect universal jurisdiction to take a role in such an environment where the notion of 'human rights' was not free from political abuse to condemn rival States. Therefore, it is not surprising that States were reluctant to accept universal jurisdiction when they mistrusted the rule of law in other States. In sum, the rule of the dominance of territorial jurisdiction, avoiding interference in the domestic affairs of other States, the political climate, the absence of trust in proceedings in foreign courts, and the difficulty in achieving agreement on the interest of the international community, all acted against the general acceptance of universal jurisdiction.

4 The Third Period: The Expansion of Universal Jurisdiction in the 1970s and 1980s

4.1 The Expansion of Universal Jurisdiction in Conventional International Law since the 1970s

An increase in terrorist activities – especially criminal acts directed against aircraft – since the late 1960s posed a serious threat to life and to the viability of international civil aviation. It heightened the attention of the international community and as a result produced new conventions to prohibit such acts, enhancing international cooperation between States for the objective of prosecuting and punishing offenders. New instruments against terrorist acts on aircraft were drafted, starting with the Tokyo Convention in 1963, followed by the Hague Hijacking Convention in 1970, and the Montreal Convention for the Suppression of Unlawful Acts against the Safety of Civil Aviation in 1971. As explained in Chapter II, the adoption of new instruments was not confined to that of criminal acts on board aircraft, but for other criminal acts and human rights violations as well, such as torture.

This increase in international legislation was due to the failure of the classical jurisdictional regime to effectively prosecute and punish these crimes. There were significant needs to be able to respond effectively to new types of crime committed in a situation where jurisdiction was difficult to determine, to capture and prosecute efficiently those criminals fleeing abroad. Because of these needs, States agreed to establish a jurisdictional system that was different from the classical jurisdictional regime. These needs are somewhat similar to the situation leading to the formation of customary rules on the universal jurisdiction over the crime of piracy. Crimes such as hijacking an aircraft are unlikely to be efficiently prosecuted and punished if there is sole reliance on territorial jurisdiction as was the case with the crime of piracy. Since I have already explained the phenomenon of the expansion of jurisdiction (including universal jurisdiction) using the Torture Convention as an example in Chapter II, in this section I will take conventions concerning hijacking as examples in elaborating upon the expansion of universal jurisdiction.

Universal jurisdiction was first incorporated in the Hague Hijacking Convention in 1970. Article 4(2) reads:

> 'Each Contracting State shall ... take such measures as may be necessary to establish its jurisdiction over the offence in the case where the alleged offender is present in its territory and it does not extradite him pursuant to [the Convention].'

Article 7 further provides:

> 'The Contracting State in the territory of which the alleged offender is found shall, if it does not extradite him, be obliged, without exception whatsoever and whether or not the offence was committed in its territory, to submit the case to its competent authorities for the purpose of prosecution. Those authorities shall take their decision in the same manner as in the case of any ordinary offence of a serious nature under the law of that State.'

This is impressive since the Tokyo Convention of 1963, which was drafted before the Hague Hijacking Convention, did not refer to universal jurisdiction or the principle *aut dedere aut judicare*. Furthermore, the Tokyo Convention barely allowed for multiplicity of jurisdiction only in exceptional manner. The Tokyo Convention laid down the jurisdiction of a State where the aircraft was registered as the main jurisdiction, and others as limited exceptions. It included nationality jurisdiction, passive personality jurisdiction and protective jurisdiction, but did not mention universal jurisdiction among the exceptions.[68] Compared to this convention, the Hague Hijacking Convention was innovative in providing various jurisdictions with obligatory universal jurisdiction,[69] providing the principle of *aut dedere aut judicare*, and including a provision

---

68 Art. 4 of the Tokyo Convention reads as follows:
'A Contracting State which is not the State of registration may not interfere with an aircraft in flight in order to exercise its criminal jurisdiction over an offence committed on board except in the following cases:
(a) the offence has effect on the territory of such State;
(b) the offence has been committed by or against a national or permanent resident of such State;
(c) the offence is against the security of such State;
(d) the offence consists of a breach of any rules or regulations relating to the flight or manoeuvre of aircraft in force in such State;
(e) the exercise of jurisdiction is necessary to ensure the observance of any obligation of such State under a multilateral international agreement.'

69 Some say that it is really 'an obligatory territorial jurisdiction' rather than universal jurisdiction. 'The parties to these treaties agreed both to grounds of jurisdiction and as to the obligation to take the measures necessary to establish such jurisdiction. The specified grounds relied on links of nationality of the offender, or the ship or aircraft concerned, or of the victim. ... These may properly be described a treaty-based broad extraterritorial jurisdiction. But in addition to these were the parallel provisions whereby a State party in whose jurisdiction the alleged perpetrator of such offences is found, shall prosecute him or extradite him. By the loose use of language the latter has come to be referred to as

to allow extradition among States so as not to require a special bilateral treaty to be concluded before the extradition. Various conventions on crimes and human rights violations subsequent to the Hague Hijacking Convention have followed the example and have incorporated universal jurisdiction in their articles.

Modelled after the Hague Hijacking Convention, many conventions concerning international crimes or gross human rights violations thereafter included similar provisions. However, there are some problems related to universal jurisdiction under these conventions. Many conventions oblige State Parties to enact appropriate legislation for various jurisdictions, but do not go further to oblige the actual exercise of jurisdiction. Also, the conventions do not obligate States to prosecute but only to refer the case to a competent domestic authority. In other words, many conventions do not explicitly provide a prohibition on arbitrary decisions by denying prosecution or manipulative proceedings (e.g. providing an unfairly light punishment) in order to protect the person in question through the abuse of the principle of *ne bis in idem*. There may be no need to specify such an obligation since States generally have the obligation to act in good faith. However the awareness of such abuse and danger only became apparent later, and some new deterrent provisions were therefore incorporated in conventional international law, including the ICC Statute.

4.2 Efforts to Prescribe Universal Jurisdiction over Genocide in International Law in the 1970s and 80s

It may be observed that the phenomenon at the level of conventional international law explained above has encouraged the proposition that universal jurisdiction over the crimes specified in the treaties has become customary international law. In addition, many proposed to apply universal jurisdiction to other crimes of a comparable serious nature. I will now consider how the expansion of universal jurisdiction has impacted upon our assessment of universal jurisdiction over genocide.

As for the crime of genocide, although there is no doubt that genocide is no less heinous than other crimes prohibited in multilateral conventions providing for universal jurisdiction, the Genocide Convention itself does not provide for universal jurisdiction. It was considered to be contradictory not to allow universal jurisdiction for such gross and serious human rights violations as genocide while other crimes of lesser gravity came were subject to universal jurisdiction.

In addition to the analogy with other crimes, the inability of States to exercise territorial jurisdiction effectively and the resulting *de facto* impunity compelled scholars and activists to seek more effective measures. It is noted that only a few prosecutions had taken place in accordance with Article 6 of the Genocide Convention up

"universal jurisdiction", though this is really an obligatory territorial jurisdiction over persons, albeit in relation to acts committed elsewhere.' The Joint Separate Opinion of Judges Higgins, Kooijmans and Buergenthal to the ICJ judgment on 14 February 2002, Case Concerning the Arrest Warrant of 11 April 2000 (Democratic Republic of the *Congo* v. *Belgium*), para. 41.

to this period. The trial of a former dictator in Equatorial Guinea, and the trials of Khmer Rouge leaders Pol Pot and Ieng Sary *in absentia* in Cambodia[70] were rare cases of genocide prosecuted by territorial States. These two cases have been criticized for their highly politicised nature and the lack of fundamental elements of due process. As such, they have been denounced as being weak precedents.[71] Indeed, it is obvious that the number of actual prosecutions was out of proportion compared to the number of incidents which were suspected of being genocide.

In order to change this trend of impunity, several efforts were made to include universal jurisdiction over genocide in both conventional and customary international law. Below, I will illustrate how these legislative efforts failed.

4.2.1 The Ruhashyankiko Report in the 1970s

Even after the adoption of the Genocide Convention, crimes alleged to be genocide were being committed all over the world. The virtual ineffectiveness of the prohibition and the non-enforcement of the Genocide Convention were manifest. As a result, a discussion was raised in the UN to contemplate measures to improve the Convention. It was discussed in the Commission on Human Rights under the UN Economic and Social Council.

From 1973 to 1975, 'The Study on the Question of the Prevention and Punishment of the Crime of Genocide' was undertaken by the Special Rapporteur Nicodème Ruhashyankiko under the auspices of the UN Sub-Commission on Prevention of Discrimination and Protection of Minorities.[72] One of Ruhashyankiko's recommendations was to incorporate universal jurisdiction into the Genocide Convention in order to make it more effective. He advised that if a new international instrument on the prohibition and punishment of genocide were to be considered (since no international criminal tribunal existed at that time), universal punishment should be similarly addressed. Ruhashyankiko expressed the same doubt which originally instigated the drafting of the Genocide Convention – a doubt as to the possibility of proper adjudication within a territorial State. He was convinced that incorporating universal jurisdiction would enhance the effective application of the Genocide Convention. He explained that adopting universal jurisdiction would not automatically oblige States to prosecute the crime of genocide, and that this was simply a choice. He advised that universal jurisdiction should be provided alongside the principle of *aut dedere aut*

70 For an in-depth study of the punishment of the Khmer Rouge leaders including the efforts to put them on trial after the Second Period, see Steven R. Ratner and Jason S. Abrams, *Accountability for Human Rights Atrocities in International Law: Beyond the Nuremberg Legacy* (Oxford University Press, 2001), pp. 267-328.

71 Steven R. Ratner and Jason S. Abrams, *ibid.*, p. 168.

72 Special Rapporteur Ruhashyankiko submitted three reports: first on 25 June 1973, next on 17 June 1974, and lastly on 25 June 1975. I will analyse the last report which included the context of the former two reports. Study of the Question of the Prevention and Punishment of the Crime of Genocide, study prepared by Mr. Nicodeme Ruhashyankiko, UN Doc.E/CN.4/Sub.2/416 (1975).

judicare, so that States would have a choice in deciding whether to extradite or prosecute.[73]

The Sub-Commission discussed his report, but contrary to the intentions of the rapporteur, the discussion became to a political dispute over whether or not to omit the reference to the certain alleged cases of genocide in the past – it soon became a place for a heated debate over whether or not the Armenian massacre in 1916 constituted a crime of genocide, and whether or not it should be mentioned as a precedent for genocide in the report. The discussion entailed and stimulated the political sensitivity of the States involved in that incident and, as a consequence, there was hardly any discussion on the actual measure for the prohibition and punishment of genocide. As a result, the Commission only managed to conclude that the report should be widely distributed after some amendments in the light of the discussions.[74] The debate in the Commission illustrated how a discussion on genocide may end up as political and emotional confrontation. Due to the dispute over the evaluation of a historical account among some members, the discussion ended up in a deadlock, forcing the entire discussion on the effective enforcement of the prohibition of genocide to be set to aside.

4.2.2 The Whitaker Report in the 1980s

For many years, the subject of the study of genocide became almost taboo, and it was only in the 1980s that it was re-examined. The Sub-Commission decided to undertake a study on genocide once again, and Benjamin Whitaker was appointed as the Special Rapporteur on this occasion. He submitted his reports in 1984 and 1985.[75] He was expected to take into consideration all the relevant developments which had taken place after the previous report submitted by Ruhashyankiko.[76] This meant that Whitaker had to take into consideration the expansion of national jurisdictions which had taken place since the 1970s. Therefore, this re-examination of the study of genocide was a perfect opportunity to acknowledge universal jurisdiction over genocide under international law.

However, this opportunity was once again ruined by the heated arguments over past situations. The Special Rapporteur himself commented upon past precedents which had been expressly omitted from the report by Ruhashyankiko. In the report by Whitaker, he presented his views, recognising that some past massacres did constitute the crime of genocide. It was obvious that such a remark would invoke vigorous reactions from the States involved, as indeed it had done during the discussion of Ruhashyankiko's report in the 1970s. As expected, the remark by Whitaker gave rise to a heated political discussion on the perception of history, taking up a substantial part of time allocated

73 The Ruhashyankiko Report, *ibid.*, paras. 211, 278, 627.

74 E/CN.4/SR. 1520, p. 7.

75 Revised and Updated Report on the Question of the Prevention and Punishment of the Crime of Genocide, study prepared by Mr. B. Whitaker, UN Doc. E/CN.4/Sub.2/1985/6 (1985).

76 E/CN.4/1983/SR.48/Add.1, para. 155.

for the discussion of his report. Consequently, some members criticised the Special Rapporteur for drawing the Sub-Commission into this discussion instead of the main topic of how to prevent genocide and what measures should be taken against it. It was criticised that if 'the Sub-Commission were instrumental in setting up an international court or tribunal, it would have rendered some service to mankind. However, the Special Rapporteur's action in going beyond his terms of reference and including an irrelevant paragraph had led to a long debate on unnecessary aspects of the question instead of a discussion on the prevention and punishment of the crime of genocide. The aim should be to look to the future, not the past, and to seek reconciliation not bitterness.'[77]

As a result, there was no thorough discussion on the enforcement system for the punishment of genocide. However, some comments were made within the Sub-Commission in support of stronger measures. The majority of the members were pessimistic concerning the possibility of establishing an international criminal court even though the need for such a court was voiced within the Sub-Commission. They seemed to place more hope in universal jurisdiction. Before the preparation of his report, Whitaker had distributed a questionnaire to the UN member States and various international organizations;[78] the sixth question asked for their opinion on drafting an additional protocol to the Genocide Convention. The underlying motive of this question was to ask whether it would be possible and appropriate to broaden the jurisdiction beyond territorial jurisdiction by means of an additional protocol.[79] It was proposed that because the crime of genocide was often committed by a government authority, it was unthinkable to expect the same authority to try suspects in a domestic court, and it would be better to allow all States to prosecute those suspects who had fled abroad.[80]

Some members opposed this recommendation, stating that there was no need to additionally provide for universal jurisdiction since Article 6 of the Genocide Convention already provided for international criminal jurisdiction.[81] They also claimed that it was a great mistake to expand the interpretation beyond the meaning of the Convention when it was first drafted. Moreover, Article 16 of the Convention, they argued, laid down measures to amend the Convention and it was thus inappropriate to amend it through the adoption of an additional protocol.[82]

Special Rapporteur Whitaker advised member States to adopt domestic laws allowing the prosecution of suspects if they decided not to extradite them to other States.[83] As for universal jurisdiction, he observed that the crime of genocide could be subject to 'universal jurisdiction *aut dedere aut punire*', as is the case with the crime

77 Statement by Mr. Chowdhury, E/CN.4/Sub.2/1985/SR.19, para. 33.
78 UN Doc. E/CN.4/Sub.2/1984/40.
79 See the statement by Mr. Dahak, UN Doc. E/CN.4/Sub.2/1984/SR.4, para. 19.
80 See the statement by Mr. Deschenes, *ibid.*, paras. 8-11.
81 For example, see the statement by Mr. Roche, UN Doc. E/CN.4/Sub.2/1984/SR.3, para. 22.
82 See statement by Mr. Martinez, UN Doc. E/CN.4/Sub.2/1984/SR.4, para. 33.
83 UN Doc. E/CN.4/Sub.2/1985/6, para. 63.

of piracy.[84] He mentioned Article 8 of the Torture Convention (1984) in comparison, and stated that genocide was nothing less than torture and he therefore recommended a similar provision for the crime of genocide.[85] He put forward both the proposal for adjudication by an international organ and for setting universal jurisdiction, and criticised any State which would not adopt either one.[86]

In sum, both Special Rapporteurs of the UN Sub-Commission on Prevention of Discrimination and Protection of Minorities considered universal jurisdiction to be a measure to enhance the effectiveness of the Genocide Convention. Both had recommended universal jurisdiction in conjunction with the principle of *aut dedere aut judicare*. The universal jurisdiction proposed by them seemed to be of a primary obligatory nature. They advised that a new international instrument in the form of a protocol should be adopted providing universal jurisdiction in lieu of widening the interpretation of the Convention. The option of expanding the interpretation without a new protocol was rejected because it would add a new meaning to the provisions which the Signatory States of the Convention had not intended.

However, their reports containing this recommendation fell somewhat short of actually drafting such an instrument. Hence there was no conventional international law enacted that allowed for universal jurisdiction over genocide during this period. Although unsuccessful, these efforts implied that it was recognized that the mere existence of the Genocide Convention was not enough to bring about the intended treaty objective and that something had to be done to prevent and punish genocide. It is worth noting that these reports prepared in the 1970s and the 1980s considered that universal jurisdiction over genocide should be newly legislated into conventional international law, but not as a codification of customary international law, implying that it had not yet achieved customary status during this period. As a result of the failure of their recommendations, there is no new convention or additional protocol to the Genocide Convention explicitly providing for universal jurisdiction over genocide.

4.3 Restatement (Third) of the American Foreign Relations Law

Next, let us analyse how the Restatement of the Law (Third) of Foreign Relations Law of the United States[87] (hereafter: the Third Restatement) came to accept universal jurisdiction over crimes other than piracy. Although the Third Restatement is a work by a group of scholars and is not binding law, it nevertheless has a great influence as an authoritative and prominent interpretation. It is cited by many scholars and court rulings as evidence that universal jurisdiction has become a part of customary international law.

84 *Ibid.*, para. 64.
85 *Ibid.*, para. 64.
86 *Ibid.*, para. 89.
87 *Restatement of the Law (Third) of Foreign Relations Law of the United States* (American Law Institute Publishers, 1987), (referred in this study as Third Restatement).

The Third Restatement refers to universal jurisdiction in Paragraph 404.[88] Paragraph 404 provides as follows:

> 'A state may exercise jurisdiction to define and punish certain offenses recognized by the community of nations as of universal concern, such as piracy, slave trade, attacks on or hijacking of aircraft, genocide, war crimes, and perhaps terrorism, even where none of the bases of jurisdiction indicated in § 402 is present.'[89]

From the wording, it seems that the Third Restatement provides for primary permissive universal jurisdiction. As the rationale, therefore, the Commentary on Paragraph 404 explains that since the end of World War II the crime of genocide has become the subject of universal jurisdiction.[90] In support of this opinion, it mentions UN General Assembly Resolution 96(I) of 1946 which unanimously condemned genocide, and also the fact that the Genocide Convention has been ratified by many States. This interpretation by the Third Restatement coincides with the reasoning held by the Israeli court in the Eichmann Trial which was introduced earlier in this chapter.

It is interesting to note the timing of when the Restatement declared that universal jurisdiction over genocide had become customary international law. It was admitted for the first time in the Third Restatement which was published in 1987. The former versions of the Restatement – the First and the Second (1962) Restatements – commented otherwise. For instance, the Second Restatement expressly provided that piracy was the only crime which was subject to universal jurisdiction. The Second Restatement stated that crimes other than piracy were not subject to universal jurisdiction under international law.[91] In short, within the versions of the Restatement, universal jurisdiction was admitted only in limited sense in 1962, but was subsequently admitted in a more expanded form in 1987. This means that in 1962 – in that same year the Supreme Court of Israel delivered its decision in the Eichmann Trial – the Restatement did not acknowledge universal jurisdiction for crimes other than piracy. It is likely that the change in interpretation from the Second Restatement to the Third Restatement was brought about by the development of international law and the expansion of national jurisdictions since the 1970s as I illustrated in Chapter II. The Third Restatement must have taken the phenomenon of the expansion of national jurisdictions into consideration. That is why Paragraph 404 of the Third Restatement included attacks on aircraft, hijacking, and other terrorist activities – international crimes which were newly prohibited by multilateral conventions and had become subject to universal jurisdiction through these conventions.

---

88 The Third Restatement, p. 254. § 404 is entitled 'Jurisdiction to Prescribe'; however, by § 423 which recognises judicial jurisdiction for those crimes within prescriptive jurisdiction, we can contemplate adjudicatory jurisdiction based on § 404.

89 The jurisdictional bases in § 402 are territorial jurisdiction, nationality jurisdiction, and protective jurisdiction. See *ibid.*, § 402.

90 *Ibid.*, p. 256.

91 *Ibid.*, p. 257.

4.4 State Responses: The U.S. Legislation in the 1980s

In the light of the acknowledgement of universal jurisdiction over genocide and other crimes in the Third Restatement, one might presume that the United States must have strongly supported the notion of universal jurisdiction since the Restatement is considered to be an accumulation of international law applicable to the United States. The reality was different, however. Although the Third Restatement published in 1987 explicitly acknowledged universal jurisdiction over genocide and other crimes, the actual domestic legislation in the United States did not lay down such broad jurisdiction in the 1980s.

Of course, some laws were enacted in accordance with obligations under multilateral conventions which the United States had ratified. For example, in line with its obligation under the Hague Hijacking Convention, a federal law was adopted in 1974 laying down universal jurisdiction for the crime of hijacking.[92] Yet, for crimes not specified in conventions as being subject to universal jurisdiction (such as the crime of genocide) the United States remained passive. The federal law adopted in 1987 to implement the Genocide Convention only determined jurisdiction for crimes committed within American territory or committed by a U.S. citizen.[93] In other words, it only provided for territorial jurisdiction and nationality jurisdiction for the crime of genocide. In this law, the United States did not interpret Article 6 of the Genocide Convention so as to limit the national jurisdiction only to territorial jurisdiction, but it also allocated itself nationality jurisdiction, although it did not go further to lay down universal jurisdiction.

As for universal jurisdiction over genocide, some people mention that the United States has the Alien Tort Claims Act[94] which allows the domestic courts of the United States to deal with civil cases for acts committed in breach of international law. This Act allows a civil suit for serious human rights violations in breach of international law, including genocide committed abroad by foreigners, to be heard by American courts.[95] Comparing this Alien Tort Claims Act with the above-mentioned criminal legislation for genocide, it is obvious that criminal jurisdiction was much more narrowly defined. The difference in the scope of jurisdiction seems to derive from the difference between a civil case and a criminal case. In a civil case, courts and other

92 For example, Antihijacking Act of 1974, Pub.L.93-366, 88 Stat.409. Act for the Prevention and Punishment of the Crime of Hostage-Taking, 1984, 18 U.S.C. 1203. For an article discussing domestic legislation and cases of universal jurisdiction within the Untied States, see, Hary M. Osofsky 'Domesticating International Criminal Law: Bringing Human Rights Violators to Justice' *Yale Law Journal* Vol.107 No.1 (Oct. 1997).

93 Genocide Convention Implementation Act of 1987 (the Proxmire Act), Pub.L.No.100-606, 102 Stat. 3045-46.

94 Alien Tort Claims Act, 28 U.S.C. sec. 1350.

95 Several cases have been dealt with under the Alien Tort Claims Act. Examples of cases before the 1990s include *Tel-Oren* v. *Libyan Arab Republic*, 726 F. 2d 774, 781, 788 (D.C.Cir.1984), cert. denied, 470 U.S. 1003 (1985), and also *Filartiga* v. *Pena-Irala*, 630 F. 2nd 876, 890 (2d Cir.1980).

national authorities are in a neutral or non-involved position and a court merely decides on the issue of compensation. However, in a criminal case, the national authority is involved in a prosecuting role, being responsible for proving a crime in pursuit of justice.[96] Unless such an effort to pursue proceedings is recognised as amounting to a national interest, this will not be the case. This is one of the reasons why States are reluctant to allocate universal jurisdiction. Consequently, notwithstanding the Third Restatement, universal jurisdiction was not provided for in the domestic law adopted in the same year when the Third Restatement was issued in the United States.

4.5 Demjanjuk Case

Despite the lack of legislation prescribing universal jurisdiction for genocide at the international level (and the national level as well for the United States) there is a case of universal jurisdiction over genocide which was decided in the United States' courts in the 1980s. It is the Demjanjuk Case,[97] in which the U.S. courts allowed the extradition of a suspect to another State based on the recognition of the latter State's universal jurisdiction.

The issue of universal jurisdiction came into the picture in the Demjanjuk case after an extradition request had been made by Israel for John Demjanjuk who was present in the territory of the United States.[98] He was suspected of killing tens of thousands of people, mostly Jews, by operating a gas chamber while he was working in a Nazi concentration camp in Poland during World War II.[99] Israel had issued an arrest warrant against him on 18 October 1983 based on its domestic law – the Nazis and Nazi Collaborators (Punishment) Law. This Israeli domestic law employs a similar definition of genocide as the Genocide Convention, as I explained earlier in this chapter when introducing the Eichmann Trial. Demjanjuk was suspected of the same category of crime as Eichmann.

The U.S. courts discussed the extradition of Demjanjuk to Israel. Demjanjuk raised objections as to the legality of Israeli jurisdiction. He pleaded that Israel had no

96 See, Hary M. Osofsky, *supra* note (92), pp. 217-218.

97 The Northern District Court of Ohio and the Sixth Circuit Court of Appeals denied Demjanjuk's petition for a writ of *habeas corpus* submitted after certification of his extradition to Israel. The Supreme Court denied Demjanjuk's petition for *certiorari* in 1986. In Matter of Extradition of Demjanjuk, 612 F. Supp. 544 (N.D. Ohio), aff'd sub nom. *Demjanjuk* v. *Petrovsky*, 776 F. 2d 571 (6th Cir.1985), cert. denied, 475 U.S. 1016, 89 L. Ed. 2d 312, 106 S. Ct. 1198 (1986). There were court proceedings before those cited above concerning the denaturalisation of Demjanjuk. See note below.

98 Demjanjuk was originally from the Ukraine, but became a U.S. citizen. But after proof of his relationship with the Nazi secret police, his naturalization was cancelled. *United States* v. *Demjanjuk*, 518 F. Supp. 1362 (N.D.Ohio, 1981), aff'd, 680 F.2d 32 (6th Cir.), cert. denied, 459 U.S. 1036, 103 S. Ct. 447, 47 L.Ed.2d 602 (1982). His arrest warrant was issued by Israel while his deportation was being argued in the U.S. For details of his naturalization and denaturalisation proceedings, see Rena Hozore Reiss 'The Extradition of John Demjanjuk: War Crimes, Universality Jurisdiction, and the Political Offense Doctrine' *Cornell International Law Journal* Vol. 20 No. 2 (Summer 1987), pp. 284-290.

99 In Matter of Extradition of Demjanjuk, 603 F. Supp., at 1467.

jurisdiction over him because he was neither an Israeli national nor an Israeli resident; because the alleged crime was committed in the territory of Poland, not Israel; and because the nation of Israel did not exist at the time of the alleged commission of the crime.[100] But the District Court and the Court of Appeals both recognised that Israel enjoyed universal jurisdiction under international law and accordingly gave permission for his extradition.

The reasoning adopted by the District Court in determining Israeli jurisdiction can be summarised as follows. The District Court held that international law allows any State to prosecute crimes that are common enemies to the human race and in which all States have an interest in their punishment. It reasoned that many court precedents in the Allied States after World War II support the notion that any person who commits war crimes or crimes against humanity would be subject to universal jurisdiction.[101] The court also cited the Third Restatement as evidence. In the light of such evidence, the court found that jurisdiction over the suspected 'murders' allegedly committed by Demjanjuk was based on the domestic law intended to punish war crimes and crimes against humanity, and that the international community recognised universal jurisdiction over such crimes. The defence did not present evidence to prove that the exercise of jurisdiction by Israel would constitute a violation of international law,[102] and no other State had requested his extradition, hence there was no conflict as to jurisdiction. In addition, it is possible to argue that Israel had jurisdiction based on protective jurisdiction and passive personality jurisdiction, but the court held that because it was admitted that Israel had universal jurisdiction in accordance with international law, there was no need to further contemplate the other aspects of Israeli jurisdiction.[103]

The Court of Appeals maintained the same reasoning as the District Court. It explained that the Nuremberg Military Tribunal and other trials conducted mainly by the Allied States after the surrender of the Axis States constituted precedents for universal jurisdiction. The court affirmed that national jurisdiction beyond territorial limitations was generally admitted.[104] Under universal jurisdiction, the nationalities of the suspect and the victim or the place of the commission of the criminal act were not important. The alleged crime in this case was a crime under international law or a crime against humanity. Therefore, there was an assumption that the State prosecuting such a crime was acting on behalf of all other States. Irrespective of the status of Israel as a nation at the time when the crime was committed, Israel or any other State could pursue the interest of all States by prosecuting the perpetrator of such crimes. Therefore, the court concluded that the fact that Israel did not exist as a nation at the time of

100 *Demjanjuk* v. *Petrovsky*, p. 580.
101 In Matter of Extradition of Demjanjuk, p. 556.
102 In Matter of Extradition of Demjanjuk, p. 558.
103 *Ibid.*
104 *Demjanjuk* v. *Petrovsky*, p. 582.

the commission of the alleged crime did not preclude Israel from exercising its jurisdiction based on universal jurisdiction.[105]

Following the above decisions and the approval of the Supreme Court, the United States extradited Demjanjuk to Israel.[106] The following points are worth noting in relation to the issue of universal jurisdiction. First, it is relevant in the Demjanjuk case that universal jurisdiction over the crime of genocide was treated as a jurisdiction which is recognised under international law without much discussion. Notice that in the Demjanjuk Case, neither passive personality jurisdiction nor protective jurisdiction were examined in any depth by the courts as the jurisdictional bases. The courts in the Demjanjuk Case recognised Israeli jurisdiction based solely on universal jurisdiction. Compared to the Eichmann Trial in which the courts acknowledged two other jurisdictions (protective and passive personality jurisdiction) in addition to universal jurisdiction as the jurisdictional bases, we can observe a shift of emphasis toward universal jurisdiction. The difference in emphasis signifies that universal jurisdiction over genocide had gradually been accepted over the years. It is also interesting that the U.S. courts recognised universal jurisdiction not as an individual State interest, but as an interest of all States, and that a State exercising universal jurisdiction was acting not in its own interest, but in the interest of all States.

Second, it is astonishing that the decisions of the U.S. courts depart from the usual understanding of universal jurisdiction. To be more precise, the courts recognized universal jurisdiction *in absentia*. Ordinarily, universal jurisdiction is exercised by a State where a suspect is present. On the contrary, the above decisions recognised that Israel, which did not have Demjanjuk in custody, was entitled to universal jurisdiction. If the courts had followed the ordinary understanding of universal jurisdiction which considers universal jurisdiction to be a jurisdiction which is exercised by a State where a suspect is present, it would not have found that Israel had jurisdiction based on universal jurisdiction. This would constitute a contradiction because the extradition of the suspect was requested based on a jurisdiction that is usually claimed and admitted only after the suspect is in custody in that country. As explained earlier, universal jurisdiction was supplemental in the classical jurisdictional regime, thereby not having an active role in asserting jurisdiction. But the U.S. courts implied a different understanding. They recognised that universal jurisdiction has an active character, according to which the extradition of a suspect could be requested from custodial States. Consequently, with the approval of Demjanjuk's extradition, universal jurisdiction in *absentia* was introduced. Universal jurisdiction *in absentia* can be asserted by any State in the international community and is not limited to States where a suspect is actually

105 *Ibid.*, pp. 582-583.

106 Demjanjuk was extradited to Israel in 1986. After his extradition, court proceedings commenced in Israel concerning his criminal responsibility, but he was acquitted by the Supreme Court in 1993 after sufficient doubts had been raised as to whether he was the same person who had perpetrated the crime. For a discussion on his release, see, Mordechai Kremnitzer 'The Demjanjuk Case', in Yoram Dinstein and Mala Tabory ed., *War Crimes in International Law* (Martinus Nijhoff Publishers, 1996).

present. The Demjanjuk Case affirmed that States could request the extradition of a suspect based on such a base of jurisdiction.

The consequence of approving universal jurisdiction *in absentia* may considerably expand the scope of national jurisdiction. However, how readily this notion of universal jurisdiction in *absentia* was accepted among States (even in the United States where the above judgments were delivered) at that time is highly dubious, especially in the light of its liberal and innovative character. Universal jurisdiction in *absentia* was not a common understanding even in the United States since the domestic legislation for punishing genocide does not even incorporate the traditional universal jurisdiction. Some have also criticized the Demjanjuk Case as an example 'of the danger that some states will exploit universal jurisdiction for political ends.'[107]

In sum, as for proceedings against the crime of genocide in the United States, although the Alien Tort Law allowed universal jurisdiction in civil cases, there was no law for criminal cases. Some authors have criticized the United States as breaching international law by not implementing even the ordinary universal jurisdiction.[108] However, there were a number of precedents noting the existence of universal jurisdiction over the crime of genocide or hijacking, with reference to the Third Restatement.[109] Regarding universal jurisdiction in *absentia*, there seemed to be a lack of consistency between the courts' ruling in the Demjanjuk case and the law concerning serious crimes.

4.6 Concluding Observations on the Third Period

The phenomenon of the expansion of national jurisdiction has been observed among many conventions since the 1970s. This change was caused by the inability of the classical jurisdictional regime to effectively prosecute and punish international crimes. In other words, the shortcoming of relying on territorial jurisdiction and of the extradition system based on the principle of reciprocity led to a reconstruction of the jurisdictional regime. Universal jurisdiction also expanded considerably along with the increase in conventions prohibiting international crimes and gross human rights violations. Many conventions expressly allowed, and some expressly obliged, universal jurisdiction. Through these provisions, the nature of universal jurisdiction underwent some changes. Unlike the supplemental permissive universal jurisdiction tolerated under the classical jurisdictional regime, universal jurisdiction had become a primary jurisdiction and universal jurisdiction was even obligatory in many conventions.

---

107 Geoffrey Robertson, *Crimes Against Humanity: The struggle for Global Justice* (London: Allen Lane 1999).

108 See, for example, Lee A. Steven 'Genocide and the Duty to Extradite or Prosecute: Why the United States is in Breach of Its International Obligations' *Virginia Journal of International Law* Vol. 39 (Winter 1999), pp. 446-447.

109 For example, *U.S.* v. *Yunis*, 681 F. Supp.896 (D.D.C. 1988), aff'd 924 F.2A 1086, 1091 (D.C.Cir. 1991).

Furthermore, the development in conventional international law instigated some proposals to prepare a new instrument to specify universal jurisdiction over genocide. However, those proposals were buried under political confrontation, leaving one to speculate as to the nature of universal jurisdiction over genocide under customary international law.

However, influenced by the expansion of universal jurisdiction in conventional international law and by the development of international human rights law, some courts and many academic authors came to recognize universal jurisdiction as customary international law. For example, the Third Restatement noted this development for the first time in its publication in 1987. In the Demjanjuk Case, the U.S. courts recognized universal jurisdiction *in absentia*. The great steps forward in conventional international law promoted and facilitated the acceptance of universal jurisdiction among scholars and States. The notion of the obligation of a State towards the international community, and the interest of the international community as a whole, was beginning to settle within the minds of States constituting the international community. It was in 1970 that the ICJ admitted the obligation *erga omnes* in the Barcelona Traction Case. One could say that the notion of the interest of the international community had grown and begun to be accepted among States. With this gradual change, universal jurisdiction became more acceptable.

However, this gradual change did not give rise to many actual prosecutions of gross human rights violations through universal jurisdiction. The few cases that involved universal jurisdiction, e.g., the Demjanjuk Case and the Barbie Case,[110] concerned crimes which had been committed during the Second World War, and not contemporary atrocities which were occurring during this period. The political climate in the international community was such that court proceedings in other States remained the subject of mistrust. The more expanded application of universal jurisdiction in practice comes in the next period. The sceptical attitude toward universal jurisdiction which prevailed in the third period can be observed in the work of Bowett in 1982. Bowett recognized that the underlying rationale for universal jurisdiction is a universal interest in punishing serious crimes and upholding a community interest in the maintenance of law and order, yet he concluded as follows:

> 'Despite its superficial attractions, the thesis neither finds general support in State practice, nor does it commend itself as a very practical proposition. For it overlooks the very real difficulties of criminal trial outside the territory of the State where the crime is committed: difficulties of evidence, of the availability of witnesses, and even of

110 Klaus Berbie Case, French Court of Cassation, 6 October 1983, 26 January 1984, and 20 December 1985. For a summary of the case, see International Law Reports Vol. 78 (1985), pp. 125-148. For an examination of the prosecution of the Barbie Case in the 1980s, see Guyora Binder 'Representing Nazism: Advocacy and Identity at the Trial of Klaus Barbie' *Yale Law Journal* 98 (May 1989). The war crimes trials of Paul Touvier and Maurice Papon in France and the trial of Imne Finta in Canada are other examples of the prosecution of war crimes committed during the Second World War.

language. The idea is much more an argument for extradition than for universal jurisdiction.'[111]

5 The Fourth Period: The Spread of Universal Jurisdiction from the 1990s to the Present

5.1 The Ad Hoc Tribunals and Universal Jurisdiction against Crimes related to Yugoslavia and the Rwanda Crisis

In the 1990s, the jurisdictional system underwent a great transition in conjunction with the development of international criminal and humanitarian law. *Ad hoc* tribunals (the ICTY and ICTR) were established. Nothing in the Statute of these ad hoc tribunals suggest the exercise of universal jurisdiction by States, but indirectly these tribunals have made a great impact on the development of universal jurisdiction. The establishment and application of international criminal jurisdictions have reaffirmed the great concern in ending impunity and establishing accountability for gross human rights violations. States are obliged to cooperate with *ad hoc* tribunals in accordance with the UN Security Council Resolutions. But apart from a legal obligation, there has been a great moral awareness among many States. Being endorsed by the interest of the international community in prosecuting and punishing such crimes, States have begun to take actions themselves not only for crimes related to the former Yugoslavia or Rwanda but for other cases as well. The overall incentive in ending impunity has led to numerous exercises of national jurisdiction and, in a few cases, universal jurisdiction. Also, the fact that the International Law Commission included the idea of universal jurisdiction in its Draft Codes of Crimes Against Peace and Security of Humankind can be interpreted as one of the results of this general trend.

5.2 The Pinochet Case

The most celebrated case in the 1990s that drew attention to universal jurisdiction may be the Pinochet Case.[112] The Pinochet Case is regarded as a very important case in measuring the development of international criminal law. The issuing of an arrest warrant by Spain against Pinochet symbolized the recognition of the interest of the international community in ending the impunity of individuals who have committed gross human rights violations. The case drew international attention when Augusto

111 D.W. Bowett, *supra* note (29), p. 13.

112 The Pinochet Case includes many court proceedings in various States such as Britain, and States that requested the extradition of Pinochet including Spain and Chile. This study will selectively examine the discussion related to universal jurisdiction. For the proceedings after Pinochet's release and his return to Chile, see Adam Isaac Hasson 'Extraterritorial Jurisdiction and Sovereign Immunity on Trial: Noriega, Pinochet, and Milosevic – Trends in Political Accountability and Transnational Criminal Law' *Boston College International and Comparative Law Review* Vol. XXV No. 1 (Winter 2002), pp. 148-149.

Pinochet, the former President of Chile, was arrested in the U.K. on 16 October 1998, in accordance with the arrest warrant issued by Spain. Pinochet was suspected of breaching international law by having committed acts of genocide and terrorism. The alleged crimes had been committed mostly in Chile; however, the allegation of human rights violations against Pinochet and other military and political leaders had been unsuccessful in Chile. With some Spanish nationals among the victims, Spain showed an interest in the case and started an investigation which resulted in the request for Pinochet's extradition, who was visiting the U.K. at that time.[113] The main issue discussed by the British court was the legality of Pinochet's arrest and whether or not he enjoyed immunity as the former head of State and a permanent Senator.[114] For the purpose of this study, I will concentrate on the question of whether the Spanish authorities had jurisdiction, especially universal jurisdiction, over the case under international law.

Could Spain prosecute a crime which had been committed outside Spanish territory by a foreigner? The jurisdictional basis under international law which Spain could employ in the Pinochet case was passive personality and universal jurisdiction provided under the Torture Convention. In addition to torture, Spain considered claiming its universal jurisdiction over alleged genocide. The Spanish claim of jurisdiction over the case was based on its domestic law laying down jurisdiction for crimes such as piracy, genocide, terrorism and hijacking, irrespective of the place where such crimes had occurred.[115] However, it was argued within Spain that the alleged acts committed by Pinochet did not constitute the crime of genocide, but rather the crime of torture over which Spain does not have jurisdiction when it has been committed abroad by foreigners.[116] Also, some argued that for the crime of genocide allegedly committed by Pinochet in Chile, Spain would only be precluded from exercising its jurisdiction when Chile or an international judicial organ – the territorial State or the international criminal court (although not yet in existence at that time) as prescribed in Article 6 of the Genocide Convention – commenced prosecution.[117] On this point, the Spanish

---

113 For details as to how the investigation was started in Spain, see Naomi Roht-Arriaza 'Pinochet Precedent and Universal Jurisdiction' *New England Law Review* 35 (Winter 2001), pp. 311-312.

114 The English High Court admitted the immunity of Pinochet as a former head of state. However, the House of Lords overturned the decision of the lower court and denied his immunity.

115 See the explanation of the Spanish legislation by Luis Benavides 'The Universal Jurisdiction Principle: Nature and Scope' *Annuario Mexicano de Derencho International* Vol. 1 (2001), pp. 73-78. He cites the original text of the Spanish law and explains how Article 23.4 of the Ley Orgánica del Poder Judicial (del 1 de Julio 1985) allows Spain to exercise jurisdiction over genocide, terrorism, piracy, illegal control of aircraft, counterfeiting of foreign currency, prostitution, drug trafficking, and any other crime under the treaties to which Spain is a party.

116 See, Julio Barboza 'International Criminal Law' *Recueil des Cours* Tome 278 (1999), p. 171 note 4.

117 William J. Aceves 'Liberalism and International Legal Scholarship: The Pinochet Case and the Move Toward a Universal System of Transnational Law Litigation' *Harvard International Law Journal* Vol. 41 No. 1 (Winter 2000), pp. 162–164. See also, Richard J. Wilson 'Prosecuting Pinochet: International Crimes in Spanish Domestic Law' *Human Rights Quarterly* Vol. 21 No. 4 (November 1999), pp. 957–958.

national court (*Audiencia Nacional*) ruled that it could investigate and exercise universal jurisdiction over crimes committed in Chile.[118] Together with this assertion, the Spanish decision stated that, because more than fifty Spanish nationals had been victims of the crime, a request for Pinochet's extradition could be justified.[119] Since Spain had modified its initial request for extradition based on alleged crimes including genocide, concentrating mainly on the alleged crime of torture, the British courts did not decide on this issue. Accordingly, the British courts dealt with the issue of the obligation of the U.K. under the 1984 Torture Convention to either prosecute or extradite a person alleged to have committed torture.[120]

There was also opposition outside Spain. In response to the Spanish investigation into Pinochet, South American States including Chile vigorously opposed jurisdiction in third States. Chile and Argentina initially criticized the arrest of Pinochet as a violation of State sovereignty.[121] Chile emphasized that the arrest was an intrusion into its State sovereignty and expressed its position that it did not recognize the jurisdiction of a foreign court over acts committed within its territory.[122] In contrast, the majority of the European States supported the arrest on the basis of human rights. Such support triggered extradition requests from other European States as well, e.g., from Switzerland, France and Belgium.[123] To put it succinctly, at the initial stage, there were disputes among States as to the legality of the arrest and the exercise of jurisdiction, and

118 Decision of the Spanish Audiencia National. See Maria del Carmen Marquez Carrasco and Joaquin Alcaide Fernandez 'In re Pinochet: Initiation of Criminal Proceedings Against Former President of Chile for Offenses While in Office' *American Journal of International Law* Vol. 93 (1999), p. 690. See also Mary Griffin 'Ending the Impunity of Perpetrators of Human Rights Atrocities: A Major Challenge for International Law in the 21st Century' *International Review of the Red Cross* No. 838 (June 2000), p. 382. See also, Naomi Roht-Arriaza, *supra* note (113), p. 313. Roht-Arriaza summarized the Spanish decision as follows:

'...[T]he court agreed with the characterization of the crimes committed as genocide... The court found that the lack of express authorization for universal jurisdiction in the 1948 Genocide Convention did not mean such jurisdiction was barred, as it was consistent with the intent of the drafters.'

119 See Maria del Carmen Marquez Carrasco and Joaquin Alcaide Fernandez, *ibid.*, p. 691.

120 Arts. 4, 5, and 7 of the Torture Convention.

121 It was observed that when a Spanish investigating team requested Argentina to provide documents and testimony by victims living in Argentina, the Argentine government refused, claiming it to be a violation of Argentine sovereignty. See, Naomi Roht-Arriaza, *supra* note (113), p. 312. Roht-Arriaza also observed that the Chilean and Argentine governments based their opposition on the argument that such foreign adjudication of crimes committed within Chile and Argentina would 'upset a delicate political consensus regarding the proper balance between truth, justice and amnesty.' *Ibid.*, 315.

122 See, William J. Aceves, *supra* note (117), p. 164.

123 See Mary Griffin, *supra* note (118). See also the *Revue de Droit Pénal et de Criminologie*, 1999, pp. 278-300. See also Suzanne Schairer and Chile Eboe-Osuji 'The Jurisdiction to Prosecute Foreigners for Crimes Against Humanity Committed Abroad' *African Legal Aid Quarterly*, January-March 2000. Shairer and Eboe-Osuji compare the domestic law of Spain, France, and Belgium and how they were applied to the Pinochet Case, and then criticise the lack of harmonization among States seeking to prosecute Pinochet.

it was anticipated that it might lead to unfriendly relations developing between certain States.

Irrespective of the actual result of the Pinochet Case, in which Pinochet's extradition to Spain was refused on the grounds of his deteriorating health, some regard the Pinochet Case as the birth of a regime of worldwide punishment.[124] There is no doubt that the Pinochet Case had a great impact on the international community in seriously considering the possibility and propriety of the exercise of national jurisdiction over gross and serious human rights violations.[125]

5.3 The ICC and Universal Jurisdiction

The effort to establish a permanent international criminal court gained momentum in the 1990s, encouraged by the establishment and functioning of the *ad hoc* tribunals. As a result, the ICC Statute[126] was adopted by the United Nations Diplomatic Conference of Plenipotentiaries on 17 July 1998. Concerning the importance of national jurisdiction to end impunity, the Preamble to the ICC Statute reads as follows:

> '[...] Affirming that the most serious crimes of concern to the international community as a whole must not go unpunished and that their effective prosecution must be ensured by taking measures at the national level and by enhancing international co-operation,
> Determined to put an end to impunity for the perpetrators of these crimes and thus to contribute to the prevention of such crimes,
> Recalling that it is the duty of every State to exercise its criminal jurisdiction over those responsible for international crimes [...]'

One of the basic principles of the ICC is complementarity. The ICC will only exercise its jurisdiction when national legal systems are 'genuinely unable or unwilling' to exercise jurisdiction. Under the principle of complementarity, the ICC Statute expressly states that the ICC and States have concurring jurisdiction and that national courts are the primary forums for prosecuting crimes.

Contrary to the interpretation of some scholars, the Preamble itself does not prescribe universal jurisdiction since it does not mention on which jurisdictional basis States must rely. However, recognizing the importance of the interest of the international community as signified in the Preamble, States have begun to consider universal jurisdiction for those crimes which are subject to the ICC jurisdiction. Consequently, many States began to consider expanding their national jurisdiction as well while

124 William J. Aceves, *supra* note (117), pp. 170-171. Aceves mentions other examples, such as the case in Canada in which Canada deported a Rwandan on the basis of his participation in the act of genocide; and the German Supreme Court upholding the jurisdiction of a lower court in a case of genocide where a Serbian had allegedly played a role in an act of ethnic cleansing committed in Bosnia.

125 For the effect of the Pinochet Case in Argentina and Chile and other Latin American States, see Naomi Roht-Arriaza, *supra* note (113), pp. 315-318.

126 UN Doc. A/CONF. 183/9.

preparing to ratify the ICC Statute. In fact, some States prepared their national legislation to broaden their jurisdiction. For instance, Belgium amended its law to incorporate definitions of crimes under international law, such as genocide, in order to explicitly lay down universal jurisdiction over these crimes.[127] In addition, some scholars, in recommending the United States to prepare for universal jurisdiction for crimes subject to ICC jurisdiction, have pointed to the need to close the gap between the jurisdiction of the ICC and the United States.[128] It has also been said that, by doing so, the United States can pre-empt the ICC jurisdiction, including its jurisdiction over American nationals under the principle of complementarity.[129]

5.4 Greater Expectations as Regards Universal Jurisdiction and Some Results

Since the 1990s, a substantial increase in the prosecution of gross and serious violations of human rights in domestic courts may be observed compared to the previous period. For instance, a large number of prosecutions are taking place in the domestic courts of Rwanda. Together with the continuing pursuit of crimes committed during World War II,[130] the campaign to end impunity has led to a re-examination of human rights violations that occurred in the past in order to determine whether they are suitable to be tried. For example, the United States enacted a law in May 1994 to investigate the genocide committed in Cambodia,[131] reaffirming that the prosecution of the crime of genocide constitutes an international interest. Many scholars and States have expressed their appreciation of universal jurisdiction as an effective measure to end impunity and have encouraged States to exercise it. For example, the Organization of American States advised its Member States to exercise universal jurisdiction against the crime of genocide, crimes against humanity, and war crimes, as well as to ratify the ICC Statute.[132]

In addition, universal jurisdiction was recognized when the UN established national courts to prosecute gross human rights violations in East Timor. The special panel established within the District Court in Dili in East Timor is explicitly entrusted with universal jurisdiction. UNTAET, which constructed the judicial system in East Timor

127 See, 'Belgium: Act Concerning the Punishment of Grave Breaches of International Humanitarian Law' *International Legal Materials* Vol. 38 (July 1999), p. 922. The Belgian law which provides for universal jurisdiction is studied in detail later in this chapter.

128 See Douglass Cassel 'Empowering United States Courts to Hear Crimes Within the Jurisdiction of the International Criminal Court' *New England Law Review* 35 (Winter 2001).

129 See Douglass Cassel, *ibid.*, pp. 436-439.

130 For example, see, Christopher Amerasinghe 'The Canadian Experience', Leila Sadat Wexler 'The French Experience', and Graham T. Blewitt 'The Australian Experience', Mark S. Zaid 'The U.S. War Crimes Act of 1996'. All these articles are in Cherif Bassiouni ed., *International Criminal Law: Vol. V Enforcement* (2nd ed.) (Transnational Publishers, 1999).

131 Cambodian Genocide Justice Act, 22 U.S.C. 2656 Part D, Section 571–574.

132 See, the *1998 and 1999 Annual Reports of the Inter–American Commission on Human Rights*. Also, see, OEA/Ser/L/V/U/.101 Doc.69, and Doc.70 (December 8, 1998).

in accordance with the power entrusted by the UN Security Council, placed the crime of genocide, war crimes, crimes against humanity, murder, sexual offences, and torture within the exclusive jurisdiction of the District Court in Dili. And, at the same time, UNTAET promulgated in its Regulation No. 2000/15 that the court shall have universal jurisdiction with regard to the crime of genocide, war crimes, crimes against humanity and torture. Then it defined universal jurisdiction as follows:

> '2.2. For the purposes of the present regulations, "universal jurisdiction" means jurisdiction irrespective of whether:
> (a) the serious criminal offence at issue was committed within the territory of East Timor;
> (b) the serious criminal offence was committed by an East Timorese citizen; or
> (c) the victim of the serious criminal offence was an East Timorese citizen.'

This signifies the international recognition of universal jurisdiction.

Some cases were actually commenced in some domestic courts concerning gross violations of human rights including genocide. After the Pinochet Case, many other cases began to be investigated for possible trial. Victims of gross human rights violations began to look for the better forum to file their complaints, sometimes entrusting their hope in the exercise of universal jurisdiction by a third State rather than the more traditional jurisdiction such as territorial jurisdiction.

Unfortunately, one can observe a gap between the high expectations of victims and scholars and the actual outcome achieved by the exercise of universal jurisdiction in reality. I will introduce three cases in which universal jurisdiction did not result in a successful completion of criminal proceedings. Ironically, although universal jurisdiction was expected to ameliorate prosecution and to end impunity, all the three examples noted below failed to do so. It is observed that the case law has largely remained cautious in relying on universal jurisdiction.[133] Some people maintain that the gradual, but steady expansion of the exercise of universal jurisdiction is likely to be a permanent trend in the struggle for international justice,[134] but, at the current stage, there seems to be some difficulty in moving forward with such a trend, as illustrated next.

5.4.1 The Guatemalan Massacre Case

The complaint filed to a Spanish court on 2 December 1999 by Nobel Peace Prize winner Rigoberta Menchù concerning the massacres in Guatemala was a result of the growing expectations as regards universal jurisdiction and it was instigated in the hope of following the precedent set in the Pinochet Case. The complaint accused eight for-

---

133 See the Joint Separate Opinion of Judges Higgins, Kooijmans, and Buergenthal in the Case Concerning the Arrest Warrant of 11 April 2000, *supra* note (69), para. 22.

134 Jelena Pejic 'Accountability for International Crimes: From conjecture to reality' *International Review of the Red Cross* Vol. 84 No. 845 (March 2002), p. 24.

mer political and military leaders of Guatemala of acts of genocide, torture, terrorism, and other crimes committed during the Guatemalan internal strife, especially those acts which had been committed during the late 1970s and the early 1980s. This case was another case of universal jurisdiction *in absentia* just like the Pinochet Case. However, in its decision on 13 December 2000, the Spanish national court (Audiencia Nacional) dismissed the complaint, finding that insufficient evidence had been presented to conclude that Guatemala itself could not deal with the case.[135] The court's reasoning is based on two findings: (1) universal jurisdiction is supplemental to territorial jurisdiction, and (2) at the time, there were no legal obstacles to prosecution in Guatemala and the inactivity and denial of the Guatemalan judicial authorities to exercise jurisdiction had not been established.[136] I will examine these two findings in detail below.

First, the Spanish court concluded that universal jurisdiction is supplemental to territorial jurisdiction based on its unique interpretation of the Genocide Convention. It construed that Article 6 of the Genocide Convention:

> 'imposes the subsidiarity of the exercise of jurisdictions other than those mentioned by the provision [Article 6 of the Genocide Convention], so that the judicial authorities of a State should abstain from exercising jurisdiction over acts constitutive of genocide that would be tried by the courts of the country in which they occurred or by an international criminal tribunal.'[137]

The same interpretation had been expressed in earlier findings by the same court, but, in this case, the court went further to assert that the subsidiarity of universal jurisdiction forms a part of international *jus cogens*.[138] Therefore, the Spanish court construed that the supplemental nature is imperative not only within the exercise of universal jurisdiction in Spain, but in any other State as well. However, as Cottier criticizes, even Article 6 of the Genocide Convention and Article 17 of the ICC Statute which the court recklessly presented as evidence of this do not support such a finding.[139] Although the court's legal reasoning may be considered to be somewhat poorly consti-

135 See Tom Scheirs 'Relatives of Murdered Belgian Priests Initiate Criminal Investigation into Crimes Against Humanity while Spanish Court Dismisses Complaint of Rigoberta Menchu' in Section VIII: Enforcement of International Human Rights, *International Enforcement Law Reporter* Vol. 17 No. 3 (March 2001). For the problem of prosecuting the massacres in Guatemala, see Nathanael Heasley, Rodger Hurley, Kara E. Irwin, Andrew H. Kaufman, Nadine Moustafa, and Alain Personna 'Impunity in Guatemala: The State's Failure to Provide Justice in the Massacres Cases' *American University International Law Review* Vol. 16 (2001).

136 See Michael Cottier 'Correspondents' Reports Spain', in H. Fischer and Avril McDonald eds., *Yearbook of International Humanitarian Law* Vol. 3: 2000 (T.M.C. Asser Instituut, 2002), pp. 587-594.

137 The citation from the decision is the translation found in Michael Cottier, *ibid.*, p. 589.

138 Decision of the Audiencia Nacional, Criminal Chamber, Plenary Session, shelving the proceedings regarding the case of Guatemala, Appeal Record No. 115/2000, Preliminary Proceedings 331/99, Central Court of Instruction No. 1, Madrid, 13 December 2000. See the translation by Michael Cottier, *supra* note (136), p. 589, and also the translation by Amnesty International, *ibid.*, p. 694.

139 See, Michael Cottier, *ibid.*, p. 593.

tuted, it does not detract from the fact that Spain interprets universal jurisdiction to be a supplemental jurisdiction. Also, this case symbolizes a clear preference for territorial jurisdiction, reaffirming that territorial jurisdiction is the primary jurisdiction for the purpose of prosecution.

Having determined that universal jurisdiction is supplemental, the Spanish court then examined the situation of Guatemalan territorial jurisdiction to see whether or not supplemental universal jurisdiction should be exercised by Spain. The court asserted that supplemental universal jurisdiction can be exercised when there is sufficient evidence to show that territorial jurisdiction cannot be exercised. In this regard, the Spanish court examined Guatemalan domestic law and the work carried out by the Guatemalan Truth Commission and it saw no legal obstacle for Guatemala to exercise territorial jurisdiction over the crime of genocide. In addition, it also checked whether there is any 'judicial inactivity or prosecutorial inefficiency for reasons of governmental pressure or factual powers', and concluded that 'we cannot infer judicial inactivity by virtue of the time passed, as was possible in the cases of Chile and Argentina for the passing of years since the military dictatorships ended'.[140]

Based on these findings, the Spanish court decided not to exercise its supplemental universal jurisdiction. It is interesting to note that, consequently, while the possibility of exercising universal jurisdiction *in absentia* by the Spanish courts is not denied, Spain delimits universal jurisdiction by characterizing it as a supplemental jurisdiction.

On 25 February 2003, the Spanish High Court emphasised again that universal jurisdiction is to be supplemental to other jurisdiction. Furthermore, the court ruled that universal jurisdiction can be exercised only when there is a nexus between the case and Spain, namely the Spanish nationality of the victims, or the presence of the suspect in Spain.[141]

5.4.2 The Hissène Habré Case

Senegal indicted the former Chadian President Hissène Habré on 3 February 2000 and placed him under house arrest.[142] This was the first time that a third State in Africa had exercised its jurisdiction over a former head of State of another State. Hissène Habré, who ruled Chad from 1982 to 1990, was charged with crimes against humanity and complicity in torture. Later, the charge of crimes against humanity was dropped since there was no Senegal law for any prosecution under this charge. Furthermore, the

---

140 The citation is a translation found in Michael Cottier, *ibid.*, p. 590.

141 For the introduction of this case, see Antonio Cassese 'Is the Bell Tolling for Universality? A Plea for a Sensible Notion of Universal Jurisdiction' *Journal of International Criminal Justice* Vol. 1 No. 3 (December 2003), p. 590.

142 See 'Senegal Court Charges Ex-Chad Leader with Torture' in Section VII: Enforcement of International Human Rights, *International Enforcement Law Reporter* Vol. 16 No. 3 (March 2000). See also Frederic Kirgis 'The Indictment in Senegal of the Former Chad head of State' ASIL Insights, February 2000, http://www.asil.org/insights/insigh41.htm.

Court of Appeals and also the Supreme Court of Senegal denied the indictment based on the charge of torture, ruling that Senegal lacks the necessary domestic legislation.[143] Senegal is a party to the Torture Convention, yet it had not prepared domestic legislation enabling Senegal courts to prosecute torture crimes committed abroad by a foreigner. Charges against Hissène Habré are now being considered by Belgium.

5.4.3 The Bouterse Case

In the Netherlands, the case against Desi Bouterse entailed some discussion as to the exercise of Dutch judicial authority on the basis of universal jurisdiction *in absentia*.[144] Desi Bouterse was suspected of ordering his military personnel to execute 15 people in Surinam in December 1982. Complaints were filed in 1996 and 1997 to the Dutch authorities by relatives of the victims who live in the Netherlands. Considering that the relatives had been seeking the initiation of proceedings against the suspect for years, the decision of the Court of Appeal in Amsterdam in November 2000 ordering the commencement of proceedings against him indicated the influence of the interest of the international community in ending the impunity of gross violations of human rights.

Finding a legal and appropriate basis of jurisdiction for the case proved to be a problem. With the past colonial relationship between Surinam and the Netherlands, the suspect and victims were thought to have Dutch nationality at the outset of proceedings in the Netherlands, as the Court of Appeal found some indications that at least one of the victims and possibly more had Dutch nationality.[145] In addition, the Court of Appeal acknowledged that having a large number of people of Surinamese origin living in the Netherlands, the alleged crime shocked not only the relatives of the victims but also society at large in the Netherlands.[146] Considering these factors, the Netherlands seemed to have at least nationality jurisdiction and passive personality jurisdiction under international law, but the transition of nationality from Dutch to Surinamese caused confusion. Although the complaint was dealt with based on the Dutch nationality of the suspect at the outset of the proceedings, after doubts were raised about his nationality, more emphasis was placed on universal jurisdiction over torture, war crimes or crimes against humanity. The Court of Appeal affirmed its jurisdiction over Bouterse finding that States had competence to exercise universal jurisdiction over crimes against humanity as customary international law stood when

143 See Jelena Pejic, *supra* note (134), p. 25.

144 For details, see Pita J.C. Schimmelpenninck van der Oije 'A Surinam Crime Before a Dutch Court: Post-Colonial Injustice or Universal Jurisdiction?' *Leiden Journal of International Law* Vol. 14 No. 2 (2001). See also Harmen van der Wilt 'The Prosecution of Crimes Against Humanity: Some Reflections on the Dutch Approach' *African Legal Aid Quarterly*, January-March issue (2000), pp. 21-22.

145 See the Decision of the Court of Appeal of Amsterdam in the Case of Desi Bouterse, 3 March 2000, para. 4.2., translated by Peter Kell, published in H. Fischer and Avril McDonald eds., *Yearbook of International Humanitarian Law* Vol. 3: 2000 (T.M.C. Asser Instituut, 2002), p. 682.

146 See *ibid.*, p. 682.

the crime was committed in 1982. It dismissed a proposition that prosecution would not be possible and admissible as long as the suspect is not in the Netherlands, finding insufficient evidence to support this argument.[147] As to the relation with the territorial jurisdiction of Surinam, while noting that Surinam itself is obliged to prosecute offences that were committed in its territory, the Court of Appeal speculated that Bouterse would not be prosecuted in Surinam in the foreseeable future.[148] Yet, the court did leave room for suspending the proceedings in the Netherlands if Surinam were to decide to exercise its jurisdiction.[149]

One reasoning that gave rise to a substantial dispute was the decision of the Court of Appeal to apply the Dutch law to the incidents retroactively. Since the alleged crime had occurred before 1984 – the year that the Torture Convention was adopted by the UN General Assembly and well before its implementation in the Netherlands in 1988[150] – the propriety of a trial in the Netherlands was doubted. Consequently, the Supreme Court reversed the finding of the Court of Appeal and denied jurisdiction over Bouterse on the ground of the non-retroactivity rule.[151]

The Supreme Court of the Netherlands also questioned the nexus between the Netherlands and the alleged crime. As mentioned above, the Court of Appeal authorized the initiation of proceedings notwithstanding the fact that Bouterse was not on the territory of the Netherlands.[152] But, on this point, the Supreme Court noted that, because Bouterse was still in Surinam and none of the victims were Dutch nationals, it lacked a direct link with the Dutch legal order. It concluded that prosecution in the Netherlands for acts of torture committed abroad was possible only 'if one of the conditions of connection provided for in that Convention for the establishment of jurisdiction was satisfied, for example if the accused or the victim was Dutch or fell to be regarded as such, or if the accused was on Dutch territory at the time of his arrest.'[153] Therefore, it can be observed that the Supreme Court denied the commencement of procedures based on universal jurisdiction *in absentia* which the Court of Appeal had supported. The Bouterse Case is an example of other legal norms halting

---

147 See *ibid.*, para. 5.4.

148 See para. 3.1 of the Decision of the Court of Appeal of Amsterdam in the Case of Desi Bouterse, 20 November 2000, *supra* note (145), p. 687.

149 See *ibid.*, para. 3.4., p. 687.

150 Law Concerning the Application of the Convention Against Torture and Cruel, Inhuman or Degrading Treatment or Punishment, 29 September 1998, Stb. 478. This law entered into effect on 20 January 1989. See Pita J.C. Schimmelpenninck van der Oije, *supra* note (144), pp. 463-466.

151 The decision of the Supreme Court of the Netherlands, 18 December 2001, No. 00749/01. See Tom Scheirs 'Dutch Supreme Court Bars Prosecution of Former Surinamese Head of State Bouterse' in Section: Enforcement of International Human Rights, *International Enforcement Law Reporter* Vol. 17 No. 2 (December 2001).

152 For the problem of trial in *absentia*, see Pita J.C. Schimmelpenninck van der Oije, *supra* note (144), pp. 473-474.

153 This citation from the ruling by the Dutch court is the translation cited in the Separate Opinion of President Guillaume to the ICJ judgment on 14 February 2002, Case Concerning the Arrest Warrant of 11 April 2000 (Democratic Republic of the *Congo* v. *Belgium*), para. 12.

the exercise of universal jurisdiction as there was no international conflict in his prosecution since Surinam did not oppose the exercise of jurisdiction by the Netherlands.[154]

One common feature in the Hissène Habré Case and the Bouterse Case was that both cases lacked domestic legislation that explicitly attributes universal jurisdiction over the crime to national courts. On the other hand, some States have begun to actively prepare their domestic legal environment for trying crimes such as genocide and war crimes. The most liberal measure is to be found in the legislation of Belgium. I will present the Belgian law next.

5.5 Universal Jurisdiction in Belgium

5.5.1 The Belgian Law of 1993 and 1999

Belgium adopted a domestic law in 1993[155] to punish grave breaches of the Geneva Conventions of 1949 and Additional Protocols I and II. According to this law, the Belgian courts have jurisdiction irrespective of the place of the commission of such offences as well as the nationality of the suspect or victim. In February 1999, Belgium amended the law to include explicitly genocide and crimes against humanity.[156] It was asserted that those crimes were already subject to Belgian jurisdiction before that amendment as crimes punishable under customary international law. But the amendment in 1999 contributed to making it explicit that these crimes fall under Belgian jurisdiction, and also in expressing strong support for the ICC by incorporating the definition of those crimes adopted in the ICC Statute. As a result, universal jurisdiction over genocide became laid down in the law in Belgium. What is extraordinary is that Belgium attributed to itself universal jurisdiction *in absentia*. As a result, Belgium enabled itself to hear any case in the world which is suspected of constituting a crime listed in the law, even without the presence of suspects.

Following the law, a number of complaints accusing foreigners currently or formerly in high positions of gross human rights violations were submitted in Belgium. Among these are complaints against Ariel Sharon; Abdoulaye Yerodia Ndombasi, the former Foreign Minister of Congo; and Hissène Habré, the former President of Chad. The only case so far successfully concluded through the exercise of universal jurisdic-

---

154 The Surinamese government was said to have expressed its preference for a Dutch trial over a trial in Surinam because it feared that even if a conviction could be obtained, the government doubted that a prison in Surinam could securely detain Bouterse. See 'Dutch and Surinam Both Bring Criminal Charges Against Former Head of State Bouterse' in Section IX: Extraterritorial Jurisdiction and International Human Rights, *International Enforcement Law Report* Vol. 17 No. 1 (January 2001).

155 Loi relative à la répression des infractions graves aux Conventions internationales de Genève du 12 août 1949 et aux Protocoles I et II du 8 juin 1977, additionnels à ses Conventions, *Moniteur Belge* No. 157 (5 August 1993), at 17751.

156 Loi du 10 febrier 1999 No. 57 (23 March 1999), at 9286 ; the translation of this Belgian Act can be found in 38 *International Legal Materials* 918 (1999).

tion is the prosecution of four Rwandans, including two Catholic nuns, for taking part in the murders of Tutsi tribe members by Hutu militia in 1994.[157] In this case, the crime had been committed in Rwanda and both the suspects and the victims were Rwandan nationals.

However, the wide scope of universal jurisdiction attributed to the Belgian courts provoked some conflicts with other States as complaints flooded in from all over the world requesting the Belgian authorities to investigate and to commence proceedings. One example of the conflicts is introduced next.

5.5.2 The ICJ Case Concerning the Arrest Warrant of 11 April 2000

On 17 October 2000, the Democratic Republic of the Congo filed an application against Belgium to the ICJ concerning the arrest warrant issued by Belgium against its Minister of Foreign Affairs at that time, Yerodia Abdoulaye Ndombasi. After deliberation, the ICJ upheld his immunity and ordered Belgium to cancel the arrest warrant. Although the ICJ did not rule on the legality of universal jurisdiction *in absentia* asserted by Belgium, this question was discussed at the hearings and the judges displayed their different views in their individual opinions.

Belgium stated at the hearing that it also had clear and reasonable links with the acts in question because of the Belgian nationality or residence of the victims of those acts.[158] Thus, it can be said that the arrest warrant was based on passive personality jurisdiction. Despite this, universal jurisdiction was still disputed by the judges of the ICJ. Some judges stated that universal jurisdiction *in absentia* has no basis in international law, while others approved it.

For instance, *ad hoc* Judge Bula-Bula stated as follows:

> '[p]uisque le différend international portait sur des prétentions contradictoires entre les immunités en question et la compétence dite universelle, par sa décision, la Cour a *implicitement* rejeté l'allégation de cette compétence dans la présente affaire.'[159]

---

157 For the decision of the Belgian courts denying the request to dismiss the case, see Eric David 'Correspondents' Reports Belgium (Proceedings against Vincent Ntezimana, Alphonse Higaniro, Consolata Mukangango (Sister Gertrude) and Julienne Mukabutera (Sister Maria Kisito), Decisions of 28 March of the Council Chamber (Chambre du conseil) and of 27 June 2000 of the Indictments Chamber (Chambre des mises en accusation)', in H. Fischer and Avril McDonald eds, *Yearbook of International Humanitarian Law* Vol. 3: 2000 (T.M.C. Asser Instituut, 2002), pp. 429-450.

158 See, the ICJ Case Concerning the Arrest Warrant of 11 April 2000, Order of 8 December 2000 concerning the request for the indication of provisional measures, para. 25.

159 The Separate Opinion of Judge M. Bula-Bula to the same case, para. 108.

President Guillaume concluded that '[u]niversal jurisdiction *in absentia* is unknown to international conventional law.'[160] He held that 'international law knows only one true case of universal jurisdiction: piracy.'[161] He further noted as follows:

> 'International criminal law has itself undergone considerable development and constitutes today an impressive legal *corpus*. ... But at no time has it been envisaged that jurisdiction should be conferred upon the courts of every state in the world to prosecute such crimes, whoever their authors and victims and irrespective of the place where the offender is to be found. To do this would, moreover, risk creating total judicial chaos. It would also be to encourage the arbitrary for the benefit of the powerful, purportedly acting as agent for an ill-defined "international community". Contrary to what is advocated by certain publicists, such a development would represent not an advance in the law but a step backward.'[162]

Moreover, President Guillaume added:

> 'States primarily exercise their criminal jurisdiction on their own territory. ... Additionally, they may exercise jurisdiction in cases of piracy and in the situations of subsidiary universal jurisdiction provided for by various conventions if the offender is present on their territory. But apart from these cases, international law does not accept universal jurisdiction; still less does it accept universal jurisdiction *in absentia*.'[163]

Judge Rezek was of the same opinion. He concluded that an examination of international law demonstrates that, as it currently stands, that law does not permit the exercise of criminal jurisdiction by domestic courts in the absence of some connecting circumstance with the exercising State. Judge Rezek noted in particular that the Geneva Conventions do not enshrine any notion of universal jurisdiction *in absentia*, and that such jurisdiction had never been claimed by the Spanish courts in the Pinochet case. Judge Oda also praised the decision of the Court on this issue, stating that the law was not sufficiently developed in this area.

On the other hand, Judges Higgins, Kooijmans, Buergenthal, and Van den Wyngaert affirmed universal jurisdiction *in absentia* on the basis that there was no law prohibiting it. For instance, Judge Van den Wyngaert stated that '[t]he term "universal jurisdiction" does not necessarily mean that the suspect should be present on the territory of the prosecuting State. Assuming the presence of the accused, as some authors do, does not necessarily mean that it is a legal requirement.'[164] She explained that there is no conventional or customary international law prohibiting universal jurisdiction *in absentia*. In examining customary international law, she stated that

160 Separate Opinion of President Guillaume, para. 9.
161 Separate Opinion of President Guillaume, para. 12.
162 Separate Opinion of President Guillaume, para. 15.
163 Separate Opinion of President Guillaume, para. 16.
164 Dissenting Opinion of Judge Van den Wyngaert, para. 53.

'even where national law requires the presence of the offender, this is not necessarily the expression of an *opinio juris* to the effect that this is a requirement under international law.'[165] She held that a lack of practice on universal jurisdiction *in absentia* cannot be seen as evidence of an *opinio juris*.[166] Furthermore she concluded as follows:

> 'It may be *politically* inconvenient to have such a wide jurisdiction because it is not conducive to international relations and national public opinion may not approve of trials against foreigners for crimes committed abroad. This does not, however, make such trials illegal under international law. .... A *practical* consideration may be the difficulty in obtaining the evidence in trials of extraterritorial crimes. Another practical reason may be that States are afraid of overburdening their court system.'[167]

The legality of universal jurisdiction *in absentia* under international law will be examined in the next chapter. Yet, the difference in opinions among the ICJ judges shown above evidences that the scope of various rules on jurisdiction is still ill-defined. When States start to consider whether they should exercise universal jurisdiction in the present jurisdictional system where multiple jurisdictions co-exist, there is a possibility of resulting conflict with other jurisdictions.

5.5.3 Amending the Belgian Law in 2003

The Belgian law allowing the universal jurisdiction *in absentia* of the Belgian courts has affected diplomatic relations with some States, and it has resulted in opposition toward the law. Recently, Belgium decided to restrict its controversial law. On 2 April 2003, the Lower House of the Belgian parliament approved amendments that adds some requirements for the exercise of universal jurisdiction *in absentia*, and discussion in the Upper House followed.[168] The amendment was passed on 23 April 2003.[169] Reflecting the ICJ judgment introduced above, this amended law clearly states that there shall be no prosecution of a person who have immunity, such as Heads of State, heads of government, and foreign ministers of foreign affairs during their terms of office.[170] Concerning universal jurisdiction, three changes prescribed in Article 16(2) are important. First, under Article 16(2), the alleged serious violation of international humanitarian law shall be the one 'committed against a person who, at the time of the

---

165 Dissenting Opinion of Judge Van den Wyngaert, para. 55.
166 Dissenting Opinion of Judge Van den Wyngaert, para. 56.
167 Dissenting Opinion of Judge Van den Wyngaert, para. 56.
168 See Andrew Osborn 'Sharon Made Safe by Belgian Vote on War Crime Law' *The Guardian* (London), 3 April 2003, p. 16.
169 For the French text and translation, see, 'Belgium's Amendment to the Law of June 15, 1993 (As Amended by the Law February 10, 1999 and April 23, 2003) Concerning the Punishment of Grave Breaches of Humanitarian Law', *International Legal Materials* Vol. 42 No. 5 (September 2003), pp. 1258-1283.
170 Article 13, *ibid.*

commission of the acts, is a Belgian national or against a person who has been effectively, habitually, and legally residing in Belgium for at least three years.'[171] Therefore, the nexus based on nationality or residence of victims, which is a rationale for passive personality jurisdiction, is incorporated. Second, any prosecution which includes the preliminary investigation phase may only be undertaken at the request of the Federal Prosecutor.[172] Third, it is especially interesting that the Federal Prosecutor may decide not to proceed in the following situation:

> 'from the specific circumstances of the case, it appears that, in the interest of the proper administration of justice and in compliance with Belgium's international obligations, this case should be put before either the international courts, or before the court of the place where the acts were committed, or before the court of the State of which the perpetrator is a national, or the court of the place where he may be found, and to the extent that this court is independent, impartial, and fair, as may result from relevant international commitments binding on Belgium and that State.'[173]

This allows Belgian courts to hold passive attitude in exercising jurisdiction when there is any other foreign court. This requirement can be construed as altering Belgian universal jurisdiction *in absentia* to supplemental jurisdiction.

Furthermore, the Belgian law was amended more radically in 5 August 2003.[174] The new law requires a foreigner who wishes to submit a case to be residence in Belgium for a minimum of 3 years. Consequently, it can be construed that the Belgian law disposed universal jurisdiction and instead, placed emphasis on passive personality jurisdiction.

5.6 Concluding Observations on the Fourth Period

The world has faced dramatic legal and political changes in the fourth period. These changes have promoted and advanced considerably the awareness and recognition of the interest of the international community and its significance in maintaining international peace, compared to the former periods. The discussions on human rights, State responsibility, and the Draft Code of Crimes Against Peace and Security of Humankind were among the factors that influenced the acceptance of universal jurisdiction. With the success of the collective response and international cooperation in the 1991 Gulf War, there was renewed respect and expectations for the UN security system and other international enforcement mechanisms. The end of the Cold War prompted the former East and West to come closer, but disrupting ethnic conflicts threatened the

171 Article 16(2), the first paragraph of the new subparagraph 1 bis, *ibid.*

172 Article 16(2), the second paragraph of the new subparagraph 1 bis, *ibid.*

173 Article 16(2), the new subparagraph 1 bis (4), *ibid.*

174 The Belgian law of 5 August 2003, *Moniteur Belge* (7 August 2003), at 40506-40515. Can be found at http://www.moniteur.be.

peace and security of the international community. Witnessing the atrocities caused by ethnic conflicts, States renewed their determination to end impunity and to promote peace and security together with the promotion of human rights. States invested in efforts to construct a better jurisdictional regime.

The establishment of the international criminal courts boosted the progress of international humanitarian and criminal law more than ever. It has convinced States of the importance of recognizing the interest of the international community in ending impunity. As a result, the more active acceptance of universal jurisdiction has been observed in this period. For example, the Cairo-Arusha Principles on Universal Jurisdiction Respect of Gross Human Rights Offences admits that it is 'the well established and generally accepted principle that gross human rights offences are of legitimate concern to the international community, and give rise to prosecution under the principle of universal jurisdiction.[175] It states that the principle of non-interference in the internal affairs of States should be interpreted in the light of the above principle.

However, the actual exercise of universal jurisdiction has encountered many problems because the international political and domestic legal environments are not fully prepared to facilitate it. Even taking into consideration some cases related to universal jurisdiction in Europe, Scheffer states that '[u]niversal jurisdiction is not a broadly adhered-to standard. Everyone talks about universal jurisdiction, but almost no one practices it. ... The evidence of state practice on universal jurisdiction is sparse...'[176] In the Pinochet Case[177] and the Ocalan Case[178] (which drew the attention of the international community to accountability for crimes other than those committed in the former Yugoslavia and Rwanda) although the suspect had been detained subject to an arrest warrant issued by foreign States, the actual extradition to the requesting State was not without dispute concerning its legality. The fact that the ICJ has been requested to rule on the disputes resulting from universal jurisdiction in more than one case indicates the extent of universal jurisdiction being controversial.[179] Likewise, despite the gradual acceptance of appreciating universal jurisdiction as a measure to

175 Africa Legal Aid (AFLA), the Cairo-Arusha Principle on Universal Jurisdiction in Respect of Gross Human Rights Offences: An African Perspectives, adopted at the Follow-up Expert Meeting held at Arusha, 18-20 October 2002, http://www.afla.unimaas.nl/en/act/index.html, principle 6.

176 David Scheffer 'Opening Address' (Symposium: Universal Jurisdiction: Myths, Realities, and Prospects' *New England Law Review* 35 (Winter 2001), p. 233. Similarly, Bassiouni concludes that '[t]he sum total of national experience, whether in legislative or judicial practice, does not evidence that the application of universal jurisdiction in state practice has risen to the level of customary international law.' M. Cherif Bassiouni, *supra* note (1), p. 148.

177 For details on the situation leading to the issuance of the arrest warrant by Spain, see, Richard J. Wilson, *supra* note (117), and for details on the Pinochet case, see, William J. Aceves, *supra* note (117).

178 For details on the case of Abdullah Ocalan, the Kurdish leader extradited to and prosecuted in Turkey, see Hanz Chiappetta 'Rome, 11/15/1998: Extradition or Political Asylum for the Kurdistan Workers Party's Leader Abdullah Ocalan?' *Pace International Law Review* Vol. 13 (Spring 2001).

179 Concerning universal jurisdiction, after conclusion of the Case Concerning the Arrest Warrant of 11 April 2000, the ICJ is requested to rule on the Case Concerning Certain Criminal Proceedings in France (Republic of the *Congo* v. *France*).

end impunity, its actual exercise faced many problems in many cases. The theoretical and practical challenges that universal jurisdiction is facing today will be studied in the next chapter.

6 Conclusions

In this chapter, I have illustrated the development of universal jurisdiction from classical international law to the present. Under classical international law, universal jurisdiction was generally conceived as a supplemental permissive jurisdiction. Universal jurisdiction over piracy was admitted under two rationales: the seriousness of the crime under international law, and the absence of national or international jurisdiction capable of effectively prosecuting those serious crimes. Owing to the strong incentive among States to prosecute and punish piracy and recognition that to do so serves the common interest among many States, and also to the fact that it was unlikely to conflict with the traditional jurisdictional regime, it was possible to develop a primary universal jurisdiction over piracy under customary international law. But for other crimes, universal jurisdiction was supplemental.

Modern international law started to construct a different jurisdictional regime. 'The contemporary trends, reflecting international relations as they stand at the beginning of the new century, are striking. The movement is towards bases of jurisdiction other than territoriality.'[180] For instance, the idea of employing universal jurisdiction to prosecute and punish war crimes and genocide was presented after the Second World War. However, under the strong influence of the rules governing the classical jurisdictional regime, States were reluctant to accept it. This reluctance began to weaken from the 1970s onwards after the expansion of universal jurisdiction in conventional international law. By prescribing a custodial State's right to prosecute coupled with the principle of *aut dedere aut judicare*, many conventions prohibiting crimes and gross human rights violations have laid down universal jurisdiction with an obligatory character. Also, universal jurisdiction in conventional international law seems to have overcome the supplemental characteristic and has become a primary jurisdiction. This expansion of universal jurisdiction in conventional international law has influenced the formation of customary international law. As a result, the idea of universal jurisdiction gradually gained support as the notion of the interest of the international community as a whole developed. However, the active exercise of universal jurisdiction came later when the international community was forced to reconsider the jurisdictional system in order to respond to the terrible atrocities committed in the early 1990s. The establishment of international criminal courts encouraged States to exercise their jurisdiction over the same categories of crimes. The determination to end impunity and to serve the interest of the international community has led many cases to be tried by

180 The Joint Separate Opinion of Judges Higgins, Kooijmans, and Buergenthal, in the Case Concerning the Arrest Warrant of 11 April 2000, *supra* note (69), para. 47.

domestic courts. 'Universal jurisdiction has become the preferred technique by those seeking to prevent impunity for international crimes.'[181] However, the active exercise of universal jurisdiction in recent years has encountered some problems. These problems will be discussed in the following chapter.

Observing the development of universal jurisdiction, one has to remember that it is still in transition under international law and thus requires continuous study and review in the future. For example, we will be compelled to consider universal jurisdiction in conjunction with the future prospect of international criminal courts. As some States vehemently oppose the jurisdiction of the new ICC, the notion of national jurisdiction and its theoretical relationship with the international criminal jurisdiction is seriously questioned as well.

---

181 M. Cherif Bassiouni, *supra* note (1), p. 82.

CHAPTER IV
UNIVERSAL JURISDICTION IN A CONCEPTUAL CONTEXT

1 INTRODUCTION

Chapter III elucidated the historical development of the notion of universal jurisdiction. In the light of the observations in that chapter, the present chapter will study the status of universal jurisdiction under international law today. This chapter is composed of two parts. Each part answers a particular question: the first part, 'what is universal jurisdiction?', the second, 'what is the legal status of universal jurisdiction under international law?'.

The first part studies the notion of universal jurisdiction. Here, the notion of universal jurisdiction will be dissected and its components analysed. As pointed out earlier, there is diversity in the perception of the notion of universal jurisdiction among scholars and States, creating conceptual chaos. I will emphasise the need to distinguish between universal jurisdiction and universal jurisdiction *in absentia*, and then between ordinary universal jurisdiction and *international criminal jurisdiction* (the jurisdiction of international criminal courts). The second part analyses the legal status of universal jurisdiction under conventional and customary international law.

2 WHAT IS UNIVERSAL JURISDICTION?

2.1 Universal Jurisdiction and Universal Jurisdiction *in Absentia*

2.1.1 Definitions

Throughout history, universal jurisdiction was substantiated as a jurisdiction exercised by a State having no relation to the crime in question except for the presence of the suspect on its territory. However, some interpret universal jurisdiction to be a jurisdiction exercised by a State irrespective of any factors, even irrespective of the fact that the suspect is not to be found in that State. In this study, this is referred to as '*universal jurisdiction in absentia*.' For example, Principle 13 of the 'Brussels Principles Against Impunity and for International Justice' defines universal jurisdiction as 'the right of a state to institute legal proceedings and to try the presumed author of an offence, irrespective of the place where the said offence has been committed, the nationality or the place of residence of its presumed author or of the victim.' Then it explains that '[t]his jurisdiction is exercisable, in accordance with the rules of fair trial, regardless of whether or not the presumed author is present on the territory of the forum state.'

One difference between ordinal universal jurisdiction and universal jurisdiction *in absentia* is that the former is recognised only for a State in which a suspect is present, and the latter is attributable to virtually any State in the world since it requires no nexus between the crime and the State claiming jurisdiction. With regard to the lack of a nexus, some regard universal jurisdiction *in absentia* as a purified form of universal jurisdiction. They believe that universal jurisdiction *in absentia* approaches the ideal that every State in the international community has an interest in ending impunity concerning gross violations of human rights and that every State should eagerly implement all the means possible to achieve this end. As such, universal jurisdiction *in absentia* may be regarded as a kind of *actio popularis*, since it virtually allows all States to prosecute and punish individuals notwithstanding the total lack of a nexus between the State and the crime. Because these States are considered to be acting on behalf of the international community and not in their own specific national interest, it is an action for the good of the international society.

Some may reason that the distinction between universal jurisdiction and universal jurisdiction *in absentia* is meaningless since a State which initially only has universal jurisdiction *in absentia*, may eventually obtain ordinary universal jurisdiction if it succeeds in obtaining the custody of a suspect who is located abroad as the result of its arrest warrant or extradition request. Therefore, they might interpret a State action based on universal jurisdiction as an effort to obtain the custody of a suspect in order to exercise universal jurisdiction. In the ICJ's Case Concerning the Arrest Warrant of 11 April 2000, Judges Higgins, Kooijmans and Buergenthal seemed to take universal jurisdiction *in absentia* as the original form of universal jurisdiction, and they then denied the presence of the suspect as a prerequisite by pointing out the inconsistency and variation in people's discussions on exactly when the presence of a suspect is required. These judges concluded that '[a]n examination of national legislation, cases and writings reveals a wide variety of temporal linkages to the assertion of jurisdiction. This incoherent practice cannot be said to evidence a precondition to any exercise of universal criminal jurisdiction.'[1] And as for jurisdiction prescribed in various conventions, the judges contended that by the 'loose use of language' it has come to be referred to as 'universal jurisdiction', though 'this is really an obligatory territorial jurisdiction over persons, albeit in relation to acts committed elsewhere.'

This study, however, believes that it is meaningful to make the distinction between ordinary universal jurisdiction and universal jurisdiction *in absentia*. One major reason for this is because each has different status in conventional and customary international law. More specifically, the practice of universal jurisdiction *in absentia* is not widely

1 See Principle 13 of the 'Brussels Principles Against Impunity and for International Justice', adopted by the Brussels Group for International Justice, following on from the colloquium 'The Fight Against Impunity: Stakes and Perspectives' (Brussels, 11-13 March, 2002). See the Joint Separate Opinion of Judges Higgins, Kooijmans, and Buergenthal in the ICJ Judgment of 14 February 2002 in the Case Concerning the Arrest Warrant of 11 April 2000 (Democratic Republic of the *Congo* v. *Belgium*), paras. 41, 54.

practiced or accepted, and its legality is seriously questioned, compared to ordinary universal jurisdiction, as I will explain later.

Since international law mostly concerns relations between States, this study examines jurisdiction from the viewpoint of when a State can legally assert that it has such jurisdiction against other States. Because this study examines jurisdiction at the international level, attention should be given not only to the trial stage, but also to the moment when a matter can be considered as an international issue, such as when a State claims its jurisdiction over a suspect by requesting extradition and expects the requested State to recognize its jurisdiction as being legitimate. With this in mind, it is observed that ordinary universal jurisdiction is based on the presence of a suspect within its territory before a State claims jurisdiction over the relevant case, while universal jurisdiction *in absentia* does not. Understanding universal jurisdiction as a jurisdiction without any nexus to the case except the presence of a suspect, it is contradictory to allow a State to submit an extradition request based on universal jurisdiction that can be asserted only after the extradition is competed and this State in question obtains the actual custody of the person sought.

In sum, there is no doubt that both forms of universal jurisdiction are envisaged to serve the interests of the international community as a whole by replacing impunity with accountability. However, I believe that making a distinction will help to clarify and establish more solid rules at least for ordinary universal jurisdiction and thereby contribute to the formation of a stable system to end impunity.

2.1.2 The Different Status under International Law

An essential distinction relates to their legal status, the realm of their acceptance among States. In short, ordinary universal jurisdiction is seen to have more solid evidence of recognition under international law than universal jurisdiction *in absentia*.

Historically, universal jurisdiction was normally exercised based on the nexus of the presence (and often the custody) of a suspect within the territory of the exercising State. Many contemporary treaties and conventions prescribe universal jurisdiction in the form of an obligation upon States *where a suspect is present*. Also, many States which have incorporated universal jurisdiction into their domestic law require the presence of a suspect within their territory, or some other form of nexus to it. For example, the Canadian Crimes Against Humanity and War Crimes Act of 2000 manifestly requires the presence of a suspect in Canada for prosecuting crimes committed abroad.[2] And in Germany, the courts have generally required some connection with

2 Section 8 of Crimes Against Humanity and War Crimes Act of 2000 prescribes the presence of a suspect as the requirement for prosecution based on any non-territorial jurisdiction as follows.
'8. A person who is alleged to have committed an offence under section 6 or 7 may be prosecuted for that offence if
(a) at the time the offence is alleged to have been committed,
(i) the person was a Canadian citizen or was employed by Canada in a civilian or military capacity,

Germany to be established before they extend their jurisdiction. For example, in some cases, the courts have found a link between alleged crimes and Germany through the presence of the accused or his permanent residence or domicile on German territory.[3] This connection requirement is made in order override the principle of non-interference in the affairs of another State.[4] Yet it is observed that the German courts have tended to view the interests of the international community as a sufficient basis to outweigh this principle.[5]

Moreover, many conventions allow the custodial State to enjoy discretion in deciding whether to extradite or exercise jurisdiction itself. This discretion has allowed universal jurisdiction to develop from being supplemental to primary. The fact that the discretion granted to the custodial State is so broad confirms the greater responsibility vested upon custodial States. This nexus is crucial in creating a rule in international law that attributes a right and, even more so, an obligation upon States to exercise universal jurisdiction over gross violations of human rights. To formulate an acceptable equation of universal jurisdiction is important and useful in clarifying the role of States in exercising it within the jurisdictional regime and promoting States to act in conformity. I will explain the importance of this nexus later.

In contrast, however, no convention explicitly prescribes universal jurisdiction *in absentia*. Hence, universal jurisdiction *in absentia* is not a direct consequence of the expansion of national jurisdiction under conventional international law. Of course, the fact that there is no specific provision for this under conventional international law does not preclude it from becoming part of customary international law. In fact, the U.S. courts in the Demjanjuk Case recognized universal jurisdiction *in absentia* by extraditing the suspect to Israel. However, theoretically, universal jurisdiction *in absentia* is extraordinary even within the modern jurisdictional regime since there is no connection between the exercising State and the actual case. It is only the recognition of the interest of the international community that promotes its exercise. There is no support from the principle of State sovereignty or the exclusiveness of territorial sovereignty. Partially due to this theoretical disparity, and also due to the lack of

---

(ii) the person was a citizen of a state that was engaged in an armed conflict against Canada, or was employed in a civilian or military capacity by such a state,

(iii) the victim of the alleged offence was a Canadian citizen, or

(iv) the victim of the alleged offence was a citizen of a state that was allied with Canada in an armed conflict; or

(b) after the time the offence is alleged to have been committed, the person is present in Canada.'

3 For example, see the Decision of the Bavarian Higher Regional Court (Munich) of 23 May 1997, Bayerisches Oberstes Landesgericht, 23 May 1997, re D., 3 St 20/96. See also, the Decision of 15 December 1999 by the Bavarian Higher Regional Court (Munich), Bayerisches Oberstes Landesgericht, 15 December 1999, re K., 6 St 1/99.6 St 1/99. A summary of these cases can be found at the homepage of the International Red Cross, http://www.icrc. org/ihl-nsf.

4 See The Tadic Case, Decision of 13 February 1994 by the German Federal Court of Justice (BGH-Ermittlungsrichter), re Tadic, 1 BGs 100/94.

5 See the Tadic case and others.

specific provisions recognizing universal jurisdiction *in absentia*, States have been less than passionate in recognizing such jurisdiction. In my view, it would be easier to create more solid rules in both conventional and customary international law for ordinary universal jurisdiction.

2.2 The Different Characteristics of Universal Jurisdiction

As the notion of universal jurisdiction has gained attention, some scholars have tried to categorize variations thereof, but they have been less successful in describing the different characteristics which universal jurisdiction might entail. In this study, universal jurisdiction is categorised by two aspects which differentiate its nature. The first aspect is whether it is permissive or obligatory. The second aspect is whether it is supplemental or primary. These categorizations are made in order to facilitate our understanding of the evolution of the notion of universal jurisdiction from the classical jurisdictional regime to the present.

Universal jurisdiction may be understood as a right pertaining to a State. In this study, universal jurisdiction which is perceived as a right is termed 'permissive universal jurisdiction.' Permissive universal jurisdiction means that States are not obliged to exercise universal jurisdiction but are entitled to do so if they desire. In this study, a further categorization is made in respect of the principle of *aut dedere aut judicare*. If a State can freely decide and exercise universal jurisdiction without regard to other forms of national or international jurisdiction, it can be categorized as *primary permissive universal jurisdiction*. A State exercises primary permissive universal jurisdiction when it decides freely to do so, not affected by the existence of other entities having legitimate jurisdiction (including territorial jurisdiction) over the same case. On the other hand, if a State is first required to exhaust domestic remedies to extradite or surrender a suspect for trial in another State or the international criminal courts before deciding to exercise its universal jurisdiction over a case, it is categorized as *supplemental permissive universal jurisdiction*. The latter universal jurisdiction is described as being 'supplemental' because it can be exercised only after the jurisdictions of other States or international institutions fail, thereby providing supremacy to other bases of jurisdiction and itself being a secondary rather than primary jurisdiction. Consequently, the difference between *primary* and *supplemental* universal jurisdiction is whether a State has freedom to decide to exercise it or rather its freedom is limited by the prerequisite of giving preference to other bases of national or international jurisdiction.

Sometimes, universal jurisdiction is considered to be more than a right. It may be an obligation imposed on States for certain types of crimes. Then it is categorised as *obligatory universal jurisdiction*. *Primary obligatory universal jurisdiction* means that States are obliged to exercise universal jurisdiction irrespective of other national jurisdictions. *Supplemental obligatory universal jurisdiction* means States are obliged to exercise universal jurisdiction to avoid impunity when the effort to extradite suspects to other States or international criminal courts has failed. The essential difference between supplemental and primary obligatory universal jurisdiction therefore is that the executing State first has to endeavour to entrust suspects to be tried in other States or in international criminal courts. Therefore, a State with supplemental obligatory universal jurisdiction does not have the discretion to decide whether or not to extradite or prosecute. In both primary and supplemental obligatory universal jurisdiction, the obligation on States can be lifted if States extradite or surrender suspects to other States or to international criminal courts. It is important to note that the status of these kinds of universal jurisdiction having an obligatory character depends on the status of the principle *aut dedere aut judicare* under customary international law.[6]

2.3 The Rationales for Universal Jurisdiction

Chapter III illustrated how universal jurisdiction over piracy developed based on two rationales. The first rationale was criminality under international law in which piracy was recognized as *delicta juris gentium* – it is the seriousness of the crime at issue, the prosecution and punishment of which gives rise to the common interest among the members of the international community or the interest of the international community as a whole. The second rationale was the absence or uncertainty of a jurisdiction capable of being effectively exercised over the crime in question. In the case of piracy, universal jurisdiction was less likely to be in conflict with other jurisdictions such as territorial jurisdiction or jurisdiction of the flag State. For crimes other than piracy, however, the absence or uncertainty of other jurisdictions was not as obvious as the crime of piracy. As a result, only when functioning jurisdictional systems failed to bring justice was universal jurisdiction expected to step in. Under the classical jurisdictional regime, universal jurisdiction for crimes other than piracy was to function as a supplement to other jurisdictions, and this can be seen as the influence of the second rationale. Nonetheless, many advocates of universal jurisdiction today do not pay much attention to these two rationales. I will examine them from the perspective of modern international law.

2.3.1 Reduced Emphasis on the Second Rationale

Many of the arguments to establish universal jurisdiction for crimes other than piracy show a tendency to concentrate on the first rationale – the seriousness of the crime in question – while ignoring the second. Many scholars determine whether or not a crime is subject to universal jurisdiction based solely on the gravity of the crime.[7] For

---

6 However, one must remember that the principle of *aut dedere aut judicare* in itself does not connote permission for universal jurisdiction, as I explain in a separate section.

7 Van der Vyver argues that the requirement of universal jurisdiction must be considered according to the seriousness of the crime instead of the lack of territorial jurisdiction. Johan D. Van der Vyver 'Prosecution and Punishment of the Crime of Genocide' *Fordham International Law Journal* Vol. 23 (1999), p. 322.

instance, Mann explained universal jurisdiction as arising from the character of crimes. His only criterion was that the crimes constitute attacks upon the international order.[8] The Third Restatement also stated that '[a]n international crime is presumably subject to universal jurisdiction'.[9] Various courts have evaluated universal jurisdiction based on the seriousness of the crime.

Some court precedents relating to universal jurisdiction seem to support this trend. The Eichmann Trial and the Demjanjuk Case noted in Chapter III and the ICTY judgment[10] are some examples thereof. For example, in the Pinochet Case, Lord Millet stated that there were two main conditions for applying universal jurisdiction: one was the breach of an absolute norm under international law so as to constitute *jus cogens*; the second was the seriousness of the crime in that it amounted to an attack on the international legal order itself[11] – both conditions therefore relying on the seriousness of the crimes in question. In these arguments, the strong emphasis on the first rationale is expressed while the second rationale is hardly mentioned.

In contrast, Sunga recognizes the existence of the second rationale as well. However, he associates each rationale with a different crime category. He distinguishes the rationale for piracy and for war crimes by acknowledging only the second rationale (absence or uncertainty of effective jurisdiction) for piracy and the first rationale (seriousness of the crime) for war crimes. He explains that for piracy it was the unusual circumstance of the situation in which piracy was committed on the high sea which rendered it a crime under universal jurisdiction, whereas for war crimes it is their serious character.[12]

2.3.2 The Effects of a Reduced Emphasis on the Second Rationale: Primacy and Analogy

As the reliance on the second rationale – a lack of effective jurisdiction or uncertainty as to the whereabouts of legitimate jurisdiction – diminished, the emphasis on respect for other national jurisdictions faded. In other words, the universal jurisdiction envisaged becomes a jurisdiction that can be exercised irrespective of the existence of other

8 See, F.A. Mann 'The Doctrine of Jurisdiction in International Law' *Recueil des Cours* Tome 111 (1964-I), p. 95.

9 Art. 404 of the Third Restatement, p. 257.

10 *Prosecutor* v. *Anto Furundzija*, *International Legal Materials* Vol.38, p. 349-350. The ICTY held that all States have an obligation to either extradite or to investigate, prosecute and punish a suspect within their territory. The judgment stated as the reason for this the fact that the prohibition of torture is a *jus cogens*, and it would be contradictory to preclude the prosecution and punishment of perpetrators while prohibiting the States' power to sign treaties. It also referred the seriousness of the crime by citing the Eichmann Trial and the Demjanjuk case to support its reasoning.

11 Opinion of Lord Millett in Ex Parte Pinochet, see, *International Legal Materials* Vol. 38, pp. 649-650.

12 Lyal S. Sunga, *Individual responsibility in International Law for Serious Human Rights Violations* (Martinus Nijhoff Publisher, 1992), p. 103.

jurisdictions. Therefore, it can be said that ignoring the second rationale has contributed to transforming universal jurisdiction into primary jurisdiction.

Another effect is that analogy has become a popular means by which to expand the number of categories of crime that are subject to universal jurisdiction. If the second rationale can be disregarded as indeed is done by many authors, then universal jurisdiction would be established by the mere recognition of the seriousness of the crimes in question. And in doing so, many employ the technique of analogy. One of the most common analogies justifies universal jurisdiction as an obligation on the part of States for the crime of genocide since other crimes (such as apartheid or torture) are subject to universal jurisdiction under the relevant conventions. They compare the seriousness of the crimes and conclude that, because the crime of genocide is no less serious than these treaty crimes, genocide should also be subject to obligatory universal jurisdiction under customary international law.

Nevertheless, one should be cautious in relying too heavily on a simple analogy between the seriousness of crimes. Even though the seriousness of a crime may be equal to that of a treaty crime which is prescribed to be subject to universal jurisdiction, it cannot be automatically deduced that the former crime should be subject to universal jurisdiction in the same manner. Not an analogy, but a careful examination of each category of crime in both conventional and customary international law is required in order to establish universal jurisdiction for the category of crime in question. Moreover, it is reiterated that the mere fact that a crime falls within the category of 'international crime' or 'crime under international law' does not necessarily give rise to universal jurisdiction. For example, Higgins points out that although Article 19 of the International Law Commission (ILC) Draft Articles on State Responsibility included a serious breach of the right of self-determination as well as a serious breach of the duty to prohibit massive pollution as crimes under international law, these crimes do not give rise to universal jurisdiction.[13]

2.3.3 Reduced Emphasis on the First Rationale

There is a trend of easing the requirement of the seriousness of the crime – the first rationale, as well. Since the 1970s, conventions that have accepted universal jurisdiction are not limited to those concerning the serious crimes tantamount to crimes under international law. The conventions concerning relatively less serious crimes such as drug trafficking have also prescribed universal jurisdiction. The reduced emphasis on the seriousness of the crime may signify how widely the notion of universal jurisdiction has achieved acceptance in conventional international law.

However, one should be careful not to presume that the tendency of conventional international law to reduce the emphasis on the first rationale can be observed in

13 See, Rosalyn Higgins, *Problems and Process: International Law and How We Use It* (Clarendon Press, 1994), p. 62.

domestic law as well. In reality, the arrangement of universal jurisdiction as prescribed in conventional international law is not fully reflected at the national level. Within the domestic laws of many States and in their opinion, universal jurisdiction is still an exceptional jurisdiction, just as it was in the classical jurisdictional regime.

It should also be remembered that the 'expansion' of universal jurisdiction observed in conventional international law may indicate the general direction of the development of international law, but it may not be identical to the level of customary international law. The difference between conventional and customary international law may be observed in relation to the level of the seriousness of the crimes with which universal jurisdiction may be associated. While conventions that lay down universal jurisdiction for crimes such as drug trafficking relate to the common interest of States, they may not quite fall within the interest of the international community as a whole. On the contrary, customary international law recognizes universal jurisdiction as being related to more serious crimes, the prohibition of which constitutes *jus cogens* and *erga omnes*, and the interest of the international community as a whole. Therefore, in analyzing the status of universal jurisdiction, the difference between conventional international law and customary international law must be kept in mind.

2.3.4 The Relevance of Rationales

It can be said that the reduced emphasis on the two rationales has followed the general direction of the development of international law, encouraged by the 'expansion' of universal jurisdiction under conventional international law. Although States generally have discretion in deciding what kind of jurisdiction to uphold, general jurisdiction in the classical jurisdictional regime was territorial jurisdiction. Under the dominance of territorial jurisdiction in practice, other forms of jurisdiction had to be justified. This was especially true in the case of universal jurisdiction since it is a jurisdiction with a considerably weak nexus to a crime; therefore it required some justifications – the two rationales mentioned above – before it could be exercised. However, this has changed over the years. Now, many conventions explicitly encourage States to extend their national jurisdiction beyond territorial jurisdiction. As illustrated in the preceding chapters, especially after the 'expansion' of national jurisdiction under conventional international law since the 1970s, international law has encouraged States to adopt a variety of jurisdictions including universal jurisdiction. Hence, non-territorial jurisdiction today does not require such an extensive search for the necessary justification as it did under the classical jurisdictional regime. Due to the expansion of national jurisdiction, many consider the rationales underlying universal jurisdiction to be less significant.

In my view, however, the two rationales for universal jurisdiction are still relevant and valuable in the modern jurisdictional regime. This is because although universal jurisdiction has started to be widely accepted in conventional international law, the determination of universal jurisdiction in customary international law requires more careful consideration. Many rules on jurisdiction are still not in the evident form of written law. Moreover, although the jurisdictional system is changing, it is still greatly influenced by rules that dominated the classical jurisdictional regime. Since universal jurisdiction is still to be established and placed firmly within the modern jurisdictional regime, it is important to ascertain the precise meaning and value of universal jurisdiction. I consider that both rationales are important in determining the application of universal jurisdiction. Crimes which are subject to universal jurisdiction should be crimes constituting 'acts which damage vital international interests', 'impair the foundations and security of the international community', and 'violate the universal moral values and humanitarian principles that lie hidden in the criminal law systems adopted by civilized nations'.[14] As for the second rationale, the absence or uncertainty of effective jurisdiction is not only a historical consideration, but a practical and contemporary one as well. In order to successfully implement universal jurisdiction within the measures to end impunity, it is important to adjust to the existing jurisdictional system. Therefore, although the second rationale is not as strongly emphasized as it was in the classical jurisdictional regime, it is still important to take notice.

In addition, the two rationales serve to determine the appropriateness of universal jurisdiction. Even though a particular exercise of universal jurisdiction may be considered to be legal, its appropriateness may be denied in the event of a jurisdictional conflict with other States. In determining the appropriateness of exercising universal jurisdiction in a particular situation, the two rationales may be taken into consideration. I will elaborate this point later in Chapter VI.

2.4 The Source of Universal Jurisdiction

Some scholars categorise universal jurisdiction by its source. They contend that there are three forms of universal jurisdiction: *unilateral* universal jurisdiction, *delegated* universal jurisdiction, and *absolute* universal jurisdiction,[15] and explain each as follows. 'Unilateral universal jurisdiction' is described as jurisdiction exercised by a State 'acting without delegation of jurisdiction over the matter by the State that is linked to the crime, and in the absence of any delegation (fictive or real) on behalf of the international community at large.'[16] 'Delegated universal jurisdiction' is exercised when the 'original judicial competence over a crime belongs to another State, that either renounces it, yields, or delegates its jurisdiction in favour of the State where the perpetrator is found.'[17] 'Absolute universal jurisdiction' is exercised when a State has

14 These words are quoted from the evaluation of the seriousness of crimes by the Israeli court in the Eichmann Trial. See the judgment by the Israeli Supreme Court in the Eichmann Trial, in E. Lauterpacht ed., *International Law Reports* Vol. 36 (Butterworths, 1968), p. 291.

15 See, Nicolaos Strapatsas 'Universal Jurisdiction and the International Criminal Court' *Manitoba Law Journal* Vol. 29 No. 1. See, M. Henzelin, *Le Principe De L'universalité en Droit Pénal International: Droit et obligation pour les États de poursuivre et juger selon le principe de l'universalité* (Helbing & Lichtenhahn, 2000), p. 2.

16 See, Nicolaos Strapatsas, *ibid.* See, M. Henzelin, *ibid.*

17 See, Nicolaos Strapatsas, *ibid.* See, M. Henzelin, *ibid.*

'exercised jurisdiction over a crime the nature of which affects the interests of all States and justifies its repression as a matter of international policy, even against the wishes of the State having territorial or any other form of jurisdiction.'[18] This categorization is interesting from a theoretical perspective but may be somewhat confusing. It seems to rely on the source of jurisdiction (whether that power derives from the exercising State itself or from another State or from the international community), but there is a considerable overlap among them since, in practice, States rarely explain the source of their universal jurisdiction, and even when they do, they may cite more than one source. Furthermore, this categorization does not illuminate the differences in the character or the consequences of universal jurisdiction in each category. In this study, the different categorizations of universal jurisdiction (*i.e.*, permissive/obligatory, and supplemental/primary) are employed, but below I will also elucidate my views concerning the issue of the source of universal jurisdiction.

2.4.1 Territorial or Other National Jurisdiction?

The category of 'delegated universal jurisdiction' introduced above seemingly bases itself on *the representational rule*.[19] According to the theory of the representational rule, 'a state acquires the power to exercise extraterritorial jurisdiction based on a delegation of jurisdiction by the territorial state (or other state with jurisdiction based on active or passive personality or on the protective principle) to the forum state, either expressly or impliedly, when the forum state takes the initiative independently of another state with jurisdiction.'[20] This theory explains that when the extradition of a suspect to a territorial State or other States is not requested, the State having custody of the suspect may proceed to try him or her in its courts since the others have abandoned their right to exercise jurisdiction and, by doing so, have implied their consent to prosecution in the custodial State. One author refers to this phenomenon as 'delegated universal jurisdiction' and explains that the 'original judicial competence over a crime belongs to another State, that either renounces it, yields, or delegates its jurisdiction in favour of the State where the perpetrator is found.'[21] The consequence of adopting this interpretation is that the supplemental character of that jurisdiction becomes intrinsic. Since such a jurisdiction is exercised only after some efforts to give priority to the jurisdictions of other States.

---

18 See, Nicolaos Strapatsas, *ibid*. See, M. Henzelin, *ibid*.

19 The representational rule is sometimes referred to as 'the principle of the vicarious (or representative) administration of justice', or the 'substitutionary principle'. See Albin Eser 'Common Goals and Different Ways in International Criminal Law: Reflections from a European Perspective' *Harvard International Law Journal* Vol. 31 No. 1 (Winter 1990), p. 119. See also, Jürgen Meyer 'The Vicarious Administration of Justice: An Overlooked Basis of Jurisdiction' *Harvard International Law Journal* Vol. 31 No. 1 (Winter 1990), pp. 115-116.

20 Amnesty International 'Universal Jurisdiction: The duty of states to enact and implement legislation' (September 2001), AI Index: IOR 53/002/2001, p. 18.

21 Nicolaos Strapatsas, *supra* note (15), p. 7.

Section 7(2) No. 2 of the German Penal Code lays down the principle of *representative administration of criminal justice* (Prinzip der stellvertretenden Strafrechtspflege)[22] which allows the German authorities to exercise jurisdiction in cases where requests for extradition have been denied or extradition is otherwise impossible. This form of jurisdiction is prescribed separately in different provisions from those providing for universal jurisdiction against genocide and other crimes subject to universal jurisdiction under treaties and conventions.[23] Hence it can be interpreted that under the German Penal Code, jurisdiction based on the representational rule is distinguished from universal jurisdiction.

So, what then are the differences between universal jurisdiction and a jurisdiction based on the representational rule? The first such difference is the gravity of crimes subject to these jurisdictions. As is evident from the first rationale of universal jurisdiction, universal jurisdiction under international law is recognised for serious crimes, the prosecution and punishment of which are believed to be within the common interest of States or, moreover, the interest of the international community as a whole. In comparison, the representational rule is used to justify the exercise of national jurisdiction over lesser crimes. In fact, under international law, there is no basis generally recognised for States to exercise jurisdiction over lesser crimes that have no relation to the exercising States. Therefore, the justification for the exercise of jurisdiction must come from other bases enjoyed by other States, and that is how the representational rule is formulated. In contrast, universal jurisdiction needs no such theoretical formulation because universal jurisdiction itself is recognised as one of the bases of national jurisdiction under international law. Wolfrum also points out the difference as follows:

> 'The norms based upon the principle of vicarious administration of justice are to be differentiated from those arising from the principle of universality, since the ability to prosecute under vicarious administration is dependent on the liability to punishment at the site of the offence and on the question of extradition, which is not the case under universal jurisdiction. This stems from the fact that each principle pursued a different objective. The principle of vicarious administration of justice allows another State to enforce a criminal law norm which the original State itself could have enforced, whereas a State enforces a criminal law norm under the principle of universality because the world community has determined the offence to be generally punishable.'[24]

In sum, the representational rule is employed to justify national jurisdiction over lesser crimes when there is no basis of jurisdiction, especially that of territorial jurisdiction. Because, as mentioned earlier, conventional international law is becoming more lenient concerning the seriousness of crimes subject to universal jurisdiction, the practical

22 Sect. 7(2) No. 2 of the Strafgesetzbuch (German Penal Code).

23 Sect. 6 of the Strafgesetzbuch (German Penal Code).

24 Rudiger Wolfrum 'The Decentralized Prosecution of International Offenses Through National Courts', in Yoram Dinstein and Mala Tabory eds., *War Crimes in International Law* (Martinus Nijhoff publisher, 1996), p. 236.

difference between universal jurisdiction and jurisdiction based on the representational rule is becoming almost insignificant from the point of view of implementing the treaty-based obligation to exercise universal jurisdiction. Yet, the principle of representative administration is one explanation for non-territorial jurisdiction and not for the notion of universal jurisdiction under international law.

One should remember that when we look back in history at how universal jurisdiction emerged and developed, it was not characterised as the delegation of territorial or other forms of jurisdiction. On the contrary, the crime of piracy became subject to universal jurisdiction because there was an absence of or uncertainty concerning which jurisdiction – including territorial jurisdiction – was capable of effectively prosecuting such a crime. Therefore, it was not a delegation of territorial jurisdiction, but rather the absence of such. As to other categories of crime, it is true that under the classical jurisdictional regime, universal jurisdiction was supplemental in character. Yet, it only required an effort to give priority to the jurisdiction of other States and did not require the explicit or implicit permission from a territorial State or others. If universal jurisdiction was understood as a delegated jurisdiction of other States, then the courts exercising universal jurisdiction could be required to obtain consent from another State for the delegation of power, and might also be required to apply the domestic law of the State that had delegated its jurisdiction. However, the issue of the applicable law was not generally considered in relation to universal jurisdiction. States exercising universal jurisdiction base themselves on and also apply their own national law and international law, rather than the corresponding domestic law of a territorial State. Moreover, especially concerning the crimes of gross human rights violations under consideration in this study, States exercising universal jurisdiction are not acting in the place of territorial States in order to protect the interest of those territorial States. They are acting in their own interest. The benefits of prosecuting and punishing such grave crimes are shared by all States and they have also become an interest of the international community as a whole. Therefore, universal jurisdiction is not an entrusted form of territorial jurisdiction or other national jurisdiction. The prerequisite of the failure of extradition to other States prescribed in the domestic law of some States can be understood as the attribution of a supplemental character to universal jurisdiction, rather than an indication of the source of universal jurisdiction.

2.4.2 Acting on Behalf of the International Community

Compared to the narrow understanding of universal jurisdiction as delegated territorial or other bases of national jurisdiction, there is a totally opposite approach to the source of universal jurisdiction. Rather than interpreting that States exercising universal jurisdiction are acting according to delegated power from the territorial State, many interpret the fact that they are acting on behalf of the international community. Henzelin categorises this as 'absolute universal jurisdiction'. The ILA report explains that '[d]omestic courts and prosecutors bringing the perpetrators to justice are not acting on behalf of their own domestic legal system but on behalf of the international legal order.'[25] The decisions in the Eichmann Trial and the Demjanjuk Case adopted the same view.[26]

Wolfrum's notion of a *decentralised enforcement mechanism* plays a role in this interpretation. He interprets that the criminal jurisdiction inherent to the international community is exercised through the State's jurisdiction. His interpretation has influenced the understanding that States are acting on behalf of the international community, and that States are justified in exercising universal jurisdiction *in absentia*. However, the gap between this theory and practice is evident. In practice, States exercise universal jurisdiction in accordance with their domestic law, applying their domestic penal law and procedural law. Therefore the actual practice varies and is not uniform. Universal jurisdiction is exercised by the national courts. Thus, the justification that a State is acting on behalf of the international community does not change the source and the fact that it is an individual State taking action.

2.5 Universal Jurisdiction and the Jurisdiction of International Criminal Courts

Many authors define universal jurisdiction as including jurisdiction exercised by international criminal courts. For instance, Scharf and Fischer define it as 'the authority of domestic courts and *international tribunals* to prosecute certain crimes, regardless of where the offense occurred, the nationality of the perpetrator, or the nationality of the victim [emphasis added].'[27] Similarly, many other scholars assume universal jurisdiction to be the same as the international criminal jurisdiction exercised by international judicial organs such as the ICTY, ICTR, and the ICC.[28] But they rarely contemplate the reasons for or the consequence of this integration in theory and terminology. Such an interpretation increased after the drafting of the ICC Statute, possibly influenced by discussions on the scope of the ICC jurisdiction in comparison with the exercise of universal jurisdiction by States.[29] What is more confusing is that

---

25 International Law Association 'Final Report on the Exercise of Universal Jurisdiction in Respect of Gross Human Rights Offences', prepared by the Committee on International Human Rights Law and Practice, submitted to London Conference (2000), p. 3.

26 See the judgment by the Israeli Supreme Court in the Eichmann Trial, *supra* note (14), p. 300. See also Chapter III of this study for the explanation of each case.

27 'Foreward' by Michael P. Scharf and Thomas C. Fischer, for the Symposium: Universal Jurisdiction: Myths, Realities, and Prospects, *New England Law Review* Vol. 35 No. 2 (Winter 2001), p. 227. However, not all the articles from the same symposium appearing within the same issue of the periodical follow this definition. Some articles only discuss ordinal universal jurisdiction. The article by Leila Nadya Sadat makes the distinction by creating the two terms 'universal international jurisdiction' and 'universal inter-state jurisdiction'. See Leila Nadya Sadat 'Redefining Universal Jurisdiction' *New England Law Review* Vol. 35 No. 2 (Winter 2001).

28 For example, see Bartram S. Brown 'The Evolving Concept of Universal Jurisdiction' *New England Law Review* Vol. 35 No. 2.

29 For example, the proposal submitted by the German delegation to the Preparatory Committee on the Establishment of an International Criminal Court, A/AC.249/1998/DP.2 (23 March 1998). For the influence of universal jurisdiction on the drafting of the ICC Statute, see my article, 'The Meaning of

there are other variations when using the term 'universal jurisdiction.' Some use the term 'universal jurisdiction' to express what is understood to be the 'automatic jurisdiction' of the ICC,[30] which means that a State accepts the jurisdiction of the ICC by ratification and any other additional consent is not required from this State when the ICC commences proceedings in a case. On the other hand, some people use the term 'universal jurisdiction' of the ICC to mean jurisdiction free from any form of State consent. Therefore, they conclude that the ICC is not granted 'universal jurisdiction' because the ICC requires consent from the territorial State or the State of the nationality of the suspect. Notwithstanding the increased attention to and the discussion on 'universal jurisdiction', there is deep confusion as to the real meaning of universal jurisdiction.

Unlike the broad interpretations of 'universal jurisdiction' discussed above, this study uses the term 'universal jurisdiction' to envisage a jurisdiction exercised by States. The jurisdiction exercised by international criminal courts is thus excluded from its meaning, and is referred to as '*international criminal jurisdiction*' in order to differentiate. In this section I will examine whether the theoretical integration proposed by many scholars is legally appropriate. The practical and procedural aspects of the relationship between national jurisdiction (including universal jurisdiction) and the jurisdiction of international criminal courts is prescribed in the relevant statutes and rules of procedure of each international court.[31] It is important to dwell on this point because it relates to the expected role which universal jurisdiction is to play within the whole jurisdictional system. For instance, one may assert that those States exercising

---

the State Consent Precondition in Article 12(2) of the Rome Statute of the International Criminal Court: A Theoretical Analysis of the Source of International Criminal Jurisdiction' *Netherlands International Law Review* Vol. XLIX Issue 2 (2002), pp. 175-180.

30 For example, an article explains that '[a]ny state or international tribunal can punish perpetrators of international crimes such as genocide on the basis of universal jurisdiction.' Accordingly, the article includes a discussion on the various trials in domestic courts as well as on the various international criminal courts. It explains that pursuant to the ICC Statute, 'a ratifying state accepts ICC jurisdiction over all crimes referred to in Article 5 of the Statute, effectively creating universal jurisdiction over these crimes.' See Evo Popoff 'Inconsistency and Impunity in International Human Rights Law: Can the International Criminal Court Solve the Problems Raised by the Rwanda and Augusto Pinochet Cases' *George Washington International Law Review* Vol. 33 (2001), pp. 384, 389.

31 The practical problems arising from the concurrent jurisdiction will not be considered at length in this section. For example, some scholars point to the irony of allowing major criminals who have committed heinous crimes to be tried in the international criminal courts that are often recognised to have higher standards of human rights protection, more comfortable custodial conditions, and no death penalty compared to the domestic courts of many States. The problem of the allocation of cases between national and international courts and the question of uniformity in the enforcement of international law are other problems which need to be studied. For an analysis of the practical problems, see for example, Madeline Morris 'Complementarity and Conflict: States, Victims, and the ICC' in Sarah B. Sewall and Carl Kaysen eds., *The United States and the International Criminal Court* (Rowman and Littlefield Publishers, 2000), pp. 203-204. See, also, Madeline Morris 'The Trial of Concurrent Jurisdiction: The Case of Rwanda' *Duke Journal of Comparative and International Law* Vol. 7 (Spring 1997), p. 365 and note 91 on that page.

universal jurisdiction, especially universal jurisdiction *in absentia*, enjoy the same authority as international criminal courts and that the same law will be applied to them. In the following pages, I will argue that although the idea of universal jurisdiction and the idea of international criminal jurisdiction have some similarities in their goal and rationales, the two jurisdictions should not be regarded as being the same. They should be distinguished to avoid confusion in practice. In order to explain this, I will first elucidate the similarities between the ideas of universal jurisdiction and international criminal courts as evidenced in many instances throughout history. Secondly, I will examine two schools of thought: One asserting that international criminal jurisdiction is the compilation of the universal jurisdiction of States; and the second which is based on the reversed reasoning that the universal jurisdiction of States derives from international criminal jurisdiction and that States are exercising jurisdiction in the place of the international criminal courts.

2.5.1 The Similarities in Objectives and Rationales

First of all, universal jurisdiction of States and international criminal jurisdiction have been considered to serve the same goal. For example, during the drafting of the Genocide Convention, proposals for both the universal jurisdiction of States and for an international criminal court were raised and discussed in correlation, sometimes proposed together, and at other times as one replacing the other. Both proposals were triggered by a conjecture that there is a great possibility that a territorial State may not be capable of effectively prosecuting and punishing the crime of genocide – a highly political crime which often involves government authorities. In other words, both the notions of universal jurisdiction and the establishment of an international criminal court were intended to overcome the deficiency of the traditional jurisdictional system based on territorial jurisdiction in order to punish criminals and to end impunity.

These two proposals shared not only a common goal, but they were presented as having similar underlying rationales. Both proposals were justified as being in the interest of the international community. The proponents of each proposal argued that because of the gravity of the crime of genocide, such jurisdiction should be admitted as a means to ensure that genocide would not go unpunished due to the unwillingness of States to exercise territorial jurisdiction. Both the notions of universal jurisdiction and of an international criminal court were extraordinary from the point of view of the classical jurisdictional regime, which was based on the national jurisdiction exercised by States to serve their own interests under the nexus rule and on the dominance of territorial jurisdiction. The gravity and seriousness of the crime and the lack of any other national jurisdiction capable of effectively prosecuting crimes were the two rationales for universal jurisdiction as well as for establishing an international criminal court to convince States to depart from the rules which were dominant in the classical jurisdictional regime.

The two proposals were often proposed for other matters in a similar manner to the discussion on the drafting of the Genocide Convention, but were rarely adopted simultaneously except in the Apartheid Convention and in other recent conventions. The ILC's Draft Code of 'Crimes Against Peace and Security of Mankind' prepared in 1996[32] employed both proposals in its provisions, with the intention of creating a concurrent jurisdictional system.[33]

In addition to sharing a common goal and rationales, these two proposals influenced each other in the pursuit of this goal. The acceptance of universal jurisdiction in conventions has strengthened the idea of the interest of the international community and the fight against impunity, facilitating the establishment of international criminal courts. *Vice versa*, the establishment of *ad hoc* tribunals and their jurisdiction over certain crimes has served as a justification and an encouragement for States to exercise their national jurisdiction against such crimes.[34] Moreover, the jurisdiction of *ad hoc* tribunals instigates the codification and formation of customary international law concerning individual accountability for gross human rights violations. The recognition of the interest of the international community heightened by the above line of development brought about the establishment of a permanent international criminal court. In sum, one can observe that the idea of universal jurisdiction and of international criminal courts have influenced each other. History shows that the idea of universal jurisdiction gained support when international criminal courts were unable to be established, resulting in the incorporation of universal jurisdiction within conventional international law.

2.5.2 Schools of Thought that Consider Universal Jurisdiction and International Criminal Courts to be Theoretically Identical

The close relationship between the ideas of universal jurisdiction and of international criminal courts in the history of the effort to end impunity for gross violations of human rights has been described above. However, there is a recent trend in some scholarly writing seeking to associate universal jurisdiction with the international criminal jurisdiction on a theoretical level. Below, I will introduce two schools of thought that conclude that universal jurisdiction is identical to international criminal jurisdiction in theory. In simple terms, the first school of thought advances international criminal jurisdiction as the delegation of national jurisdiction from States, while conversely the second school of thought argues that the universal jurisdiction of States

32 Report of the International Law Commission, *UN GAOR* 51st Session, Supplement No.10 (A/51/10).

33 *Ibid.*, Article 8, and p. 45.

34 International Committee of the Red Cross '*International Criminal Court: State consent regime* vs. *Universal jurisdiction*'. Cases referred there are: Third Chamber of the Eastern Division of the Danish High Court, '*The Prosecution* vs. *Refik Saric*' (Decision of November 25, 1994), Case No. S-3396-94; Tribunal de Bruxelles, Chambre du Conseil, 'Ordonnance du 22 juillet 1996', Journal des Procès No. 310 (20 septembre 1996); and, Tribunal Militaire de Cassation (Switzerland), 'Décision du 8 juillet 1996.'

is the delegation of international criminal jurisdiction inherent to the international community as a whole.

2.5.2.1 Universal jurisdiction as the source of international criminal jurisdiction?

The first school of thought proposes that the jurisdiction of the international criminal courts is the accumulation of the universal jurisdiction of all States Parties. In other words, the international criminal courts are exercising the delegated authority provided by States.[35] Therefore, it is national jurisdiction exercised through an international body. This school of thought denies the existence of any inherent jurisdiction of the international community.

However, this school of thought may have a problem explaining the court's authority to issue an arrest warrant. Of course, if the suspect is present in the territory of States Parties or of States recognizing the court's jurisdiction, they the court may reason that it obtained jurisdiction through delegated territorial jurisdiction. But if it is to depend on the delegated power from the ordinary universal jurisdiction of States, the consequence is, that an international criminal court cannot exercise its jurisdiction unless the court itself has the suspect in custody. This is an odd interpretation and will likely to hamper the activities of an international criminal court since it would prohibit it from issuing arrest warrants in general when the whereabouts of the suspect (thereby, the any possible jurisdiction other than universal jurisdiction that can be delegated to the court) is not known. It is evident that neither the ICTY, ICTR nor the ICC are conceived to perform their mandate in this way. For its theoretical basis to be sound and in line with practice, the idea of universal jurisdiction *in absentia* must be adopted by this school of thought allowing the court to assert jurisdiction over a suspect not yet located. However, as is pointed out later in this chapter, universal jurisdiction *in absentia* is not yet a common understanding among States.

2.5.2.2 International criminal jurisdiction as the source of universal jurisdiction?

The second school of thought entails a reverse interpretation of the first one. A member of this school will argue that States prosecuting and punishing war crimes or crimes against humanity are exercising jurisdiction under the mandate of the international community. It is the decentralized enforcement mechanism contemplated by Wolfrum. Wolfrum argues that a criminal jurisdiction inherent in the international community is exercised through a State's jurisdiction.[36] His interpretation presupposes that there exists a jurisdiction inherent in the international community. He submits that universal jurisdiction allows States to recognise the international value relevant to all the constituents of the international community. He further explains that States punish

35 See my article, *supra* note (29), pp. 188-190.
36 Rudiger Wolfrum, *supra* note (24), p. 186.

crimes only when a specific violation is recognised to be infringing the protected values under conventional or customary law. When a domestic court punishes a criminal based on universal jurisdiction, that court is acting on behalf of the international community or all the member States of the relevant conventions. He refers to this as the *decentralised* implementation of international law. Because a State exercising universal jurisdiction is acting as a mechanism of the international decentralised implementation, the State is not limited by the principle of State sovereign equality and can try crimes in which a foreign State authority may be involved.[37] A State exercising universal jurisdiction may prosecute and punish acts which inflict significant damage on the international community on behalf of all the States in the international community.[38] In this case, the State is exercising jurisdiction in order to protect the interest of the international community as a whole.

However, it is not a common understanding among States to interpret universal jurisdiction as a delegated form of international criminal jurisdiction which is inherent in the international community.[39] Also, as a consequence of explaining universal jurisdiction as a delegated form of international criminal jurisdiction, this school of thought entertains the propositions which attribute to States the same powers as international criminal courts. I will explain the difference between universal jurisdiction and international criminal jurisdiction below.

2.5.2.3 Differentiating between universal jurisdiction and international criminal jurisdiction

The history of the development of universal jurisdiction has shown that although one of its rationales is the interest of the international community, universal jurisdiction has been exercised by States, not by international institutions. National courts have

---

37 Rudiger Wolfrum, *ibid.*

38 Eichmann Case, *supra* note (14), p. 304.

39 However, this does not mean the denial of the existence of international criminal jurisdiction inherent to the international community. The universal jurisdiction of States and international jurisdiction can theoretically coexist, too. For a detailed analysis of the source of international criminal jurisdiction, see my article, *supra* note (29). Another author explores a further possible theory to explain international criminal jurisdiction inherent in the international community. Tanaka considers the possibility of explaining international criminal jurisdiction through the direct delegation of power from citizens to the international community. He explains that for a State establishing national sovereingty, criminal jurisdiction which is one component of sovereign power derives from nationals, and it is entrusted to the State by its nationals to protect them. Therefore when the premise of the protection of nationals is lost, so is the basis of national criminal jurisdiction, and as a consequence, the relationship of entrustment would be dissolved. Nationals of a State is are also members of the international society as citizens, therefore when protection from the State disappears, they can entrust the power to the international community in order to fill the void of protection, thereby giving power to the institution of the international community, the international criminal courts. See, Tanaka Toshiyuki 'Principles of criminal Law and the International Criminal Court' *Human Rights International* (Published by the International Human Rights Law Association in Japan) No. 12 (2001), p. 60 [written in Japanese].

traditionally been the only entity that can prosecute individuals in the long absence of international criminal courts. During the discussions on the drafting of various instruments, States distinguished between the two proposals of universal jurisdiction and establishing an international criminal court. For example, the Genocide Convention incorporated only the latter, and rejected the proposal for universal jurisdiction. What caused this difference in the attitudes of States toward the two proposals? Why was the more radical proposal which required the establishment of a new international institution favoured in comparison to the proposal for universal jurisdiction which required no such new institution, and would thus be more easily implemented? The main reason for the rejection of the proposed universal jurisdiction may be because it would be exercised by individual States. There was serious distrust among States of proceedings within other States – the actor (holder) of jurisdiction may prove to be a decisive difference that should not be ignored.

Although there are some overlaps, these two ideas were substantiated at different points and situations in history and therefore have different rules and law applied to each. They also require different considerations in practice. For example, the ICJ treated two differently in the ICJ decision on the Case Concerning the Arrest Warrant of 11 April 2000. The ICJ examined the rules of immunity taking into consideration the relevant provisions from the charters of the Nuremberg and Tokyo Tribunals, as well as from the statutes of the ICTY, ICTR, and the ICC, which do not exempt responsibility on the basis of the suspect's official position, yet found that these provisions 'do not enable it to conclude that any such an exception exists in customary international law in regard to national courts.'[40] President Guillaume also stated that the development of international criminal courts 'was precisely in order to provide a remedy for the deficiencies of national courts, and the rules governing the jurisdiction of international courts as laid down by treaty or by the Security Council of course have no effect upon the jurisdiction of national courts.'[41] Therefore, it is very important to take note of these differences in order for each of them to function properly and effectively.

States have developed practices and rules of universal jurisdiction, although in very vague form. To simply apply the newly emerging law governing the international criminal courts to universal jurisdiction, as some people propose, would ignore the history and the differences between national jurisdiction exercised by States and international criminal jurisdiction exercised by the international criminal courts. The consequence and the danger of such ignorance are not acceptable as far as the preci-

---

40 The ICJ Judgment of 14 February 2002 in the Case Concerning the Arrest Warrant of 11 April 2000 (Democratic Republic of the *Congo* v. *Belgium*), para. 58. The Court is also observed to be treating the international criminal courts differently from national courts when it noted that the immunities enjoyed by an incumbent or former Minister for Foreign Affairs do not preclude criminal proceedings before 'certain international criminal courts', such as the ICTY, ICTR, and the ICC. *Ibid.*, para. 61.

41 Separate Opinion of President Guillaume, Case Concerning the Arrest Warrant of 11 April 2000, *ibid.*, para. 11.

sion of the law is concerned. Such ignorance may result in imprecision and the reckless expansion of the notion of universal jurisdiction that may be unfounded in international law. Qualifying the two different jurisdictions as being the same or drawing a simple analogy between the two without careful consideration should be avoided. Hence, for example, just because the ICC can exercise its jurisdiction only if the territorial State or the State of the nationality of the suspect accepts jurisdiction does not mean that a State exercising universal jurisdiction has to obtain similar consent from these States. Although it is desirable to achieve uniformity in the application of international law, especially since it relates to individual accountability and punishment, at present the reality is that the enforcement of international criminal and humanitarian law relies largely on the judicial systems in each State administered by relevant domestic law.

In sum, it is true that the proposals for universal jurisdiction and that for international criminal jurisdiction share the same goal, and that both serve the interest of the international community. Both universal jurisdiction and international criminal jurisdiction are expected to bring about justice for gross violations of human rights when there is an absence of other effective jurisdiction capable of being exercised over the case. But the similarities in the overall objective and the rationales do not automatically lead to the conclusion that the same law and rules apply and that the two jurisdictions should be exercised in the same manner. Therefore, individuals who explain the jurisdiction of international criminal courts as universal jurisdiction must remember to note the difference in their application. This important difference explains why the establishment of the ICC is required even in the present environment where national jurisdictions including universal jurisdiction have considerably expanded.[42]

2.6 Universal Jurisdiction and the Principle of *Aut Dedere Aut Judicare*

Universal jurisdiction is most often provided coupled with the principle of *aut dedere aut judicare* in conventions. The principle of *aut dedere aut judicare* obliges the State having custody of a suspect to either extradite the person to a State having jurisdiction over the case or to instigate its own judicial proceeding. Some consider the principle of *aut dedere aut judicare* to be the same as universal jurisdiction. Although there is a considerable overlap between these two notions, in a strict theoretical sense they are

42 If the notions of universal jurisdiction and of an international criminal court both serve the same goal of ending impunity, and moreover, if universal jurisdiction *in absentia* is thought to derive from the same source as the jurisdiction of international criminal courts, one may ask why we still need international courts such as the ICC. In answering this question, one must remember that national jurisdiction and the ICC jurisdiction do not reject each other. This is evident from the provisions of the ICC Statute and the statutes of ad hoc tribunals. The concurrent jurisdictional system is already established, acknowledging the importance of both national and international jurisdiction. Both do not have exclusive jurisdiction. They are expected to work in collaboration. In fact, the corresponding statutes and rules of the ICTY, ICTR, and the ICC all provide for collaboration between States and the international criminal courts.

different notions. The objective of the principle *aut dedere aut judicare* is to avoid crimes being left unpunished because there is no extradition or prosecution. According to this principle, if there is no extradition, the State will be obligated to refer the case to its appropriate prosecuting authorities. However, this principle itself does not specify which bases of jurisdiction should be exercised. It does not imply any jurisdictional preference either. Therefore, strictly speaking, it does not matter which jurisdictional basis is employed. As long as a suspect is prosecuted within a State where the person is present in the absence of extradition, the principle of *aut dedere aut judicare* is fulfilled.

The principle of *aut dedere aut judicare* overlaps with universal jurisdiction when a State has no other nexus to the alleged crime or to the suspect other than the mere presence of the person within its territory. Under the principle of *aut dedere aut judicare*, irrespective of the lack of a close nexus, a State where a suspect is present has to exercise jurisdiction when extradition is not possible, consequently resulting in universal jurisdiction. If the State has any other nexus to the crime, then universal jurisdiction will not be an issue. Some scholars argue that the principle of *aut dedere aut judicare* is a rule under customary international law,[43] but there are those who oppose such a claim.[44]

Notwithstanding the theoretical difference between universal jurisdiction and the principle of *aut dedere aut judicare*, universal jurisdiction has been greatly affected by this latter principle. As a result, there are some notable changes in the nature of universal jurisdiction prescribed in the conventions compared to the classical jurisdictional regime. First, many conventions prescribed universal jurisdiction not merely as a right of States, but as an obligation pertaining to the State Parties. An exception can be found in the 1973 Apartheid Convention which determines permissive universal jurisdiction,[45] although many other conventions prescribe obligatory universal jurisdiction, clearly stating that a State that finds a suspect has the obligation either to extradite or to try the suspect within that State, in accordance with the principle of *aut dedere*

43 Bassiouni argues that it has already become a customary norm. M. Cherif Bassiouni, *Crimes Against Humanity in International Criminal Law* (Martinus Nijhoff Publishers, 1992), pp. 499-508. See also, Lee A. Steven 'Genocide and the Duty to Extradite or Prosecute: Why the United States is in Breach of Its International Obligations' *Virginia Journal of International Law* Vol. 39 (Winter 1999), pp. 446-450. The principle of *aut dedere aut judicare* was also argued in the Lokkerbie Case in the ICJ. See, Dissenting Opinion of Judge Weeramantry, *1992 ICJ Report*, pp. 51, 161.

44 See, M. Cherif Bassiouni and Edward M. Wise, *Aut Dedere Aut Judicare: The Duty to Extradite or Prosecute in International Law* (Martinus Nijhoff Publishers, 1995), pp. 43-69. Benavides also explains the principle of *aut dedere aut judicare* as binding only the parties to the conventions which incorporate the principle. See Luis Benavides 'The Universal Jurisdiction Principle: Nature and Scope' *Anuario Mexicano de Derencho International* Vol. 1 (2001), pp. 32-36.

45 Article 5 of the 1973 Apartheid Convention prescribes as follows:
'Persons charged with the acts enumerated in article II of the present Convention *may* be tried by a competent tribunal of any State Party to the Convention which may acquire jurisdiction over the person of the accused or by an international penal tribunal having jurisdiction with respect to those States Parties which shall have accepted its jurisdiction.' [emphasis added].

aut judicare. If the State Party which has the suspect in custody decides not to extradite the suspect to another State for any reason, that State will be under an obligation to refer the suspect to a competent authority for prosecution. Therefore, the exercise of universal jurisdiction can become an obligation.

Secondly, the conventions concerned seem to imply primary universal jurisdiction, rather than supplemental one. This is because, in obligating either to extradite or to prosecute, many conventions concerned do not prescribe any preference between them. Therefore, a custodial State can act under its own discretion in deciding whether to extradite or prosecute, allowing it to materially enjoy primary jurisdiction.

Some argue, however, that the choice between extradition and prosecution is not at the discretion of the State which has the suspect in custody. This view contends that because territorial jurisdiction is the traditional jurisdiction, the request for extradition from the territorial State must be given priority, therefore extradition rather than the prosecution in the custodial State is the normal procedure. Because extradition is preferred, it can only be denied when it conflicts with domestic law.

The treaties and conventions providing for the principle of *aut dedere aut judicare* do not contain any priority. Therefore, many authors consider that the choice is at the discretion of the custodial State.[46] Compare this to the traditional understanding of universal jurisdiction. Traditionally, universal jurisdiction was considered to be supplemental to other jurisdictions, therefore extradition to other States having a stronger nexus was the prerequisite. However, the universal jurisdiction provided under many modern conventions does not have such character. The conventions do not expressly prescribe that the State can itself prosecute only when an attempt to extradite has failed. As a result, a State can decide to prosecute the suspect itself even if there is a request for extradition from another State. This is why some make an analogy between terrorism against aircraft and piracy, since both are subject to primary universal jurisdiction.[47] In sum, we can observe that the primacy of territorial jurisdiction which was typical of the classical jurisdictional system has now disappeared. It should also be noted that the effect of allowing or obligating a certain basis of jurisdiction is not strictly limited to the State Parties to a specific convention. For instance, a convention obligating State Parties to exercise universal jurisdiction is construed as allowing State Parties to try even the nationals of non-State Parties or crimes committed within the territory of non-State Parties.[48]

Most of the time, extradition functioned as a system to assist the exercise of territorial jurisdiction. However, as a consequence of having universal jurisdiction provided together with the principle of *aut dedere aut judicare*, the system of extradition became not only a system to enhance inter-State cooperation with the objective

46 M. Cherif Bassiouni and Edward M. Wise, *supra* note (44), pp. 56-57.

47 § 404 of the Third Restatement.

48 See, Kenneth C. Randall 'Universal Jurisdiction Under International Law' *Texas Law Review* 66 (March 1998), p. 821. Randall points out that the power to try nationals of Non-Member States was vested on Member States in those multilateral conventions.

of concentrating the exercise of judicial jurisdiction in territorial States, but it also came to have the function of allocating the exercise of jurisdiction among States.[49] This new feature attributable to extradition is discussed in Chapter VI.

2.7 Jus Cogens, Obligatio Erga Omnes and Universal Jurisdiction

The notion of universal jurisdiction is often described to be in close relation with the notions of *jus cogens* and obligation *erga omnes*. Some academics presume that any act violating a peremptory norm which is *jus cogens* will *ipso facto* be the subject of universal jurisdiction, and, moreover, that the exercise of universal jurisdiction is *erga omnes*. But, in fact, these three notions are theoretically different although there is a close connection in the discussion concerning which crime becomes subject to universal jurisdiction under customary international law. I will briefly explain these notions.

2.7.1 The Notions of Jus Cogens and Obligation Erga Omnes

Jus cogens is a rule which cannot be set aside by a treaty or acquiescence by States but only by the formation of a subsequent customary rule with contrary effect.[50] It restricts the discretion and freedom of States to enter into a treaty by prohibiting them from making or adopting any instrument which violates a certain value. States cannot derogate from peremptory norms constituting *jus cogens* even of their own free will. Therefore, even if two or more States sign an international agreement to commit gross and serious human rights violations, claiming the freedom of States to create a certain rule, the agreement would be null and void for violating *jus cogens*. As examples of *jus cogens*, Brownlie lists the prohibition of the use of force, the law of genocide, the principle of racial non-discrimination, crimes against humanity, and the rules prohibiting the trade in slaves and piracy.[51]

Obligatio erga omnes amounts to 'the obligations of a state towards the international community as a whole', as explained by the ICJ.[52] The ICJ held that 'an essential distinction should be drawn between obligations of a State towards the international community as a whole, and those arising vis-à-vis another State', and proclaimed as follows:

49 See Chapter VI. See also Souzi Yamamoto, *Kokusai Keijihou* (Sanseidou, 1991) [in Japanese], p. 196.

50 Article 53 of the Law of Treaties 1966 states that 'a treaty is void if it conflicts with a peremptory norm of general international law from which no derogation is permitted and which can be modified only by a subsequent norm of general international law having the same character.'

51 See Ian Brownlie, *Principles of Public International Law* 5th ed. (Clarendon Press, 1998), p. 515.

52 Barcelona Traction, Light and Power Co. Ltd. (*Belgium* v. *Spain*), *1970 ICJ Report*, p. 32.

> 'By their very nature the former are the concern of all States. In view of the importance of the rights involved, all States can be held to have a legal interest in their protection; they are obligations *erga omnes*.'[53]

The ICJ admitted that an obligation *erga omnes* includes acts of aggression, genocide, slavery, racial discrimination, and various fundamental principles and rules concerning respect for human rights.[54]

Bassiouni distinguishes *jus cogens* and *erga omnes* as follows:

> '*Jus cogens* refers to the legal status that certain international crimes reach, and *obligatio erga omnes* pertains to the legal implications arising out of a certain crime's characterization as *jus cogens*.'[55]

From the definitions of each concept, it is evident that universal jurisdiction is not directly deduced from the notion of *jus cogens*, and vice versa at a strict theoretical level. The *jus cogens* rule only limits States' power to make an international agreement. Therefore in itself it does not order States to exercise their enforcement power. At the same time, the prohibition of a certain act becoming *erga omnes* does not automatically subject such act to universal jurisdiction. Nor does it mean that States are obliged to exercise universal jurisdiction on such an act. Higgins denies that the ICJ was intending to provide guidance on universal jurisdiction when it affirmed the obligation *erga omnes* in the Barcelona Traction Case.[56] She makes it clear that this case was in the context not of the assertion of jurisdiction but of an examination of the law relating to diplomatic protection.[57]

2.7.2 The Correlation between Determinations of Jus Cogens and Erga Omnes

Notwithstanding the theoretical difference, the correlation between universal jurisdiction and *jus cogens* and *erga omnes* is often made because they all represent the recognition of the interest of the international community as a whole. As explained earlier, the seriousness of the crime that promulgates its prosecution and punishment to be within the interest of the international community is one of the rationales of universal jurisdiction as the notion emerged on the international plane. Consequently there is a connection between *jus cogens, erga omnes* and universal jurisdiction. There is a considerable overlap in the application of these notions especially when we look at the prohibition of the crimes which are the subject of this study, that is gross and serious violations of human rights.

---

53 *Ibid.*

54 *Ibid.*

55 M. Cherif Bassiouni 'International Crimes: *Jus Cogens* and *Obligatio Erga Omnes*' *Law and Contemporary Problems* Vol. 59 No. 4 (Autumn 1996), p. 63.

56 Rosalyn Higgins, *supra* note (13), p. 57.

57 See *ibid.*

Although the prohibition of some acts being *jus cogens* and *erga omnes* may consequently signify that States can exercise universal jurisdiction due to the interest of the international community, one must be careful not to presume the reverse by assuming that these notions overlap in all circumstances. As explained earlier, a part of universal jurisdiction under conventional international law has lost its close relation with the two traditional rationales for universal jurisdiction. In other words, universal jurisdiction in treaties and conventions is now allowed for lesser crimes and even in situations where there is another functioning and potentially effective jurisdiction exercisable by other States to try the case. For example, under relevant treaties and conventions, hostage taking and attacks on aircraft and ships, and attacks on United Nations and related personnel are subject to universal jurisdiction, but there remains a doubt in presuming that these rules have a *jus cogens* or *erga omnes* character. Therefore, universal jurisdiction under conventional international law can be exercised against acts that have not reached the level of *jus cogens* or *erga omnes* prohibition. Hence, not all crimes which are subject to universal jurisdiction under certain conventions may fall within the scope of *jus cogens* or *erga omnes* prohibitions.

However, whether or not the prohibition of certain acts falls within the scope of *jus cogens* and *erga omnes* may be relevant in ascertaining the legal status of universal jurisdiction over such acts under customary international law. This is because they may become part of the evidence indicating that a certain crime is of a serious gravity, which is the first rationale of universal jurisdiction. Hence *jus cogens* and *erga omnes* can be taken into consideration in proving the legality of universal jurisdiction under customary international law.

The motive in analysing the *jus cogens* and *erga omnes* character in relation to universal jurisdiction is typically to prove the seriousness of the crime and hence to provide States with justification for exercising *permissive universal jurisdiction*, and sometimes to argue in support of *obligatory universal jurisdiction*. First, the indication of *jus cogens* and an obligation *erga omnes* are regarded as signs of permission for universal jurisdiction. In the Furundzia Case, the ICTY found the prohibition of torture to be *jus cogens* and then proclaimed as follows:

> 'Indeed, it would be inconsistent on the one hand to prohibit torture to such an extent as to restrict the normally unfettered treaty-making power of sovereign States, and on the other hand bar States from prosecuting and punishing those torturers who have engaged in this odious practice abroad. This legal basis for States' universal jurisdiction over torture bears out and strengthens the legal foundation for such jurisdiction found by other courts in the inherently universal character of the crime. It has been held that international crimes being universally condemned wherever they occur, every State has the right to prosecute and punish the authors of such crimes.'[58]

58 *Prosecutor* v. *Furundzia*, Case No. IT-95-17/1-T, the ICTY Trial Chamber II, Judgment of 10 December 1998, para. 156.

Furthermore, some academics present the *jus cogens* and *erga omnes* rule as evidence of *obligatory universal jurisdiction* under customary international law. Bassiouni states that:

> 'recognizing certain international crimes as *jus cogens* carries with it the duty to prosecute or extradite, the non-applicability of statutes of limitation for such crimes, and universality of jurisdiction over such crimes irrespective of where they were committed, by whom (including Heads of State), against what category of victims, and irrespective of the context of their occurrence (peace or war). Above all, the characterization of certain crimes as *jus cogens* places upon states the *obligatio erga omnes* not to grant impunity to the violators of such crimes.'[59]

In my view, the seriousness of the crime is only one of the rationales for universal jurisdiction. The real need for the exercise of universal jurisdiction arises from the second rationale, the absence of or uncertainty concerning jurisdiction capable or willing to be exercised effectively. Therefore, even for those gross violations of human rights the prohibition of which constitutes *jus cogens* and an obligation *erga omnes*, if there is a jurisdiction capable of effectively conducting the prosecution and punishment of the crimes in question, the exercise of universal jurisdiction may not have sufficient justification to take precedence over other bases of jurisdiction. I will explain this point in Chapter VI.

3 The Legal Status of Universal Jurisdiction under International Law

Next, I will evaluate the legal status of universal jurisdiction under international law based on the observations made in Chapter III. First I will examine its status under conventional international law, and then its status under customary international law. At the end, I will specifically determine the status of universal jurisdiction over the crime of genocide.

3.1 Universal Jurisdiction under Conventional International Law

In Chapter III I introduced the phenomenon of the 'expansion' of universal jurisdiction beginning from how conventions since the Hague Hijacking Convention had universal jurisdiction incorporated into their provisions. Subsequent treaties and conventions adopted provisions allowing for a wider range of national jurisdictions to be exercised.[60] Earlier, I illustrated the 'expansion' of universal jurisdiction and its influences

59 M. Cherif Bassiouni, *supra* note (55), pp. 65-66.

60 This trend of providing for a wide range of bases of national jurisdiction can be observed not only with regard to crimes of a serious nature, but in general. Therefore, similar jurisdictional provisions can be seen in various international or bilateral or regional treaties and conventions, such as: The Montreal Convention for the Suppression of Unlawful Acts against the Safety of Civil Aviation of 23 September 1971; the New York Convention on the Prevention and Punishment of Crimes against Internationally

on conventional international law. First, the increase in the number of treaties and conventions prescribing the jurisdiction of the State where a suspect is present resulted in the notion of universal jurisdiction becoming more common in the modern jurisdictional regime. Second, these treaties and conventions departed from or ignored the two rationales of universal jurisdiction. Third, as a consequence of the treaties and conventions providing the principle of *aut dedere aut judicare* as an obligation, universal jurisdiction has become obligatory in certain situations (e.g. when States decide not to extradite a suspect who is present on their territory). Fourth, it was also made possible for universal jurisdiction to be a primary jurisdiction instead of a supplemental one. The transformation of universal jurisdiction from permissive to obligatory, and from supplemental to primary jurisdiction has been observed in conventional international law.

3.1.1 Primary Obligatory Universal Jurisdiction

As noted in Chapter III, treaties and conventions since the 1970s have actively incorporated universal jurisdiction into their provisions. Recent conventional international law shows a tendency to provide for obligatory primary universal jurisdiction. Under these conventions, State Parties have an obligation to extradite or establish their jurisdiction over a suspect who is found in their territory, and it is interpreted that they have discretion in deciding whether to extradite or prosecute. This discretion allows the State where a suspect is present to exercise universal jurisdiction if they wish, thereby allowing universal jurisdiction to become a primary jurisdiction.

On the other hand, some authors deny that universal jurisdiction can become a primary jurisdiction under these conventions and claim that it is only 'a last resort'.[61] Clark argues that, because other jurisdictions including territorial jurisdiction and nationality jurisdiction are provided in the provision prior to that setting universal jurisdiction, the former has primacy.[62] However, the fact is that there is no clear article providing for the hierarchy between various national jurisdictions. Consequently, a

---

Protected Persons, including Diplomatic Agents, of 14 December 1973; the New York Convention Against the Taking of Hostages of 17 December 1979; the Vienna Convention on the Physical Protection of Nuclear Materials of 3 March 1980; the New York Convention Against Torture and Other Cruel, Inhuman or Degrading Treatment or Punishment of 10 December 1984; the Montreal Protocol of 24 February 1988 concerning acts of violence at airports; the Rome Convention for the Suppression of Unlawful Acts Against the Safety of Maritime Navigation of 10 March 1988; the Protocol of the same date concerning the safety of platforms located on the continental shelf; the Vienna Convention Against Illicit Traffic in Narcotic Drugs and Psychotropic Substances of 20 December 1997; and the New York Convention for the Suppression of the Financing of Terrorism of 9 December 1999.

61 See Roger S. Clark 'Offenses of International Concern: Multilateral State Treaty Practice in the Forty Years Since Nuremberg' *Nordic Journal of International Law* Vol. 57 (1988), p. 59. Clark describes the universal jurisdiction contemplated in treaties with the terms 'secondary', 'fallback' or 'last resort' universal jurisdiction.

62 See Roger S. Clark, *ibid*.

State having the custody of a suspect generally has discretion in deciding whether to extradite or prosecute. This discretionary power allows universal jurisdiction to be a primary jurisdiction rather than a supplemental one.[63] There is thus the possibility of universal jurisdiction becoming a primary jurisdiction, leaving aside the aspect of whether or not it is in fact appropriate.

There is a reservation to the obligatory character of universal jurisdiction. Note that the universal jurisdiction provided in many treaties and conventions becomes obligatory only when the State does not extradite a suspect who is on its territory. If a State extradites a suspect to another eligible State for prosecution, the former State is no longer obliged to exercise universal jurisdiction over the case. No convention has prescribed that universal jurisdiction is an obligation upon States without mentioning the alternative of extradition to other States. In this sense, obligatory universal jurisdiction under conventions is somewhat selective rather than absolute. Retaining this alternative, universal jurisdiction may be regarded as having a supplemental character in its inherent nature, even though the provisions in these conventions enable it to be a primary jurisdiction.

The 'expansion' of universal jurisdiction has contributed to the gradual acceptance of the notion of universal jurisdiction worldwide. It is the influence of this development in conventional international law that has stimulated the proposition of permitting or, moreover, obligating universal jurisdiction over gross human rights violations under customary international law.

3.1.2 A Reconfirmation of the Non-exclusive Character of Jurisdiction

There is another effect of the expansion of national jurisdictions. As a result of universal jurisdiction becoming common in conventional international law, the non-exclusive character of jurisdiction has been reconfirmed. For instance, a State that has ratified a specific treaty providing for universal jurisdiction is considered to have accepted the idea of universal jurisdiction by its ratification and, therefore, cannot object to other States exercising universal jurisdiction over their nationals or over crimes that have occurred in its territory, unless it is exercised in a manner which breaches the rules of the treaty or of international law. In addition, what is more significant is that these treaties and conventions do not only limit universal jurisdiction to crimes committed in State Parties or by nationals thereof. They do not preclude the exercise of universal jurisdiction in accordance with corresponding treaty provisions

63 In fact, some States act in accordance with this interpretation. For example, concerning the provision laying down the notion of *aut dedere aut judicare* in the Torture Convention, Wilt explains the attitude of the Netherlands as follows: 'According to the Dutch interpretation of this provision, the starting of criminal proceedings does not depend on the existence (and subsequent refusal) of an extradition request. In other words: a previous denial of an extradition request is not a requirement for the exercise of jurisdiction.' Harmen van der Wilt 'The Prosecution of Crimes against Humanity: Some Reflections on the Dutch Approach' *African Legal Aid Quarterly* January-March (2000), p. 21.

even for those crimes committed in the territory of non-State Parties or acts committed by the nationals of non-State Parties. Thus, they have reinforced that no State (including territorial States) have exclusive jurisdiction over gross violations of human rights prohibited under conventions. The necessity and practice of national jurisdiction other than territorial jurisdiction has become generally accepted.

3.1.3 The Gap between the International Obligation and Reality

Although many conventions oblige States to implement universal jurisdiction, many member States have failed to adopt adequate national legislation to do so. Unfortunately, the expansion of universal jurisdiction in conventional international law is not fully reflected at the national level as envisaged by the treaties and conventions in question. For example, we only have to look at the actions of the States Parties to the Geneva Conventions. Although 'the Conventions create universal mandatory criminal jurisdiction among Contracting States',[64] a recent study by Van Elst shows that less than one in six of the parties to the Geneva Conventions have established universal jurisdiction over all grave breaches in accordance with their obligation.[65] The number which have implemented it is small compared to the total number of States that have ratified the Geneva Conventions. This mirrors the phenomenon illustrated in the last chapter, that of the few cases of prosecution pursued before the 1990s; these were mostly based on territorial jurisdiction or passive or active nationality jurisdiction rather than universal jurisdiction. This is also true of the crimes committed during the Second World War, even though alleged gross human rights violations continued to be committed in modern times, too. The failure of the prosecution of Hissène Habré in Senegal signifies the problem of the lack of appropriate domestic legislation for prosecuting these grave crimes. This inconsistency among the rules at the conventional international law level and at national level makes the recognition of customary international law difficult.

3.1.4 No Evidence of Universal Jurisdiction in Absentia

Lastly, it is worth remembering that no conventions provide for universal jurisdiction *in absentia* in their articles.[66] Conventions mention the obligation of the State where

64 *Prosecutor* v. *Tadic*, Case IT-94-1-T, Decision on Jurisdiction (2 October 1995), para. 79. Reprinted in *International Legal Materials* (1996).

65 Van Elst found that fifty-five States have provided for some kind of universal jurisdiction but only 30 of them have made it applicable to all grave breaches. Richard van Elst 'Implementing Universal Jurisdiction Over Grave Breaches of the Geneva Conventions' *Leiden Journal of International Law* Vol. 13 No. 4 (2000), pp. 831-836.

66 Some argue that the Preamble of the ICC Statute, by referring to the 'duty of every State to exercise its criminal jurisdiction over those responsible for international crimes', obliges States to exercise universal jurisdiction. But it is an unlikely presumption that States in legislating and also in signing the ICC Statute intended to incorporate and to accept universal jurisdiction *in absentia*. In 1998 when the

a suspect is found by providing that each State Party has an obligation to take measures which are necessary to establish its jurisdiction when a suspect is in its territory and it does not extradite him to another State. This provision does not apply when the suspect is not present in the territory of the executing State. This is why Judge Guillaume proclaimed that '[u]niversal jurisdiction *in absentia* is unknown to international conventional law.'[67]

It is noted that most of the domestic laws and practices of States concerning universal jurisdiction contemplate cases where a suspect is in their territory and, indeed, most often in their custody. For example, Article 689-I of the French Code of Criminal Procedure provides:

> 'Pursuant to the international conventions referred to in the following articles, any person, if present in France, may be prosecuted and tried by the French courts if that person has committed outside the territory of the Republic one of the offences specified in those articles.'[68]

In Germany, the Criminal Code (Strafgesetzbuch) contains provisions permitting the prosecution of crimes committed abroad,[69] but the German courts have been requiring the presence of the suspect on German territory, and, moreover, some additional links to Germany in order to exercise universal jurisdiction.[70]

The legislation and practice of many States envisage limiting universal jurisdiction to those crimes specifically exemplified in specific treaties as being subject to universal jurisdiction, and also limiting its exercise to cases in which the suspect is present in their territory. States are reluctant to expand their jurisdiction beyond that which they are obliged to do under specific treaties or conventions. Since universal jurisdiction *in absentia* is not prescribed in treaties and conventions, States are reluctant to enact such legislation.

ICC Statute was elaborated, there were still some States raising objections to universal jurisdiction; moreover, it was not common to interpret universal jurisdiction as capable of being exercised even by States not having the custody of a suspect. Therefore, the ICC Statute does not amount to evidence of universal jurisdiction *in absentia*.

67 Separate Opinion of President Guillaume, Case Concerning the Arrest Warrant of 11 April 2000, *supra* note (40), para. 9.

68 Cited in the Separate Opinion of President Guillaume, Case Concerning the Arrest Warrant of 11 April 2000, *supra* note (40), para. 12.

69 See, Section 6, paragraphs 1 to 9, and Section 7, paragraph 2 of the German Penal Code (Strafgesetzbuch). Article 6 of the German Penal Code provides that the German law is applicable to certain acts committed abroad, for example, genocide, and other acts which, on the basis of an international treaty which is binding on Germany, are to be prosecuted even when they have been committed abroad.

70 See REDRESS 'Universal Jurisdiction in Europe in Practice: Austria, Belgium, Denmark, France, Germany, Italy, the Netherlands, Spain, Switzerland, United Kingdom', annex. This document is available at the homepage of REDRESS: http://www.redress.org/inpract.html. See also the Separate Opinion of President Guillaume, Case Concerning the Arrest Warrant of 11 April 2000, *supra* note (40), para. 12.

However, international conventional law does not prohibit universal jurisdiction *in absentia* either. These conventions have a provision specifying that the convention 'does not exclude any criminal jurisdiction exercised in accordance with internal law.'[71] The incorporation of this provision shows the attitude of international law in allowing the multiplicity and variety of jurisdiction for the purpose of enhancing the possibility of substantiating prosecution and punishment and ending impunity. Therefore, although there is no evidence of universal jurisdiction *in absentia* in conventional international law, it does not mean that such jurisdiction is prohibited under international law.

3.2 Universal Jurisdiction Under Customary International Law

3.2.1 Is International Law a Prohibitive or Permissive Rule?

Let us now examine the status of universal jurisdiction in customary international law. Can a State legally exercise universal jurisdiction for particular crimes in the absence of a specific treaty or convention authorizing it? Before examining this question, let us first contemplate the nature of international law since this is relevant to the approach in examining the legality of the matter. Perhaps we need to ask the following simple question: 'Is a matter legal under international law so long as it is not explicitly prohibited? Or, is it only legal when specifically permitted?' The answer to this question determines the position which one takes in examining matters under international law. The conclusion which can be drawn completely differs depending on the approach taken.

The question of the nature of international law was examined by the PCIJ in the Lotus Case. In any dispute concerning conflicting jurisdictions, this question is relevant in deciding which side bears the burden of proof. The PCIJ denied that the burden of proof lay on the State claiming that it was entitled to exercise jurisdiction.[72] The PCIJ held that 'restriction upon the independence of States cannot be presumed', and emphasised State discretion by stating as follows:

> 'Far from laying down a general prohibition to the effect that States may not extend the application of their laws and the jurisdiction of their courts to persons, property or acts outside their territory, it leaves them in this respect a wide measure of discretion which is only limited in certain cases by prohibitive rules; as regards other cases, every State remains free to adopt the principles which it regards as best and most suitable.'[73]

In line with the above reasoning, it can be deduced that there are *prima facie* no limits imposed by customary international law on the extent of a State's criminal jurisdiction.

---

71 For example, Article 4(3) of the Torture Convention.

72 See, the Lotus Case, PCIJ Series A, No. 10 (1927), p. 19.

73 *Ibid.*

The PCIJ only noted that 'all that can be required of a State is that it should not overstep the limits which international law places upon its jurisdiction; within these limits, its title to exercise jurisdiction rests in its sovereignty.'[74] States are free to determine the limitation of their own jurisdiction apart from abiding by their obligations imposed by treaties or other rules under customary international law. The wide degree of freedom accorded to States concerning their jurisdiction respects the principle of State sovereignty.

Although international law allows States to have wide discretion, including the adoption of universal jurisdiction, in practice, as noted by Kamminga, States have tended to be more restrictive and are reluctant to provide for universal jurisdiction in the absence of specific permission under international law.[75] Accordingly, it is claimed that jurisdiction may not be rightfully exercised unless it is exercised under certain recognized heads of jurisdiction.[76] Carnegie stated that the burden of proof in a doubtful jurisdictional situation should rest on the State which asserts jurisdiction.[77] He stated that his view is the sounder theory from a historical viewpoint, i.e. from the practice of States. He noted that some conventions demonstrate a careful regard for the necessity of specifying circumstances in which jurisdiction may be exercised, and also that national laws generally have provisions expressly setting out the heads under which jurisdiction may be exercised, and concludes that States should normally adduce specific grounds when exercising jurisdiction over persons who are neither nationals nor residents.[78] Taking such a view, he then concluded in his article written in 1963, that 'in the present unsettled state of the law reliance can be placed only on the territoriality principle, the nationality principle and the protective principle as *general* grounds for exercising jurisdiction.'[79]

In my view, there is no contradiction in the above two understandings. First of all, in general, adjudicating jurisdiction does not have an exclusive character. Even territorial jurisdiction does not have the legal effect of nullifying other types of jurisdiction. Especially in the current jurisdictional regime, in which international law has actively invited a multiplicity of jurisdiction over a case, the legality of jurisdiction is assumed. Recent treaties and conventions provide that other types of jurisdiction under the domestic law of State Parties are allowed in addition to the various bases of jurisdiction explicitly listed in certain provisions. Therefore, *ab initio*, a State's jurisdiction

74 *Ibid.*

75 See Menno T. Kamminga 'Lessons Learned from the Exercise of Universal Jurisdiction in Respect of Gross Human Rights Offenses' *Human Rights Quarterly* Vol. 23 No. 4 (November 2001), p. 951.

76 For example, Joyner is of the opinion that 'a state may not extend its power beyond the limits of national jurisdiction without authoritative legal bases.' Christopher C. Joyner 'Arresting Impunity: The Case for Universal Jurisdiction in Bringing War Criminals to Accountability' *Law and Contemporary Problems* Vol. 59 No. 4 (Autumn 1996), p. 163.

77 See A.R. Carnegie 'Jurisdiction Over Violations of the Laws and Customs of War' *British Yearbook of International Law* 39 (1963), p. 403.

78 See, *ibid.*, p. 403-404.

79 See, *ibid.*, p. 405.

is presumed to be legal under international law. However, the classical jurisdictional regime was based on the dominance of territorial jurisdiction. The main jurisdiction was territorial, and jurisdictions other than this (such as those based on the close nexus to the crime in question) had to be justified. Although this dominance of territorial jurisdiction has been weakened in the modern jurisdictional regime which promotes and encourages various bases of jurisdiction, rules which governed the classical jurisdictional regime remain influential. Moreover, as a result of the overall development of international law, matters untouched by international law and the discretion left to States have been considerably reduced. Therefore, nowadays States are expected to indicate the evidence for the legality of their act. In a situation where more than one State claims jurisdiction, a States claiming jurisdiction must convince the others that it has an appropriate jurisdiction to try the case. In the process of justifying their jurisdiction, States often prove that their jurisdiction falls within the categories of jurisdiction recognised under international law that had developed since the classic international law regime.

To summarise, international law has given States broad but not unlimited discretion in deciding which bases of jurisdiction they uphold within their domestic law. International law does not prohibit a State from exercising its jurisdiction in a matter that has occurred outside its territory. This means that territorial jurisdiction is not an exclusive jurisdiction. As in any other case, an act of State is generally presumed to be legal until it is proven that it undermines the rights of other States or is in breach of treaty or customary international law obligations. In the event that another State objects to the exercise of jurisdiction by a State, it is natural that the latter State justifies its exercise of jurisdiction by referring to the bases and rules of jurisdiction.

It should also be remembered that merely because a jurisdiction is legal does not necessarily mean that a State has the absolute right to exercise it. The appropriateness of a particular exercise of universal jurisdiction, and the extent to which other States must respect a State exercising a particular basis of jurisdiction, are different questions. This must also be measured in relation to other national jurisdictions. This issue of measuring appropriateness will be studied in Chapter V and VI, but, for now, I will concentrate on the issue of the legality of universal jurisdiction below.

3.2.2 Is Universal Jurisdiction Illegal?

In accordance with the approach clarified above, I will first analyse whether or not there is a rule in international law prohibiting universal jurisdiction in order to determine its legality. A prominent argument against the idea of universal jurisdiction is that it undermines State sovereignty. This argument that universal jurisdiction violates State sovereignty has been raised many times in history. For example, during the drafting of the Genocide Convention, the Soviet Union and other Eastern States expressed such an opinion. What was the precise legal reasoning? Because States opposing the idea of universal jurisdiction never explained its illegality other than to claim that it was a 'violation of State sovereignty', the legal basis of their claim remains very much a matter of speculation.

The principal corollaries of the sovereignty and equality of States are understood as '(1) a jurisdiction, *prima facie* exclusive, over a territory and the permanent population living there; (2) a duty of non-intervention in the area of exclusive jurisdiction of other states; and (3) the dependence of obligations arising from customary law and treaties on the consent of the obligor.'[80] Taking these corollaries into consideration, the basis on which States denounce universal jurisdiction as a violation of State sovereignty may be that it violates the following: the rule of non-interference in the domestic matters of States, the sovereign equality of States, and the exclusiveness of territorial jurisdiction. But are these arguments legally sound?

3.2.2.1 Universal jurisdiction exercised within the territory of the exercising State

First of all, one must bear in mind that the exercise of universal jurisdiction does not constitute an exercise of sovereignty within the territory of another State. The actual exercise of jurisdiction is applied by the national court of the exercising State situated within the territory of this State, not in the territory of the State where the crime occurred. The consequence of the trial may affect the territorial State politically and socially, but the trial proceedings are not conducted in the territorial State. Therefore, universal jurisdiction is not in breach of the rule prohibiting the exercise of sovereign power within the territory of other States. And because universal jurisdiction is exercised by States having the presence of the suspect in their territory, Judges Higgins, Kooijmans and Buergenthal explained that the word 'universal jurisdiction' is used to refer to 'the jurisdiction to establish a territorial jurisdiction over persons for extraterritorial events'.[81] Therefore, universal jurisdiction does not *ipso facto*, fall within the scope of the prohibition indicated by the PCIJ in the Lotus Case, in which the PCIJ pointed out that a State may not exercise its power in the territory of another State.[82] Yet, if a State has claimed universal jurisdiction *in absentia* and has exercised its power to arrest individuals in the territory of another State without permission from the latter, such action would be in violation of the sovereignty of the latter State.[83]

80 Ian Brownlie, *Principles of Public International Law* 4th edition (Clarendon Press, 1990), p. 287.

81 Joint Separate Opinion of Judges Higgins, Kooijmans and Buergenthal, Case Concerning the Arrest Warrant of 11 April 2000, *supra* note (1), para. 42. These judges envisage universal jurisdiction not limited by the requirement of the presence of a suspect within the territory of the exercising States. Therefore, they refer to the obligation of States under many treaties to prosecute individuals in their territory as 'the inaccurately termed "universal jurisdiction principle"'. See, ibid., paras. 44, 57.

82 See Lotus Case, *supra* note (72), 18-19.

83 'A state is not allowed to send its troops, its warships, or its police forces into or through foreign territory, or its aircraft over it, or to carry out official investigations on foreign territory or to let its agents conduct clandestine operation there, or to exercise an act of administration on jurisdiction on foreign territory, without permission.' Sir Robert Jennings and Sir Arthur Watts, *Oppenheim's International Law Vol. I Peace* (9th ed.) (Longman Group UK Limited, 1992), p. 386.

3.2.2.2 Non-interference in the internal affairs of other States

Does universal jurisdiction violate the principle of non-interference in the internal affairs of other States? The answer to this depends on whether the prosecution of the relevant crime is considered to be a matter of domestic or international concern. In this regard, the Cairo Guiding Principles, especially its Preliminary Draft holds that the principle of non-interference 'should be interpreted in the light of the well established and generally accepted principle that serious violations of human rights are of concern to the international community and may give rise to prosecution under the principle of universal jurisdiction.'[84] In addition, the ICTY has held (although in relation to its jurisdiction rather than the universal jurisdiction of States) that State sovereignty cannot be an excuse for action against serious crimes. The ICTY stated that 'the sovereign rights of States cannot and should not take precedence over the right of the international community to act appropriately as they affect the whole of mankind and shock the conscience of all nations of the world.'[85] Therefore, it is observed that, increasingly, responding to gross human rights violations is recognised as being no longer in the realm of the domestic matters of a State or the sovereign prerogative, but a matter of international concern. Many crimes categorised as being of serious gravity such as genocide and crimes against humanity are considered to be a matter of international concern that they be prevented and punished. On the other side of the same coin, it is interesting to note that many people consider that universal jurisdiction should only be exercised over those crimes considered to be the most heinous by the international community.[86] As a result, they consider that an exercise of universal jurisdiction is precluded for lesser crimes.[87]

3.2.2.3 The sovereign equality of States

In the Case Concerning Certain Criminal Proceedings in France, Congo instituted proceedings against France in the ICJ accusing France for alleged

> 'violation of the principle that a State may not, in breach of the principle of sovereign equality among all Members of the United Nations, as laid down in Article 2, paragraph

84 Africa Legal Aid (AFLA) 'Preliminary draft of the Cairo Guiding Principles on Universal Jurisdiction in Respect of Gross Human Rights Offenses: An African Perspective', adopted in Cairo on July 2001, Principle 3. The finalized form of principles prepared by the Africa Legal Aid adopts different wordings.

85 Tadic, Trial Chamber, para. 42.

86 See the Joint Separate Opinion of Judges Higgins, Kooijmans, Buergenthal, the Case Concerning the Arrest Warrant of 11 April 2000, *supra* note (1), para. 60.

87 Judges Higgins, Kooijmans, and Buergenthal concluded this because the allegation by Mr. Yerodia fell within the concept of crimes against humanity, and 'would be within that small category in respect of which an exercise of universal jurisdiction is not precluded under international law.' *Ibid.*, para. 65.

> 1, of the Charter of the United Nations, exercise its authority on the territory of another State, by unilaterally attributing to itself universal jurisdiction in criminal matters'.[88]

Does universal jurisdiction infringe the principle of the sovereign equality of States? The accusation that universal jurisdiction infringes the principle of the sovereign equality of States arises because it is considered that the exercising State is interfering in the domestic matters of another State, and to put individuals on trial may be equated with judging the act of another State. The nexus between a State and a suspect may be a great concern, especially when the suspect is an agent or a high official or, more importantly, a head of State of a foreign State. Judging the act of a person in such a position may imply that his or her State has committed the crime in question, thereby actually condemning this State itself. It may respond fiercely to this as an unfriendly or unlawful act against its virtue. The consequence of State equality is that no State can claim jurisdiction over another. For this reason, States are given jurisdictional immunity from the courts of other States. This immunity is deduced not only from the principle of equality but also from the principles of the independence and the dignity of States.[89]

However, the target of universal jurisdiction in this study is individuals. Even if the prosecution of individuals might indirectly relate to the responsibility of a State in certain cases, States are not the actual defendant before the national courts exercising universal jurisdiction. Although in such a case, the exercise of universal jurisdiction may entail conflicts with the rule of immunity among others, they relate not to the illegality of universal jurisdiction as a jurisdictional basis. Rather, it is the problem of the relationship with and adjustment to other rules of international law and the means of exercising universal jurisdiction which should be considered in each individual case. It does not lead to the conclusion that universal jurisdiction is inherently in conflict with the principle of State equality.

3.2.2.4 The dominance of territorial jurisdiction

Judge Altamira acknowledged the strong position of territorial jurisdiction in the Lotus Case as follows.

> 'It is certain that amongst the most widely recognized principles of international law are the principles that the jurisdiction of a State is territorial in character and that in respect of its nationals a State has preferential, if not sole jurisdiction. Therefore, exceptions to these principles, in so far as they allow a foreign jurisdiction to be exercised over the

88 Case Concerning Certain Criminal Proceedings in France (Republic of the *Congo* v. *France*), Order on the Request for the Indication of a Provisional Measure, 17 June 2003, para. 1.

89 See Sir Robert Jennings and Sir Arthur Watts ed., *supra* note (83), pp. 341-342.

> citizens of a given State, have only been recognized in extreme cases where it has been absolutely necessary or inevitable.'[90]

However, Judge Altamira also recognised that 'the case of a general need of mankind or of a common danger (the slave trade, piracy, etc.)' is the exception to the dominance of territorial and nationality jurisdiction.[91]

Does universal jurisdiction infringe upon international law by undermining the dominance of territorial jurisdiction? The likely answer would be in the negative in the modern jurisdictional regime. Even in traditional international law, territorial jurisdiction was not an absolute rule, as observed by the PCIJ in the same case noted above. The PCIJ held as follows:

> 'Though it is true that in all systems of law the territorial character of criminal law is fundamental, it is equally true that all or nearly all these systems of law extend their action to offences committed outside the territory of the State which adopts them, and they do so in ways which vary from State to state. The territoriality of criminal law therefore is not an absolute principle of international law and by no means coincides with territorial sovereignty.'[92]

Unlike the classical jurisdictional regime, the dominance of territorial jurisdiction is not as strong a rule in the modern jurisdictional regime. For instance, many conventions since the 1970s have set a concurrent jurisdictional system of various bases of jurisdiction. Judicial jurisdiction is a right pertaining to States, and a jurisdictional basis does not have an absolute exclusive character which obliges other States to respect it while prohibiting different States from claiming jurisdiction over the same case. For instance, in preparing the Draft Code of Crimes Against the Peace and Security of Mankind, the Special Rapporteur proposed, on second reading, that consideration should be given to recognizing the priority of the territorial State's request for extradition above that of any other State. However, the drafting committee considered that this question was not ready for codification and, therefore, the draft code did not prescribe any preference between various bases of national jurisdiction.[93]

3.2.2.5 Conclusion on *a priori* illegality

From the above analysis, it can be deduced that universal jurisdiction is not *a priori* illegal under international law. It is noteworthy that Judges Higgins, Kooijmans and Buergenthal, after examining the practice of States, expressed the view that 'while none of the national case law to which we have referred happens to be based on the

---

90 Dissenting Opinion by Altamira in the Lotus Case, *supra* note (72), p. 95.

91 See the Dissenting Opinion by Altamira in the Lotus Case, *ibid.*

92 Lotus Case, *supra* note (72), p. 20.

93 See Paragraph 6 of the Commentary to Article 9 (Obligation to extradite or prosecute), Draft Code of Crimes Against the Peace and Security of Mankind, International Law Commission Report, 1996.

exercise of a universal jurisdiction properly so called, there is equally nothing in this case law which evidences an *opinio juris* on the illegality of such a jurisdiction. In short, national legislation and case law, – that is, State practice – is neutral as to the exercise of universal jurisdiction.'[94]

Of course, even if universal jurisdiction is not *a priori* illegal this presumption does not completely exclude the possibility of universal jurisdiction coming into conflict with international law. The extent to which universal jurisdiction may conflict with the notion of State sovereignty and other rules may be different according to what kind of universal jurisdiction is exercised and in what manner. Likewise, the extent to which it becomes part of customary international law is different for each type of universal jurisdiction with different characteristics. I will next examine each type of universal jurisdiction in customary international law below. Furthermore, the extent to which universal jurisdiction is acknowledged as a right or obligation under customary international law must be determined separately for each category of crime taking into account the historical and legal status of the crime, and whether or not there are *opinio juris* and State practice acknowledging universal jurisdiction for that particular category of crime.[95] Ultimately, the conclusion may be different depending on the crime under consideration. I will now examine the legality of each type of universal jurisdiction in relation to their different characteristics followed by universal jurisdiction over genocide in particular.

3.2.3 Permissive Universal Jurisdiction

Permissive universal jurisdiction has a long history, since it was recognized for the crime of piracy as well as for other crimes under the classical jurisdictional regime. For the crime of piracy, universal jurisdiction was recognised as one of primary jurisdiction. But for any other crime, under classical international law, it was understood that States were allowed to exercise universal jurisdiction only after the exhaustion of their efforts to extradite suspects to States having other jurisdictional bases. Therefore, under the classical jurisdictional regime, *primary permissive universal jurisdiction* was recognised for piracy, while only *supplemental permissive universal jurisdiction* was recognised for other crimes.

The book of the Oppenheim (9th Edition) published in 1992 stated that:

---

94 Joint Separate Opinion of Judges Higgins, Kooijmans, and Buergenthal, *supra* note (1), para. 45.

95 Benavides points out that there is a 'double *opinio juris*' requirement. He explains that '[t]he first *opinio juris* is necessary in order to recognize an unlawful act under international law as an international crime. The second *opinio juris* is required in order to consider such a crime as a crime of a particular nature and one for which universal jurisdiction can be exercised.' Luis Benavides 'The Universal Jurisdiction Principle: Nature and Scope' *Anuario Mexicano de Derecho Internacional* Vol. 1 (2001), p. 38.

> 'While no general rule of positive international law can as yet be asserted which gives to states the right to punish foreign nationals for crimes against humanity in the same way as they are, for instance, entitled to punish acts of piracy, there are clear indications pointing to the gradual evolution of a significant principle of international law to that effect.'[96]

The international environment has also significantly changed since then, promoting such evolution in international law.

Kamminga interprets that States parties to the Geneva Conventions and the Torture Convention are obliged to exercise universal jurisdiction over grave breaches and torture but, apart from the conventional obligations, States are only '*entitled* to exercise universal jurisdiction in respect of genocide, crimes against humanity, war crimes and torture' under customary international law.[97] Today, permissive universal jurisdiction against these crimes is established within customary international law and has gained the support of many. It conforms to the nature of international law in which States are generally given wide discretion in the exercise of their sovereign power.

There is no general rule prohibiting States from exercising universal jurisdiction under customary international law. However, scholars affirming universal jurisdiction as a right under customary international law do not clarify whether this universal jurisdiction is primary or supplemental. In this regard, the two rationales for universal jurisdiction should be remembered. Universal jurisdiction has developed in international law together with the two rationales: the seriousness of the crimes in question and the absence of or uncertainty concerning effective jurisdiction. Considering this second rationale, universal jurisdiction is expected to be exercised when there is no other jurisdiction that can effectively be exercised over the same case. Therefore, universal jurisdiction will retain supplemental character. Although primary permissive universal jurisdiction is not prohibited under customary international law, its appropriateness needs to be considered in this regard. Determining the appropriateness of universal jurisdiction will be discussed in Chapter VI.

In reality, States are reluctant to determine that universal jurisdiction is applicable to a wide range of categories of crime. Most often, States only lay down universal jurisdiction because of the obligation arising from specific treaties which oblige them to extend their national jurisdiction to acts committed abroad.[98] Many States are reluctant to determine for themselves even the permissive form of universal jurisdiction in general.

96 Robert Jennings and Arthur Watts eds., *supra* note (83), p. 998.
97 Menno T. Kamminga, *supra* note (75), p. 965.
98 For example, see Article 6 of the German Penal Code.

3.2.4 Obligatory Universal Jurisdiction

3.2.4.1 Support for obligatory universal jurisdiction

Recently, the argument that States have an *obligation* to exercise universal jurisdiction has gained strong authority.[99] The Draft Code of Crimes against the Peace and Security of Mankind prepared by the UN International Law Commission in 1996 stated that States shall extradite or prosecute individuals who have allegedly committed genocide, or crimes against humanity, crimes against the United Nations and associated personnel, or war crimes.[100] Scholars claim that crimes violating international order are within the interest of all States. Therefore, all States must cooperate in trying criminals committing such crimes, and such cooperation includes the obligation to extradite or prosecute.[101] It is argued that in order to fulfill their duty under international law, States must prepare their domestic legislation to achieve this end.[102] This opinion is held not only by scholars, but also by some States.[103] In support of this contention, the ICTY Appeals Chamber declared in the Blaskic Case as follows:

> 'The national jurisdictions of the States of Ex-Yugoslavia, as those of all States, are required by customary law to judge or to extradite those persons presumed responsible for grave violations of international humanitarian law.'[104]

As explained earlier, universal jurisdiction and the principle of *aut dedere aut judicare* are theoretically different in a strict sense. So even if the principle of *aut dedere aut judicare* becomes international customary law, it does not directly imply obligatory universal jurisdiction, strictly speaking. This is because the principle of *aut dedere aut judicare* does not in itself dictate which bases of national jurisdiction a State can exercise. The principle itself gives no preference to any national jurisdiction while connoting no prohibition of any either. In the extreme case that there is no extraditable State and at the same time the State having the custody of the suspect has no other

99 See for example, Principle 14 of the 'Brussels Principles Against Impunity and for International Justice', *supra* note (1). Principle 14(1) states the following: 'By virtue of international law, any state has the obligation to exercise universal jurisdiction in relation to the presumed author of a serious crime from the moment the said presumed author is present on the territory of that state.'

100 Articles 8, 9, 17, 18, and 20 of the Draft Code of Crimes Against the Peace and Security of Mankind, Report of the International Law Commission on the Work of its Forty-Eighth Session, UN Doc. A/51/10.

101 Lee A. Steven 'Genocide and the Duty to Extradite or Prosecute: Why the United States is in Breach of Its International Obligations' *Virginia Journal of International Law* Vol. 39 (Winter 1999), pp. 441-443.

102 It is argued that the United States must amend the domestic law implementing the Genocide Convention to allow for universal jurisdiction. See, Lee A. Steven, *ibid.*, pp. 462-466.

103 Belgium issued the arrest warrant against the former foreign minister of Congo based on its understanding that the exercise of universal jurisdiction is an obligation on the part of States.

104 The decision of the ICTY of 29 October 1997, case IT-95-14-AR, paragraph 29.

bases of jurisdiction over the case, the principle of *aut dedere aut judicare* may require obligatory universal jurisdiction. Since the two notions are different, it is possible that the principle of *aut dedere aut judicare* could be an obligation under customary international law while universal jurisdiction is not. But this strict theoretical analysis set aside, the two notions are understood to be closely linked. Therefore, the changing nature of the principle of *aut dedere aut judicare* into customary law is a major advancement in the realization of universal jurisdiction. While Bassiouni contends that the principle of *aut dedere aut judicare* has become a customary norm,[105] Cassese denies that international customary rules impose on States an obligation to prosecute and try the suspects of international crimes. He points out the difficulty in proving the emergence of such a customary rule and points to the lack of State practice supporting such a contention.[106]

3.2.4.2 Objections to obligatory universal jurisdiction

Many people and States express objections to the proposition that obligatory universal jurisdiction has become a part of customary international law.[107] It is true that there is not enough practice to convince States that there is a customary rule obliging them to exercise universal jurisdiction. For example, the United States does not provide for universal jurisdiction over genocide in its domestic law.[108] In addition, when in 1996 the United States enacted a new law to punish serious breaches of the Geneva Conventions, it only laid down jurisdiction for cases where the suspects or victims are U.S. nationals or members of the U.S. armed forces. As seen, the United States is reluctant to incorporate universal jurisdiction into its domestic law.[109] On the other hand, even those States which have laid down universal jurisdiction within their domestic law only admit it as a right, not as an obligation. For example, France provides for universal jurisdiction as a right.[110] The two French laws prescribing cooperation with the *ad hoc* international tribunals have been criticised by some as being focused upon French territory and its borders.[111] But the French courts are also considered to be reluctant to

---

105 See M. C. Bassiouni and E. M. Wise eds., *Aut Dedere Aut Judicare: The Duty to Extradite or Prosecute in International Law* (Martinus Nijhoff Publishers, 1995), pp. 20-25.

106 See Antonio Cassese, *International Law* (Oxford Press, 2001), p. 264.

107 See for example, Cherif Bassiouni and Edward Wise, *supra* note (105), p. 54. Also, Lyal S. Sunga, *The Emerging System of International Criminal Law: Developments in Codification and Implementation* (Kluwer Law International, 1997), p. 254.

108 Genocide Convention Implementation Act of 1987 (the Proximire Act), 18 U.S.C. 1091-1093 (1994).

109 Those who interpret universal jurisdiction as an obligation on the part of States criticize the position of the United States. See, Mark S. Zaid 'The U.S. War Crimes Act of 1996' in M. Cherif Bassiouni ed., *International Criminal Law: Vol. V Enforcement* (Transnational Publishers, 1999).

110 See, Brigitte Stern 'La compétence universelle en France: le cas des crimes commis en ex-Yougoslavie et au Rwanda' *German Yearbook of International Law* Vol. 40 (1997), p. 298.

111 See, *ibid.*

recognize universal jurisdiction in customary law.[112] In reality, many of the States that have enacted domestic law allowing for universal jurisdiction have done so not because they recognize it as a legal obligation under customary international law, but in response to public opinion or requirements in treaties.[113]

After examining the present situation it can be concluded that primary obligatory universal jurisdiction permitted under treaties has not as yet necessarily become customary international law. In order to convince States of the changes to the classical jurisdictional regime and traditional universal jurisdiction (of which the supplemental and exceptional character has remained), the change from the supplemental character to the primary one requires it to be specified in writing. An explicit provision even for crimes under international law is required in order to convince many reluctant States about universal jurisdiction. It is my understanding that a new obligation on the part of a State should be prescribed in law, but not necessarily a new right. There seems to be no consensus among States concerning the obligation of universal jurisdiction under customary international law. In sum, States have a right to exercise universal jurisdiction under customary international law, but there is still a doubt as to whether it can be assumed that it is recognised as constituting an obligation on the part of States.

Consequently, it is difficult to prove that States have a general obligation to exercise universal jurisdiction even for those heinous crimes which have recently emerged. However, the law concerning universal jurisdiction is evolving with rapid speed, and it would not be surprising to see it become a norm in customary international law in the very near future. An argument in support of obligatory universal jurisdiction is presented next.

3.2.4.3 The Responsibility of States concerning universal jurisdiction deriving from their territorial Sovereignty

For the purpose of encouraging law to crystallize, I here elucidate my proposition regarding obligatory universal jurisdiction. Although the exercising State is not the State where the crime is committed, there is another possible territorial link between the State and the suspect. In this regard, it can be said that universal jurisdiction is somewhat based on the territorial sovereignty of the exercising State. Let me elucidate this point further.

A State generally has exclusive power over its territory, and extends its control over persons, property and many other matters within its territory. This exclusive power over its territory entails not only rights but some obligations upon the State. These obligations are recognised in different forms by some international courts. Concerning State responsibility for acts of private persons on its territory, an arbitrary tribunal supported the proposition that 'a State owes at all times a duty to protect other States

112 See, Brigitte Stern 'In re Javor' *American Journal of International Law* Vol. 93 (1999), pp. 525, 529.
113 See, Lee A. Steven, *supra* note (101), p. 440 and note 72.

against injurious acts by individuals from within its jurisdiction.'[114] Also the ICJ referred to 'every State's obligation not to allow knowingly its territory to be used for acts contrary to the rights of other States' in the Corfu Channel case.[115] Similarly, due to the absolute character of a State's control over its territory, it may be possible to find a State responsible for allowing a situation of impunity within its territory.

According to the principle of State sovereignty, it is within the power of a State to control who enters and stays in its territory. It is presumed that by his or her presence in its territory, a suspect is under its control, at least at a theoretical level. Since such control is recognized to be exclusive by territorial sovereignty, it is solely the responsibility of this State where the suspect is present if any criminal enjoys freedom there. To allow the presence of a criminal without accountability being attributed to him or her would mean that the control of this State is insufficient, implying that it has failed to establish a law-abiding environment within its territory. By allowing such a person to enjoy his or her unreasonable freedom from justice within the area of its exclusive sovereign power, this State could be condemned by the international community not only for its lack of active contribution to international justice, but also for its acquiescence in the gross and serious violations of human rights which have been committed. It would thereby be in violation of its obligation to act in *good faith* as a respectable member of the international community. Consequently, such a State could face the legal and political disgrace of being labelled a safe haven for criminals, a State with low human rights standards, and a non-law-abiding nation. Although many scholars deny that universal jurisdiction can be derived from the sovereignty of States,[116] in my view this reasoning reinforces the standpoint that States have an obligation to exercise universal jurisdiction and could convince States to exercise jurisdiction over the crime or else extradite or surrender suspects.

3.2.5 Universal Jurisdiction in absentia

Some assert that a State may prosecute persons regardless of their nationality, the place where the crime was committed, the nationality of the victim, and even when the suspect is not on its territory. This is universal jurisdiction *in absentia*. I will analyse its status under customary international law next.

---

114 The Trail Smelter Arbitration, *RIAA*, iii, p. 1963.

115 The Corfu Channel case, ICJ Reports 1949, p. 22.

116 For example, Henzelin notes that 'le principe de l'universalité ne peut être déduit des composantes même de l'Etat ou des fondements de la souveraineté. Qui plus est, le principe de l'universalité ne peut pas non plus être déduit de la somme des principes issus des composantes de l'Etat.' Marc Henzelin, *supra* note (15), p. 137.

3.2.5.1 Support for universal jurisdiction *in absentia*

Some have adopted the position that proper 'universal jurisdiction' is universal jurisdiction *in absentia*, according to which *any* State can assert jurisdiction, and they therefore reject the requirement of the presence of the suspect in the exercising State. Cassese explains two rationales for universal jurisdiction *in absentia*. The first is when the crime is of such gravity and magnitude that it warrants universal prosecution and repression. The second is when 'the exercise of this jurisdiction does not amount to a breach of the principle of sovereign equality of States, nor does it lead to undue interference in the internal affairs of the State where the crime has been perpetrated'.[117] But the extent to which States accept these rationales and hold *opinio juris* on the matter is questionable. The evidence that it is gaining support among States with *opinio juris* is scarce as I will mention later.

Some States have actually enacted universal jurisdiction *in absentia* in their domestic law. For example, Spain has a domestic law allowing for the prosecution of non-nationals abroad who have committed genocide, terrorism, or other crimes which Spain is obliged to prosecute under international treaties even if the crime was committed outside Spanish territory. The request for the extradition of Pinochet was made in accordance with a decision to prosecute him under this law. Belgium also has a domestic law which allows universal jurisdiction *in absentia*. The Belgian law of 3 February 1999 explicitly added genocide and crimes against humanity to crimes which are subject to universal jurisdiction, in addition to grave breaches of the 1949 Geneva Conventions and the 1977 Protocols which were already subject to Belgian universal jurisdiction under the Belgian law of 16 June 1993. Furthermore, Cassese claims that universal jurisdiction *in absentia* is permitted by the German Supreme Court and under the Italian Criminal Code and he concludes that universal jurisdiction *in absentia* is legally admissible.[118]

Even in the absence of domestic legislation, some domestic courts have accepted universal jurisdiction *in absentia*. For example, in the Demjanjuk Case, the American courts acknowledged Israel's universal jurisdiction *in absentia* by extraditing the suspect to Israel.

---

117 See, Antonio Cassese, *supra* note (106), p. 262.

118 Cassese notes that the German Supreme Court, in its judgment of 21 February 2001, accepted that universal jurisdiction *in absentia* may be employed whenever the obligation to prosecute is provided in an international treaty which is binding upon Germany. He also notes that Article 7.5 of the Italian Criminal Code may be construed to the effect that suspects may be prosecuted even if they do not find themselves on Italian territory, provided that (i) the crimes are envisaged in international treaties ratified by Italy and (ii) under these treaties the Italian courts may exercise jurisdiction. See, Antonio Cassese, *supra* note (106), p. 262.

3.2.5.2 Opposition to universal jurisdiction *in absentia*

On the other hand, universal jurisdiction *in absentia* is controversial since it ignores the nexus rule, and its intention is to oblige a State, not an international organization, to use its domestic legal proceedings for the purpose of protecting the interest of the international community as a whole.

Because universal jurisdiction *in absentia* is different from the universal jurisdiction normally prescribed in various treaties and conventions, one cannot presume the acceptance of the former from the general acceptance of the latter. We must specifically search for an *opinio juris* and State practice which allow universal jurisdiction *in absentia*.

In the law and practice, States allowing universal jurisdiction tend to limit it to cases in which a suspect is present on their territory. For example, the Canadian legislation which implements the ICC Statute strengthens Canada's ability to ensure that it is not a safe haven for criminals, and universal jurisdiction is thereby provided. This allows Canada to prosecute anyone who is present in Canada and who has committed a crime.[119] France has taken similar measures. Although Article 689 of the French Criminal Procedure Code does not mention the requirement of the presence of the suspect within French territory, sub-article 689-1 prescribes that those suspects who are found in France and who have committed certain crimes can be prosecuted and sentenced by the French courts.[120] The French courts however, have specified that the accused must be present on the French territory.[121] Also, the Swiss Penal Code grants universal jurisdiction for genocide but it specifically states that the Swiss courts can only enforce this jurisdiction if the suspect is in Switzerland and cannot be

119 The Crimes Against Humanity and War Crimes Act, adopted on 29 June 2000, which entered into force on 29 October 2000. The Act incorporates territorial jurisdiction, active nationality jurisdiction, passive nationality jurisdiction, and universal jurisdiction. For some situations, active and passive nationality jurisdictions are extended to include other persons who are associated with a State that was engaged in an armed conflict against Canada or was an ally of Canada in an armed conflict. See UN Doc. E/CN.4/2002/102/Add.1.

120 Article 689 of the French Criminal Procedure Code provides: 'Les auteurs ou complices d'infractions commises hors du territoire de la République peuvent être poursuivis et jugés par les juridictions françaises (...) lorsqu'une convention internationale donne compétence aux juridictions françaises pour connaître l'infraction.' On the other hand, Article 689-1 provides : 'En application des conventions internationales visées aux articles suivants, peut être pousuivie et jugée par les juridictions françaises, si elle se trouve en France, toute personne qui s'est rendue coupable hors du territoire de la République de l'une des infractions énumérées par ces articles ...'
For these articles and an analysis of the French legislation on universal jurisdiction, see Brigitte Stern, *supra* note (110), p. 288.

121 The Decision of the Appeal Court of 24 November 1994. The Court stated: 'la compétence des juridictions françaises résulte d'un élément objectif et matériel de rattachement, consistant en la présence des auteurs présumés sur le sol français'. For this citation and an analysis of this case, see Brigitte Stern, *ibid.*, p. 293.

extradited.[122] As a final example, it is interesting to note that unlike Spain which claimed universal jurisdiction *in absentia* over Pinochet, the Danish Minister of Justice decided not to do so. Denmark concluded that Danish authorities were not authorised under Danish law to request his extradition because Pinochet was not a Danish citizen nor was he present in Denmark, after reviewing a request lodged by 15 Chileans (nine of whom were Danish citizens) living in Denmark.[123]

Furthermore, it should be noted that universal jurisdiction in absentia may provoke some oppositions from the States involved in the case. For instance, when Belgium issued an arrest warrant for a case which Belgium had no nexus, thereby asserting universal jurisdiction *in absentia*, it caused an conflict with Congo which was the State of the nationality of the suspect. This conflict had to be solved by the ICJ as the Case Concerning the Arrest Warrant of 11 April 2000. It is also important to note that after this ICJ judgment, Belgium amended its domestic law toward abolishing universal jurisdiction *in absentia*.

Universal jurisdiction *in absentia* may be claimed to result in an arbitrary determination of the forum. It may also be argued that it is inhumane to try a suspect and to subject him to a long prison sentence in a foreign country to which that person has no connection. In the case of ordinary universal jurisdiction, suspects are within the territory of the State exercising universal jurisdiction usually after his or her voluntary entry into this State.[124] In contrast, in the case of universal jurisdiction *in absentia*, suspects cannot foresee which State will claim jurisdiction. Suspects will neither be able to know which State will issue an arrest warrant in the future, and thereby to which State they may be extradited, nor under which national law they will be prosecuted, what kind of punishment may be imposed, and in which State they will have to serve the sentence.

122 See Article 264 of the Swiss Penal Code (Code pénale suisse). Article 264 was added under the new title, 'Titre douze bis: Délits contre les intérêts de la communauté internationale' and it entered into froce on 15 December 2000. It provides that genocide 'est également punissable celui qui aura agi à l'étranger, s'il se trouve en Suisse et qu'il ne peut être extradé.' The Swiss Penal Code is available online at http://www.admin.ch/ch/f/rs/3.html.

123 Decision by the Minister of Justice, 29 January 1999. A summary thereof can be found in Peter Otken 'Correspondents' Reports Denmark', in H. Fischer and Avril McDonald eds, *Yearbook of International Humanitarian Law* Vol. 3: 2000 (T.M.C. Asser Instituut, 2002), p. 469.

124 In examining the case of Swiss universal jurisdiction over war crimes committed in Rwanda, Reydams dismisses the accusation of an arbitrary determination of the forum by emphasizing that in this case the defendant had come to Switzerland voluntarily, and that his immediate family still lived in Switzerland. He concludes that '[i]t is by no means clear that it would be more humane to send him back to Rwanda either for trial or to serve his sentence.' Luc Reydams '*Niyonteze* v. *Public Prosecutor*, Tribunal militaire de cassation (Switzerland), April 27, 2001' *American Journal of International Law* Vol. 96 No. 1 (January 2002), p. 236.

3.3 Conclusion Concerning the Legality of Universal Jurisdiction

In this section, I have examined the status of universal jurisdiction with different characteristics under customary international law. From the above analysis, I conclude that universal jurisdiction is not in general prohibited under international law, and is thereby legal. In the absence of a specific rule prohibiting universal jurisdiction and in accordance with the wide discretion given to States in choosing what kind of jurisdiction they provide in their domestic law, it can be said that permissive universal jurisdiction, including that of universal jurisdiction *in absentia,* is indeed legal. Although even universal jurisdiction *in absentia* is not prohibited under international law in the modern jurisdictional regime, it is not yet acknowledged as an obligation on the part of every State constituting the international community.

The fact that universal jurisdiction is not *a priori* illegal does not dismiss the actual possibility of it being exercised in violation of international law or in an inappropriate manner and thus undermining its validity. It also does not have the effect of nullifying other States' bases of jurisdiction, which may also be legal under the wide freedom given to States. With various bases of jurisdiction being allowed under international law, the question of the appropriateness thereof and of deciding which State should actually exercise its jurisdiction must be examined separately from the point of view of the legality of universal jurisdiction in general.

Before agreeing with the proposition of obligatory universal jurisdiction, according to which States would be obliged to exercise universal jurisdiction, one must substantiate a specific rule in that respect in order to establish some responsibilities of States. Obligatory universal jurisdiction is provided in many treaties and conventions, hence State Parties to these instruments are obliged to exercise universal jurisdiction when they do not extradite a suspect to other States. Apart from the obligatory universal jurisdiction in conventional international law, at the time of this analysis in this study, it is difficult to establish without doubt whether there is a customary rule which obliges States to exercise universal jurisdiction over gross violations of human rights. Such a rule may be in the process of being formed at the time of writing.

As concluded, universal jurisdiction in general is not illegal nor is it prohibited by customary international law, yet the propriety of its exercise is a different question. How far other States must respect the exercise of universal jurisdiction by a State is yet another question. I will consider the propriety of universal jurisdiction in Chapter VI in correlation with the guiding rules for determining venue of a trial.

4 The Status of Universal Jurisdiction over Genocide

So far, I have examined the status of universal jurisdiction in general. However, in determining the legality of any actual exercise of universal jurisdiction, it is imperative to be more specific and examine the status of universal jurisdiction for the given crime of the case in question. Lord Slynn of Hadley in the first Pinochet Case noted:

> 'It does not seem ... that it has been shown that there is any State practice or general consensus let alone a widely supported convention that all crimes against international law should be justiciable in national courts on the basis of the universality of jurisdiction ...'[125]

Therefore one has to examine the status of universal jurisdiction for each category of crime. In this study, I will specifically examine universal jurisdiction over genocide below.

4.1 Does the Genocide Convention Prescribe Universal Jurisdiction?

Some argue that universal jurisdiction was admitted in the Genocide Convention. This is the opinion expressed by Judge Lauterpacht in a case at the ICJ.[126] Judge Lauterpacht interprets that Article 1 of the Genocide Convention[127] allows the establishment of universal jurisdiction against the crime of genocide by prescribing that genocide 'is a crime under international law'. He expressly observes that States can exercise universal jurisdiction over acts committed outside a State's territory by a foreigner.[128]

However, the intention of Article 1 of the Genocide Convention is to reaffirm that genocide is a crime under international law and to make Member States realize that the law applies irrespective of whether the crime is committed in a time of war or peace. The wording of that provision does not expressly mention universal jurisdiction. Moreover, in carefully examining the *travaux préparatoires* with regard to Articles 1 and 6, it is apparent that it is not appropriate to interpret Article 1 as having the intention to recognize universal jurisdiction. It is not a logical composition of the provisions to set it in Article 1 and never to mention universal jurisdiction in the provision specifically providing for judicial jurisdiction.

Judge Lauterpacht offered no reason for, or any elaboration on, his interpretation. His reasoning is therefore a matter of speculation. It is likely, for instance, that his conclusion was based on his recognition of the crime of genocide as a 'crime under international law'. Not only Judge Lauterpacht, but also many others equate 'crime

---

125 House of Lords, 25 November 1998, *R.* v. *Bartle*; ex parte Pinochet.

126 Separate Opinion of Judge Lauterpacht in the Case of Application of the Convention on the Prevention and Punishment of the Crime of Genocide (*Bosnia and Herzegovina* v. *Yugoslavia* (Serbia and Montenegro), Further Requests for the Indication of Provisional Measures, 13 September 1993, *1993 ICJ Reports*, p. 325.

127 Art. 1 of the Genocide Convention provides as follows.
'The Contracting Parties confirm that genocide, whether committed in time of peace or in time of war, is a crime under international law which they undertake to prevent and to punish.'

128 His logic was based on the interpretation that the purpose of Art. 1 'is to permit parties, within the domestic legislation that they adopt, to assume universal jurisdiction over the crime of genocide – that is to say, even when the acts have been committed outside their respective territories by persons who are not their nationals.' Separate Opinion of Judge Lauterpacht, the Case of Application of the Convention on the Prevention and Punishment of the Crime of Genocide (*Bosnia and Herzegovina* v. *Yugoslavia* (Serbia and Montenegro), *supra* note (126), p. 325.

under international law' as a subject of universal jurisdiction. They argue that universal jurisdiction emerges automatically from the simple fact that genocide is a crime under international law. In the Eichmann trial, the judgment held that universal jurisdiction is permitted based on the gravity of the crime, the fact that the alleged crime is a crime under international law, and the existence of serious interests of the international community.

There is no doubt that the crime of genocide is serious and is a crime under international law. Its prevention and prosecution are in the interest of the international community. Yet, the fact that a particular crime is a 'crime under international law' does not necessarily connote that universal jurisdiction is automatically allowed. Because States at the time of drafting the Genocide Convention unanimously recognized genocide as a 'crime under international law' but rejected the proposals of universal jurisdiction during the drafting procedures, the notion of 'crimes under international law' was not bound together with the allowing of universal jurisdiction at this period in time.

4.2 Universal Jurisdiction over Genocide under Customary International Law

In this dawn of the twenty-first century, no one dares to claim that universal jurisdiction against the crime of genocide is unlawful under international law. It has often been implied that universal jurisdiction against genocide is allowed under customary international law. But exactly when did it become a part of customary international law? Indeed, what is the exact rule that has become part of customary international law? These questions have rarely been asked despite the fact that many people claim that universal jurisdiction against genocide is not in breach of international law. Even though many scholars contend that it is part of customary international law, it is evident that, in practice, States until recently had been reluctant to prosecute and punish suspects alleged to have committed suspected genocide with the exception of those crimes committed during World War II. In the light of the contradictory practice, how can we say that universal jurisdiction is a norm?

It would be interesting to ascertain the time at which universal jurisdiction became recognised as falling within the realm of customary international law. Such an analysis may well illustrate the development of international law. With this in mind, let us analyse the influence of customary international law on universal jurisdiction over the crime of genocide, in accordance with the periodic division used in this study.

4.2.1 Article 6 of the Genocide Convention and Customary Law

There is no clear provision under conventional international law for universal jurisdiction against genocide. Article 6 of the Genocide Convention prescribes only territorial jurisdiction and the jurisdiction of an international criminal court. Contrary to the belief of some,[129] territorial jurisdiction is not an exclusive jurisdiction over genocide. Therefore, in examining customary norms, there is no need to be concerned about the possibility of conflict with this provision. Article 6 of the Genocide Convention does not preclude the subsequent development of customary international law.

4.2.2 The Second Period (Post-WWII to the end of the 1960s)

There is an argument that there was already a customary law with respect to universal jurisdiction against genocide when the Genocide Convention was elaborated.

Some academics interpret that universal jurisdiction was already customary international law at the time when the Genocide Convention was adopted in 1948. They reason that even though Article 6 did not provide for universal jurisdiction, it did not deny that universal jurisdiction over genocide was recognized under customary international law. They argue that universal jurisdiction was already established under customary international law as a result of the prosecutions conducted by the Allied States after the Second World War.

However, such an assessment of the post-WWII trials as precedents for universal jurisdiction is doubted, as explained earlier. Furthermore, whereas one has to prove the existence of the repeated customs and *opinio juris* in order to hold that universal jurisdiction over genocide has become part of customary international law, such customs and *opinio juris* were not yet found in 1948. The *opinio juris* expressed by States during the drafting of the Genocide Convention suggests that universal jurisdiction was not regarded as customary international law at that time. This is apparent from the rejection of proposals to incorporate universal jurisdiction. Even the Iranian proposal for universal jurisdiction, as only a supplement to territorial jurisdiction, was rejected. Moreover, in discussions on the explanatory note for interpreting Article 6, an opinion was expressed that universal jurisdiction should not be allowed by broadening the interpretation of the provision.[130] It can be seen that at the time of drafting the Genocide Convention, States not only rejected the possibility to provide for universal jurisdiction in the convention, but expressed their view that universal jurisdiction was not part of customary international law. In addition, considering that the term 'genocide' created by Lemkin was still fairly new at that time,[131] it is doubtful that sufficient time had elapsed for customary international law have been formed.

In sum, universal jurisdiction against genocide was not readily accepted among States in 1948. There is insufficient evidence of *opinio juris* or practice for universal jurisdiction over genocide to conclude that it had already become customary interna-

---

129 See James E. Fawcett 'The Eichmann Case' *British Yearbook of International Law* Vol. 38 (1962), p. 205.

130 See *UN General Assembly Official Records*, 3rd Session, C. 6, 131st meeting, p. 686. See also 132nd meeting, p. 698.

131 'Genocide' was a new term created by Raphael Lemkin in order to classify the Nazis holocaust. See Raphael Lemkin, *Axis Rule in Europe* (Carnegie Endowment for International Peace, 1944), p. 70.

tional law at that time. Much more so, a conclusion to the contrary seems to be more appropriate. Even supplemental permissive universal jurisdiction, which was a very weak entitlement tolerated under the classical jurisdictional regime, was rejected during the drafting. The discussion during the drafting procedures of the Genocide Convention does not provide any evidence of the existence of customary law in this respect.

Another reason they present is based on the analogy which is made between piracy and genocide. In their view, genocide is not inferior to piracy in gravity and seriousness, thus genocide should be subject to universal jurisdiction just like piracy. Also, during the drafting procedures of the Genocide Convention, many delegates expressed their awareness that genocide might not be effectively punished by the classical jurisdictional system based on territorial jurisdiction.

However, as explained above, the fact that a crime constitutes a 'crime under international law' does not necessarily imply that universal jurisdiction applies *ipso facto*. The Genocide Convention is a good example. Therefore it was not very likely that customary international law supported such an argument at that time.

Of course, compared to piracy, it can be argued that genocide has the same or a stronger rationale for requiring universal jurisdiction to be exercised. First of all, there was no question that the crime of genocide is a serious crime. In addition, it was feared that there would be no effective jurisdiction over genocide if left under the classical jurisdictional regime with the supremacy of territorial jurisdiction. Thus one may be tempted to conclude that genocide became subject to universal jurisdiction just as piracy had done. However, there are differences between piracy and genocide that influence the views of States on the application of universal jurisdiction. In the case of the crime of genocide, there is the possibility of undermining the dominance of territorial jurisdiction. This is because, unlike piracy, acts of genocide are generally committed within the territory of a State. Therefore, most of the time there would be a State with territorial jurisdiction in the case of genocide, and if universal jurisdiction were to be adopted, it would conflict with and possibly undermine the exercise of territorial jurisdiction. This conflict with the traditional rule downgraded the support for universal jurisdiction in relation to genocide and other crimes. It is also noteworthy that the comparison with piracy included in the draft of UN General Assembly Resolution 96(I)[132]

132 See, William A. Schabas, *Genocide in International Law* (Cambridge University Press, 2000), pp. 42-47. The draft resolution (UN Doc. A/BUR/50) included the following remark.
'Whereas the punishment of the very serious crime of genocide when committed in time of peace lies within the exclusive territorial jurisdiction of the judiciary of every State concerned, while crimes of a relatively lesser importance such as piracy, trade in women, children, drugs, obscene publications are declared as international crimes and have been made matters of international concern;
... the United Nations Assembly ... invite the [Social and Economic] Council to study this problem and to prepare a report on the possibilities of ... recommending, *inter alia*, that genocide and related offences should be dealt with by national legislations in the same way as other international crimes such as piracy, trade in women, children and slaves, and others.'

was later omitted and therefore does not appear in the adopted resolution. Consequently, an analogy with piracy was not expressed in the resolution.

In sum, considering that the idea of universal jurisdiction was rejected during the drafting procedures, and the fact that there was insufficient time for a customary rule to have materialized since the crime of 'genocide' had been newly created by the Genocide Convention, it can be concluded that at the time of drafting the Genocide Convention in the late 1940s, there was no customary law amounting to universal jurisdiction against genocide. Furthermore, taking into account the influence of rules in the classical jurisdictional regime, even the proposition that permissive universal jurisdiction amounting to customary law for genocide is difficult to uphold. Therefore, we must consider subsequent developments.

There is another opinion that universal jurisdiction against genocide had become customary international law by the 1960s. As evidence of this, one might refer to the Eichmann Trial. There is reason to contend that the Eichmann Trial admitted permissive universal jurisdiction since there was no conflicting claim of jurisdiction over the case. It is observed that the court in the Eichmann Trial recognised the supplemental character of universal jurisdiction. The Israeli Supreme Court held that there is a 'limitation upon the exercise of universal jurisdiction ... namely that the State which has apprehended the offender must first offer to extradite him to the State in which the crime was committed'.[133]

On the other hand, there was also evidence against the recognition of primary permissive universal jurisdiction or obligatory universal jurisdiction over genocide during this period. It is a fact that, even though there were many crimes which allegedly constituted the crime of genocide, States were reluctant to exercise universal jurisdiction against them with the exception of those committed during World War II. From such a reluctant attitude and practice on the part of States, it is obvious that universal jurisdiction was regarded as not being an obligation at that time. To prove this point, it is noted that the Second Restatement published in 1962 – the same year as the Eichmann Trial was concluded – did not even provide for universal jurisdiction for crimes other than piracy. Overall, universal jurisdiction over genocide, even of a permissive nature, was the subject of doubt during this period.

4.2.3 The Third Period (the 1970s and the 1980s)

Next to the Eichmann Trial, the Third Restatement published in 1987 is most often mentioned as evidence of a customary norm. The Third Restatement recognises that universal jurisdiction against genocide is accepted under customary international law. Yet the Third Restatement is not clear as to whether its universal jurisdiction departs from the traditional sense. It is also unclear whether it declared its recognition as a

---

Observing the elimination of those sentences, Schabas concludes that the UN General Assembly resolution did not recognise universal jurisdiction for genocide. See, *ibid.*, p. 46.

133 The Eichmann Trial, *supra* note (14), p. 302.

right or an obligation. Additionally, the failure of the efforts at the UN to prescribe universal jurisdiction over genocide comes to mind when analysing this period. As illustrated in Chapter III, even though an additional protocol to provide universal jurisdiction was proposed, it did not come to fruition. It is noteworthy that the two Special Rapporteurs in the 1970s and the 1980s recommended such legislation by means of an additional protocol, instead of claiming universal jurisdiction over genocide to be part of customary international law. Therefore, the proposed universal jurisdiction which was considered together with the principle of *aut dedere aut punicare* was not regarded as a rule of customary international law at the time when the study was conducted in the UN during the 1970s and 1980s.

During this period, permissive universal jurisdiction had begun to be recognised in theory. Yet, in practice, custom and *opinio juris* that affirm universal jurisdiction against genocide were scarce, and the idea of elaborating new law prescribing universal jurisdiction against genocide did not result in such law. Therefore, permissive universal jurisdiction against genocide rested solely on the fact that there was no law prohibiting it. This was far from active recognition. In terms of obligatory universal jurisdiction, the same type of universal jurisdiction incorporated in treaties and conventions was not recognised under customary law during the 1970s and 1980s.

4.2.4 The Fourth Period (the 1990s to the present)

In my view, it was in the 1990s that universal jurisdiction over genocide started to be established under customary international law. It was the influence of the expansion of universal jurisdiction in conventional international law and also the establishment of *ad hoc* international tribunals that promoted the recognition of universal jurisdiction as a measure for ending impunity. The ICTY and the ICTR and also the ICC admitted a jurisdictional system where various national jurisdictions and international jurisdiction could coexist. These international criminal courts encourage States to take an active role in enforcing international criminal and humanitarian law. States are encouraged to prepare legislation and to exercise not only territorial, but also various other bases of jurisdiction over gross violations of human rights.[134] The ICJ also ruled in the Case of the Application of the Genocide Convention that the obligation to punish genocide is an *erga omnes* obligation, thus not limited by territoriality.[135] On many occasions, the international community has expressed the opinion that it is desirable to have a concurrent jurisdictional system. These aspirations for a concurrent jurisdictional regime in which various bases of jurisdiction are allowed have diminished the dominance of territorial jurisdiction and increased the acceptance of universal jurisdic-

134 See, Question of the Impunity of Perpetrators of Human Rights Violations, UN Doc. E/CN.4/Sub.2/1997/20/Rev.1 (1997), Principles 20, 21.

135 Case Concerning the Application of the Convention on the Prevention and Punishment of the Crime of Genocide (*Bosnia and Herzegovina* v. *Yugoslavia*), Judgment of 11 July 1996, *I.C.J. Reports 1996*, p. 616.

tion. During the drafting of the ICC Statute, the UN International Law Commission (ILC) proposed to place genocide under the inherent jurisdiction of the ICC due to 'the character of the crime of genocide as a crime under international law for which universal jurisdiction existed as a matter of customary law for those States that were not parties to the Convention'.[136] Furthermore, in the Rome Conference, where the ICC Statute was finalised, many States stated their position admitting that universal jurisdiction against the crime of genocide falls within customary international law. This allowed the ICC to have inherent jurisdiction over genocide. The majority of the international community today holds the view that universal jurisdiction against genocide is customary international law.

Consequently, universal jurisdiction over genocide is now recognised by States in their domestic law and practice as well. The German courts arrested, prosecuted and punished many foreigners present in Germany who had committed genocide in the Former Yugoslavia.[137] Similarly, the Austrian Supreme Court held on 13 July 1994 that the Austrian courts could exercise universal jurisdiction over genocide because both the court of the territorial State and the international criminal tribunal prescribed in Article 6 of the Genocide Convention were not functioning.[138]

Now, many people presume that universal jurisdiction against genocide is a norm under customary international law. Some even assert that it is an obligation without offering much explanation. This assertion in itself demonstrates how it has become natural to allow universal jurisdiction over gross human rights violations such as genocide.

The ILC, in the discussion on the Draft Code of 'Crimes Against Peace and Security of Mankind' of 1996, recognised obligatory jurisdiction over genocide for all States, stating that it is customary international law.[139] The ILC explained that this position is justified because of the nature of genocide as a crime against international law. In addition, Article 9 of the draft code provided the obligation of *aut dedere aut judicare*. According to this article, States having custody of a suspect have an obligation either to extradite or prosecute within its domestic courts. The draft code did not clarify the order of supremacy between these two choices, and therefore left it to the

136 The ILC seems to assume that crimes under international law become subject to universal jurisdiction, but no evidence for this is presented. See the Report on the Work of the 43rd Session of the International Law Commission, UN Doc. A/51/10, *ILC Yearbook 1996*, Vol. II(2), 29.

137 For example, the decision of 30 April 1999 by the Third Criminal Senate of the Federal Court of Justice, and its subsequent revision by the German Federal Constitutional Court, see Cristina Hoß and Russel A. Miller 'German Federal Constitutional Court and Bosnian War Crimes: Liberalizing Germany's Genocide Jurisprudence' *German Yearbook of International Law* Vol. 44 (2001). See also, International Law Association, *supra* note (25), appendix, pp. 26-27. See also, REDRESS, *supra* note (70), pp. 31-34.

138 Judgment of the Oberster Gerichstshof concerning the case against Dusko Cvjetkovic, Vienna, 13 July 1994; see the summary of this case in REDRESS, *ibid*, annex.

139 Report of the International Law Commission on the Work of its Forty-Eighth Session, UN Doc. A/51/10, pp. 42, 46-47.

discretion of the custodial State. There was a proposal to give supremacy to the request for extradition from the territorial State, but this was ultimately rejected.[140]

4.3 Conclusion on universal jurisdiction over genocide

As already explained, the domination of territorial jurisdiction under the classical jurisdictional regime was so strong that international law recognised other national jurisdictions only on a limited basis. Therefore, it was only after the weakening of the dominance of territorial jurisdiction that it began to be widely accepted that States had a right to exercise universal jurisdiction.

In sum, at the time of drafting and adopting the Genocide Convention, there was no customary international law relating to universal jurisdiction over genocide. However, as time passed and the political and legal environment of the international community changed, expectations grew with regard to universal jurisdiction as an ideal measure to prosecute and punish criminals more effectively and to deter the continued occurrence of the crime of genocide. Although the Eichmann Trial in the 1960s had a great influence in drawing attention to these expectations, the case itself cast some doubt as a precedent for universal jurisdiction. In fact, it is very likely that permissive jurisdiction against genocide became customary international law somewhat later than during the 1960s. It is likely that it became customary international law after the influence of the inclusion of universal jurisdiction in many multilateral treaties in the 1970s. Although it is now recognised that universal jurisdiction against genocide is a norm under customary international law, there is still some ambiguity as to its nature. There is no sound evidence to presume that it is recognised as being more than a right pertaining to States. Also, the practices of States are too divergent to evidence the acceptance of universal jurisdiction *in absentia* in genocide. It seems to be that the recognition of universal jurisdiction over genocide as an obligation is still in a formative stage. Yet this does not preclude new developments in the law. The *opinio juris* and the practices of States must be carefully followed in the future.

140 *Ibid.*, pp. 53-54.

Chapter V
Guiding Rules by which to Solve Jurisdictional Conflicts

1 Introduction

In the preceding chapters, I have illustrated the development of the modern jurisdictional regime, noting the phenomenon of the 'expansion' of national jurisdictions, especially universal jurisdiction. As the result of the expansion of national jurisdictions, the modern jurisdictional regime is now composed of multiple national and international jurisdictions which exist concurrently. The concurrence of multiple jurisdictions may have some advantages, but, at the same time, it may also cause some problems. This chapter contemplates the problems arising from this concurrence, and identifies some guiding rules under international law to resolve jurisdictional conflicts.

With this objective, the present chapter is composed of three parts. The first section notes and describes the problem of competing jurisdictional claims. In the second section an example of a jurisdictional dispute is presented in order to demonstrate the complexity and significance involved in the conflict. After illustrating the need for clarifying international law in this respect, this study compiles some rules that may be taken into consideration when deciding which State should exercise jurisdiction over a particular case.

2 Concurrent Jurisdictional Regime

2.1 The Multiplicity of National and International Jurisdictions

First, it should be reiterated that the modern jurisdictional regime is composed of multiple national and international jurisdictions. Concerning national jurisdictions, international law recognises five bases: territorial, nationality, passive personality, protective, and universal jurisdiction. Ever since the 'expansion' of national jurisdictions in international conventional law, a variety of bases of national jurisdiction have been expressly acknowledged and sometimes placed as an obligation as far as States are concerned. Rather than discouraging a particular basis of jurisdiction, international law tends to encourage States to prepare many jurisdictional bases with the aim of enhancing the possibilities for punishing of criminals. Therefore, in the present day, it is most likely that there is more than one national jurisdiction that can be legally exercised over a case.

The establishment of international criminal jurisdictions also contribute to the multiplicity of jurisdictions. From the end of the twentieth century to the dawn of the twenty-first century, several international courts were established to pursue individual accountability for gross violations of human rights. The two *ad hoc* tribunals – the ICTY and ICTR – were created by the UN Security Council. The ICC was created by an international treaty to function on a permanent basis. In addition, some 'internationalised' tribunals were created to try serious crimes committed in specific regions. The international community has made an effort to obtain justice for gross violations of human rights committed during a civil war or in a situation where governmental authorities and systems have collapsed, such as in Sierra Leone, East Timor, and Kosovo – atrocities which might have gone unpunished due to the lacunae in effective jurisdiction if they had been committed decades ago.

2.2 The Objective and the Advantage of Concurrent Jurisdictional Regimes

As summarized above, it is observed that international law has actively established the concurrence of multiple jurisdictions, both national and international, which can be exercised over a case. This concurrence can be seen as the manifestation of the great concern of the international community to end the impunity of gross human rights violations, and has been promoted by the development of international human rights law as well as that of international criminal and humanitarian law.

The concurrent jurisdictional structure constituted by various national and international criminal jurisdictions has been constructed with the aim of eliminating safe havens for criminals. The objective is to close jurisdictional gaps and to overcome other defects that had existed in the classical jurisdictional regime, namely those caused by the failure of territorial jurisdiction to effectively prosecute and punish serious crimes. In the modern jurisdictional regime, jurisdictions are clearly envisaged to be non-exclusive, hence co-existing with each other. The current legal situation of plural jurisdictions is seen as desirable because it greatly increases the possibilities and likelihood of prosecution. Hence, even if one jurisdiction fails to be exercised, there may be another basis of jurisdiction that could be exercised to bring about prosecution. It is expected, as a result, that criminals will not be able to escape the manifold net of jurisdiction.

2.3 Problem Inherent in a Concurrent Jurisdictional Regime

On the other hand, having more than one court (domestic or international), each with a lawful jurisdictional basis may cause some difficulties. These difficulties mainly arise from the problem of ascertaining which court, among all those having lawful jurisdiction, should actually exercise jurisdiction and proceed with prosecution. Jurisdictional problems within a concurrent jurisdictional regime may occur in the form of a *negative conflict* or *positive conflict*.[1] A *negative conflict* occurs when there is no State or other entity (including international criminal courts) which is willing to prosecute the particular case in question. On the other hand, a *positive conflict* occurs when there is more than one State or entity willing to prosecute the same case.

2.3.1 Negative Conflicts

A *negative conflict* arises when no jurisdiction is asserted even though a crime has been committed. The adverse effect of a negative conflict is obvious – the prevalence of impunity. Ultimately, the impunity of gross violations of human rights is harmful to future peace and justice and is against the interests of the international community.

The most obvious cause of negative conflicts is the lacuna of jurisdiction, that is, the absence of any jurisdiction that can be legally asserted over the crime in question. Therefore, in order to prevent negative conflicts, it is beneficial to recognize various bases of jurisdiction, thereby filling this lacuna. Even in the classical jurisdictional regime in which territorial jurisdiction was dominant, the problem of the lacuna of jurisdiction was recognized, and some bases of jurisdiction were expanded in response. The development of universal jurisdiction over piracy is one example. As explained in Chapter III, one rationale behind the development of universal jurisdiction was the lacuna of effective jurisdiction capable of being exercised over the crime of piracy.

Nevertheless, substantiating the law by recognizing as many bases of jurisdiction as possible is not enough to eliminate certain gaps in criminal prosecution.[2] In addition to filling the lacuna of jurisdiction, the actual exercise of jurisdiction must be promoted. For this end, it is beneficial to oblige States to exercise jurisdiction. Therefore, States should be urged to comply with treaties that oblige them to legislate and to enact various national jurisdictional laws. They are also encouraged to take an active role in ending impunity through applying such laws as well as through their cooperation with others for this purpose. In order to prevent negative conflicts, it is recommended that future conventions relating to crime prevention and punishment should include

1 See Principle 15 of the 'Brussels Principles Against Impunity and for International Justice', adopted by the Brussels Group for Intenational Justice, following on from the colloquium entitled 'The Fight Against Impunity: Stakes and Perspectives' (Brussels, 11-13 March, 2002).

2 Eser highlights the jurisdictional gaps and overlaps created by the 'American territoriality principle' and 'European extraterritorialism', and notes that 'given that domestic cases will continue to receive preference in the daily work of practitioners, one may doubt if the extension of substantive law will really eliminate gaps in criminal prosecution.' He calls for improvement by remarking that '[i]f not, the remaining function of extraterritorial substantive law would do no more than symbolize state authority and allow itself to be misused for purely political purposes.' Albin Eser 'Common Goals and Different Ways in International Criminal Law: Reflections from a European Perspective' *Harvard International Law Journal* Vol. 31 No. 1 (Winter 1990), p. 125.

provisions for recognizing various bases of jurisdiction as well as obliging States to exercise jurisdiction.[3]

Another factor that may provoke negative conflicts is uncertainty concerning the law. In which situation does customary international law impose an obligation upon States to prosecute offences?[4] Clarifying the existence and content of this obligation would put pressure on States to comply, and it would thereby prompt States to exercise jurisdiction in order to prosecute and punish these crimes.

Finally, the lack of systematic international supervision is indicated as being one factor behind States' failure to exercise jurisdiction.[5] In order to persuade States to exercise jurisdiction, the ILA report concerning universal jurisdiction encourages the supervisory body of the Torture Convention to undertake a more aggressive role as regards universal jurisdiction and to adopt a 'general comment' on the matter.[6] The same report further recommends that the UN Security Council should undertake a monitoring role by urging Member States to exercise universal jurisdiction.[7]

2.3.2 Positive Conflicts

A *positive conflict* of jurisdiction arises, on the other hand, when more than one State or other entity claims jurisdiction over the same case. The problem of positive conflicts is often dismissed as being insignificant compared to that of negative conflicts. This is because having more than one court willing to try the case at least ensures that a trial will indeed take place somewhere. For instance, one textbook on international law assesses the significance of the problem as follows:

> '[I]t is only in relatively few cases that overlapping claims to jurisdiction cause serious problems, usually where the states concerned attach importance to the assertion of their competing claims, and more often in criminal cases (where the element of public authority is more evident) than in civil cases. Usually the coexistence of overlapping

---

3 For example, in addition to Article 5 acknowledging various bases of jurisdiction, the Torture Convention prescribes in Article 11 that '[e]ach State Party shall ensure that its competent authorities proceed to a prompt and impartial investigation, wherever there is reasonable ground to believe that an act of torture has been committed in any territory under its jurisdiction.'

4 For example, Cassese notes the judgment of 20 October 2000 upheld by the French Court of Appeal concerning the prosecution of Qadaffi, which cited the preamble of the ICC Statute as evidence of the obligation to prosecute international crimes. But as for the emergence of a customary rule imposing obligations to prosecute or to extradite, Cassese concludes that supporting State practice is lacking. See Antonio Cassese, *International Law* (Oxford Press, 2001), pp. 264-265.

5 International Law Association 'Final Report on the Exercise of Universal Jurisdiction in Respect of Gross Human Rights Offences', prepared by the Committee on International Human rights Law and Practice, submitted to London Conference (2000), p. 18. See also, Menno T. Kamminga 'Lessons Learned from the Exercise of Universal Jurisdiction in Respect of Gross Human Rights Offenses' *Human Rights Quarterly* Vol. 23 No. 4 (November 2001), pp. 961-963.

6 International Law Association, *ibid.*, p. 18. See also, Menno T. Kamminga, *ibid.*, p. 962.

7 International Law Association, *ibid.*, p. 19. See also, Menno T. Kamminga, *ibid.*, pp. 962-963.

jurisdiction is acceptable and convenient; and forbearance by states in the exercise of their jurisdictional powers avoids conflict in all but a small (although important) minority of cases.'[8]

Nonetheless, a positive conflict has the potential of becoming a dispute of a significant magnitude. Some recent jurisdictional conflicts have evolved into serious disputes between States, so as to require the intervention of the UN Security Council and/or referral to the ICJ. The clash of jurisdictional claims in the Lockerbie Case will be examined later in this chapter to illustrate the danger of a positive conflict.

2.4 The Need for Rules Concerning Jurisdiction

Which State should exercise jurisdiction in order to end impunity? How can the competing assertions made by different States to apply and enforce their law to a particular event or person be resolved? Both negative and positive conflicts of jurisdiction require some clarification of international law on this point.

Before examining the rules by which to resolve jurisdictional conflicts, it should be reiterated that this study as a whole mainly concerns national jurisdiction. Accordingly, the issue of the relations between various international criminal jurisdictions, as well as between national and international criminal jurisdiction is outside the scope of this study. This chapter examines the relations among various national jurisdictions. The relationships between national and international criminal jurisdictions are fairly easy to perceive compared to those between national jurisdictions, since there is more explicit law and a substantial amount of scholarly debate and review. The statutes and rules of each international criminal court have explicit provisions regarding this issue. For example, the Statutes of the ICTY and the ICTR provide for the supremacy of their jurisdiction over national jurisdictions,[9] while the ICC Statute proclaims the principle of complementarity in its Preamble and provisions.[10] On the other hand, the problem of conflict among national jurisdictions, although existing for much longer in history than international criminal jurisdictions, has still not been extensively considered. Explicit rules still remain to be defined. The confusion and uncertainty concerning the law has caused disputes among States. No criminal should be able to avoid accountability by taking advantage of uncertainty concerning international law, and consequently, of national borders and jurisdictional conflicts between States. For that reason

8 Sir Robert Jennings and Sir Arthur Watts eds., *Oppenheim's International Law* Vol. I Peace (9th ed.) (Longman Group UK Limited, 1992), section 136.

9 Both ad hoc Tribunals enjoy primacy over domestic courts as it is prescribed in their statutes that '[a]t any state of the procedure, the International Tribunal may formally request national courts to defer to the competences of the International Tribunal'. See Article 9(2) of the ICTY Statute and Article 8(2) of the ICTR Statute. See Bartram S. Brown 'Primacy or Complementarity: Reconciling the Jurisdiction of National Courts and International Criminal Tribunals' *Yale Journal of International Law* Vol. 23 (1998).

10 See the preamble and Article 1 of the ICC Statute.

this chapter attempts to identify the guiding rules in determining which domestic court should exercise jurisdiction.

2.5 The Applicability of International Law to Jurisdictional Problems

Since there are multiple jurisdictional bases acknowledged under international law, States sometimes have conflicting views on jurisdiction over a case. In such a case, international law should provide an answer to the question of which State should actually exercise jurisdiction. However, since the classical jurisdictional regime, international law has generally remained silent on this point. Apart from recognizing some bases of jurisdiction, international law has not laid down any rigid rules on how to exercise national jurisdiction. Consequently, States are left with wide discretion.

However, this *laissez-faire* attitude should not be interpreted as implying that international law cannot regulate the exercise of national jurisdiction. Sir Gerald Fitzmaurice in the ICJ's Barcelona Traction Case (1970) stated that international law does 'involve for every State an obligation to exercise moderation and restraint as to the extent of the jurisdiction assumed by the courts in cases having a foreign element, and to avoid undue encroachment on a jurisdiction more properly appertaining to, or more appropriately exercisable by, another State.'[11] Also, regulating relations between jurisdictions is considered to be within the fundamental objectives of international law concerning jurisdiction.[12] International law should take cognisance of the interest of the international community in ending the impunity of gross violations of human rights, while keeping in mind the objectives of international law in balancing and harmonizing each State's interest while protecting individuals from the unreasonable exercise of jurisdiction. At a glance, these objectives might appear to contradict one another. However, it is the task of international law to present a proper balance between these considerations in regulating the jurisdictional regime.

In sum, international law can and should clarify rules for the purpose of resolving problems of jurisdictional conflicts. International law is required to answer questions such as 'which State is obliged to exercise jurisdiction?' and 'which State should actually proceed with a case if there is more than one State claiming jurisdiction?', or

11 ICJ Barcelona Traction case.

12 The four fundamental objectives of the international law on jurisdiction are described as follows: 'The first is to establish limits of jurisdiction that protect the independence and sovereign equality of States by balancing each State's interest in exercising jurisdiction to advance its own policies with each State's interest in avoiding interference with its policies resulting from the exercise of jurisdiction by foreign states. The second is to recognize the interdependence of States by ensuring that effective jurisdiction exists to achieve certain common objectives of States. The third is to harmonize the rights of two or more States when they have concurrent jurisdiction, that is when each of them has jurisdiction over the same matter. The fourth is to protect individuals from unreasonable exercises of jurisdiction either by a single State or by two or more States seeking to impose conflicting or compounding obligations on the same person.' Bernard H. Oxman 'Jurisdiction of States' in Rudolf Bernhardt ed., *Encyclopedia of Public International Law* Vol. 3 (Elsevier Science, 1997), p. 56.

'is there any supremacy of any particular basis of jurisdiction over others?'. Inevitably, answers to these questions are expected to reflect the structure within the modern jurisdictional regime. Hence, they are relevant to the assessment of how the allocation of authority among States is envisaged under international law.

3 The Lockerbie Case as an Example of a Jurisdictional Dispute

In order to illustrate the significance of the problems resulting from jurisdictional conflicts, we will discuss the Lockerbie Case below.[13] I am aware that this case relates to the crime of terrorism (bombing a commercial aircraft), instead of gross violations of human rights on which this study concentrates. Nevertheless, this case deserves attention because it is a prominent example of a positive conflict of jurisdiction, exemplifying the significance and difficulty of settling jurisdictional disputes. At the same time, it indicates the new trend of international criminal law that emphasises the fair and impartial conduct of a trial, as I will explain later.

3.1 The Facts

On 21 December 1988, Pan Am flight 103 flying over Lockerbie, Scotland, exploded and killed all 259 passengers and crew on board and some residents on the ground. The subsequent investigation indicated that two Libyan nationals were suspected of planting a bomb on the aircraft.[14] After this finding, a jurisdictional conflict over the criminal trial of the two suspects arose between Libya, the United States, and the United Kingdom.

3.2 Analysis of the Jurisdictional Aspect

3.2.1 Libyan Jurisdiction over the case

Among the various bases of national jurisdiction recognised under international law, Libya had a right to exercise its jurisdiction as the State of the nationality of the suspects and as the State of the territory where the suspects were present. In other words, Libya had both nationality jurisdiction and universal jurisdiction. Libya's power to exercise jurisdiction is also specifically recognised in a relevant convention. Under the Montreal Convention for the Suppression of Unlawful Acts against the Safety of Civil Aviation of 1971 (Montreal Convention), Libya could exercise its jurisdiction based on Article 5(2) which allows the custodial State to exercise jurisdic-

13 Questions of Interpretation and Application of the 1971 Montreal Convention arising from the Aerial Incident at Lockerbie (*Libya* v. *United Kingdom*), *1992 ICJ Reports*.

14 Abdel Basset Ali al-Megrahi and Lamen Khalifa Fhimah were suspected of planting the bomb, acting as agents of Libya. Hence, Security Council Resolution 731 referred to the suspects as Libyan 'officials'.

tion, and also based on Article 5(3) which specifically provides that the convention does not exclude any other form of national jurisdiction exercised in accordance with domestic law.

In response to the allegation made by the U.S. and the U.K. about two Libyan suspects, Libya decided to initiate proceedings in its domestic courts.[15] Because Libya decided to exercise its jurisdiction over this case, it refused the American and British requests for the extradition of the suspects. According to the principle of *aut dedere aut judicare* embodied in Article 7 of the 1971 Montreal Convention, a State Party in the territory of which the alleged offender is found shall, if it does not extradite that person, submit the case to its competent authorities for the purpose of prosecution. Since Libya itself initiated domestic proceedings, it was not obliged to extradite the two suspects. Furthermore, Libya argued that it was not obliged to extradite its own nationals under international law and also under Libyan domestic law which does not permit the extradition of nationals in the absence of an extradition treaty.[16] If the matter had been handled strictly according to the Montreal Convention, Libya could have adhered to its decision to conduct proceedings itself.

In addition to expressing its intention to instigate criminal proceedings against the two suspects itself, Libya asked the U.S. and the U.K. to assist in its investigation.[17] Under Article 11(1) of the 1971 Montreal Convention, States Parties are obliged to provide assistance to States conducting criminal proceedings. Accordingly, Libya asked the Security Council to urge the U.S. and the U.K. to hand over the dossiers in the investigation to the two Libyan judges in order to complete the investigation in Libya.[18] But this Libyan request was not fulfilled.

3.2.2 The Jurisdiction of the U.S. and the U.K. over the Case

It is important to note that the U.S. and the U.K. also had legitimate a concern as regards this case. The Scottish courts issued a warrant for the arrest of the two suspects on 13 November 1991.[19] The U.S. also indicted the two suspects before a grand jury

---

15 See 'Letter Dated 18 January 1992 From the Permanent Representative of the Libyan Arab Jamahiriya to the United Nations Addressed to the President of the Security Council', *International Legal Materials* Vol. 31 (1992), pp. 728-729.

16 See the Dissenting Opinion of Judge Weeramantry, 1992 ICJ Reports, p. 51. Libyan Criminal Code (28 November 1953), Articles 8-10, and Criminal Procedure Code (28 November 1953), Articles 493-510.

17 See 'Letter Dated 18 January 1992 From the Permanent Representative of the Libyan Arab Jamahiriya to the United Nations Addessed to the President of the Security Council', *supra* note (15), p. 729.

18 See 'Letter dated 18 March 1992 from the Secretary of the People's Committee for Foreign Liaison and International Cooperation of the Libyan Arab Jamahiriya addressed to the Secretary-General' *International Legal Materials* Vol. 31 (1992), p. 741. This request was made after the adoption of UN Security Council Resolution 731(1992).

19 See Announcement by the Lord Advocate of Scotland on 14 November 1991, *International Legal Materials* Vol. 31 (1992), pp. 718-721.

in the District of Columbia on 14 November 1991. The U.S. and the U.K. issued a joint declaration on 27 November 1991, demanding that Libya must surrender the suspects for trial and accept responsibility for the actions of its officials, to disclose all information relating to the alleged crime, and to pay appropriate compensation.[20]

With regard to the jurisdiction to try the suspects, both the U.S. and the U.K. had a legally sound jurisdiction to do so under general and conventional international law.[21] The U.S. could claim jurisdiction over this case because it was an American airline that was bombed and American nationals were among the victims. Therefore, the U.S. had jurisdiction based on the registration of the aircraft as prescribed in Article 5(b) of the 1971 Montreal Convention, and based on passive nationality jurisdiction recognized under general international law. The U.K. could also claim jurisdiction since the plane had crashed in Lockerbie, Scotland, and British nationals were among the victims. Therefore, the United Kingdom had territorial jurisdiction recognized by Article 5(a) of the 1971 Montreal Convention, and passive nationality jurisdiction.

Although no extradition treaties were in force at the time of the dispute between Libya and the UK or between Libya and the U.S., the 1971 Montreal Convention to which all three States were parties provides provisions that can be utilized as a legal basis for extradition. Therefore, in a strict legal sense, the absence of extradition treaties between these States did not preclude the surrender of a suspect from Libya to the U.K. or the U.S.

Contrary to the demands of the U.S. and the U.K., however, Libya expressed its intention to prosecute the suspects under the Libyan domestic judicial system. Libya was determined to conduct the trial under the Libyan legal system, and it invited observers from the U.S., the U.K., and international organizations to observe the conduct of the trial in Libya.[22]

3.3 Mutual Distrust of Conducting a Trial in a Fair and Impartial Manner

As explained above, all three States involved had one or more lawful basis of national jurisdiction over the bombing, and claimed their jurisdiction accordingly. Hence, it was a situation of a positive jurisdictional conflict. This positive conflict of jurisdiction deteriorated into a vehement dispute, made worse by the unfriendly relations and

---

20 1992 ICJ Reports, p. 11, para. 28. See the text of the U.K.-U.S. Joint Declaration, *International Legal Materials* Vol. 31 (1992), p. 723.

21 There were other States with possible jurisdictional bases, such as Malta or Germany where the bomb was transferred. But the visible positive conflict of jurisdiction arose between these three States: Libya, the U.S. and the U.K.

22 See 'Texts of Reports by the Secretary-General Pursuant to Paragraph 4 of Security Council Resolution 731 (1992)', *International Legal Materials* Vol. 31 (1992), p. 734. Colonel Qadafi suggested inviting judges from the United States, the United Kingdom and France, as well as representatives of the League of Arab States, the Organization of African Unity and the Organization of the Islamic Conference to observe the trial in Libya. See also the Dissenting Opinion of Judge Weeramantry, 1992 ICJ Report, p. 51.

mutual distrust between the States involved. On the one side, the U.S. and the U.K. denied that Libya had the capacity to conduct the trial of the Libyan suspects who were alleged to have acted as the agents of the Libyan government. On the other hand, Libya insisted on conducting the trial itself without foreign interference, arguing that the suspects could not receive a fair trial in the U.S. or the U.K.[23] With deep distrust dividing them, these States were unable to reach an agreement on the venue for the trial.

As a compromise, it was proposed to have a third party involved in the conduct of the trial in order to eliminate the suspicion of an arbitrary trial. Libya, which insisted on domestic proceedings, proposed several alternatives as the dispute escalated. For instance, Libya proposed the possibility of a trial in another third country, mentioning Malta and any Arab country.[24] Libya proposed that it would hand over the two suspects to the Office of the United Nations Development Programme in Tripoli for questioning, and that the UN should then undertake to form a legal committee 'made up of judges whose probity and impartiality are well attested in order to inquire into the facts, ascertain whether the charges made against the two suspects are well founded and conduct a comprehensive inquiry.'[25] If the committee found the charge to be well-founded, then Libya would not oppose handing over the suspects to a third party. In so doing, Libya added that the UN Secretary-General 'should endeavour to provide all legal and judicial guarantees for the conduct of a just and fair trial based on the International Bill of Human Rights and the principles of international law.'[26] However, this proposal did not lead to the settlement of the dispute. The U.S. and the U.K. insisted on the extradition of the two suspects, while Libya remained determined to avoid a trial in the U.S. or the U.K. The deep distrust among all the States involved caused this jurisdictional conflict to evolve into a serious international dispute.

3.4 Different Forums to Settle the Dispute

In order to settle this dispute, both the UN Security Council and the ICJ were called upon. The U.S. and the U.K. pursued their argument against Libya in the UN Security Council with the purpose of forcing Libya to extradite the suspects. On the other hand, Libya requested the ICJ to confirm its sovereign right to try the suspects itself, and that Libya was being subjected to illegal interference and its sovereignty was being violated.

---

23 See Thomas W. Lippman 'U.S., Britain Announce Plan for Pan Am Trial', The Washington Post, 25 August 1998.

24 See 'Further report by the Secretary-General Pursuant to Paragraph 4 of Security Council Resolution 731 (1992), UN Doc. S/23672. Reprinted in *International Legal Materials* Vol. 31 (1992), p. 736.

25 'Letter dated 27 February 1992 from the Secretary of the People's Committee for Foreign Liaison and International Cooperation of the Libyan Arab Jamahiriya addressed to the Secretary-General', annexed to 'Further report by the Secretary-General Pursuant to Paragraph 4 of Security Council Resolution 731 (1992)', UN Doc. S/23672. Reprinted in *International Legal Materials* Vol. 31 (1992), pp. 736-737.

26 *Ibid.*, p. 738.

The UN Security Council promptly acted in response to this matter. On 21 January 1992, the UN Security Council adopted Resolution 731 (1992). This resolution urged Libya to immediately provide a full and effective response to the requests to cooperate in establishing responsibility for the terrorist acts. And a few weeks after Libya had instituted proceedings at the ICJ, the UN Security Council adopted Resolution 748 (1992) on 31 March 1992. This resolution found the failure of Libya to comply with resolution 731 as a 'threat to international peace and security', and, acting under Chapter VII of the UN Charter, it imposed sanctions against Libya. Similarly, the Security Council again urged Libya to surrender the suspects in Resolution 883 (1993).

On the other hand, Libya referred its claim to the ICJ on 3 March 1992. By an Order dated 14 April 1992, the ICJ rejected the request for provisional measures submitted by Libya, finding that the circumstances of the case were not such as to require the exercise of its power to indicate provisional measures.[27] Notwithstanding the preliminary objections submitted by the U.K., the ICJ did find that it had jurisdiction over the case in the Judgment of 27 February 1998.[28] However, the three parties later notified the ICJ that they had 'agreed to discontinue with prejudice the proceedings', and the case was removed from the ICJ's List on 10 September 2003.[29]

The principal difference among the States involved is the difference in the assessment of the dispute. Libya claimed that the conflict was within the application and interpretation of the 1971 Montreal Convention, whereas the U.S. and the U.K. assessed it to be beyond this treaty and within the international concern relating to international peace and stability, which is within the authority of the UN Security Council. The U.S. and the U.K. contended that the government involvement in the criminal act placed the conflict in a different arena, beyond the Montreal Convention. In a sense, this contention is convincing since the convention is based on the presumption that a State Party will conduct a trial in a *bona fide* manner. The Montreal Convention gives attention to acknowledging various jurisdictions, but not to the manner of conducting a trial. If a State itself is involved in the crime in a malicious manner, then the State may be held accountable under the provision on State responsibility.

3.5 Final Solution: The Special Trial in the Netherlands

Nearly a decade later, the jurisdictional conflict was resolved in an extraordinary manner. The parties to the dispute agreed to prosecute the two suspects in a Scottish tribunal, physically located in the Netherlands, which was especially established for the Lockerbie incident. A domestic trial to be convened on foreign territory was an unusual practice, and had no legal basis under international law, hence special treaties

27 Case concerning Questions of interpretation and application of the 1971 Montreal Convention Arising from the Aerial Incident at Lockerbie (*Libyan Arab Jamahiriya* v. *UK*), Order of 14 April 1992.

28 Case concerning Questions of Interpretation and Application of the 1971 Montreal Convention arising from the Aerial Incident at Lockerbie (*Libyan Arab Jamahiriya* v. *UK*), Judgment of 27 February 1998.

29 See ICJ Press Release 2003/29.

were concluded between the States involved.[30] As a result, Scotland exercised its right to exercise jurisdiction outside Scottish territory, which is just as extraordinary as the Netherlands allowing a foreign State (not an international organization) to exercise its sovereign right of jurisdiction within Dutch territory. The Scottish court announced its verdict on 31 January 2001, finding one suspect guilty and acquitting the other.[31]

3.6 Implications of the Lockerbie Case

The following implications can be deduced from the Lockerbie Case. First, it illustrates how difficult it is to erase the fear of bias. This is especially so when States claiming jurisdiction over the same case are embroiled in unfriendly or antagonistic relations. The actual or possible presence of bias undermines the confidence in justice. Especially when the political climate of the international society is unstable, the mere suspicion of bias or of vengeance influencing the conduct of the trial degrades the integrity of justice and the rule of law, not only for the specific case in question, but as a whole. However, when such suspicion is mutually expressed by the States claiming jurisdiction, the quest for justice becomes trapped within the labyrinth of an inter-State dispute. At the time of the Lockerbie Case, there was no international criminal jurisdiction in existence. Hence there was no alternative but to try the case in a domestic court of a certain State. As for the decision in which State a trial should be conducted, this is up to the States themselves. Even today, there is no institution specifically to allocate criminal cases among States. Consequently, the States involved in the Lockerbie Case used all the political and legal power they could employ to support their claim for jurisdiction.

Second, the Lockerbie Case established that securing a fair and impartial trial could be a matter of international concern. Charney comments on the Lockerbie Case as follows:

> 'While this case may be unique, the situation demonstrates the growing pressure on states to conduct bona fide criminal proceedings regarding alleged offenders or to turn them over to others who will. Few states will have the fortitude even of Libya to resist that pressure.'[32]

It should be noted that in the Lockerbie Case the Security Council consequently adopted resolutions under Chapters VI and VII of the UN Charter, even imposing

30 For details of the legal arrangements for the Scottish court to be established in the Netherlands, see Ilias Bantekas, Susan Nash and Mark Mackarel eds., *International Criminal Law* (Cavendish Publishing, 2001), pp. 275-288.

31 *Her Majesty's Advocate* v. *Abdelbaset Ali Mohamed Al Megrahi and Al Amin Khalifa Fhimah*, No. 1475/99, High Court of Justiciary at Camp Zeist, the Netherlands. The judgment is available at: www.scotcourts.gov.uk/html/ lockerbie.htm.

32 Jonathan I. Charney 'International Criminal Law and the Role of Domestic Courts' *American Journal of International Law* Vol. 95 (2001), p. 123.

sanctions against Libya, all for the purpose of securing a trial. The fact that the Security Council became involved implies that the pressure on States to ensure impartiality is recognised as being of international concern. In my opinion, this case is tantamount to the declaration by the international community that securing the exercise of jurisdiction by States is not enough, and that fairness and impartiality in its exercise must also be achieved. In other words, not only the realization of a trial, but also the manner in which it is conducted falls within the interest of the international community. This is a manifestation of a great change in international law since it is now the case that how a State exercises jurisdiction is no longer exclusively within the realm of a State's discretion. The Lockerbie Case provides evidence that the quality of a trial is also beginning to be closely supervised under modern international law.

Third, the case illustrates a problem concerning the means available for solving a jurisdictional conflict. Who decides the venue of the trial in the first place, and who determines the lawfulness of this decision or the opposing claims of other States? The U.K. and the U.S. presumed that Libya was *mala fide*, not capable of conducting proceedings in a fair and impartial manner, but the correctness of their assessment was not examined. Considering that it had not been proved by any judicial body that Libya had breached international law in this particular instance, the Security Council risked being accused of selectively and arbitrarily using its enforcement power against such a State.

Finally, it is remarkable that the disputing States agreed that Scottish law and judges should preside. This final solution signifies that the States gave preference to territorial jurisdiction over other jurisdictional bases. This implies that, although not exclusive, territorial jurisdiction is still recognized as a major jurisdiction, possibly preceding others.

4 General Observations on Rules Governing the Concurrence of National Jurisdictions

Having explained the importance of clarifying international law in order to prevent and solve jurisdictional conflicts, this section provides some general observations before searching for some guiding rules to resolve jurisdictional conflicts.

4.1 A Prerequisite: Legality

First of all, as a prerequisite in determining which State should exercise jurisdiction, the jurisdiction claimed by a State must be lawful and capable of being exercised in a lawful manner under international law in order to be able to compete with other jurisdictions. If a particular jurisdiction is in breach of international law, it has no standing against any other jurisdiction.

A jurisdiction claimed by a particular State is considered to be legal unless it is prohibited by international law. However, many authors determine legality by whether the asserted jurisdiction falls within one of the particular bases of jurisdiction recognized under international law. It should be reiterated that in the case of gross violations of human rights, international law tends to encourage, rather than discourage States to establish and exercise their jurisdiction to prosecute and punish offenders. There are general presumptions in favour, rather than prohibiting non-territorial jurisdiction. Therefore, even if one considers that a jurisdiction can only be legal when there is a specific international law allowing such jurisdiction, most likely a jurisdiction claimed by a State will be presumed to be legal under modern international law.

The prerequisite of legality may be raised when considering the compatibility of a particular jurisdiction with other principles of international law. Jurisdiction must be able to be exercised in a lawful manner. For example, Brownlie distinguishes between territorial jurisdiction and non-territorial jurisdiction, and lays down special criteria for the latter to be legal. He states as follows:

> 'Extra-territorial acts can only lawfully be the object of jurisdiction if certain general principles are observed:
> (i) that there should be a substantial and bona fide connection between the subject-matter and the source of the jurisdiction;
> (ii) that the principle of non-intervention in the domestic or territorial jurisdiction of other states should be observed;
> (iii) that a principle based on elements of accommodation, mutuality, and proportionality should be applied. Thus nationals resident abroad should not be constrained to violate the law of the place of residence.'[33]

However, Brownlie notes that these principles may not apply in the case of crimes against international law.[34] Hence he admits that the gravity of a crime may alter the applicability of the above principles restricting the legality of non-territorial jurisdiction.

The lawfulness of an exercise of jurisdiction may be affected by the particular circumstances of each case, so they should be examined separately. Certain situations may lead to particular jurisdictions being legal while others are in breach of international law. For example, the ICJ ruled that the immunities enjoyed by an incumbent or former Minister for Foreign Affairs preclude any criminal prosecution against that person, thereby limiting the power of States to exercise jurisdiction. According to the ICJ judgment,[35] such a person enjoys no criminal immunity under international law in

---

33 Ian Brownlie, Principles of Public International Law 4th ed. (Clarendon Press, 1990), p. 310.

34 Brownlie explains that although the relations of customary law and general principles of law to jurisdiction are 'emanations of the concept of domestic jurisdiction and its concomitant, the principle of non-intervention in the internal affairs of other states' still applies. However, these basic principles do not apply to or are not very helpful in the case of crimes against international law. Ian Brownlie, *ibid.*, pp. 310-311.

35 ICJ Judgment of 14 February 2002 in the Case Concerning the Arrest Warrant of 11 April 2000 (*Democratic Republic of the Congo* v. *Belgium*), para.61. The ICJ listed four circumstances in which criminal prosecution against an incumbent or former Minister for Foreign Affairs is not precluded by the immunities. The four circumstances are (1) prosecution in their own countries; (2) after the waiver of the immunity by the State which they represent or have represented; (3) for a former Minister,

his or her State, therefore that State can exercise jurisdiction while other States may not, unless with the waiver of immunity by the former State. Also, other issues such as amnesty,[36] and statutes of limitation may be considered in determining the lawfulness of an exercise of jurisdiction.

To sum up, for a jurisdiction claimed by a State to be able to compete with other jurisdictions, it must be capable of being exercised lawfully under international law. However, in most situations where the legality of the jurisdiction is in doubt, the domestic authority refrain itself from taking any action, thereby terminating the proceedings before it yields an international conflict.[37]

4.2 Difficulty in Finding Rules Concerning the Venue of a Trial

Under international law, jurisdiction generally does not have an exclusive character,[38] thus concurrence of jurisdiction is maintained. But identifying some international law rules for determining the venue of a trial is difficult for many reasons. The first difficulty relates to the fact that the rules are not prescribed in a written or compiled form in either conventional or customary international law.

Another reason for this difficulty lies in the discretion granted to States in deciding whether or not to exercise their national jurisdiction over a case. Some treaties and conventions oblige State Parties to incorporate various bases of national jurisdiction into their domestic law, but do not oblige them to actually initiate criminal proceedings and to prosecute and punish a crime. States have discretion in deciding whether or not to exercise their jurisdiction, and over which crime, whom to prosecute and when to do so. The criteria which will trigger a State to exercise its jurisdiction over a case are considered to be within the discretion of each State and political and policy considerations may influence its choice.[39]

---

prosecution for acts other than those committed in an official capacity during his or her period of office; (4) prosecution before certain international criminal courts such as the ICTY, ICTR, and ICC. For a discussion on immunity within national courts, see Matthias Ruffert 'Pinochet Follow Up: The End of Sovereign Immunity?' *Netherlands International Law Review* Vol. XLVIII, 2001/2.

36 See, Roman Boed 'The Effect of a Domestic Amnesty on the Ability of Foreign States to Prosecute Alleged Perpetrators of Serious Human Rights Violations' *Cornell International Law Journal* Vol. 33 No. 2 (2000). See also, Massimo Starita 'Amnesty for Crimes Against Humanity: Coordinating the State and Individual Responsibility for Gross Violations of Human Rights' *Italian Yearbook of International Law* Vol. 9 (1999).

37 The French court (Cour de cassation) reversed the decision of the lower Cour d'appel and ackonwledged the immunity of the Libyan leader Muammar Al Qadaffi, thereby dismissing the criminal proceedings against him for a terrorist attack on a French aircraft in 1989. See Matthias Ruffert, *supra* note (35), pp. 173-174.

38 Brownlie also notes that jurisdiction is 'not based upon a principle of exclusiveness: the same acts may be within the lawful ambit of one or more jurisdictions.' See Ian Brownlie, *supra* note (33), p. 311.

39 For example, in relation to grave breaches of the Geneva Conventions or Additional Protocol I, common law States require the consent or authorization of the Attorney General or the Director of Public Prosecutions before bringing such a charge before the ordinary criminal courts. See Anna Segall,

This margin of discretion creates another difficulty as far as extradition is concerned. As I will explain later in this chapter and more extensively in Chapter VI, the decision on the venue of a trial is more or less in the hands of a State where a suspect is present. This is because a State where a suspect is present has the power to decide whether or not and to which State it will extradite the suspect, whereas many States do not allow a trial *in absentia*, requiring the presence of a suspect to continue prosecution. Therefore, at an initial stage, a custodial State has the power to virtually determine the venue of a trial. Regarding this power, a margin of discretion is preserved in most extradition treaties, and the decision by a custodial State is usually made *quasi-judicial / quasi-executive*, taking into consideration its foreign policy as well as other factors, including non-legal ones. Therefore, it is difficult to determine any rigid legal rules even within domestic law, and especially, under international law.

These difficulties exist in clarifying rules concerning the venue of a trial, but this study will tentatively consolidate some guiding rules by collecting evidence scattered over related law and relevant rules in international law.

4.3 Obligation Under Conventional Law

First of all, if a treaty encompasses a particular jurisdictional system, State Parties are obliged to respect this and to act accordingly. Indeed, many treaties and conventions provide for various bases of national jurisdiction, envisaging a concurrent jurisdictional regime and obliging State Parties to prepare domestic law enabling these jurisdictional bases. However, they often do not clarify the relations between the various bases of jurisdiction in their provision. For example, the Torture Convention acknowledges various jurisdictional bases – territorial jurisdiction, nationality jurisdiction, passive nationality jurisdiction, universal jurisdiction, and any other jurisdiction exercised in accordance with national law. Having said this, however, it does not have a provision clarifying the hierarchy between these jurisdictions. Some may interpret that supremacy is provided by the order of listing, but there is no proof of this. Overall, conventional international law is silent as to the hierarchy between jurisdictional bases.

4.4 Customary International Law

General international law does not prohibit any basis of national jurisdiction. Instead, it allows States to enjoy discretion in deciding what kind of jurisdiction they choose to incorporate in their domestic law. It also does not expressly state or establish any clear-cut customary law spelling out the order or supremacy among various bases of national jurisdiction. Therefore, we must rely on other norms to discover any implications for resolving jurisdictional problems. In order to identify some rules providing

---

Punishing Violations of International Humanitarian Law at the National Level: A Guide for Common Law States (International Committee of the Red Cross, 2001), p. 129.

guidance for solving jurisdictional conflicts, this study will devote particular attention to extradition law and the views of some scholars.

5 Looking for Evidence of Guiding Rules

5.1 Extradition Law

The rules and principles concerning extradition are fairly well-developed in international law. They are a reliable source in searching for some guiding rules in the event of concurrent jurisdictions. In my opinion, the rules concerning the handling of competing extradition requests deserve close examination.[40] This is because how a State decides on the supremacy of certain competing extradition requests reflects its understanding of the supremacy of jurisdiction. Therefore, this study takes into consideration those rules that provide guidance as to what to do when there are multiple extradition requests.

For example, Article 10 of the Extradition Treaty between the U.K. and the U.S. concluded on 1931 provides as follows:

> 'If the individual claimed by one of the High Contracting Parties in pursuance of the present Treaty should be also claimed by one or several other Powers on account of other crimes or offences committed within their respective jurisdictions, his extradition shall be granted to the Power whose claim is earliest in date, unless such claim is waived.'[41]

Compared to this, recent extradition treaties concluded by the U.S. list more factors to be considered. For example, the extradition treaty concluded between Hong Kong and the U.S. provides:

> ARTICLE 11 Concurrent Requests
> 'If the surrender of a fugitive offender is requested concurrently by one of the Parties and a State or States with which the United States of America or Hong Kong, whichever is being requested, has arrangements for the surrender of fugitive offenders, the executive authority of the requested Party shall make its decision having regard to all the circumstances, including the relevant provisions of such arrangements, the place of commission of the offences, their relative seriousness, the respective dates of the requests,

40 The law concerning extradition has in major respects been largely uniform and settled since classical international law. The Third Restatement explains that extradition was 'generally goverened by treaty and subject to various limitations. A network of bilateral treaties, differing in detail but having considerable similarity in principle and scope, has spelled out these limitations, and in conjunction with state legislation, practice, and judicial decisions has created a body of law with substantial uniformity in major respects.'

41 Extradition Treaty between the United States and the United Kingdom, signed at London on 22 December 22, 1931, 47 Stat. 2122; TS 849; 12 Bevans 482; 163 LNTS 59.

> the nationality of the fugitive offender, the nationality of the victim, and the possibility of subsequent surrender to another jurisdiction.'[42]

Similarly, Article 17 of the European Convention on Extradition (1960)[43] provides some guidance in the case of conflicting requests as follows:

> 'If extradition is requested concurrently by more than one State, either for the same offence or for different offences, the requested Party shall make its decision having regard to all the circumstances and especially the relative seriousness and place of commission of the offences, the respective dates of the requests, the nationality of the person claimed and the possibility of subsequent extradition to another State.'

One can also gain an insight from the ICC Statute. Although it prescribes the concurrence of national and international jurisdiction rather than competition between national jurisdictions, there is evidence of some criteria in giving priority to competing requests which may reflect a common understanding of the hierarchy between jurisdictions. Article 90 of the ICC Statute prescribes that, concerning competing requests for the extradition and surrender of the same person, priority should be given to the surrender request from the ICC. However, in a case where the requested State is under an existing international obligation to extradite the person to a requesting State which is not a Party to the ICC Statute, the same article prescribes as follows:

> '... [T]he requested State shall consider all the relevant factors, including but not limited to:
> (a) The respective date of the requests;
> (b)The interests of the requesting State including, where relevant, whether the crime was committed in its territory and the nationality of the victims and of the person sought ...'[44]

Many extradition treaties list the exceptions under which a State will not be obliged to extradite, or, furthermore, is actually prohibited from doing so. It can be argued that these provisions reflect those rules which are also relevant to the determination of the venue of a trial. By examining these provisions I will demonstrate later in this chapter how the human rights of a suspect become one criterion to be taken into consideration when deciding which jurisdiction supersedes others.

Not only the provisions of actual extradition treaties, but also the opinions of scholars are examined in this study as evidence of the rules concerning the venue of a trial. The materials examined include scholarly evaluations under classic international law as well as modern international law. For example, the International Commission of Jurists compiled various extradition laws and in 1912 proclaimed as follows:

---

42 Agreement for the Surrender of Fugitive Offenders between Hong Kong and the United States, reprinted on *International Legal Materials* Vol. 36 No. 4 (July 1997), p. 842.
43 European Convention on Extradition, entered into force on 18 April 1960, ETS No. 24.
44 Article 90(6) of the ICC Statute.

> 'If several nations request the extradition of the same person for the same act, the nation in whose territory the offense has been committed shall be given preferential attention; if the extradition is requested for different acts, the nation to be given preference shall be the one in which the gravest offense has been committed, in the opinion of the nation of refuge; or if the acts are of equal gravity, the first nation to request extradition shall be given the preference. When all the requests are presented on the same day, that of prior date shall prevail; if all are of equal date, the nation requested shall determine the order to be followed. ...'[45]

Also, the Draft Extradition Convention adopted by the International Law Association in 1928 stated as follows:

> 'Art. 13 Should several States demand the extradition of a person, either for the same or for different acts, the State applied to shall decide at its discretion which application shall rank first. In this case it shall be taken into consideration that preference is usually given in the first place to the State where the crime or offence is committed and in the second place to the application in respect of a crime or offence liable to a more severe punishment.
>
> If an application is made to surrender a person who is not a national either of the State or of one of the States making the application, the State applied to may in the first place notify the State of which the person is a national, and if this State does not demand the extradition, the State applied to shall decide at its discretion to which State it shall grant the extradition.'[46]

Another example is the compiled extradition law reported by Charles Burdick, which was drafted following an extensive study of various bilateral extradition treaties as well as the domestic law of States. It prescribes as follows:

> 'Article 8 Conflicting Requisitions
>
> (a) When a requested State receives from two or more States requisitions for the same person for the same act, the requested State shall, in extraditing the person claimed, give preference to that requesting State in whose territory the act was committed. If the act was committed in the territory of more than one requesting State or in the territory of a non-requesting State, the requested State shall extradite the person claimed to the requesting State whose requisition is first received. ...'[47]

---

45 'Project for an American Extradition Convention drafted by the International Commission of Jurists at Rio de Janeiro, 1912', Article 12, printed in *Supplement to the American Journal of International Law* Vol. 29 No. 1 & 2 (January and April, 1935), p. 303.

46 'Draft Extradition Convention Approved by the International Law Association in 1928', printed in *Supplement to the American Journal of International Law* Vol. 29 Nos. 1 & 2 (January and April, 1935), p. 311.

47 See Article 8 of the 'Draft Convention on Extradition', *Supplement to the American Journal of International Law* Vol. 29 Nos. 1 and 2 (January and April 1935), pp. 22-23.

An examination of extradition law and scholarly literature reveal that, ever since the classical jurisdictional regime, some criteria have been noted which are of assistance to a requested State with competing extradition requests to make a decision. It also illustrates that preference is generally given to territorial jurisdiction and nationality jurisdiction if the suspect is present in its territory. I will take into the consideration the observation deduced from the rules and principles concerning extradition in compiling guiding rules for deciding the venue of a trial.

5.2 The Third Restatement

One effort to compile and clarify factors to be relied upon in determining the appropriateness of a jurisdiction can be found in Section 403 of the Third Restatement. The Third Restatement determines that, in addition to the requirement that a jurisdiction must correspond to one of a jurisdictional bases recognized under international law, the exercise of jurisdiction must not be 'unreasonable'. Section 403 of the Third Restatement states as follows:

> § 403. Limitations on Jurisdiction to Prescribe
> '(1) Even when one of the bases for jurisdiction under § 402 is present, a state may not exercise jurisdiction to prescribe law with respect to a person or activity having connections with another state when the exercise of such jurisdiction is unreasonable.
> (2) Whether exercise of jurisdiction over a person or activity is unreasonable is determined by evaluating all relevant factors, including, where appropriate:
> (a) the link of the activity to the territory of the regulating state, i.e., the extent to which the activity takes place within the territory, or has substantial, direct, and foreseeable effect upon or in the territory;
> (b) the connections, such as nationality, residence, or economic activity, between the regulating state and the person principally responsible for the activity to be regulated, or between that state and those whom the regulation is designed to protect;
> (c) the character of the activity to be regulated, the importance of regulation to the regulating state, the extent to which other states regulate such activities, and the degree to which the desirability of such regulation is generally accepted;
> (d) the existence of justified expectations that might be protected or hurt by the regulation;
> (e) the importance of the regulation to the international political, legal, or economic system;
> (f) the extent to which the regulation is consistent with the traditions of the international system;
> (g) the extent to which another state may have an interest in regulating the activity; and
> (h) the likelihood of conflict with regulation by another state.
> (3) When it would not be unreasonable for each of two states to exercise jurisdiction over a person or activity, but the prescriptions by the two states are in conflict, each state has an obligation to evaluate its own as well as the other state's interest in exercising

> jurisdiction, in light of all the relevant factors, Subsection (2); a state should defer to the other state if that state's interest is clearly greater.'[48]

The Third Restatement maintains that this requirement of *reasonableness* has not only become part of the U.S. law of foreign relations, but also a rule of international law.[49] On the other hand, other authors argue that the rule of reasonableness is not a rule of international law, but, instead, merely a manifestation of comity.[50] However, the Third Restatement explains that the rule of reasonableness is different from a requirement of 'comity', because the rule of reasonableness applies regardless of the status of relations between the State exercising jurisdiction and the other State whose interests may be affected. Moreover, it is not conditional upon reciprocity.[51]

Section 403 (3) of the Third Restatement envisages a positive conflict of jurisdiction – a situation where there is more than one State claiming jurisdiction over the same case or person. In that case, it requires each State to evaluate its own interests in exercising jurisdiction as well as those of the other State. If such an evaluation concludes that one State has 'clearly a greater' interest in its exercise, then other States should defer to it. In weighing the interests of a foreign State, 'a court in the United States may take into account indications of national interest by the foreign government, whether made through a diplomatic note, a brief amicus curiae, or a declaration by government officials in parliamental debates, press conferences, or communiqués.'[52]

5.3 The Princeton Principles

Principle 8 of the Princeton Principles is another example of a compilation of rules concerning modern concurrent jurisdiction regimes. It states as follows:

> Principle 8 on the Resolution of Competing National Jurisdictions
> 'Where more than one state has or may assert jurisdiction over a person and where the state that has custody of the person has no basis for jurisdiction other than the principle of universality, that state or its judicial organs shall, in deciding whether to prosecute or extradite, base their decision on an aggregate balance of the following criteria:
> (a) multilateral or bilateral treaty obligations;
> (b) the place of commission of the crime;
> (c) the nationality connection of the alleged perpetrator to the requesting state;
> (d) the nationality connection of the victim to the requesting state;

---

48 The American Law Institute, *Restatement of the Law: The Foreign Relations Law of the United States Vol. 1* (American Law Institute Publishers, 1987), (referred in this study as Third Restatement), pp. 244-245.

49 Third Restatement, *ibid.*, p. 245.

50 See in M. Cherif Bassiouni ed., *International Criminal Law Vol. II: Procedural and Enforcement Mechanisms*, 2nd ed., (Transnational Publishers, 1999), p. 175.

51 Third Restatement, *supra* note (48), p. 246.

52 Third Restatement, *ibid.*, p. 251.

(e) any other connection between the requesting state and the alleged perpetrator, the crime, or the victim;
(f) the likelihood, good faith, and effectiveness of the prosecution in the requesting state;
(g) the fairness and impartiality of the proceedings in the requesting state;
(h) convenience to the parties and witnesses, as well as the availability of evidence in the requesting state; and
(i) the interests of justice.'

It lists the criteria to be considered by a custodial State in deciding whether to extradite or exercise universal jurisdiction. It can be summarised that the Princeton Principles propose to consider the nexus between the State and the crime (criteria (a)-(e)), and the manner of conducting a trial in order to enable a better and effective administration of justice (criteria (f)-(i)).

5.4 The Brussels Principles

The Brussels Principles Against Impunity and for International Justice, which were adopted following an international conference in which many scholars and lawyers participated, propose to resolve jurisdictional conflicts as follows:

> 'Positive conflicts of jurisdiction that may ensue from the exercise of universal jurisdiction in the case of serious crimes should be settled through consultations or negotiations between the states concerned, and taking into account all relevant circumstances, in particular, the gravity of the crime, the place where it occurred, the date on which the proceedings were initiated, the place of residence of the victims, the nationality of the presumed author, or the observance of the rules governing the right to a fair trial.'[53]

These proposals and others put forward by scholars, together with the interpretation of other rules under international law, demonstrate that jurisdiction should not be exercised unreasonably, and its appropriateness should be measured and compared to that of other jurisdictions.

6 Compilation of Guiding Rules

Taking into consideration the extradition law and various scholarly works and proposals, this section reviews and compiles the criteria to be used in assessing the appropriateness of jurisdiction. Some of these criteria may not amount to legally binding standards in a strict sense, but together they serve to indicate some guiding principles.

53 Principle 15(2) of the 'Brussels Principles Against Impunity and for International Justice', *supra* note (1).

6.1 The Nexus Rule

The nexus rule is relied upon in various situations to determine the legality of the jurisdiction as well as its appropriateness. This study notes that the nexus rule has been associated with the preference for territorial jurisdiction, as explained below. I will examine how the nexus rule can be associated with the responsibility of States to exercise jurisdiction over a case.

It is generally understood that States asserting jurisdiction should have some *nexus* (link) with the crime. In this study, this is referred to as *the nexus rule*. As evidenced above, the law and practice of extradition as well as the opinions of scholars take into consideration the relationship between a crime and the State claiming jurisdiction over it. For example, the Third Restatement notes that the nexus is one of the relevant factors in deciding upon the reasonableness of the jurisdiction. It takes special cognisance of territorial and active nationality jurisdiction.[54]

Within the U.S. legal system, the term 'sufficient nexus test' is used to refer to a requirement of a sufficient nexus between defendants and the U.S., even for a crime committed in the U.S.; therefore, the nexus serves as an additional requirement for territorial jurisdiction which is sufficient enough to comply with standards of due process and fairness.[55] However, 'the nexus rule' referred to in this study suggests that it is generally believed that the stronger the nexus, the stronger the interest of a State in prosecution, and that this State can thereby maintain its claim of jurisdiction against, and prevail over, other States.

6.1.1 Preference for Territorial Jurisdiction

Many authors employ the nexus rule to suggest a hierarchy among various bases of jurisdiction, which should consequently resolve positive conflicts of jurisdiction. For example, Bassiouni, seemingly based on this idea, suggests such a hierarchy and lists bases of national jurisdiction in their order of supremacy: territorial jurisdiction, followed by nationality jurisdiction, and finally passive personality jurisdiction.[56]

The nexus rule is most often employed as evidence of the supremacy of territorial jurisdiction. Territorial jurisdiction has a long history of being acknowledged as the most common basis for the exercise of jurisdiction. The Harvard Research concluded that all States assert criminal jurisdiction on the basis of territory and nationality, whilst the Third Restatement states that '[t]erritoriality is considered the normal, and nationality an exceptional, basis for the exercise of jurisdiction.'[57] Territorial jurisdic-

54 Section 403(2)(a) and (b) of the Third Restatement.

55 See M. Cherif Bassiouni ed., *International Criminal Law Vol. II Procedure and Enforcement Mechanisms*, 2nd ed. (Transnational Publishers, 1999), p. 89.

56 See M. Cherif Bassiouni, *International Criminal Law: A Draft International Criminal Code* (1980), p. 145.

57 The Third Restatement, p. 238.

tion was believed to lead to the most efficient administration of justice.[58] Its supremacy is based on the long history of the dominance of territorial jurisdiction under the classical jurisdictional regime.

Evidence of the dominance of territorial jurisdiction can also be found in extradition law.[59] Under the classical jurisdictional regime, the overwhelming majority of extradition treaties concerned offences committed outside the territory of a requested State.[60] Many treaties specifically allowed States to refuse extradition for crimes committed within their territory. In addition, many extradition treaties gave preference to the extradition request of the territorial State. Even today, extradition law seems to give a somewhat a preferential status to territorial jurisdiction.

The preference for territorial jurisdiction was also affirmed by many scholars under classical international law. For example, the ninth section of the Resolution adopted by the Institute of International Law in 1880 stated that '[i]f there are several requests for extradition for the same act, preference should be given to the State upon whose territory the offense was committed.'[61] A similar acknowledgment of preference for territorial jurisdiction can be seen in many other documents such as the Draft Extradition Convention approved by the International Law Association in 1928.[62] The Draft Convention on Extradition prepared by Burdick which was published in a journal in 1935 also gave territorial jurisdiction priority in several respects, namely in the refusal of extradition requested by a non-territorial State,[63] or for crimes committed on the territory of the requested State.[64] Territorial jurisdiction was also given preference

58 See the comment on Article 7 of the 'Draft Convention on Extradition', *Supplement to the American Journal of International Law* Vol. 29 Nos. 1 and 2 (January and April 1935).

59 For example, the Institute of International Law stated that preference is given to the territorial State over the State of nationality of the suspect. It asserted as follows: '6. Between countries whose criminal legislations rest upon similar bases and which have mutual confidence in their judicial institutions, extradition of nationals would be a means of assuring good administration of penal justice because it should be considered as desirable that the jurisdiction of the *forum delicti commissi* be so far as possible called upon to render judgment.' See, 'Resolution Adopted by the Institute of International Law (Oxford, 9 September 1880)', printed in *Supplement to the American Journal of International Law* Vol. 29 No. 1 & 2 (January and April, 1935), p. 300.

60 See 'Draft Convention on Extradition', *Supplement to the American Journal of International Law* Vol. 29 Nos. 1 and 2 (January and April 1935), p. 86.

61 'Resolution Adopted by the Institute of International Law (Oxford, 9 September 1880)', printed in *Supplement to the American Journal of International Law* Vol. 29 Nos. 1 & 2 (January and April, 1935), p. 300.

62 See Article 13 of Draft Extradition Convention Approved by the International Law Association in 1928, *supra* note (46), p. 311. It stated as follows:
'Art. 13 Should several States demand the extradition of a person, either for the same or for different acts, the State applied to shall decide at its discretion which application shall rank first. In this case it shall be taken into consideration that preference is usually given in the first place to the State where the crime or offence is committed ….'

63 Article 3(b) of 'Draft Convention on Extradition', *Supplement to the American Journal of International Law* Vol. 29 Nos. 1 and 2 (January and April 1935), p. 21.

64 Article 3(a) of 'Draft Convention on Extradition', *ibid.*

where competing extradition requests were involved.[65] This was explained as the inevitable consequence of the universal acceptance of territoriality as the primary basis of competence.[66] In sum, the preferential status of territorial jurisdiction clearly existed. However, it should be noted that the strong preference for territorial jurisdiction does not preclude other jurisdictions being found more reasonable following the consideration of other rules, which will be elucidated upon next.

6.1.2 Nationality Jurisdiction

It is noted that even under the classical jurisdictional regime, one situation is generally recognized as justifying the refusal of an extradition request from a territorial State: when the person who is the subject of extradition is a national of a requested State. International law neither prohibits nor obliges the extradition of nationals in general. It is argued that there is a custom which allows a State to refuse extradition when the suspect is its national. This means that the State of which a suspect is a national may defeat territorial jurisdiction of another State when the suspect is present within its territory. Therefore, it can be construed that the State having both a nexus of nationality and the presence of the individual is in a strong position to compete against other jurisdictions, even the territorial jurisdiction of another State.

In general, nationality jurisdiction is widely recognized and accepted, alongside territorial jurisdiction. As a result, respect for nationality jurisdiction has been expressed in various instruments, even in the Statute of the ICC. Article 12 of the ICC Statute provides due respect for national jurisdiction by providing the consent of the territorial State or the State of the nationality of a suspect as a prerequisite for the exercise of ICC jurisdiction.[67] Another example of the manifestation of respect for nationality jurisdiction can be seen in the Statute of the Special Court for Sierra Leone which provides that peacekeepers who have 'transgressed' would, in the first instance, be subject to the jurisdiction of their sending State.[68]

---

65 See Article 8 of 'Draft Convention on Extradition', *ibid.*, pp. 22-23.

66 See 'Draft Convention on Extradition', *ibid.*, p. 86.

67 This does not mean that the ICC exercises national jurisdiction deferred from the territory or State of the nationality of a suspect. See my article, 'The Meaning of the State Consent Precondition in Article 12(2) of the Rome Statute of the International Criminal Court: A Theoretical Analysis of the Source of International Criminal Jurisdiction' *Netherlands International Law Review* Vol. XLIX, Issue 2 (2002), pp. 159-193.

68 See Article 1(2) of the Statute of the Special Court for Sierra Leone, UN Doc. 2002/246. However, in accordance with Article 1(3), if the sending State is unwilling or unable to investigate or prosecute, then the Special Court of Sierra Leone can exercise its jurisdiction upon the authorisation of the UN Security Council. Article 1 prescribes as follows:
Article 1 Competence of the Special Court
'1. The Special Court shall, except as provided in subparagraph (2), have the power to prosecute persons who bear the greatest responsibility for serious violations of international humanitarian law and Sierra Leonean law committed in the territory of Sierra Leone since 30 November 1996, including those leaders who, in committing such crimes, have threatened the establishment of and implementa-

6.1.3 *Exceptions to the Nexus Rule*

The exception to the requirement of a nexus is universal jurisdiction *in absentia*. Unlike ordinary universal jurisdiction claimed by a State where a suspect is present, universal jurisdiction *in absentia* can be claimed by any State with no connection to the crime in question.

As explained in the preceding chapter, this form of jurisdiction is not prohibited under international law. Furthermore, it is maintained that some offences are so heinous and harmful to the foundations of humanity, that the perpetrators of such offences are *hostis humani generis* – the enemies of all humankind. For such offences, it is argued that no limitation should be set by any territorial boundary or nationality.

In the light of the nexus rule, however, universal jurisdiction *in absentia* is in a relatively weak position compared to others in the competition for jurisdiction over a case. The lack of a nexus implies that the State has a weaker interest compared to other States having a stronger nexus to the crime in question. Therefore, in accordance with the nexus rule, jurisdiction other than universal jurisdiction *in absentia* is likely to be given preference, and will be considered to be appropriate. In the case of a positive conflict, a State claiming universal jurisdiction *in absentia,* notwithstanding the existence of other States willing to exercise their jurisdiction, should have a good reason to dismiss the possibility of a trial in States having a stronger nexus. It may be desirable to rely on more ordinary jurisdiction than on universal jurisdiction *in absentia* at the present stage of the development of international law and the international community since the implementation of pure universality is not yet widely or readily accepted by the international community.

6.1.4 *The Nexus Rule and Responsibility*

Above, the nexus rule is described as a rule that may indicate preference for a particular jurisdiction, thereby solving positive conflicts of jurisdiction. Moreover, the nexus rule can be employed to resolve a negative conflict of jurisdiction as well. Most often, the nexus rule is discussed in relation to the *right* of States to exercise their jurisdiction. Therefore it appears to be irrelevant to a situation where no State exercises its right. However, in my opinion, the nexus rule can be employed to strengthen the enforcement mechanism of international law by considering it in association with the

---

tion of the peace process in Sierra Leone.
2. Any transgressions by peacekeepers and related personnel present in Sierra Leone pursuant to the Status of Mission Agreement in force between the United Nations and the Government of Sierra Leone or agreements between Sierra Leone and other Governments or regional organizations, or, in the absence of such agreement, provided that the peacekeeping operations were undertaken with the consent of the Government of Sierra Leone, shall be within the primary jurisdiction of the sending State.
3. In the event the sending State is unwilling or unable to genuinely to carry out an investigation or prosecution, the Court may, if authorized by the Security Council on the proposal of any State, exercise jurisdiction over such persons.'

responsibility of States. In other words, the nexus can imply not only the stronger interest of States and their right over the matter, but also their responsibility. It may be reminded that one of the new trends in international criminal law is that jurisdictions are increasingly provided for in treaties, not just as rights, but as obligations. In addition, the prosecution and punishment of gross violations of human rights are beginning to be perceived as an obligation on the part of States. I consider that the nexus rule would be useful in materializing a concrete and practical rule for obliging States to act. Unfortunately, the responsibility of *all* States in the international community to prosecute and punish gross human rights violations is still an abstract notion which is not yet fully reliable as an effective measure to end impunity. Therefore, individual States, rather than the international community as a whole, are heavily relied upon. In this present situation, naming particular States to be subject to greater responsibility than others may contribute to attaining real prosecution and punishment. In my opinion, States with a stronger nexus should have greater responsibility in realizing the interest of the international community in ending impunity by means of their special connection with the crime in question.

However, the above proposition should not be interpreted as precluding other States with a weaker nexus from exercising jurisdiction or from being obliged to exercise jurisdiction. For instance, as I explained in the previous chapter, in addition to those States with a strong nexus such as territoriality or nationality, the responsibility of a State where a suspect is present may be deduced from the notion of State sovereignty.

6.2 Weighing of Interests

In resolving a positive conflict of jurisdiction, the interests of the States involved may be compared. Indeed, the need for balancing certain interests is one origin of international law. The fundamental objectives of international law concerning jurisdiction are to establish limits of jurisdiction to protect the independence and sovereign equality of States, and to balance each State's interest in exercising jurisdiction in order to advance its own policies with each State's interest in avoiding interference with its policies resulting from the exercise of jurisdiction by foreign States, and also to harmonize the rights of two or more States when they have concurrent jurisdiction.[69] In short, it is understood that jurisdiction rests upon reconciling a State's interest in a particular case with other States' interests.[70]

The Third Restatement incorporates the weighing of interests as one of the criteria in deciding upon reasonableness. Lagodny also includes this as one criterion of 'quality', giving preference to the jurisdiction with the '*best quality*' in deciding which State should be the one to exercise jurisdiction. He explains 'quality' as follows:

---

69 Bernard H. Oxman, *supra* note (12), p. 56.

70 See Edwin D. Dickinson 'Jurisdiction with Respect to Crime', work conducted for Harvard Research in International Law, *Supplement to the American Journal of International Law* Vol. 29 (1935), pp. 435, 443-447.

> 'The criteria for the "quality" are not at all confined to the principles of jurisdiction (territoriality, personality, etc.) but – also if not mainly – include the interests of the prosecution (e.g., in which state is the most important evidence?) and those of the individual (e.g., where is the domicile?).'[71]

A similar criterion is recognised by Strapatsas, who observes that academics propose to solve the issue of *forum conveniens* by means of two criteria: The first is the effective link and the second is to compare and weigh the interests of States. He notes that in the case of several competing jurisdictions, the State that has the least interest in comparison with the others should yield to them.[72] He explains that this criterion is the preferable link theory to which the test of 'reasonableness' is applied in order to determine which State has the most interest in the matter.[73] In sum, it is considered that the State with the greater interest in prosecuting a crime should be the one to conduct a trial, and other States should defer to it.

Unlike the rule of reasonableness proposed by the Third Restatement, in my opinion it should be more than a simple comparison of national interests. In weighing and balancing interests, I think that various interests should be taken into consideration – not only those of individual States, but also those of the international community, peace and stability, integrity and administration of justice, the victims and suspects, etc.

Some activists argue that the status accorded to the individual interest of States is contrary to globalization. They may argue that the prosecution of gross violations of human rights should not be influenced by the individual national interest which is often based on egotistical claims of jurisdiction and which ultimately benefit a selfish State. However, the consideration of interests other than those of individual States does not mean that every individual State interest contradicts the interest of the international community. A State claiming jurisdiction might have various reasons for desiring a trial within its legal system, but such interests may simultaneously serve the interest of the international community. For instance, it may be that a State has a strong interest in conducting a trial itself in order to save its reputation as a State governed by the rule of law. Or it may signify the interest of a State in building trust and confidence within the State. Adjudicating a case in its domestic courts may be desired in order to prove and convince its nationals that the government authority and themselves have now recovered or established a peaceful environment governed by the rule of law. A State has an interest in taking measures which it ultimately considers to be in the best interest of its citizens, and it may be in the interest of the State to comfort victims by

---

71 See Otto Lagodny 'Comparative Overview', in Albin Eser, Otto Lagodny and Christopher L. Blakesley eds., *The Individual as Subject of International Cooperation in Criminal Matters: A Comparative Study* (Nomos Verlagsgesellschaft, Baden-Baden, 2002), pp. 739-740.

72 See Nicolaos Strapatsas 'Universal Jurisdiction and the International Criminal Court' *Manitoba Law Journal* Vol. 29 No. 1, p. 4.

73 See, Nicolaos Strapatsas, *ibid.*, note 23 on p. 4.

showing that justice can be done before their very eyes. This may be aspired to as a means by which to contribute to building peace in a particular region. My point is that the interest of the international community may bring about the best result by taking into consideration these interests which are particular to a certain State, rather than ignoring them.

Having observed that various interests not limited to that of an individual State should be considered in comparing the interests in prosecution, the determination of which jurisdiction is more appropriate compared to others depends on the situation of each case. In situations where the jurisdiction of a State is not effectively exercised against gross violations of human rights, then the interests of justice and of the international community as a whole may compel other States to exercise jurisdiction. Therefore, the conclusion deriving from this criterion depends on each individual situation.

6.3 Comparing the Gravity of the Crime

It is often considered that when there is more than one State claiming jurisdiction over a person, the claim based on the gravest offence should be given preference. This criterion of the gravity of charges has been asserted in scholarly works and treaties since the time of classical international law as a means of resolving the problem of competing extradition requests from several States. For example, the tenth section of the resolution adopted by the Institute of International Law in 1880 describes how competing requests for extradition should be resolved:

> '10. If the same person is demanded by several States by reason of different offenses, the requested State will in general have regard to the relative gravity of these offenses.
> In case of doubt concerning the relative gravity of the offenses, the requested State will take into account priority of demand.'[74]

The International Commission of Jurists also proclaimed in 1912 that 'if the extradition is requested for different acts, the nation to be given preference shall be the one in which the gravest offense has been committed in the opinion of the nation of refuge'.[75] Similarly, the Draft Extradition Convention approved by the International Law Association in 1928 listed 'the application in respect of a crime or offence liable to a more severe punishment' as the second consideration following the preference for territorial jurisdiction.[76] More recently, the UN Sub-Commission on Human Rights

74 'Resolution Adopted by the Institute of International Law (Oxford, 9 September 1880)', printed in *Supplement to the American Journal of International Law* Vol. 29 Nos. 1 & 2 (January and April, 1935), p. 300.

75 See, 'Project for an American Extradition Convention drafted by the International Commission of Jurists at Rio de Janeiro, 1912', Article 12, printed in *Supplement to the American Journal of International Law* Vol. 29 Nos. 1 & 2 (January and April, 1935), p. 303.

76 'Draft Extradition Convention Approved by the International Law Association in 1928', *supra* note (46), p. 311.

proclaimed that it believes that 'the highest priority should be given, independently of the circumstances in which these violations were committed, to legal proceedings against all individuals responsible for war crimes and crimes against humanity, including former heads of State or Government – whose exile serves as pretext for their impunity – in order, by example, to prevent future human rights violations.'[77] This criterion favouring proceedings in more grave crimes may overlap with the criterion of the weighing of interests, since the prosecution and punishment of such a grave crime is within the interest of the international community.

6.4 The Date of Initiating the Proceedings

The rule of 'first come, first served' is upheld in the extradition practice of many States and also in many extradition treaties.[78] The existence of this rule has been acknowledged by academics for a long time. For instance, with respect to competing extradition requests, in addition to giving supremacy to territorial jurisdiction and also the jurisdiction based on the allegation of a gravest offence, the International Commission of Jurists proclaimed in 1912 that 'the first nation to request extradition shall be given the preference. When all the requests are presented on the same day, that of prior date shall prevail; if all are of equal date, the nation requested shall determine the order to be followed. ...'[79]

6.5 Fairness and Impartiality of a Trial

6.5.1 Emphasis on Fairness and Impartiality

Lastly, this chapter examines a more controversial rule that may be considered in solving jurisdictional conflicts: the fairness and impartiality of a trial. It is beginning to be accepted that a trial should be conducted in a place where the human rights of suspects can be duly respected. The consequence is that States are expected to discourage the request for the extradition of a suspect made by a State lacking the minimum guarantees, and to give preference to the extradition request made by other States which can meet such requirements. This is a fairly new criterion compared to the others described above which originated in the classical jurisdictional regime. In my opinion, this criterion has become one of the guiding rules because international law

77 'Role of universal or extraterritorial competence in preventive action against impunity', UN Sub-Commission on Human Rights resolution 2000/24 (18 August 2000).

78 For example, Article 17 of the European Convention on Extradition (ETS No. 24) which entered into force on 18 April 1960 includes 'dates of the request' as one of factors to be taken into consideration in the case of conflicting requests.

79 'Project for an American Extradition Convention drafted by the International Commission of Jurists at Rio de Janeiro, 1912', Article 12, printed in *Supplement to the American Journal of International Law* Vol. 29 Nos. 1 & 2 (January and April, 1935), p. 303.

has generally started to emphasise the fairness and impartiality of trials. This emphasis on fairness and effectiveness derives from a belief that the prosecution and punishment of crimes only yields benefits if the proceedings were fair and effective. Hence, let us observe this recent trend before examining it as a criterion in solving jurisdictional conflicts.

The emphasis on fairness and impartiality in conducting a trial can be seen in many international instruments and practices. For instance, the Torture Convention prescribes in Article 7(3) that any person who is suspected of committing the crime of torture 'shall be guaranteed fair treatment at all stages of the proceedings.' Although the Montreal Convention lacked such a provision, it is noted that, in the Lockerbie Case introduced earlier in this chapter, the response of the UN Security Council demonstrated the new trend in international law which emphasizes fairness and impartiality during a trial.

Today's law and practice of extradition also demonstrates some evidence of emphasis being placed on fairness and impartiality. Under conventional and customary international law, States are prohibited from extraditing individuals in certain situations, such as when a charge is based on a political offence. But more recently, it has been recognized that States should not extradite individuals if they risk having their rights violated upon extradition. Principle 10(1) of the Princeton Principles contends that a State shall refuse an extradition request 'if the person sought is likely to face a death penalty sentence or to be subjected to torture or any other cruel, degrading, or inhuman punishment or treatment, or if it is likely that the person sought will be subjected to sham proceedings in which international due process norms will be violated and no satisfactory assurance to the contrary are provided.'[80]

The refusal of extradition based on the likelihood of sham proceedings is justified because the interest of the international community in ending impunity can only be served through a fair and impartial trial. In addition, it can also be explained with the logic of the Soering Case in which it was established that the act of extraditing a person to a State where a violation of human rights is foreseen constitutes a violation of the obligation to respect human rights.[81] Although this logic is rarely upheld in reality, theoretically it can be construed that the right to a fair and impartial trial is so fundamental that a State may not extradite a person to a State where it is foreseen that the person in question will face a violation of this right, otherwise it can find itself to be in violation of the individual's human rights.

6.5.2 The Influence of the Fair Trial Requirement on International Criminal Courts

The new trend of requiring fairness and impartiality is also reflected in, and enhanced through the Statutes of the international criminal courts. Since these Statutes concern

---

80 *The Princeton Principles on Universal Jurisdiction* (Princeton University, 2001).

81 See *Soering* v. *UK*, Judgment of 7 July 1989 of the European Court of Human Rights, Application No. 14038/88.

international criminal jurisdiction, one may criticize them as being irrelevant to this study which deals mainly with national jurisdictions. However, I will briefly introduce the relevant provisions of the Statutes because I consider it is important to note that the emphasis on the fairness and impartiality of a trial is a development of international law in general, not limited to national or international criminal jurisdiction alone. In my opinion, the concern expressed over the manner in which a trial is conducted characterizes a new direction of the development of international criminal law – the effort to assure fairness and impartiality in addition to filling the lacuna of jurisdiction to prosecute and to punish gross violations of human rights.

The Statutes of the *ad hoc* tribunal of the ICTY and ICTR provide that they have primacy over the national courts of all States. This primacy includes the capacity to retry a person even if the person has been convicted in a national court. Article 10(2) of the ICTY Statute and Article 9(2) of the ICTR Statute provide that the ICTY and ICTR can try a person once tried in a national court if the national proceedings were not impartial or independent, were designed to shield the accused from the trial in the ICTY or ICTR, or the case was not diligently prosecuted.

The emphasis on fairness and impartiality is more explicit in the ICC Statute. The ICC will admit a case if it finds that States are unwilling or unable to conduct a trial in the case. Article 17 of the ICC Statute provides as follows:

> 'Article 17 Issues of admissibility
> 1. Having regard to paragraph 10 of the Preamble and article 1, the Court shall determine that a case is inadmissible where:
> (a) The case is being investigated or prosecuted by a State which has jurisdiction over it, unless the State is unwilling or unable genuinely to carry out the investigation or prosecution;
> (b) The case has been investigated by a State which has jurisdiction over it and the State has decided not to prosecute the person concerned, unless the decision resulted from the unwillingness or inability of the State genuinely to prosecute;
> (c) The person concerned has already been tried for conduct which is the subject of the complaint, and a trial by the Court is not permitted under article 20, paragraph 3;
> (d) The case is not of sufficient gravity to justify further action by the Court.
> 2. In order to determine unwillingness in a particular case, the Court shall consider, having regard to the principles of due process recognized by international law, whether one or more of the following exist, as applicable:
> (a) The proceedings were or are being undertaken or the national decision was made for the purpose of shielding the person concerned from criminal responsibility for crimes within the jurisdiction of the Court referred to in article 5;
> (b) There has been an unjustified delay in the proceedings which in the circumstances is inconsistent with an intent to bring the person concerned to justice;
> (c) The proceedings were not or are not being conducted independently or impartially, and they were or are being conducted in a manner which, in the circumstances, is inconsistent with an intent to bring the person concerned to justice.
> 3. In order to determine inability in a particular case, the Court shall consider whether, due to a total or substantial collapse or unavailability of its national judicial system, the

State is unable to obtain the accused or the necessary evidence and testimony or otherwise unable to carry out its proceedings.'

These provisions noted above are an example of the interest of the international community in substantiating fair and impartial trials in order to end impunity.

6.5.3 The Content of the Criterion

The principle that a trial must be conducted in a fair and impartial manner is well accepted. While the importance of fair trials is hardly controversial, the precise content of this principle has given rise to some dispute. A fair trial can be conceived to contain two aspects. First, to ensure the human rights of a suspect, and second, in structural terms, as an institutional guarantee for maintaining a judicial mechanism free from bias.

6.5.3.1 The Human Rights Aspect

There are many treaties and conventions acknowledging the right to a fair and impartial trial as one of the fundamental human rights. Article 10 of the Universal Declaration of Human Rights prescribes that '[e]veryone is entitled in full equality to a fair and public hearing by an independent and impartial tribunal, in the determination of his rights and obligations and of any criminal charge against him.' In addition, the lengthy Article 14 of the International Covenant on Civil and Political Rights (ICCPR) guarantees the right to a fair trial as follows:

> '1. All persons shall be equal before the courts and tribunals. In the determination of any criminal charge against him, or of his rights and obligations in a suit at law, everyone shall be entitled to a fair and public hearing by a competent, independent and impartial tribunal established by law. The press and the public may be excluded from all or part of a trial for reasons of morals, public order (ordre public) or national security in a democratic society, or when the interest of the private lives of the Parties so requires, or to the extent strictly necessary in the opinion of the court in special circumstances where publicity would prejudice the interests of justice; but any judgement rendered in a criminal case or in a suit at law shall be made public except where the interest of juvenile persons otherwise requires or the proceedings concern matrimonial disputes of the guardianship of children.
> 2. Everyone charged with a criminal offence shall have the right to be presumed innocent until proved guilty according to law.
> 3. In the determination of any criminal charge against him, everyone shall be entitled to the following minimum guarantees, in full equality:
> a. to be informed promptly and in detail in a language which he understands of the nature and cause of the charge against him;
> b. to have adequate time and facilities for the preparation of his defence and to communicate with counsel of his own choosing;
> c. to be tried without undue delay;

d. to be tried in his presence, and to defend himself in person or through legal assistance of his own choosing; to be informed, if he does not have legal assistance, of this right; and to have legal assistance assigned to him, in any case where the interests of justice so require, and without payment by him in any such case if he does not have sufficient means to pay for it;
e. to examine, or have examined, the witnesses against him and to obtain the attendance and examination of witnesses on his behalf under the same conditions as witnesses against him;
f. to have the free assistance of an interpreter if he cannot understand or speak the language used in court;
g. not to be compelled to testify against himself or to confess guilt.
4. In the case of juvenile persons, the procedure shall be such as will take account of their age and the desirability of promoting their rehabilitation.
5. Everyone convicted of a crime shall have the right to his conviction and sentence being reviewed by a higher tribunal according to law.
6. When a person has by a final decision been convicted of a criminal offence and when subsequently his conviction has been reversed or he has been pardoned on the ground that a new or newly discovered fact shows conclusively that there has been a miscarriage of justice, the person who has suffered punishment as a result of such conviction shall be compensated according to law, unless it is proved that the non-disclosure of the unknown fact in time is wholly or partly attributable to him.
7. No one shall be liable to be tried or punished again for an offence for which he has already been finally convicted or acquitted in accordance with the law and penal procedure of each country.'

It is recognized that the right to be tried by an independent and impartial court is 'an absolute right that may suffer no exception.'[82] The Human Rights Committee has stated 'that a situation where the functions and competences of the judiciary and the executive are not clearly distinguishable or where the latter is able to control or direct the former is incompatible with the notion of an independent and impartial tribunal within the meaning of Article 14, paragraph 1, of the Covenant.'[83]

Also, the European Convention on Human Rights provides the right to a fair trial in Article 6.[84] It is also recognized with respect to extradition. Some people assert that

---

82 Comm. No. 263/1987, *Gonzalez del Rio* v. *Peru*, views of 28 October 1992, CCPR/C/46/D/263/1987, para. 5.2.

83 *Oló Bahamonde* v. *Equatorial Guinea*, Communication No. 468/1991, UN Doc. CCPR/C/49/D/468/1991 (1993).

84 The European Convention on Human Rights prescribes as follows:
'Article 6 Right to a Fair Trial
1. In the determination of his civil rights and obligations or of any criminal charge against him, everyone is entitled to a fair and public hearing within a reasonable time by an independent and impartial tribunal established by law. Judgment shall be pronounced publicly but the press and public may be excluded from all or part of the trial in the interests of morals, public order or national security in a democratic society, where the interests of juveniles or the protection of the private life of the parties so require, or to the extent strictly necessary in the opinion of the court in special circumstances where

it is a part of customary international law with *jus cogens* character to deny extradition where the individual is in serious danger of being tried by a 'tribunal d'exception', or being subjected to inhuman or degrading treatment, or where the criminal justice system in the requesting State falls short of the basic rights and guarantees contemplated by the European Convention of Human Rights and Fundamental Freedoms or the UN Covenant on Civil and Political Rights.[85] Also, Article 3 of the UN Model Treaty on Extradition prescribes that extradition shall not be granted in the following circumstances:

> '(a) If the offence for which extradition is requested is regarded by the requested State as an offence of a political nature;
> (b) If the requested State has substantial grounds for believing that the request for extradition has been made for the purpose of prosecuting or punishing a person on account of that person's race, religion, nationality, ethnic origin, political opinions, sex or status, or that that person's position may be prejudiced for any of those reasons;
> (c) If the offence for which extradition is requested is an offence under military law, which is not also an offence under ordinary criminal law;
> (d) If there has been a final judgement rendered against the person in the requested State in respect of the offence for which the person's extradition is requested;
> (e) If the person whose extradition is requested has, under the law of either Party, become immune from prosecution or punishment for any reason, including lapse of time or amnesty;
> (f) If the person whose extradition is requested has been or would be subjected in the requesting State to torture or cruel, inhuman or degrading treatment or punishment or if that person has not received or would not receive the minimum guarantees in criminal proceedings, as contained in the International Covenant on Civil and Political Rights, article 14;
> (g) If the judgement of the requesting State has been rendered in absentia, the convicted person has not had sufficient notice of the trial or the opportunity to arrange for his or

---

publicity would prejudice the interests of justice.
2. Everyone charged with a criminal offence shall be presumed innocent until proved guilty according to law.
3. Everyone charged with a criminal offence has the following minimum rights:
a. to be informed promptly, in a language which he understands and in detail, of the nature and cause of the accusation against him;
b. to have adequate time and facilities for the preparation of his defence;
c. to defend himself in person or through legal assistance of his own choosing or, if he has not sufficient means to pay for legal assistance, to be given it free when the interests of justice so require;
d. to examine or have examined witnesses against him and to obtain the attendance and examination of witnesses on his behalf under the same conditions as witnesses against him;
e. to have the free assistance of an interpreter if he cannot understand or speak the language used in court.'

85 See Dominique Poncet and Paul Gully-Hart 'Legal Framework of Extradition in Europe', in M. Cherif Bassiouni ed., *International Criminal Law Vol. II: Procedural and Enforcement Mechanisms*, 2nd ed. (Transnational Publishers, 1999), pp. 284-285.

> her defence and he has not had or will not have the opportunity to have the case retried in his or her presence.'[86]

Similarly, Principle 20 of the Brussels Principles Against Impunity and for International Justice recommends concluding a treaty with universal reach in relation to extradition and judicial co-operation. At the same time, it proposes as follows:

> '3. The treaty should likewise provide for:
> a) the refusal to extradite a person to a state where he or she would run the risk of being sentenced to death; however, such an extradition could be authorized if sufficient guarantees are provided that the sentence in question will not be executed.
> b) the refusal to extradite when there are serious grounds to believe that:
> i. the person liable to be extradited will be subjected to torture or to sentences or treatments deemed inhuman or degrading;
> ii. the extradition request was submitted with a view to prosecuting or punishing a person because of his or her race, religion, nationality or political views, or that the situation of the person in question is likely to be aggravated for one of these reasons.
> iii. The person liable to be extradited has been the object or will be the object of a flagrant denial of justice.
> 4. In case of application of the *aut judicare* principle, the said treaty should provide for the transfer of the presumed authors before national jurisdictions that respect the principles of a fair trial.'

It is contended that since the right to a fair and impartial trial is recognized as a human right it should be considered in extradition procedures as well. However, given that fairness and impartiality is to be considered in determining the appropriateness of the exercise of jurisdiction and the venue of a trial, there is difficulty in determining the accurate standard. As the provisions cited above demonstrate, numerous rights are proclaimed. Should all of them be considered as human rights criteria to be taken into consideration in assessing the appropriateness of a particular jurisdiction? If only some of them, which one? Even the minimum guarantees of human rights for a suspect are composed of various different rights. For example, Article 11 of the Draft Code of Crimes Against the Peace and Security of Mankind extensively prescribes the minimum guarantees as follows:

> '1. An individual charged with a crime against the peace and security of mankind shall be presumed innocent until proved guilty and shall be entitled without discrimination to the minimum guarantees due to all human beings with regard to the law and facts and shall have the rights:
> (a) in the determination of any charge against him, to have a fair and public hearing by a competent, independent and impartial tribunal duly established by law;

86 Model Treaty on Extradition, adopted by the UN General Assembly, A/RES/45/116 (14 December 1990), annex.

> (b) to be informed promptly and in detail in a language which he understands of the nature and cause of the charge against him;
> (c) to have adequate time and facilities for the preparation of his defence and to communicate with counsel of his own choosing;
> (d) to be tried without undue delay;
> (e) to be tried in his presence, and to defend himself in person or through legal assistance of his own choosing; to be informed, if he does not have legal assistance, of this right; and to have legal assistance assigned to him and without payment by him if he does not have sufficient means to pay for it;
> (f) to examine, or have examined, the witnesses against him and to obtain the attendance and examination of witnesses on his behalf under the same conditions as witnesses against him;
> (g) to have the free assistance of an interpreter if he cannot understand or speak the language used in court;
> (h) not to be compelled to testify against himself or to confess guilt.
> 2. An individual convicted of a crime shall have the right to his conviction and sentence being reviewed according to law.'[87]

It may be disputed whether all the above minimum guarantees should be considered or some of them. In addition, there may be an argument as to whether or not to consider the possible punishment by death when determining the appropriateness of jurisdiction. In the Niyonteze Case, Switzerland proceeded with the prosecution in its domestic courts of a Rwandan for war crimes in violation of common Article 3 of the 1949 Geneva Conventions and of Additional Protocol II, even though it had received an extradition request from Rwanda.[88] Swiss domestic law prohibits extradition if the requesting State cannot guarantee that the person will not be subject to the death penalty, and Rwandan domestic law, specifically enacted in response to the genocide crisis, provides the death penalty for certain categories of crimes. Consequently, it can be observed that Switzerland gave preference to its universal jurisdiction over the territorial jurisdiction of Rwanda. However, such a determination based on the possibility of the death penalty may be criticized from States which retain such a penalty for grave crimes. The content of the criterion is still a point of argument.

6.5.3.2 The Institutional Guarantee

It is undeniable that fairness and impartiality are vital, and great efforts are being made to ensure that this principle is one of the human rights pertaining to suspects. However, when they are considered as one of the criteria in evaluating the appropriateness of a

87 Draft Code of Crimes Against the Peace and Security of Mankind, Report of the International Law Commission on the Work of its Forty-Eighth Session, UN Doc. A/51/10.

88 *Niyonteze* v. *Public Prosecutor*, Swiss Tribunal militaire de cassation, 27 April 2001, the judgment can be found at http://www.vbs.admin.ch/internet/OA/d/urteile.htm.
See Luc Reydams '*Niyonteze* v. *Public Prosecutor*' *American Journal of International Law* Vol. 96 No. 1 (January 2002).

national jurisdiction in order to compare it with others, the emphasis seems to be placed on institutional guarantees, rather than on the human rights aspect. The institutional guarantees are, namely, the requirement of a prosecutorial and judicial institution free from any undue influence. Therefore, the common understanding is that a trial should not be influenced by political considerations or any other discriminatory prejudice. Most notably, fairness and impartiality are achieved through an institution with an appropriate structure (such as a sound composition of judges) to guarantee non-biased proceedings, in an environment free from undue interference from political/military power, while the independence of the judiciary is maintained.

6.6 Summarising of the Guiding Rules

In sum, the following considerations should be taken into account in deciding the venue of a trial in the case of a jurisdictional conflict. First of all, the particular exercise of jurisdiction by a State must not be unlawful. Although States generally have a wide discretion in deciding which jurisdictional bases to uphold, this presumption of the legality of jurisdiction exercised by States does not justify the exercise when it has taken place in breach of other rules and principles of international law. Hence, the jurisdiction in question must be able to be exercised in accordance with international law.

After the legality of each jurisdictional claim is confirmed, then relevant conventional international law should be referred to in order to find any indication of rules for resolving jurisdictional conflicts. Relevant treaties and conventions should be examined to discover whether any particular jurisdictional hierarchy has been established within their provisions.

In the absence of any specific conventional rules, one should proceed to examine the appropriateness of each jurisdiction in order to determine the venue of a trial. In doing so, the nexus rule in particular is taken into consideration. While States with a stronger nexus to the crime have a stronger interest in its prosecution, at the same time, I consider that they bear a stronger responsibility in pursuing the accountability of the crime. Hence the interest as well as the responsibility of a relevant State may be assessed through the nexus rule.

Weighing and comparing interests is also considered to be one of the methods to determine which jurisdiction has priority. In my opinion, the interests to be compared are not limited to that of the national interest of individual States. For instance, in comparing the interests of States in the prosecution of a crime, the possible impact of justice should be acknowledged. This is because it serves the interest of the international community as a whole to conduct a trial at the best venue where justice can serve the present and future peace and deterrence of such crimes. This is especially so since future deterrence is one of the reasons why ending impunity is considered to be so vital. Deterrence can be accomplished to some extent, through prosecution and punishment in any court, but one State may be more capable of doing so more effectively and significantly than others by its particular location or the accessibility of victims, the media, or other factors. These considerations may support the preference for territorial jurisdiction or, on the contrary, it may give preference to other bases of jurisdiction depending on each particular circumstance.

The assertion of jurisdiction for serious crimes may also prevail over other jurisdictions based on the allegation of a lesser crime. Or one may refer to a more pragmatic and objective rule of 'first come, first served', giving priority of jurisdiction to the State which first initiated the procedure. Lastly, the ability of each authority to prosecute in a fair and impartial manner is now beginning to be considered as one of the relevant criteria. This last criterion is important in the interest of justice, and signifies a new trend in international criminal law. However, it also gives rise to some debate as to its content and adequacy.

Consideration of these criteria may not result in an obvious definitive answer. Some criteria may suggest one answer while others point in a different direction. Rather than being legal rules to be strictly applied, they are likely to function as a guideline in evaluating and weighing the conflicting claims of jurisdiction.

7 Tentative Conclusions

This chapter has addressed the problem of jurisdictional conflicts, and has tentatively compiled some rules to be utilized in determining which jurisdiction should be exercised. In addition to solving jurisdictional conflicts between States, these guiding rules may function to compel certain States to exercise jurisdiction or to leave the case in the hands of another State. Indeed, the decision to initiate proceedings is taken by a State itself, but the guiding rules may be taken into consideration by a State in deciding to claim its jurisdiction over a case.

The rules exemplified in this chapter may not be rigidly applied in certain situations. However, that does not entirely deny their existence as the sources of some can be found all the way back in the law and practice under the classical jurisdictional regime. On the other hand, some of these rules reflect new developments under modern international law, namely, the interest of the international community, the emphasis on the fairness and impartiality of a trial, and increased respect for human rights. The assurance of fairness and impartiality is one of the contemporary objectives of international criminal law. In this regard, because of its innovative, leap-frogging from rules and principles that had been dominant under the classical jurisdictional regime, the consideration of the assurance of a fair trial and other human rights has given rise to disputes. The guiding rules in evaluating the appropriateness of a jurisdiction require further contemplation. In the next chapter, I will tentatively apply these guiding principles to determine the appropriateness of non-territorial jurisdiction in general, and also some new developments of international criminal law that are appearing in relation to the guiding rules.

CHAPTER VI
SOME EFFECTS RELATING TO THE APPLICATION OF THE GUIDING RULES

1 INTRODUCTION

In Chapter V, this study presented and analysed some guiding rules that are useful in determining the venue of a trial in order to resolve jurisdictional conflicts. Next, this chapter will tentatively apply the guiding rules. The aim of this chapter is to reveal the role of non-territorial jurisdiction, including universal jurisdiction within the modern jurisdictional regime. In addition to reiterating the *status quo* of the modern jurisdictional regime, an examination of some effects of the guiding rules enable us to observe some new changes and interpretation that may determine the future development of rules concerning the coordination and method of exercising jurisdiction over serious violations of human rights.

The first part of this chapter tentatively applies the guiding rules to non-territorial jurisdiction in general. This part will test a conservative contention advanced by some States, which upholds that jurisdictions other than territorial jurisdiction should not be exercised. Contrary to this contention, the application of the guiding rules demonstrates that the appropriateness of exercising non-territorial jurisdictions is not generally denied *a priori*, even though the preference for territorial jurisdiction that was persistent in the classical jurisdictional regime has also been maintained to some degree in the modern jurisdictional regime.

The second part of this chapter applies the guiding rules to universal jurisdiction. I will illustrate how the rationales of universal jurisdiction have an influence on the role expected to universal jurisdiction.

The third part of this chapter turns to some effects of the guiding rules. The first concerns the issue of the decision-maker. Who applies the guiding rules? It is interesting to note that with the examination of this issue, a new function that is attributable to extradition becomes apparent. This chapter notes another peripheral effect involving the principle of *ne bis in idem*. The principle of *ne bis in idem* has changed today to disregard a sham trial as a preceding trial that deters a subsequent trial for the same crime from taking place under this principle.

2 APPLICATION OF THE GUIDING RULES TO NON-TERRITORIAL JURISDICTION

This section applies the guiding rules to non-territorial jurisdiction in general – any jurisdiction other than territorial jurisdiction, often referred to by many authors as 'extra-territorial jurisdiction'. This examination is conducted in order to verify the argument that the supremacy of territorial jurisdiction compels States to refrain from exercising any other jurisdiction. Through examining this extreme argument, this section intends to reiterate the concurrent composition of jurisdictions on which today's modern jurisdictional regime is based and its oppositions.

First, I will summarise the major criticism levelled against non-territorial jurisdiction. In sum, the proponents of territorial jurisdiction criticise, first, the fact that other jurisdictions undermine the interest of the territorial State as well as that of the international community. Then they question the ability of the relevant State to prepare a case and to conduct a trial without violating human rights. Secondly, I will examine the appropriateness of non-territorial jurisdiction through applying the guiding rules.

2.1 Arguments Against the Exercise of Non-territorial Jurisdiction

2.1.1 Legality

It is argued that non-territorial jurisdiction is against the principle of non-intervention in the domestic affairs of a State. The proponents of the supremacy of territorial jurisdiction argue that the exercise of non-territorial jurisdiction violates State sovereignty. Although the principle of non-intervention and State sovereignty have been mentioned on many occasions, such contentions rarely explain how these principles could be violated by non-territorial jurisdiction.

2.1.2 Causing Instability and Damaging Peace within a State

It is argued that States should avoid exercising non-territorial jurisdiction because it might destabilize the ongoing democratic transition in a State where the crime was committed. Therefore, other States should allow a territorial State to deal with the situation. Kissinger highlights in a cynical tone the example of post-Franco Spain in which wholesale criminal trials of human rights violations in the recent past were avoided, and he raises a doubt as to why the same attempt by Chile to give priority to national reconciliation over criminal accountability should not be allowed in the Pinochet Case.[1]

In addition, the exercise of non-territorial jurisdiction might contradict the will of the State where the crime occurred. The State where the crime was committed might choose other measures for accountability such as a truth and reconciliation commission, another investigatory commission, or a compensation mechanism (i.e. civil proceedings), instead of criminal proceedings. It is understood that which one of the various accountability mechanisms or a combination thereof is the most appropriate in a given post-conflict situation will 'depend on a variety of factors such as the ultimate goals of the parties to the previous conflict, their willingness to reconcile, the

1 See Henry Kissinger 'The Pitfalls of Universal Jurisdiction' *Foreign Affairs* July/August 2001.

extent of the harm done, the duration of the conflict, as well as other external and internal circumstances that may bring about, in the best of cases, reconciliation, and in the worst cases, partitions.'[2] Taking this into account, some authors deduce that any decision and action concerning prosecution should be left to a territorial State.

2.1.3 Danger of Causing New Disputes

It is also argued that the exercise of non-territorial jurisdiction will lead to a new dispute among States.[3] This is because the exercise of non-territorial jurisdiction may be considered to be a manifestation of the distrust of the judicial system of a territorial State. Such an action may be construed as being unfriendly, and can trigger a vehement response from the territorial State, aggravating the bilateral relationship. A trial in a foreign domestic court may damage the pride of a territorial State, as exemplified in the case of Pinochet where it was suggested that it might be better to try Pinochet in an international judicial body because a trial in a Spanish or British court might undermine the trust and pride of Chile, resulting in hatred among Chilean nationals.[4]

Furthermore, there is another aspect that may give rise to political friction and confrontation between States. A conviction for an act constituting a gross violation of human rights such as genocide may in some cases be interpreted as suggesting the responsibility of the relevant State. For instance, if a person is found guilty of such a crime while acting as an agent of a State, then the involvement of the State and its responsibility are implied by the conviction.

In addition, the lack of clarity in relation to rules concerning jurisdictional hierarchy is sometimes employed in the argument to support the supremacy of territorial jurisdiction. It is argued that, without the recognition of the dominance of territorial jurisdiction, the jurisdictional regime would be without a clear-cut jurisdictional order, and it would consequently increase and complicate disputes among States claiming jurisdiction over the same case.

---

2 Christopher C. Joyner and M. Cherif Bassiouni eds. (Association Internationale de Droit Pénal), *Reining in Impunity for International Crimes and Serious Violations of Fundamental Human Rights: Proceedings of the Siracusa Conference 17-21 September 1998* (Nouvelles Études Pénales, 1998).

3 Röling argued this using the following example:
'[If a] Brazilian state official were prosecuted here in Italy for having tortured someone in Brazil in his official capacity: that would lead to enormous international tensions. It would mean that one government in effect condemns the other government as a criminal government. It could well lead to the severance of all relations between them. And that after the decision of just a local judge. It would really disturb peace in the world.' B.V.A. Röling and Antonio Cassese, *The Tokyo Trial and Beyond* (Cambridge: Polity Press 1993), p. 95.

4 Diana Woodhouse ed., *The Pinochet Case: A Legal and Constitutional Analysis* (Hart Publishing, 2000), pp. 127-129.

2.1.4 *Arbitrary Prosecution*

It is also argued that non-territorial jurisdiction is vulnerable to abuse by States. States might initiate proceedings driven by a political intention to incriminate an individual, to exterminate political or military opponents, or to condemn an unfriendly State. Such an arbitrary prosecution damages not only the diplomatic relations between the relevant States, but also the credibility of justice and the enforcement of international law.

2.1.5 *Possibility of Undermining the Suspect's Rights*

Another argument contends that a trial outside a territorial State is undesirable because it may undermine the human rights of a suspect. Trials abroad force suspects to face an unfamiliar legal system. As a result, suspects are likely to suffer difficulties in understanding the proceedings, seeking appropriate guidance, and gathering documents and evidence from a place possibly far away from the scene of the crime. Suspects may be subdued by not understanding the language used in proceedings. In addition to the inequality of arms, suspects may be subject to undue stress and suffering as a result. Therefore, it is contended that exercising of non-territorial jurisdiction should be avoided because it results in undue strain on defendants, both materially and psychologically, possibly violating their human rights.

2.1.6 *Problems with the Gathering of Evidence*

Evidentiary problems are highlighted by many authors.[5] Undoubtedly, a State needs sufficient evidence to prosecute effectively. However, a State asserting non-territorial jurisdiction may have some difficulties in obtaining access to sites, evidence, and witnesses since these are most likely to be under the control of a territorial State. Without cooperation from a territorial State, conducting search and seizures, examining crime scenes, obtaining material evidence and documents, as well as interviewing victims and witnesses may be difficult, and it would hinder the progress of the proceedings. It may result in investigations ending up in a deadlock and cases being terminated. In the Gabrez Case, the Swiss court acquitted a citizen from the former Yugoslavia for violations of the laws and customs of war, noting the insufficiency of the evidence.[6]

Moreover, there may be an excessive burden on a State asserting non-territorial jurisdiction. In prosecuting crimes abroad, often numerous documents have to be translated. The costs may be substantial not only for the translation of documents, but also

5 For example, Bruce Broomhall 'Towards the Development of an Effective System of Universal Jurisdiction for Crimes Under International Law' *New England Law Review* 35 (Winter 2001), pp. 412-414.

6 In re G., Tribunal militaire, Division 1, 1997. See Andreas R. Ziegler 'In re G.' *American Journal of International Law* Vol. 92 (1998).

for carrying out investigations abroad. Consequently, an investigation and prosecution based on non-territorial jurisdiction is expected to be much more expensive and time-consuming than proceedings based on territorial jurisdiction.

2.1.7 Lack of Specialized Institutions

Kamminga points out that investigating and prosecuting crimes committed abroad requires special skills and he concludes that special machinery should be established for this purpose.[7] His suggestion is based on concern as regards the ability of the domestic institution, such as the ability to interrogate in a proper manner or to gather enough evidence, which may require special knowledge of international criminal and human rights law as well as international humanitarian law in order to prosecute properly and effectively. Although Kamminga mentions this problem for the purpose of increasing the efficiency of exercising universal jurisdiction, in contrast to his intention, however, his suggestion is often employed to degrade non-territorial jurisdiction because few States have such a specialized institution within their territory.

2.2 Evaluating Non-territorial Jurisdiction in Accordance with the Guiding Rules

Above, I have briefly introduced the major points of criticism which are levelled against the exercise of non-territorial jurisdiction. In the light of these criticisms, one might hastily conclude that non-territorial jurisdiction is inherently inadequate and should not be exercised. However, I will next examine the appropriateness of non-territorial jurisdiction in accordance with the guiding rules and I will conclude otherwise. In fact, some situations do require the active exercise of non-territorial jurisdiction, rather than relying exclusively on territorial States. Having said that, it is important to keep in mind that there are a number of different bases of jurisdiction that are included under the term 'non-territorial jurisdiction' as used in this study. It includes, for example, nationality jurisdiction that is fairly widely accepted and practised, as well as universal jurisdiction which retains a generally supplemental character in my opinion. Therefore, it may be dangerous to discuss the diverse bases of jurisdiction that have a different nature under one heading, but this section does so in order to illustrate once again how the expansion of national jurisdiction has also endorsed jurisdictions other than territorial jurisdiction. Hence this section should not be read as ignoring the

---

7 ILA recommendation #7, prepared by Kamminga, states as follows:
'States should improve their capacity to investigate and prosecute human rights offences on the basis of universal jurisdiction by establishing specialised machinery for this purpose, by widening the admissibility of written evidence (*proces-verbal*), by making arrangements for the conduct of rogatory missions abroad, by allowing courts to take evidence by video-link, and by establishing witness protection programs.' Committee on International Human Rights Law and Practice 'Final Report on the Exercise of Universal Jurisdiction in Respect of Gross Human Rights Offences' International Law Association, London Conference (2000), pp. 12, 21. See also Menno T. Kamminga, *ibid.*, p. 954.

differences and diversity of bases of non-territorial jurisdiction. I will examine especially universal jurisdiction later.

2.2.1 *Legality*

As explained in Chapter V, it must be established that a jurisdiction in question is legal under international law before proceeding to an examination of its appropriateness. With regard to legality, it is evident that territorial jurisdiction is not the sole basis of jurisdiction which is legal under international law. It has also been acknowledged that non-territorial jurisdiction is not unlawful. Non-territorial jurisdiction is presumed to be legal due to the lack of international law prohibiting the exercise of non-territorial jurisdiction in general.[8] Moreover, the prohibition and prosecution of gross violations of human rights have been recognized to constitute international concerns. Non-territorial jurisdiction is not *per se* in breach of the principle of the sovereign equality of States, the principle of territorial sovereignty, or the principle of non-intervention in the same manner as I explained the legality of universal jurisdiction in Chapter IV. To contradict this assertion, some might point to the judgment of the ICJ in the Case Concerning the Arrest Warrant of 11 April 2000.[9] In this case, the ICJ ordered the cancellation of the arrest warrant issued by Belgium based on universal jurisdiction *in absentia*. In the application, the Democratic Republic of Congo indeed accused Belgium of violating 'the principle whereby a State may not exercise its authority on the territory of another State and the principle of sovereign equality among all members of the UN'. However, it should be noted that the ICJ did not decide on the legality of universal jurisdiction *in absentia*. Its conclusion was based on the breach of international law concerning the absolute immunity attributed to an incumbent Minister for Foreign Affairs. Therefore, the illegality was not declared to be inherent to universal jurisdiction *in absentia*, but merely as a result of the situation in this particular case (the suspect was an incumbent Minister for Foreign Affairs of Congo) and inconsistency with other principles under international law, namely the principles concerning immunity. Hence this ICJ case does not constitute a ruling on the *a priori* illegality of non-territorial jurisdictions in general. In light of this ICJ judgment, it is shown that the general presumption of the legality of non-territorial jurisdiction does not preclude it from being illegal after a thorough examination of the particular situation in each case or when it is in conflict with other principles of international law.

2.2.2 *Particular Rules in Conventions*

In deciding which jurisdiction should be actually exercised in a particular case, if there is a particular convention that is relevant to the case and if such a convention pre-

---

8 Concerning the issue of understanding international law as a prohibitive law or permissive law, see Chapter IV.

9 For the detail of this ICJ case, see Chapter III.

scribes a certain jurisdictional rule, then this should be respected among the States parties to the convention. Because this section is devoted to a general consideration rather than a specific case, it will not refer to particular treaties or conventions for guidance. However, it must be reiterated that the bases of non-territorial jurisdiction are widely recognised, and this has been a general trend in international criminal law especially since the expansion of national jurisdiction in the 1970s. For instance, the Torture Convention recognises and indeed obliges nationality jurisdiction, passive nationality jurisdiction and universal jurisdiction in addition to territorial jurisdiction.[10] Conventional international law does not deny the appropriateness of non-territorial jurisdiction in general, indeed it tends to indicate otherwise.

2.2.3 *The Nexus Rule*

According to the nexus rule, territorial States may be seen as having the strongest nexus. Even today, there is a strong presumption in favour of territorial jurisdiction and this may be observed in the practice of States. For instance, when Tanzania received the extradition requests for Ntuyahaga from both Rwanda and Belgium, it decided to extradite him to the territorial State, Rwanda.[11] It is noted that in this case, Belgium not only had universal jurisdiction over the suspect, but also passive nationality jurisdiction since Ntuyahaga was suspected of killing Belgian peace-keepers. Another example is the refusal of the Spanish court to exercise universal jurisdiction over a case of genocide in Guatemala. While confirming that Spain has power to exercise universal jurisdiction, the Spanish national court decided not to exercise it based on its conclusion that there were no legal obstacles to prosecution under the territorial jurisdiction

10 Article 5 of the Convention against Torture and Other Cruel, Inhuman or Degrading Treatment or Punishment (referred as the Torture Convention) prescribes as follows:
'1. Each State Party shall take such measures as may be necessary to establish its jurisdiction over the offenses referred to in article 4 in the following cases:
(a) When the offenses are committed in any territory under its jurisdiction or on board a ship or aircraft registered in that State;
(b) When the alleged offender is a national of that State;
(c) When the victim is a national of that State if that State considers it appropriate.
2. Each State Party shall likewise take such measures as may be necessary to establish its jurisdiction over such offenses in cases where the alleged offender is present in any territory under its jurisdiction and it does not extradite him pursuant to article 8 to any of the States mentioned in paragraph 1 of this article.
3. This Convention does not exclude any criminal jurisdiction exercise in accordance with internal law.'

11 The Ntuyahaga case illustrates a situation of concurrent jurisdiction and the defendant's forum shopping. Ntuyahaga gave himself up to the ICTR, hoping to escape arrest and extradition to Rwanda where he was likely to be given the death penalty. However, his forum shopping did not go beyond this stage when the ICTR dropped the charges and released him. See the ICTR, Decision on the Prosecutor's Motion to Withdraw the Indictment, *Prosecutor* v. *Ntuyahaga*, 18 March 1999, ICTR-98-40-T, reprinted in 38 *ILM* (1999) 866.

of Guatemala, and because the inactivity and the refusal of the Guatemalan judicial authorities to exercise jurisdiction over the alleged acts had not been established.[12]

Nevertheless, States other than a territorial State have a nexus as well and have long been recognised as having such nexus. It should be remembered that other bases of jurisdiction have been recognized even under the classical jurisdictional regime in which territorial jurisdiction was dominant. The interests of States other than territorial States have prompted the development of various bases of national jurisdiction to materialise and to be recognized under international law.

Nationality jurisdiction is the most widely accepted among non-territorial jurisdictions. It is recognised that States whose national is a suspect may have a strong nexus and a substantial interest in interfering with the treatment of its nationals. Therefore, even some international criminal courts exemplify their respect for such States. For instance, Article 12 of the ICC Statute provides that the ICC needs to obtain the acceptance of a territorial State or a State of the nationality of the suspect in question in order for it to exercise its jurisdiction. Also, the Special Court for Sierra Leone recognized the nationality jurisdiction of the State contributing its personnel to the peace keeping operation, and specifically gave priority thereto over and above the jurisdiction of the Special Court.

In sum, to some extent there is still a general preference for territorial jurisdiction, but the presumption of such a preference does not deny the fact that other jurisdictions have been recognized widely as well. Therefore, following other criteria included in the guiding rules should also be taken into consideration before giving precedence on territorial jurisdiction.

2.2.4 Weighing and Comparing the Interests

One criterion that can be considered in solving jurisdictional conflicts is to give priority to a State having a greater interest in prosecution. The interest in the prosecution and punishment of a crime is not necessarily exclusive to territorial States. In fact, other States can have a comparable interest to that of territorial States, and the recognition of such interest formed the backbone of the development of the various bases of non-territorial jurisdiction under international law. Therefore, the existence of the interests of States other than territorial States have been recognised even under the classical jurisdictional regime.

---

12 See Decision of the Criminal Division of the Spanish National Court (Sala de lo Penal de la Audiencia Nacional Espanola), Madrid, 13 December 2000 (Plenary Session, Appeal Record 115/2000 on the Preliminary Proceedings 331/99, Central Court of Instruction No. 1), introduced in Michael Cottier 'What Relationship Between the Exercise of Universal and Territorial Jurisdiction? The Decision of 13 December 2000 of the Spanish National Court Shelving the Proceedings Against Guatemalan Nationals Accused of Genocide', in Horst Fischer, Claus Kreß, Sascha Rolf Lüder eds., *International and National Prosecution of Crimes Under International Law: Current Developments* (Berlin Verlag Arno Spitz GmbH, 2001).

Today, in addition to the individual interests of States, there is the interest of the international community as a whole in cases of gross violations of human rights. It is within the interest of the international community to end the culture of impunity and to establish accountability for gross violations of human rights. As I will explain below, non-territorial jurisdiction may contribute to fulfilling the interest of the international community. This is because if jurisdiction were to be limited only to territorial jurisdiction, there is a great likelihood of leaving some lacunae in the exercise of jurisdiction, thereby engendering many negative conflicts of jurisdiction – situations where there is no State which exercises jurisdiction over a crime. It was feared that impunity would prevail if prosecutions of serious crimes were left exclusively in the hands of a territorial State. As an example of the fear of prevailing of impunity, this study has pointed to the motive behind the drafting of the Genocide Convention in Chapter III. It was anticipated that a trial in a territorial State would not be forthcoming in reality or even if a trial were to be conducted, there would be a great danger that it would not be fair and impartial. Such anticipation is strong in a situation where the authorities in the region are responsible for or acquiescence in the commission of violations, or where credible legal systems cease to exist after a total or partial collapse of governmental control during a violent conflict.

It is said that impunity may result from political constraints arising from 'the need to continue to live with (and perhaps to share power with or even to work toward reconciliation with) the perpetrator population or constituency.'[13] Morris notes the halting of the accountability process against the former military regime in Argentina and the amnesty provided in relation to apartheid in South Africa as an exemplification of political constraints.[14] Kritz notes that trials in the domestic courts of the States in the region of the former Yugoslavia were viewed as a method of continuing the conflict rather than as a method of advancing accountability and reconciliation. This is because such trials aggravated the tension and suspicion that already existed between the confronting States on each side.[15] After the Municipal Court in Belgrade delivered its judgment on 21 September 2000, which sentenced *in absentia* 14 NATO leaders including US President Bill Clinton and UK Prime Minister Tony Blair to 20 years in prison each for crimes committed during the NATO bombing campaign

13 Madeline H. Morris 'International Guidelines Against Impunity: Facilitating Accountability' *Law and Contemporary Problems* Vol. 59 No. 4 (Autumn 1996), p. 30.

14 Madeline H. Morris, *ibid*. She points out that threats of military insurrection halted the prosecution efforts under the Alfonsin government investigation of human rights abuses committed under the former military regime in Argentina. She concludes that 'precarious balances of power sometimes involving military threats often place political constraints upon the degree of accountability that is sought.'

15 See Neil J. Kritz 'Coming to Terms with Atrocities: A Review of Accountability Mechanisms for Mass Violations of Human Rights' *Law and Contemporary Problems* Vol. 59 No. 4 (Autumn 1996), pp. 136-137.

against Yugoslavia, the new Serbian justice minister criticised it as being a farce of a trial and expressed the intention to reverse the judgment.[16]

Cottier notes as follows:

> '...[T]he exercise of jurisdiction should not be deferred to the territorial State unless certain conditions are fulfilled, namely that the deferral will not result in the impunity of the perpetrator. A deferral thus should not take place unless the competent authorities of the territorial State are willing and able to genuinely prosecute the crimes concerned, and do not, for instance, intend to shield the perpetrator from responsibility for his or her acts. If a deferral to the territorial State's jurisdiction would clearly, or even only likely, result in the impunity of the perpetrator, this would not serve the interests of justice and the international community.'[17]

Indeed, national jurisdictions based on a nexus other than territoriality have been sought and desired in order to avoid negative jurisdictional conflicts and arbitrary and unfair trials. Hence, it is concern over the shortcomings of a jurisdictional regime which relies heavily on territorial jurisdiction that has enhanced non-territorial jurisdiction. Recalling that one rationale behind the birth of universal jurisdiction over piracy was, as I explained in Chapter III, the absence or the uncertainty of the whereabouts of jurisdiction capable of prosecuting and punishing criminals in an effective manner, it is no surprise that non-territorial jurisdiction has long been regarded as a solution to such shortcomings. The international community has increasingly accepted various national jurisdictions, especially universal jurisdiction, as it becomes increasingly aware of the interest of the international community as a whole. For instance, the UN Sub-Commission on the Promotion and Protection of Human Rights has invited 'all Governments to cooperate in a reciprocal manner even when there is no treaty to facilitate the task of legal authorities dealing with proceedings initiated by victims acting either within the framework of the principle of universal competence as recognized in international law or under a domestic law which establishes an extraterritorial legal competence, in particular because of the nationality of the victim or of the perpetrator'.[18]

It should not be considered that allowing non-territorial jurisdiction denotes ignorance of the interest of the region. Peace and stability in the region affected by the violence in question should indeed be taken into consideration in exercising non-territorial jurisdiction. Unlike the criticisms noted earlier, there may be a situation where a trial outside the territorial State may actually serve the interest of peace as well as justice, and that this is coherent with both the regional and international interests.

---

16 See Jann K. Kleffner 'Correspondents' Reports Federal Republic of Yugoslavia', in H. Fischer and Avril McDonald eds, *Yearbook of International Humanitarian Law* Vol. 3: 2000 (T.M.C. Asser Instituut, 2002), p. 494.

17 Michael Cottier, *supra* note (12), pp. 851-852.

18 'Role of universal or extraterritorial competence in preventive action against impunity', UN Sub-Commission on the Promotion and Protection of Human Rights resolution 2000/24 (18 August 2000).

It is probable that, in view of the interest of the administration of justice, it is efficient and feasible to rely on territorial jurisdiction. This is because in order to exercise non-territorial jurisdiction, States must make an extra effort in order to gain access to evidence, victims, witnesses and suspects – all of which are most likely to be located abroad. It is more efficient to defer proceedings to a State which has sufficient evidence to convict a person, and in most cases, this is territorial jurisdiction. However, even taking into consideration the efficacy and feasibility of proceedings, the possibility of non-territorial jurisdiction being exercised should not be dismissed out of hand since these problems may be resolved by legal assistance. If problems such as the difficulty of obtaining evidence or cooperation are the result of the reluctant attitude of States, namely that of a territorial State, it should be reminded that many treaties and conventions prohibiting serious crimes contain provisions encouraging and often obliging the ratifying States to cooperate with each other in bringing perpetrators to justice. For example, Article 9 of the Torture Convention prescribes as follows:

> Article 9 '1. States Parties shall afford one another the greatest measure of assistance in connection with criminal proceedings brought in respect of any of the offenses referred to in article 4, including the supply of all evidence at their disposal necessary for the proceedings.
> 2. States Parties shall carry out their obligations under paragraph 1 of this article in conformity with any treaties on mutual judicial assistance that may exist between them.'

In sum, the individual State interest as well as its contribution to the interest of the international community can be found in the exercise of non-territorial jurisdiction. As a result of the rapid development of international criminal law, and especially since the 'expansion' of national jurisdiction since the 1970s, the acceptance of non-territorial jurisdiction has increased dramatically. The adequacy of non-territorial jurisdiction is not generally denied. On the contrary, non-territorial jurisdiction may be regarded as being more desirable than territorial jurisdiction depending on the situation in a particular case, after taking into consideration the interests of States, of the international community, of justice, and of peace.

2.2.5 Fairness, Impartiality, and the Observance of Human Rights

While States must conduct a trial in a fair, impartial and independent manner and respect the human rights of suspects, the exercise of non-territorial jurisdiction has been the target of criticism as being vulnerable to arbitrary influence. Academic researches such as the Princeton Principles are aware of the possibility of a State abusing and arbitrarily exercising its criminal jurisdiction, including universal jurisdiction, and consequently, they specifically include suggestions for legal and judicial safeguards to help to deter such potential abuse. In addition to the prevention and prohibition of such abuse at the trial stage, similar attention should be given at the initiation stage of the proceedings. A State should endeavour to maintain a fair and clear position in selecting which case it will pursue in order to exercise its non-territorial jurisdiction. It is true that expecting non-territorial jurisdictions to prosecute all the perpetrators of international criminal acts committed all over the world is impractical. In the light of this, some permit selective prosecution and the use of 'exemplary trials'.[19] However, in such cases, it is added that the criteria to be used in selecting cases must reflect appropriate distinctions based upon degrees of culpability, sufficiency of evidence, and other relevant factors in order to avoid the risk of arbitrariness.

It may be recalled that non-territorial jurisdiction has developed considerably due to the concern over the possible arbitrary action or non-action of territorial States. Gross human rights violations committed in a systematic manner are often suspected to have been committed by, or subject to the tolerance of, a territorial State. Cynically, the closer the nexus of a State to the crime in question, the less likely it is that that State would be viewed by other States involved as being capable of conducting a trial in an impartial manner. The risk of political influence steering the proceedings functions as a caution both against territorial and non-territorial jurisdiction in many cases.

Needless to say, all States must take all possible measures to ensure that the human rights of a suspect will not be undermined. This is especially so in proceedings which are subject to non-territorial jurisdiction because it may be difficult for the defendant to prepare his or her defence in a judicial system and culture which is foreign to him or her, and he or she will be forced to gather and locate evidence and witnesses in a distant State. No criminal proceedings should be dependent on such difficulties which undermine the defence of the accused, but rather on a fair and impartial determination of the conduct of accused. Although this danger is persistent, the actual ability of a court to conduct a fair and impartial trial should be assessed in each case. Irrespective of territorial or non-territorial jurisdiction, States should be aware of their responsibility to guarantee a fair and impartial trial in exercising any jurisdiction.

---

19 See Principle 6 and the commentary thereon in 'Draft Guiding Principles for Combating Impunity for International Crimes (Revised 30 October 1997)', in Christopher C. Joyner and M. Cherif Bassiouni eds. (Association Internationale de Droit Pénal), *supra* note (2). The Principle 6 states as follows:
'Principle 6. The Appropriate Role of Prosecutorial Discretion
A. States may exercise discretion in determining how many and who among alleged perpetrators of crimes under international law are to be brought to justice, provided the selection criteria are not arbitrary. It is especially important that the most culpable perpetrators and the leaders responsible for planning or supervising their abuses be prosecuted.
B. States may delay prosecutions for a reasonable amount of time until, for example, a new government is secure enough to take such action against members of the former regime, or a new government has the judicial resources to undertake fair and effective prosecutions. The need for such delay should be balanced against the rights of victims, alleged perpetrators, and the effect on testimony and evidence to be used at trial.'

2.2.6 Other Criteria

Just as the ability of a court to conduct a trial in a fair and impartial manner and respecting the human rights of the suspect should be determined with respect to each individual case, the same is true for other criteria. The gravity of the crime charged or the date when proceedings are initiated should be analysed based on each relevant fact within a case.

2.2.7 General Assessment

From the above observations, the conclusion can be drawn that non-territorial jurisdiction, including universal jurisdiction, is not *a priori* inadequate. This conclusion is supported by the wide recognition of non-territorial jurisdiction in the modern jurisdictional regime, especially after its expansion since the 1970s. Among the various bases of non-territorial jurisdiction, nationality jurisdiction has the longest and widest acceptance in the law and practice of States. Compared to nationality jurisdiction, universal jurisdiction is found to be wanting in nexus, although they are both bases of non-territorial jurisdiction. However, even the supplemental character that can be attributed to universal jurisdiction does not entirely deny its appropriateness. On the contrary, some situations compel the exercise of non-territorial jurisdiction in order to end impunity. These bases of jurisdiction have been appreciated as one of the solutions to negative conflicts of jurisdiction. Therefore, rather than totally dismissing the possibility of a trial by means of non-territorial jurisdiction, the appropriateness of these bases jurisdiction should be determined with respect to each case.

3 How should Universal Jurisdiction be Exercised?

Next, I will contemplate the role that universal jurisdiction is expected to play. Since universal jurisdiction is one form of non-territorial jurisdiction, the analysis of its appropriateness overlap with that of non-territorial jurisdiction in general conducted in the section above. However, as I mentioned, appropriateness of each basis of jurisdiction should be measured individually, in light of the particular situation in question. Although it is difficult to assess the appropriateness without a specific case in question, this study tentatively apply the guiding rules to universal jurisdiction in general in order to show its general character. This section examines the appropriateness of exercising universal jurisdiction in relation to other jurisdictions. The concluding observation regarding the appropriateness of exercising of universal jurisdiction shows the role universal jurisdiction is expected to play.

3.1 Why the Exercise of Universal Jurisdiction is Desirable

I have described why universal jurisdiction is not *a priori* illegal under international law in Chapter IV. But this does not minimize the fact that universal jurisdiction is rather unusual considering the dominance of territorial jurisdiction which had dominated the classical jurisdictional regime as well as the nexus rule which is still relevant in the modern jurisdictional regime. Even compared to other non-territorial jurisdictions, universal jurisdiction has relatively weak nexus to cases. So how has it come to be endorsed on such an odd basis as national jurisdiction? Let us now address the appropriateness of universal jurisdiction.

Many people and organizations have voiced the need for universal jurisdiction. For instance, the International Council on Human Rights Policy notes many reasons for making use of universal jurisdiction. The objectives are to obtain justice, to deter violations of rights, to support the rule of law, to promote social reconciliation, to reveal the truth, and to register international concern and protect society.[20]

In my view, the two rationales of universal jurisdiction illustrate the basic objective. Due to the seriousness of the crimes in question, the prosecution and punishment of such acts constitute an interest of the international community as a whole. There is a great need to end impunity for these acts in order to restore and establish a peaceful environment and to deter such acts in the future. The importance of ending impunity is recognised, but to achieve this goal, there is a need to fill the lacuna which is present in jurisdiction. The absence of effective jurisdiction capable of prosecuting these acts is one of the shortcomings deriving from the dominance of territorial jurisdiction, as explained in Chapter II of this study. This was the very reason why universal jurisdiction has developed in practice and in the law. It was hoped that universal jurisdiction would serve to fill this lacuna and to replace impunity with accountability. Therefore, the seriousness of the crimes in question and the absence of or uncertainty concerning effective jurisdiction have compelled States to exercise universal jurisdiction. In my opinion, these historic rationales of universal jurisdiction are still relevant today. Universal jurisdiction has to be exercised when there is no other jurisdiction that is capable of effective prosecution.

3.2 Some Problems in Exercising Universal Jurisdiction

Now that I have established that universal jurisdiction is generally not illegal under international law and that some situations call for its exercise, I will examine some of the problems relevant to the exercise of universal jurisdiction. These problems might affect the assessment of the appropriateness of exercising universal jurisdiction. At the extreme end of the scale, some people seem to blindly worship universal jurisdiction as an ultimate solution for ending impunity. But some scholars draw attention to the

20 International Council on Human Rights Policy, *Hard Cases: Bringing Human Rights Violators to Justice Abroad – A Guide to Universal Jurisdiction* (International Council on Human Rights Policy, 1999), pp. 9-16.

dangers of providing a blank cheque to States regarding universal jurisdiction.[21] Their warning can be summarized as follows.
First, universal jurisdiction may not be exercised as a result of:
- the absence or inadequacy of national legislation;
- the lack of willingness on the part of States to exercise universal jurisdiction;
- difficulty in obtaining cooperation from other States;
- problems of evidence gathering;
- inhibition by immunity or amnesty given by other States; or
- the lack or ineffectiveness of systematic international supervision to compel States to exercise jurisdiction.

Second, they point out that even if States start to exercise universal jurisdiction more often, its exercise may be problematic because there are dangers of:
- undermining fairness and impartiality in proceedings;
- causing instability and damaging peace within a State or between States; or
- undermining the suspect's rights.

It is noted that most of the problems listed above are relevant not only to universal jurisdiction, but to any national jurisdiction, especially non-territorial jurisdiction. Therefore, I will concentrate on those that are especially problematic for universal jurisdiction in this section, namely, the lack of willingness on the part of States, the absence or inadequacy of national legislation, and the danger of hampering impartiality. The first two are problems that may hamper States in initiating the exercise of universal jurisdiction while the third is a problem that may be apparent in exercising universal jurisdiction.

3.2.1 The Lack of Willingness on the Part of States

Cassese notes that 'it is a fact that national courts are not inclined to institute proceedings for crimes that lack any territorial or national link with the State' and 'short-term objectives of national concerns seem still to prevail'.[22] Moreover, States may be

---

21 For both the legal and political obstacles to prosecution based on universal jurisdiction, see Pita J.C. Schimmelpenninck van der Oije 'A Surinam Crime Before a Dutch Court: Post-Colonial Injustice or Universal Jurisdiction?' *Leiden Journal of International Law* Vol. 14 No. 2 (2001), pp. 458-461, pp. 463-474. Teple Fett Kearns 'Breaking the Shackles of the Past: The Role and Future of State Sovereignty in Today's International Human Rights Arena' 25 *Nova Law Review*, p. 521. See also Bruce Broomhall, *International Justice and the International Criminal Court: Between Sovereignty and the Rule of Law* (Oxford University Press, 2003), pp. 118-126. For the various normative and practical reasons for impunity, see Christopher C. Joyner 'Redressing Impunity for Human Rights Violations: The Universal Declaration and the Search for Accountability' *Denver Journal of International Law and Policy* Vol. 26 (Summer 1998). See also 'Universal Jurisdiction: The duty of states to enact and enforce legislation' (Amnesty International, September 2001), p. 29.

22 Antonio Cassese, *International Law* (Oxford Press, 2001), p. 268.

reluctant to exercise universal jurisdiction unless they are obligated to do so. States are also reluctant to exercise jurisdiction over a case that is not directly related to an important interest of their own. For instance, during the discussions concerning jurisdiction in the event of grave breaches of the Geneva Conventions held within the United States, concern was expressed as regards becoming involved in conflicts where U.S. interests were minor. The point was made that, rather than establishing universal jurisdiction over grave breaches of the Geneva Conventions, there are 'ample alternative venues available which are more appropriate' and that the prosecutions 'can be handled by the nations involved'.[23] Because universal jurisdiction is at odds with the classical and also with the modern jurisdictional regime to some extent as well, States are generally reluctant to prosecute on the basis of universal jurisdiction, or even to incorporate it within their domestic law. This reluctance results in the non-exercise of universal jurisdiction.

Ironically, for universal jurisdiction, which has been expected to help overcome the shortcomings of territorial jurisdiction, there are now the same problems as there were with territorial jurisdiction. This is because universal jurisdiction is also exercised by States. In Chapter II, I illustrated how, because of the political nature of many of the most serious crimes, it was feared that territorial jurisdiction could not be effectively exercised to prosecute and punish such crimes. The same fear may also remain concerning universal jurisdiction. Criminals are most likely to choose a State that will be a safe haven for them as a place for escape. Hence, it may be just as difficult to conduct a trial in a State where the suspect is found as it is in the territorial State.

On the other hand, there may still be a problem when a State voluntarily exercises universal jurisdiction. In other words, there is a further danger of a political or other intention influencing the decision to exercise universal jurisdiction. This may greatly damage the credibility of universal jurisdiction. Bolton criticizes universal jurisdiction as improper meddling in the political arena as follows:

> 'The worst problem with universal jurisdiction is not in diaphanous legal footing but its fundamental inappropriateness in the realm of foreign policy. In effect (and in intention), the NGOs and theoreticians advocating the concept are misapplying legal forms in political (or military) contexts. What constitutes crimes against humanity and whether they should be prosecuted or handled otherwise – and by whom – are not questions to be left to lawyers and judges. To deal with them as such is, ironically, so bloodless as to divorce these crimes from reality. It is not merely naive, but potentially dangerous.'[24]

---

23 Discussion in the US House of Representatives in 1996, cited in Richard van Elst 'Implementing Universal Jurisdiction Over Grave Breaches of the Geneva Conventions' *Leiden Journal of International Law* Vol. 13 No. 4 (2000), p. 837.

24 John R. Bolton 'Universal Jurisdiction: Too Easily Sweeps Political Differences into Legal Arena' Legal Times (11 January 1999). This be viewed at the home page of the American Enterprise Institute for Public Policy Research, *http://www.aei.org*.

3.2.2 The Absence or Inadequacy of National Legislation

One has to bear in mind that the entity that will exercise universal jurisdiction is a State. In order for State authorities to consider the exercise of jurisdiction, they often require domestic legislation authorizing it. Not all States acknowledge the direct application (self-execution) of international law. Even in States in which international law may be directly applied, national authorities may not recognise or may have difficulty in recognising the existence of a rule in international law or may not actively respond to it, especially when it is a customary norm without any reference thereto in conventional international law.

It is observed in practice that the absence of national legislation authorizing universal jurisdiction deters its exercise. Many courts remain reluctant to exercise jurisdiction without explicit law authorizing it. As observed by the Canadian court in Finta Case, it was explained that very aim of Section 7(3.71) of the Canadian Criminal Code, which authorizes Canadian court to exercise its jurisdiction based on the presence of the suspect, was to emphasize that Canadian court has the capacity to serve as a forum for the prosecution of crimes against humanity and war crimes.[25] The same

25 The Finta Case was prosecuted in accordance with Section 7(3.71) of the Canadian Criminal Code [ad. R.S.C., 1985] which provided:
'Notwithstanding anything in this Act or any other Act, every person who, either before or after the coming into force of this subsection, commits an act or omission outside Canada that constitutes a war crime or a crime against humanity and that, if committed in Canada, would constitute an offence against the law of Canada in force at the time of the act or omission shall be deemed to commit that act or omission in Canada at that time if,
(a) at the time of the act or omission,
(i) that person is a Canadian citizen or is employed by Canada in a civilian or military capacity,
(ii) that person is a citizen of, or is employed in a civilian or military capacity, by, a state that is engaged in an armed conflict against Canada, or
(iii) the victim of the act or omission is a Canadian citizen or a citizen of a state that is allied with Canada in an armed conflict; or
(b) at the time of the act or omission, Canada could, in conformity with international law, exercise jurisdiction over the person with respect to the act or omission on the basis of the person's presence in Canada and, subsequent to the time of the act or omission, the person is present in Canada.'
R. v. *Finta*, [1994] 1 S.C.R. 701, p. 743. Concerning this provision, the court explained the aim of the Commission that drafted it as follows:
'The Commission's view, as I read it, is that new offences did not have to be created ; censure of the actual relevant acts was already provided for in the Canadian Criminal Code, as it was in the law of most civilized nations. So any such acts could have been prosecuted under the ordinary Canadian criminal provisions if committed here. What Canadian courts had to be equipped with was the capacity to hear and decide the prosecutions.' *Ibid.*, p. 745.
See Suzanne Schairer and Chile Eboe-Osuji 'The Jurisdiction to Prosecute Foreigners for Crimes Against Humanity Committed Abroad' *African Legal Aid Quarterly* January-March (2000), p. 15.

attitude that requires domestic law authorizing universal jurisdiction is taken by the courts of many other States.[26]

The absence or inadequacy of national legislation is a problem for other bases of national jurisdiction as well. But because there is a greater reluctance among States as far as universal jurisdiction is concerned, this legislative problem becomes particularly significant for universal jurisdiction.

In an effort to avoid this obstacle of domestic legislation, the Princeton Principles on Universal Jurisdiction state that for serious crimes under international law, a 'national judicial organ may rely on universal jurisdiction even if their national legislation does not specifically provide for it.'[27] Yet, in the absence of adequate legislation, national authorities are likely to be reluctant to resort to universal jurisdiction. Furthermore, the conflict with the principle of *nulla poena sine lege* may preclude the conduct of proceedings. And even when proceedings are commenced based on universal jurisdiction, a domestic court may have to find that it has no jurisdiction over the case without the presence of a domestic law providing for such authorization. For instance, in 1999, the Federal Court of Australia[28] ruled that in the absence of proper legislation, no person may be tried for genocide before an Australian court. The halted prosecution of Hissène Habré in Senegal[29] serves as another example of this. Not all States have prepared domestic legislation, thereby inviting criticism from many.[30] An ILA report points to the lack of proper domestic law, giving examples of States which have not adequately prepared legislation by limiting their jurisdiction to crimes committed during a certain period or in a specific place.[31] States are encouraged and often obliged, especially under certain conventions, to implement legislation enabling the exercise of jurisdiction.[32]

---

26 Dugard notes the British House of Lords in the Pinochet Case, the courts in Switzerland and France, and the Supreme Court of the Netherlands in the Knesevic Case. See John Dugard 'Universal Jurisdiction for Crimes Against Humanity' African Legal Aid Quarterly January-March (2000), p. 8.

27 Principle 3 of the Princeton Principles of Universal Jurisdiction.

28 *Nulyarimma and others* v. *Thompson*, Federal Court of Australia, Full Court, 1 September 1999, 39 *International Legal Materials* (2000) 20.

29 Such examples can be found not only in African States. For example, a court in Switzerland refused to exercise universal jurisdiction over genocide because the necessary legislation was lacking. See the summary of the Fulgence Niyonteze Case, International Law Association, *supra* note (7), annex, p. 28.

30 See, International Law Association, *ibid*., p. 12.

31 The examples mentioned are the law enacted in the United Kingdom in 1991 which is limited to war crimes committed by or against UK citizens or residents in Germany or German-occupied territory during the Second World War, and the French law only allowing for universal jurisdiction over crimes committed in relation to the conflicts in the former Yugoslavia and Rwanda. International Law Association, *ibid*., p. 12.

32 The need to incorporate a provision on universal jurisdiction for future conventions concerning serious violations of human rights and the importance of taking measures to implement extra-territorial domestic jurisdiction against crimes against international law even without a treaty obligation have been reaffirmed on many occasions in the United Nations. See for example, Question of the Impunity of Perpetrators of Human Rights Violations, U.N.Doc.E/CN.4/Sub.2/1997/20/Rev.1 (1997), Principles 20, 21.

3.2.3 Problems of Impartiality

There is a danger that a State will exercise universal jurisdiction based on its own ideological, political or religious interests in the case.[33] Kissinger commented that '[t]he danger lies in pushing the effort to extremes that risk substituting the tyranny of judges for that of governments; historically, the dictatorship of the virtuous has often led to inquisitions and even witch-hunts.'[34] Relying on States to exercise jurisdiction in a fair and impartial manner is indeed a tricky exercise.

Furthermore, the ILA report points out the possibility of States exercising universal jurisdiction being accused of 'jurisdictional imperialism' because it is only likely to be exercised in powerful States with regard to crimes committed in less powerful States.[35] There is indeed a concern that the majority of cases where universal jurisdiction is exercised are likely to take place in North American and European courts, whereas the majority of the persons prosecuted are likely to come from developing countries. It follows that people generally believe that a weaker State exercising universal jurisdiction over crimes committed by nationals of a powerful State is highly unlikely to occur.[36] As the term 'jurisdictional imperialism'[37] suggests, a former colonial power prosecuting a crime that had occurred in former colonies would be most vulnerable to such an accusation. The case of the prosecution of Surinamese nationals in the Netherlands[38] is one example of this. The same accusation was revealed in the opinion expressed by the Congo's *ad hoc* Judge Bula-Bula in the ICJ Case concerning the Arrest Warrant of 11 April 2000. In this case, Belgium was accused of imposing its justice on its former colony, the Congo.

The bias that may drive States to exercise universal jurisdiction will damage the credibility of universal jurisdiction. This danger has been voiced especially concerning

---

33 C. Van Den Wigngaert and others 'Commentaire de la loi du 16 juin 1993 relative à la répression des infractions graves au droit international humanitaire' *Revue de droit pénal et de criminologie*, 1994, No. 11, p. 1174. See also, Madeline H. Morris 'Jurisdiction in a Divided World : Conference Remarks' 35 *New England Law Review* (2001), pp. 337-338. Bowett explained that 'there will be a strong 'political' element in many war crimes trials, and there must be a risk of this influencing the actions of the State assuming jurisdiction. For example, if the Eichmann precedent is valid, why should not Sweden, or Poland, or Yugoslavia indict some former American serviceman for alleged war crimes in Vietnam ?' See, D. Bowett 'Jurisdiction : Changing Patterns of Authority over Activities and Resources' 53 *British YearBook of International Law* 1, p. 12 (1982).

34 Henry A. Kissinger 'The Pitfalls of Universal Jurisdiction' *Foreign Affairs* 86 (July/August 2001).

35 It notes that most cases of the exercise of universal jurisdiction have been in OECD States with respect to crimes committed outside these States. International Law Association, *supra* note (7), pp. 19-20.

36 A cynical remark made by Shadrack Gutto is the followings: 'What would happen if an African state like Djibouti would prosecute let us say a national of the United States for crimes against humanity? The prosecuting state would either be bombed or will not receive aid from the World Bank.' See, Evelyn Ankumah 'Introduction' Seminar: Universal Jurisdiction for Crimes Against Humanity *African Legal Aid Quarterly* January-March 2000, p. 5.

37 See, International Council on Human Rights Policy, *supra* note (20), p. 20.

38 The Bouterse Case, see Chapter III of this study.

universal jurisdiction in *absentia* because it allows any State to exercise jurisdiction. The selection of cases to be prosecuted may be accused of being biased.[39]

It should be noted that merely conducting a trial will not achieve real justice and end impunity. Trials must be conducted in a fair and impartial manner. Adherence to international norms regarding fair trials is considered to be an important factor especially for universal jurisdiction since universal jurisdiction risks being condemned as being exercised in a *mala fide* fashion. That is why the Cairo Guiding Principles noted precisely that '[i]n particular, the application of the principle of universal jurisdiction should not be used as a pretext to pursue foreign policy and national objectives or to pursue politically motivated prosecutions.'[40] Amnesty International's 14 Principles on the Effective Exercise of Universal Jurisdiction similarly determine that there should be no political interference.[41]

Furthermore, even without *mala fide*, a State asserting universal jurisdiction may have a problem in conducting a trial in proper manner. Van Elst casts some doubt on the reliability of prosecution based on universal jurisdiction, indicating that the court may not appropriately weigh the credibility of a witness from a different cultural background.[42] In addition, trials based on universal jurisdiction are often criticised for relying more heavily on eyewitness testimony rather than material evidence which the prosecuting States were unable to obtain due to the lack of sufficient cooperation from a territorial State.[43]

It is important to note, however, that the problem of ensuring impartiality is relevant not only to universal jurisdiction, but to other jurisdictional bases as well. The

---

39 See, International Council on Human Rights Policy, *supra* note (20), p. 17. It notes that 'for universal jurisdiction prosecutions, selectivity and allegation of bias are especially problematic. Because these cases will always have political implications, it will be hard to show that the decision to proceed in any one case (or not to proceed in another) is based on legal considerations alone, and not on political factors. Also, because so many human rights violations have gone unpunished, a sudden decision to act in one case will seem irregular and attract suspicion.' *Ibid.*

40 Preliminary Draft of the Cairo Guiding Principles on Universal Jurisdiction in respect of Gross Human Rights Offenses: An African Perspective, http://www.afla.unimaas.nl/en/act/univjurisd/preliminary principles.htm., principle 6. A similar observation is made in other writings. For example, see Principle 7 of Amnesty International's 14 Principles on the Effective Exercise of Universal Jurisdiction (published in May 1999), AI Index: IOR 53/01/99.

41 Principle 7 states as follows.
'7. No political interference. Decisions to start or stop an investigation or prosecution of grave crimes under international law should be made only by the prosecutor, subject to appropriate judicial scrutiny which does not impair the prosecutor's independence, based solely on legal considerations, without any outside interference.' Amnesty International '14 Principles on the Effective Exercise of Universal Jurisdiction' (May 1999), AI Index: IOR 53/01/99.

42 Richard van Elst, *supra* note (23), pp. 849-850.

43 Kamminga recommends some methods to gather evidence abroad and to reduce reliance on direct oral testimony, including travelling to the place of the commision of the crime to conduct on-sight investigations and interviews, and the use of written depositions and the taking of evidence by video-link. See Menno T. Kamminga 'Lessons Learned from the Execise of Universal Jurisdiction in Respect of Gross Human Rights Offenses' *Human Rights Quarterly* Vol. 23 No. 4 (November 2001), p. 960.

exercise of jurisdiction by States having a nexus to a crime can also be accused of being driven by vengeance rather than justice.[44]

3.3 When is Universal Jurisdiction Appropriate?

Universal jurisdiction is not illegal but may entail some problems depending on the manner in which it is exercised. So, how should universal jurisdiction be exercised by States? The question relates to the appropriateness of exercising universal jurisdiction as well as the role of universal jurisdiction in prosecuting gross violations of human rights within the jurisdictional regime.

3.3.1 Supplemental Universal Jurisdiction

Universal jurisdiction is construed as retaining supplemental character. Cassese holds that under customary international law, 'universal jurisdiction may only be exercised to *substitute for other countries* that would be in a better position to prosecute the offencer, but for some reason do not…'.[45]

It is noted that priority should generally be given to territorial jurisdiction. The ILA Report recommends that gross human rights offenders should preferably be brought to justice in the State in which they committed their offences.[46] It suggests that universal jurisdiction should be considered in the absence of such proceedings in such States. Many scholars contend that when the territorial State is willing and able to conduct out a *bona fide* prosecution, other States should generally defer to it.[47] They suggest retaining the supplemental characteristic of universal jurisdiction.

State practice confirms this point. Although different reasons are given by different domestic courts in various States, they seem to give some preference to territorial jurisdiction. In the Eichmann Trial, the Israeli Supreme Court confirmed that 'the State

44 Roberts notes that authors justify the international tribunal by criticising territorial jurisdiction. They say that '[n]ational prosecution may not be legalistic; instead, it may result in highly politicized trials (as in Croatia) or show trials (as in Serbia). The pressure of trying war criminals may overwhelm national judicial systems (as in Rwanda), or it may simply prefer revenge to legalism.' Roberts criticises such a view, holding that the historical record shows that States have tended to provide for an amnesty instead of trials. See Guy Roberts 'Assault on Sovereignty: The Clear and Present Danger of the New International Criminal Court' *American University International Law Review* Vol. 17 (2001).

45 Antonio Cassese 'Is the Bell Tolling for Universality? A Plea for a Sensible Notion of Universal Jurisdiction' *Journal of International Criminal Justice* Vol. 1 No. 3 (December 2003), p. 595.

46 International Law Association, *supra* note (7), pp. 20-21.

47 Randall, pp. 829-31. Christopher C. Joyner 'Arresting Impunity: The Case for Universal Jurisdiction in Bringing War Criminals to Accountability' *Law and Contemporary Problems* Vol. 59 No. 4 (Autumn 1996), pp. 165-170. Broomhall holds that '[i]f the territorial state is demonstrably willing and able to prosecute the accused in a fair manner, or if there is another, clearly more appropriate forum, the state considering universal jurisdiction should ordinarily defer to its courts.' Bruce Broomhall 'Towards the Development of an Effective System of Universal Jurisdiction for Crimes Under International Law' *New England Law Review* 35 (Winter 2001), p. 416.

which has apprehended the offender must first offer to extradite him to the State in which the crime was committed' for practical reasons, rather than a theoretical reason.[48] The Spanish Supreme Court (Audiencia Nacional) denied the need for Spain to exercise its universal jurisdiction over a genocide case committed in Guatemala by Guatemalan nationals by reasoning that Article 6 of the Genocide Convention has the effect of giving precedence to territorial jurisdiction.[49] The court also drew a parallel with the complementarity principle of the ICC and applied it to this case. The Spanish court asked itself whether Guatemala's authorities were unwilling or unable to prosecute, and then concluded that such inability or unwillingness had not been proven and that, therefore, there was no need for the Spanish courts to exercise universal jurisdiction.

On the other hand, there are other scholars who give primacy to nationality jurisdiction. Judges Higgins, Kooijmans, and Buergenthal expressed their opinion on placing some safeguards on the exercise of universal jurisdiction *in absentia*. They argued that primacy should be given to the jurisdiction of the suspect's State of nationality. Accordingly, '[a] State contemplating bringing criminal charges based on universal jurisdiction must first offer to the national State of the prospective accused person the opportunity itself to act upon the charges concerned.'[50]

Rather than giving preference to only one basis of jurisdiction, that is, either territorial or national jurisdiction, Cassese allows both. He explains that 'conditional universality' is the moderate conception of universality as a default jurisdiction, and that such 'jurisdiction may only be triggered when the territorial or national state fails to act, and provided the prosecuting state shows an acceptable link with the offence'.[51]

Taking into consideration the historical rationales of universal jurisdiction, universal jurisdiction, in my view, is expected to be exercised when there is an absence of or uncertainty concerning effective jurisdiction capable of being exercised over these crimes. Therefore, universal jurisdiction can be exercised to complement other jurisdictions. In other words, universal jurisdiction should be supplemental in character,

48 The Israeli Supreme Court denied that this is a theoretical limitation. The court held that 'the idea behind the above-mentioned limitation is not that the requirement to offer the offender to the State in which the offence was committed was designed to prevent the violation of its territorial sovereignty. Its basis is rather a purely practical one. Normally, the great majority of the witnesses and the greater part of the evidence are concentrated in that State and it is therefore the most convenient place (*forum conveniens*) for the conduct of the trial.' Then the court dismissed the application of this limitation is the case of Eichmann because the government of West Germany did not demand his extradition, and because the great majority of the witnesses and a great deal of the evidence were in Israel. The judgment by the Israeli Supreme Court in the Eichmann Trial, in E. Lauterpacht ed., *International Law Reports* Vol. 36 (Butterworths, 1968), p. 302.

49 Decision of the Audiencia Nacional (Sala de lo penal) of 13 December 2000. A summary and the text of this decision can be found on the homepage of the International Red Cross, http://www.icrc.org/. See Chapter III of this study.

50 Separate Opinion of Judges Higgins, Kooijmans, and Buergenthal, Case Concerning the Arrest Warrant of 11 April 2000 (Democratic Republic of the *Congo* v. *Belgium*), para. 59.

51 Antonio Cassese, *supra* note (45), p. 593.

and should extradite a suspect to other States having a stronger nexus to the crime that can effectively and impartially try the case. Only in the event that extradition is not possible, should a State exercise universal jurisdiction.

There are a number of arguments favouring this conclusion. To begin with, the notion of universal jurisdiction emerged in international law as an exception, in order to supplement other national jurisdictions. Therefore it would be consistent with its historical background to attribute universal jurisdiction a supplemental character. Second, it would be consistent with the goal which universal jurisdiction is expected to achieve. The goal is to establish accountability and to end impunity. Hence, if other national jurisdictions can be exercised in an effective, fair and impartial manner, there is no need to rely on universal jurisdiction. The purpose of universal jurisdiction is to deny a safe haven for criminals and to establish justice. If this can be achieved through other means, there is no need to actively exercise universal jurisdiction. In addition, from the point of view of effectiveness in fact-finding and conducting trials, a trial would be better held in a place where there is some nexus to the crime. A trial should be conducted in a place with the easiest means of retaining evidence and other procedural matters. If the judicial aid system such as extradition is sufficiently prepared for international cooperation, and the fairness and impartial conduct of a trial in the relevant States are ensured, the impunity of criminals committing crimes under international law would cease. If such an environment is achieved, then there would be no need to rely on, or to give primacy to, universal jurisdiction. One has to remember that proposals for universal jurisdiction put forward in the past intended to encourage, not to exclude, the fair and effective exercise of other national jurisdictions.

This approach may help to gain the support of States for universal jurisdiction. Similarly, universal jurisdiction may function to compel other States to exercise their jurisdiction in order to avoid foreign States from exercising universal jurisdiction over cases which occurred within the territory of the former State. Yet, there is a potential for universal jurisdiction to lose its supplemental character and to be a primary jurisdiction, since contemporary theories expressed by many scholars tend to ignore the second rationale. As international law concerning jurisdiction seems to gradually convert jurisdiction from a right into an obligation, and from supplemental to primary, as observed in conventional international law, the nature of universal jurisdiction could change its supplemental character in the near future.

3.3.2 Consideration Criteria in Deciding whether or not to Exercise Universal Jurisdiction

Scholars propose a variety of criteria to be used in determining whether or not to exercise universal jurisdiction. Broomhall explains that a State in deciding whether or not to exercise universal jurisdiction should take the following into account: the presence of the defendant, the availability of sufficient evidence, the seriousness of the acts, the situation in the territorial State, resources available to the prosecutor, and the relation to the other country.[52] Similarly, Osofsky proposes three elements which States must take into consideration.[53] The first element is whether or not any act has been taken by other States with a view to trial proceedings, and the second element is the propriety of other courts. The second element means taking into consideration the actions of the States which have a close relationship with the crimes, and whether or not the courts in such States can conduct proceedings in a fair and impartial manner. The third element is the nexus between the crime and the State; in other words, States thinking about exercising universal jurisdiction must ask themselves whether or not their courts are the most appropriate forum to conduct the trial, taking into consideration the needs of the victim and the foreign policy of that State. The Princeton Principles require a State seeking the extradition of a suspect to exercise universal jurisdiction 'in accordance with international norms and standards on the protection of human rights in the context of criminal proceedings'(Principle 1(3)) and to 'observe international due process norms including but not limited to those involving the rights of the accused and victims, the fairness of the proceedings, and the independence and impartiality of the judiciary' (Principle 1(4)) and 'in good faith and in accordance with its rights and obligations under international law' (Principle 1(5)). It requires States to obtain certain standards in order to exercise universal jurisdiction, and also to set additional safeguards against prosecutorial abuses. Furthermore, some argue that we should not encourage the exercise of universal jurisdiction by States which retain the potential application of the death penalty and other cruel, inhuman or degrading treatment, or where the suspect is foreseen to face torture.[54] We can see a considerable overlap between these proposals and the guiding rules I presented in this study.

In conclusion, as explained above, relying on the rationales of universal jurisdiction, a State, in deciding whether to exercise universal jurisdiction, should consider in addition to the guiding rules compiled in Chapter V, the character of universal jurisdiction that derives from its rationales. Therefore, in deciding whether or not to exercise universal jurisdiction in relation with other jurisdiction, a State should considers, especially when basing itself on customary international law, the presence of the suspect within its territory; and any other jurisdiction that is capable of exercising jurisdiction effectively and impartially; the possibility of extradition to States having such jurisdiction; and the ability of its own institutions to conduct proceedings in a fair and impartial manner.

---

52 Bruce Broomhall, *supra* note (47), pp. 416-418. See also Bruce Broomhall, *International Justice and the International Criminal Court: Between Sovereignty and the Rule of Law* (Oxford University Press, 2003), pp. 123-126.

53 See, Hari M. Osofsky 'Domesticating International Criminal Law: Bringing Human Rights Violations to Justice' *Yale Law Journal* Vol.107 No.1 (October 1997), pp. 222-223

54 See, International Council on Human Rights Policy, *supra* note (20), p. 20.

4 The Controversial Nature of Evaluating Appropriateness of Jurisdiction with Reference to the Guiding Rules

In the preceding sections, I have tentatively applied the guiding rules to the bases of non-territorial jurisdiction in general and also to universal jurisdiction, and have concluded that they are not *a priori* inappropriate, in contrast to the argument of some people and some States. However, the application of the guiding rules in actual practice is in reality very different. First of all, an analysis with reference to the guiding rules has to be made with a particular case in mind, rather than in general, in other words an assessment based on the factual details pertaining to the case. Secondly, the guiding rules may be considered in two stages rather than on a general basis: at the first stage, for a State in deciding whether to initiate proceedings in a particular case; and second, in deciding which State should exercise jurisdiction in a situation of jurisdictional conflict. Lastly, an evaluation of the appropriateness is made, first and foremost, by States claiming or considering whether to claim jurisdiction over a case, rather than by a third-party bystander. This is because there is no centralised system at the international level to coordinate and allocate cases among States having concurrent jurisdiction. Therefore, a State determines the appropriateness of its own jurisdiction as well as that of others, and then it decides to initiate, or to continue proceedings itself, or to extradite and defer the case to another State.

The power of a State to determine the appropriateness of its own jurisdiction is undisputed. However, when a State assesses this against that of another State in order to make a comparison, then it may be viewed as being problematic and controversial since it means that a State is allowed to judge the appropriateness of judicial proceedings in another State. In this regard, Schachter is critical in that 'it becomes almost impossible for the courts in either country to balance the conflicting interests in terms of what is reasonable.'[55] In particular, there is difficulty concerning the criteria that leave a margin of interpretation, namely, the criterion of evaluating the fairness, impartiality and adherence to human rights.

Assessing the observance of the right to a fair trial and other human rights within another State is tantamount to judging the ability of the judicial system of the latter State, and this can be criticised as undermining the principle of State equality. It is true that the ICC is entrusted with the power to determine the 'unwillingness or inability' of a State to investigate and prosecute individuals, the determination of which entails the fairness and impartiality of domestic proceedings, as a result of Article 17 of the ICC Statute. Yet, allowing a State to have a similar power may in itself lead to a dispute since the fairness and impartiality of this State in applying the guiding rules may itself be the subject of doubt.

---

55 Schachter, p. 264, see also note 48 and 269 of M. Cherif Bassiouni ed., *International Criminal Law Vol. II: Procedural and Enforcement Mechanisms*, 2nd ed., (Transnational Publishers, 1999), p. 175.

Furthermore, States are generally reluctant to review the appropriateness of another State's judicial system, fearing that they may be accused of intervening in the internal matters of the latter State and thereby risking jeopardizing friendly relations. Consequently, it is highly likely that even though this criterion may have induced a State to reach a decision one way or the other, this State may prefer not to publicly specify the reason behind its decision. By so doing, this State can avoid a complaint from the other State to the effect that it has violated the principles of State equality or of non-interference, while justifying its decision as a matter to be decided under its discretionary power.

Apart from such a fear, another reason behind the hesitation of States is the inherent difficulty in accurately assessing the propriety of a judicial system. Similar hesitation was expressed in the prominent case of *Soering* v. *UK*. The U.K. argued in the European Court of Human Rights that if a State is obliged to consider whether or not an extradited person may subsequently face human rights violations, 'it in effect involves adjudication on the internal affairs of foreign States not Parties to the Convention or to the proceedings before the Convention institutions; it entails grave difficulties of evaluation and proof in requiring the examination of alien systems of law and of conditions in foreign States; (...) it causes a serious risk of harm in the Contracting State which is obliged to harbour the protected person, and leaves criminals untried, at large and unpunished.'[56]

The possibility of a State misjudging or arbitrarily determining the criteria of the guiding rules cannot be totally ruled out. Even without *mala fides*, States do have difficulty in making an objective determination with confidence. However, this is not a problem which is only relevant to jurisdictional conflicts, but is common to other matters under international law because almost all State actions at the international level are initially determined by the acting State. Indeed, it is a general position under international law that acts of States are presumed to be legal unless otherwise prohibited under international law. The credibility of the enforcement of international law lies in preparing a mechanism to ensure that law is enforced in good faith and in accordance with international law, and, furthermore, to settle a dispute if a conflict among States does arise. Therefore, the importance lies in preparing a mechanism for resolving differences of opinion between States resulting from an evaluation concluded as a result of the application of the guiding rules, and preferably a mechanism that can re-evaluate the matters in question with some authority. There is no specialized international institution to resolve jurisdictional conflicts. Therefore, in the absence of a treaty or convention containing a specific dispute settlement measure, any dispute over jurisdiction may be resolved as any other inter-State dispute should be settled, e.g., through negotiation or a ruling by the ICJ. Any jurisdictional disputes should be settled in a peaceful manner, consistent with international law.

56 *Soering* v. *UK*, Judgment of 7 July 1989 of the European Court of Human Rights, Application No. 14038/88, para. 83.

5 Some Peripheral Effects of the Guiding Rules

5.1 Change in the Function of Extradition

As explained above, the appropriateness of a jurisdiction is first and foremost determined by the States claiming or considering to claim jurisdiction. What is extraordinary in relation to jurisdictional conflicts is that the appropriateness of jurisdiction may be determined by the State where a suspect is present. This point often goes unnoticed by some scholars, but it is important to realize the role which is vested in the State where the suspect is present under the modern jurisdictional regime. With suspect on its territory, this State virtually has the power to determine the venue of a trial through its decision on extradition. As a result, this power of a custodial State can mean that extradition is transformed into measure which is relevant to the allocation of cases between concurrent State jurisdictions. This section will now elucidate this point below.

5.1.1 The Classical Function of Extradition

Extradition means the process in which one State surrenders a person accused or convicted of a criminal offence to another State at its request for trial or punishment. Extradition is the oldest form of international cooperation in criminal matters. It is an important process for effectively exercising jurisdiction over individuals since obtaining custody is the key in activating prosecution and punishment. Hillier explains the rationale behind the law and practice of extradition as follows:

> '(a) a desire not to allow serious crimes to go unpunished. Frequently a State in whose territory a criminal has taken refuge cannot prosecute for the offence because of a lack of jurisdiction. It will therefore surrender the criminal to a State that can try and punish the offence; and
> (b) the State on whose territory the offence has been committed is the best able to try the offence because of the availability of evidence, etc.'[57]

This explanation reflects the dominance of territorial jurisdiction and illustrates extradition as a means to maintain and support it. In other words, extradition functions as a mechanism to return suspects to territorial States and therefore it is of assistance in the exercise of territorial jurisdiction. This emphasis on territorial jurisdiction can be found within many extradition treaties and State practice ever since the classical jurisdictional regime. However, in my opinion, this traditional function of extradition in reinforcing territorial jurisdiction is gradually losing its emphasis especially after the expansion of national jurisdiction under the modern jurisdictional regime.

57 Tim Hillier, *Principles of Public International Law* 2nd ed. (Cavendish Publishing, 1994), p. 138.

Extradition usually takes place under a treaty. In the absence of an extradition treaty, extradition is generally understood as a moral duty at most, not an obligation under customary international law, and therefore takes place under comity and the principle of reciprocity. Many States require the existence of an extradition treaty as a prerequisite, and in order to conduct extradition proceedings optimally, States have entered into extradition treaties, often in a bilateral form.[58] The signing of an extradition treaty signifies that the signing States have determined each other to be a State that is trustworthy for extraditing suspects. By signing an extradition treaty, a State establishes mutual trust in the judicial system of the other State, and, based upon this general credibility given in advance, the former State allows the extradition of a suspect in response to a request made by the latter State.

5.1.2 New Features

Today, with the development of technology for travelling, transnational measures are imperative for enforcing criminal law. The recent trend of international criminal law is directed towards diminishing the prerequisite of an extradition treaty before a person can be extradited. Today, many multilateral conventions that declare certain acts as a crime incorporate provisions for extradition that can take the place of extradition treaties.[59] These provisions specifically allow State Parties to extradite suspects based on the convention itself; therefore the absence of an extradition treaty may no longer be an obstacle to extradition.

In addition, the nature of extradition is changing. In general, extradition was thought to be an act of comity in the absence of an extradition treaty obligating a State to extradite to a particular State. However, many conventions regulating crimes in the modern age incorporate the principle of *aut dedere aut judicare*, obligating State Parties to either extradite or prosecute a suspect who is present within their territory. As a result, for a State Party to these conventions, extradition has changed from a matter of discretion to an obligation (if a State is not prosecuting the person itself).

58 See I. A. Shearer, *Extradition in International Law* (Manchester University Press, 1971), pp. 22, 24-34.

59 For example, Article 8 of the Torture Convention prescribes as follows:
'1. The offenses referred to in article 4 shall be deemed to be included as extraditable offenses in any extradition treaty existing between States Parties. States Parties undertake to include such offenses as extraditable offenses in every extradition treaty to be concluded between them.
2. If a State Party which makes extradition conditional on the existence of a treaty receives a request for extradition from another State Party with which it has no extradition treaty, it may consider this Convention as the legal basis for extradition in respect of such offenses. Extradition shall be subject to the other conditions provided by the law of the requested State.
3. States Parties which do not make extradition conditional on the existence of a treaty shall recognize such offenses as extraditable offenses between themselves subject to the conditions provided by the law of the requested State.
4. Such offenses shall be treated, for the purpose of extradition between States Parties, as if they had been committed not only in the place in which they occurred but also in the territories of the States required to establish their jurisdiction in accordance with article 5, paragraph 1.'

Another new feature of extradition observed under modern international law is the increased influence of international human rights law. It is noted that Sunga explains that 'the aim of the extradition treaty system is to improve inter-State cooperation in criminal matters in a manner that safeguards the human rights of the individual against the tyranny of Government, in particular, the right to freedom of political opinion and expression and the right to receive a fair trial.'[60] Because extradition directly affects the liberty of individuals, the development of international human rights law should be reflected in the practice and law of extradition. Today, respect for human rights influences the decision of a State to extradite a person to another State. For instance, Article 3(1) of the Torture Convention prohibits the extradition of a person if that person may be tortured in the requesting State. Article 3 of the Torture Convention prescribes as follows:

> '1. No State Party shall expel, return ("refouler") or extradite a person to another State where there are substantial grounds for believing that he would be in danger of being subjected to torture.
> 2. For the purpose of determining whether there are such grounds, the competent authorities shall take into account all relevant considerations including, where applicable, the existence in the State concerned of a consistent pattern of gross, flagrant or mass violations of human rights.'

The principle of *non-refoulement*, which is a principle prohibiting the deportation of refugees in certain situations, is analogically considered in situations of extradition as well.[61] Consequently, States are prohibited from handing a person over to a State where that person is likely to be subjected to torture or persecution. This is confirmed through the interpretation of other human rights instruments. It has been established that a State party to a human rights treaty has an obligation not to extradite a person to a State where it is predicted that he or she will face torture, inhuman or degrading treatment that would be a violation of Article 7 of the International Covenant on Civil

---

60 Lyal S. Sunga, *The Emerging System of International Criminal Law: Developments in Codification and Implementation* (Kluwer Law International, 1997), p. 257.

61 Article 33 of the Convention Relating to the Status of Refugees prescribes the prohibition of expulsion or return as follows:
'Article 33
1. No Contracting State shall expel or return ("refouler") a refugee in any manner whatsoever to the frontiers of territories where his life or freedom would be threatened on account of his race, religion, nationality, membership of a particular social group or political opinion.
2. The benefit of the present provision may not, however, be claimed by a refugee whom there are reasonable grounds for regarding as a danger to the security of the country in which he is, or who, having been convicted by a final judgement of a particularly serious crime, constitutes a danger to the community of that country.'
Convention Relating to the Status of Refugees, adopted on 28 July 1951 by the UN Conference of Plenipotentiaries on the Status of Refugees and Stateless Persons convened under General Assembly resolution 429 (V) of 14 December 1950, entry into force 22 April 1954.

and Political Rights[62] or Article 3 of the European Convention on Human Rights,[63] respectively.[64] In other words, if the foreseeable consequence is that an important right of the person under the Covenant or the Convention will be violated in another State's jurisdiction, a State party may itself be in violation of the Covenant or the Convention by extraditing the person to such a jurisdiction. Accordingly, some States have incorporated such due regard for human rights protection in extradition. For example, according to section 8 of the Finnish Extradition Act, a request for extradition may not be granted if the person in question may face persecution directed against his or her life or liberty or other persecution on account of his or her race, nationality, religion, political opinion or membership of a certain community or on the basis of political conditions.[65] In sum, extradition in modern times is increasingly influenced by human rights considerations.

5.1.3 The Significance of the Power to Decide

The State where the suspect is present has the power to decide some aspects that have a critical impact on the determination of the venue of a trial. It can decide (1) whether to prosecute a suspect itself, and if it chooses not to do so, then (2) to which State the suspect will be extradited.

As to the choice between extradition and a trial in its own courts, some people argue that it would be better to explore all the possibilities of extradition and to leave the possibility of a trial in the requested State as a last resort (*primo dedere secundo prosequi*).[66] However, in the absence of a treaty provision specifying otherwise, the

62 Article 7 of the International Covenant on Civil and Political Rights prescribes that '[n]o one shall be subjected to torture or to cruel, inhuman or degrading treatment or punishment. In particular, no one shall be subjected without his free consent to medical or scientific experimentation.'

63 Article 3 of the European Convention on Human Rights prescribes that '[n]o one shall be subjected to torture or to inhuman or degrading treatment or punishment.'

64 See *Soering* v. *UK*, Judgment of 7 July 1989 by the European Court of Human Rights, Application No. 14038/88. In the Soering Case, the European Court of Human Rights found that the UK's decision to extradite a German national to the U.S. where this person would be likely to be exposed to the 'death row phenomenon' amounted to inhuman and degrading treatment and an infringement of Article 3 of the European Convention on Human Rights. See also, *Ng* v. *Canada*, Views of 5 November 1993 of the Human Rights Committee under the Optional Protocol to the Covenant on Civil and Political Rights, Communication No. 469.1991. In the Ng Case, the Human Rights Committee concluded that Canada's extradition of the person in question to the U.S. without seeking and receiving assurances that the death penalty would not be imposed constituted a violation of the Covenant because the death penalty by gas asphyxiation would not meet the test of 'least possible physical and mental suffering', and thereby constituted cruel and inhuman treatment, in violation of article 7 of the Covenant.

65 Section 8 of the Finnish Extradition Act (1970/456, as amended by the Act 1999/182). See, Immi Tallgren 'Finland', in Albin Eser, Otto Lagodny, Christopher L. Blakesley eds., *The Individual as Subject of International Cooperation in Criminal Matters* (Nomos Verlagsgesellschaft, Baden-Baden, 2002), p. 177.

66 See Albin Eser 'Common Goals and Different Ways in International Criminal Law: Reflections from a European Perspective' *Harvard International Law Journal* Vol. 31 No. 1 (Winter 1990), p. 123.

decision concerning extradition is generally left to the discretion of the State where the suspect is present, therefore other States cannot demand the surrender of a suspect as their absolute right. Many conventions obliging extradition between State Parties also leave some margin of discretion to the custodial State. In general, rather than compelling States to extradite, international law has determined some rules of extradition prohibiting States from extraditing suspects in certain situations, *e.g.*, the rule of double criminality, the rule of speciality, the prohibition of extradition concerning political offences. In addition, extradition is generally refused if the requested State has reason to believe that the extradition has been requested for purposes of persecution, or if there are substantial grounds for believing that the person sought will not receive a fair trial in the requesting State.[67] Compared to these rules specifically prohibiting extradition, one can see that international law has not been active in laying down a rule that obliges a State to extradite in any given situation.

If a requested State decides not to prosecute a suspect itself, and when it has received competing requests for extradition, it has the power to decide to which State it will extradite.[68] By deciding to which State a suspect will be extradited, the requested State virtually determines the decision as to where the suspect will be tried. Note that in the Pinochet Case, the decision by the U.K. not to extradite Pinochet to Spain, based on its assessment of Pinochet's physical health, materially settled the jurisdictional question as to the venue of his trial.

In this respect, it may be recalled that under the classical jurisdictional regime, extradition was a system often used to return the suspect to the place where the crime had been committed in order to allow a trial in the territorial State. Nonetheless, as the exclusivity of territorial jurisdiction fades, extradition is now being transformed in order to serve as an initial system for allocating cases among States which claim jurisdiction.

Ultimately, with the obligation to prosecute or extradite, a State where an alleged offender is present is placed in a unique position. It is given responsibility by the mere presence of the suspect in its territory. This State will be under an obligation to take the necessary and reasonable steps to apprehend a suspect and to ensure the prosecution and trial of such an individual by a competent jurisdiction. This responsibility attributes a decision-making power to that State. Because jurisdictional provisions in many conventions do not specify any preference relating to the choice to be made in extraditing to another State or of initiating proceedings within the custodial State, this State has the ultimate power to decide which jurisdiction prevails over another.

---

67 Third Restatement, p. 571.

68 For example, Article 16 of the Model Treaty on Extradition adopted by the UN General Assembly prescribes that '[i]f a party receives requests for extradition for the same person from both the other Party and a third State it shall, at its discretion, determine to which of those States the person is to be extradited.' UN Doc. A/RES/45/116.

5.1.4 The Rule of Non-Inquiry

One may be of the opinion, however, that a requested State has no such power to apply the guiding rules. This argument may refer to the *rule of non-inquiry* as evidence of this contention. The courts in the United States take the viewpoint that a requested State should trust the criminal justice system of another State,[69] and thereby uphold the rule of non-inquiry. Under the rule of non-inquiry, U.S. domestic courts refuse to examine:

> '1. the processes by which a requested state secures evidence of "probable cause" to request extradition;
> 2. Whether the relator will receive a fair trial in the requested state;
> 3. the fairness of procedures under which a requested state secured a criminal conviction;
> 4. and the potential treatment or punishment a government may impose on a relator if returned to that country.'[70]

Under the rule of non-inquiry, a requested State cannot assess the appropriateness of the jurisdiction claimed by a requesting State. Hence it may be concluded that States cannot apply the guiding rules, especially the criterion of the fairness and impartiality of proceedings.

Nonetheless, the rule of non-inquiry does not mean that a State cannot take the guiding rules into consideration at any and all stages for the following reasons. First of all, not all States recognise the rule of non-inquiry. Certainly, it is applied by the courts in the United States, but the extradition procedure is governed by the domestic law of each individual State, and international law does not lay down precise rules and a uniform procedure on this point. Therefore, law and practice concerning extradition differ accordingly. For example, some States require that there is sufficient evidence to institute extradition proceedings, while others do not, and, furthermore, the extent of this sufficiency may vary from State to State. Although some people claim that the rule of non-inquiry is more than an American rule and has become a rule of customary international law,[71] this had not yet been proved.

Furthermore, even in the U.S., the rule of non-inquiry does not constrain the power of the Secretary of State to decide on the extradition of individuals. In the U.S., the Secretary of State has discretion to decide on any extradition which is certified by the extradition magistrate. In so doing, he or she can review the court's ruling on both the facts and the law, and may thereby refuse or grant extradition based on political or human rights considerations, or any other reason.[72] For instance, the Foreign Affairs Reform and Restructuring Act provides that the Secretary of State considers whether

---

69 See Albin Eser *supra* note (66), p. 122.
70 See M. Cherif Bassiouni ed., *supra* note (55), p. 232.
71 See M. Cherif Bassiouni ed., *ibid.*, p. 232.
72 See M. Cherif Bassiouni ed., *ibid.*, pp. 250-251.

a person to be extradited from the U.S. is 'more likely than not' to be tortured in the requesting State, in accordance with the obligation under Article 3 of the Torture Convention.[73] Therefore, it has been noted that courts in the U.S. which are limited by the rule of non-inquiry often highlight the potential human rights concerns as a guideline for the Secretary of State's decision.[74]

Similarly, a decision to extradite an individual is a quasi-executive, quasi-judicial decision in many other States as well. To generalize common extradition proceedings, upon the receipt of the extradition request from another State, the administrative authority, i.e., in most cases the Minister of Justice, considers the response to the request from a legal and political perspective.[75] Then, in many States, a domestic court decides on the legal admissibility of the extradition. Therefore, the individual who is the subject of the extradition request often has an opportunity to seek a judicial review in the requested State. The extradition hearings differ between civil and common law States. Procedures in common law States traditionally require proof of a *prima facie* case from a requesting State,[76] and many States also request that evidence be adduced in a form which is consistent with the law of the requested State before extradition is granted.[77] But in the end, in many States, the executive branch has the final say in deciding to extradite.[78] Subsequently, even if a court upholds the rule of non-inquiry, it does not prohibit the executive branch from taking a decision based on the guiding rules. Therefore, considering the criteria included in the guiding rules is not excluded by the rule of non-inquiry, and might well take place.

---

73 The Foreign Affairs Reform and Restructuring Act (FARR Act), Pub. L. No. 105-277, §2242, 1998 U.S.C.C.A.N. (112 Stat. 2681) 871.

74 See M. Cherif Bassiouni ed., *supra* note (55), p. 251.

75 See Otto Lagodny 'Comparative Overview' in Albin Eser, Otto Lagodny and Christopher L. Blakesley eds., *The Individual as Subject of International Cooperation in Criminal Matters: A Comparative Study* (Nomos Verlagsgesellschaft, Baden-Baden, 2002), pp. 701-702.

76 See Dominique Poncet and Paul Gully-Hart 'Legal Framework of Extradition in Europe', in M. Cherif Bassiouni ed., *ibid.*, p. 286.

77 See Kimberly Prost 'Extradition: The Practical Challenges?', in Rodrigo Yepes-Enriquez and Lisa Tabassi eds., *Treaty Enforcement and International Cooperation in Criminal Matters: With Special Reference to the Chemical Weapons Convention* (T.M.C. Asser Press, 2002), p. 205.

78 For example, in the United States, the U.S. State Department, which is notified by a foreign country about an extradition request, assigns the case to an Assistant U.S. Attorney, who will file a complaint against an individual. After the extradition magistrate has issued an arrest warrant and the suspect has been apprehended, the judge will hear whether the person is extraditable. After a decision by the magistrate approving the extradition, the Secretary of State can make a final decision on whether or not to extradite the person to the foreign country in question. See also the Third Restatement, p. 562. The Third Restatement states that usually the foreign ministry or the ministry of justice has some discretion to decline to surrender a particular person to a given State even after proceedings for extradition have been completed. In that case, it is 'customary to set forth reasons for refusing to extradite; one ground might be concern that the person would not receive a fair trial or would risk suffering other violations of human rights.' *Ibid.*

5.1.5 Prospects for the New Function of Extradition

This study has exemplified above how extradition can become one safeguarding procedure for ensuring the protection of human rights. As international human rights law develops, the responsibility of a requested State seems to be increasing. However, in reality, when a State receives extradition requests from multiple States, it tends to rely on more subjective criteria not requiring any in-depth assessment. States are reluctant to compare their interests and to evaluate the judicial system of another State, and to demonstrate any reluctance based on such evaluations. Some avoid any such considerations and deal with the case in a strictly first come, first served manner. And often, the extradition process takes place in accordance with a treaty obligation without any contemplation of the appropriateness of the jurisdiction claimed by the State requesting extradition. Therefore, although the decision on the venue of a trial may be in the hands of the State where the suspect is present, many States are not yet prepared to accept the role of a decision-maker by allocating cases between States. One foreseeable consequence is that, instead of becoming involved in the matter, States may heavily depend on immigration control and deportation, avoiding their responsibilities as the State where the suspect is present.

5.2 Effect on the Principle of Ne bis in Idem

This section introduces another aspect of the influence of the guiding rules, especially the criterion of the fairness and impartiality of proceedings. Let us now examine how the emphasis on fair and impartial trials has influenced the principle of *ne bis in idem*. It is now beginning to be accepted that a State cannot protect a person from being the subject of prosecution before a court in another State or an international criminal court by means of a sham trial in its domestic courts. This is observed in the proposition to exclude a sham trial from the applicability of the principle of *ne bis in idem*.

The principle of *ne bis in idem* protects individuals from being tried twice for the same crime. This principle is incorporated into the domestic law of the majority of States and various international instruments, and is recognized as being a general principle of law under international law.

There is a possibility for this principle to be abused. A person who has committed gross violations of human rights may subject him or herself to sham proceedings which are intentionally conducted to result in a dismissal of the case after an indictment, or acquittal or the imposition of relatively minor punishment not proportionate to the seriousness of the crime committed. Although in reality such arbitrary proceedings result in virtual impunity rather than accountability, from a strictly legal point of view, they do constitute a precedent. With the mere fact that the accused has been subjected criminal prosecution, the person in question can be less worried about prosecution in foreign States for the same act, under the protection of the principle of *ne bis in idem*. In this way, the person can obtain virtually full atonement with minimum sacrifice. The manipulation of judicial proceedings may be strongly suspected especially when a suspect is a high official or a person with substantial political or military influence – a very common situation for gross violations of human rights since the systematic and widespread perpetration of such crimes often requires the influence of political and/or military power.

This possibility has attracted attention as the international community becomes increasingly interested in ending impunity. It is contended that such a safeguard to protect the human rights of suspects should not be given to a person abusing this principle to evade real prosecution. The Preliminary Draft of the Cairo Guiding Principles holds that a person who has been tried and convicted or acquitted of a serious crime under international law before a national court may not be tried again, 'except if the proceedings were of a sham character.'[79] Similarly, Principle 9(1) of the Princeton Principles recognizes *non bis in idem* when 'the prior criminal proceedings or other accountability proceedings have been conducted in good faith and in accordance with international norms and standards' and '[s]ham prosecutions or derisory punishment resulting from a conviction or other accountability proceedings shall not be recognized as falling within the scope of this Principle.'

Furthermore, the international community has decided to include this notion in the actual instruments establishing international courts. For instance, Article 10(2)(b) of the ICTY Statute provides that if 'the national court proceedings were not impartial or independent, were designed to shield the accused from international criminal responsibility, or the case was not diligently prosecuted', this will not bar the ICTY from trying the case itself. Similarly, the ICC Statute provides that the ICC may try a person if the proceedings in the other court were intended to shield the person from criminal responsibility. The same emphasis is observed in Article 9 of the Statute of the Special Court for Sierra Leone which prescribes that a person tried by a national court may nevertheless be tried by the Special Court if 'the national court proceedings were not impartial or independent, were designed to shield the accused from international criminal responsibility or the case was not diligently prosecuted.'[80] Also, the rules regulating the special panels in the Dili District Court (which has exclusive jurisdiction over genocide and other serious crimes committed during the East Timor conflicts) exclude a sham trial from the application of *ne bis in idem*. As one of the general principles of criminal law, it is prescribed as follows:

> Section 11.3
> 'No person who has been tried by another court for conduct also proscribed under Sections 4 to 9 of the present regulation shall be tried by a panel with respect to the same conduct unless the proceedings in the other court:
> (a) Were for the purpose of shielding the person concerned from criminal responsibility for crimes within the jurisdiction of the panel; or

---

79 Principle 9.
80 Article 9(2)(b) of the Statute of the Special Court for Sierra Leone.

(b) Otherwise were not conducted independently or impartially in accordance with the norms of due process recognized by international law and were conducted in a manner which, in the circumstances, was inconsistent with an intent to bring the person concerned to justice.'[81]

These provisions in various instruments signify the emphasis given to the integrity of fair and impartial trials by the international community.

6 Conclusion

This chapter has examined some effects relating to the application of the guiding rules. It has shown that although the preference for territorial jurisdiction is still maintained to some extent in the modern jurisdictional regime, non-territorial jurisdiction is not *a priori* inappropriate. On the contrary, non-territorial jurisdiction is considered to be desirable in certain situations, especially in order to prevent and solve negative conflicts of jurisdiction. In exercising non-territorial jurisdiction, States are especially advised to give due consideration to the protection of the human rights of suspects and to conduct trials in a fair and impartial manner. Nevertheless, such consideration is an obligation under international law for all States, irrespective of whether it is a State with territorial or non-territorial jurisdiction.

In addition, this chapter has illuminated some effects of the guiding rules, namely the new function attributable to extradition, and the influence on the principle of *ne bis in idem.* The expectation placed on non-territorial jurisdiction and the new features of extradition and the principle of *ne bis in idem*, all signify the development of international criminal law endorsed by new concerns: first, to fill the lacuna of jurisdiction; second, to ensure the actual exercise of jurisdiction to prosecute crime; and lastly, to ensure fairness and impartiality in the exercise of jurisdiction. The last-mentioned concern has come to the fore fairly recently compared to others, and it is my belief that international law is likely to develop in this direction in the future.

81 Section 11.3 of UNTAET Regulation No. 2000/15 on the Establishment of Panels with Exclusive Jurisdiction over Serious Criminal Offences (6 June 2000).

CHAPTER VII
CONCLUSION

1 INTRODUCTION

In this concluding chapter, I will reiterate the conclusions deduced from each chapter of this study. After briefly reviewing the outline and conclusions of each chapter in the next section, I will present some observations and propositions based on these findings. These propositions are made in a concise manner, thereby avoiding any extensive elaboration which can be found in the relevant chapters of this study. My observations and propositions presented in this chapter are something more than mere summaries of each chapter. For instance, my last proposition concerning a reappraisal of territorial jurisdiction has not been extensively elaborated upon in the preceding chapters since it is my intention to do so in the future as the subject of separate research. Notwithstanding the absence of an elaborate explanation, in order to prevent readers from misunderstanding that this study ignores territorial jurisdiction, and also to complete the presentation of my understanding of the modern jurisdictional regime as a whole, I will briefly summarize the potential role of territorial jurisdiction at the end. I consider that it is ideal to have territorial jurisdiction that can be exercised in a fair and impartial manner, and assistance from the international community to this end is highly beneficial. One may say that if this could be accomplished, then there would be no need for any other form of jurisdiction, including universal jurisdiction, to be exercised. Yet, in reality there are some obstacles and the role of non-territorial jurisdiction still remains significant.

2 OVERVIEW OF THE STUDY

As explained in Chapter I, the very concern which served as the impetus for this study forward is how to end the impunity of individuals responsible for gross and serious violations of human rights. In this respect, this study has posed these central questions: *Which jurisdiction can and should be exercised for the prosecution of individuals responsible for gross and serious violations of human rights? And especially, in this regard, what is the role of universal jurisdiction?*

In order to answer the above questions, I have first clarified in Chapter II some basic knowledge and premises of the discussion by indicating the relevant principles in international law, explaining different jurisdictional bases, and describing the development and structure of the modern jurisdictional regime as a whole, taking note of the phenomenon of the expansion of national jurisdiction in particular.

Amongst the various bases of national jurisdiction, Chapter III especially draws attention to how universal jurisdiction has developed in history, thereby enlightening the prominent and innovative developments characterizing the modern jurisdictional regime. Universal jurisdiction which originated as the one which was exercisable over the crime of piracy began to be employed over time for different crimes which were severely grave, although somewhat slowly due to the friction with the traditional rules and principles such as the dominance of territorial jurisdiction. However, the change accelerated after the 1970s, when many conventions began to embrace the expansion of national jurisdictions including universal jurisdiction. This movement within conventional international law has been accomplished owing to the commitment among States to urgently prevent and punish violent crimes of terrorism. In addition, the rapid development of international humanitarian law triggered by the atrocities in Yugoslavia and Rwanda in the 1990s has exerted a great impact on practice and the conceptual notion of universal jurisdiction. Yet, the rapid change involving universal jurisdiction has provoked some resistance from States, and recently we can observe more reluctance toward its active exercise.

Thereupon, in Chapter IV, I have explained the notion of universal jurisdiction in detail. Its relations to international criminal jurisdiction (that is, the jurisdiction of international criminal courts), and to the rules of *jus cogens* and *obligatio erga omnes* are explained in order to remove common misunderstandings maintained by some who regard these different notions as being the same as or included in the notion of universal jurisdiction. As to the notion of universal jurisdiction itself, Chapter IV explicates its definition, and its rationales and sources. Furthermore, within the same notion of universal jurisdiction, this study points to the need to differentiate it from universal jurisdiction *in absentia*, as well as its different nature. This study has categorized its nature by two aspects: The first aspect is whether it is *permissive* or *obligatory*, and the second is whether it is *supplemental* or *primary*. These distinctions are made in order to facilitate our understanding concerning the evolution of the notion of universal jurisdiction from the classical jurisdictional regime to the present.

In addition, based on the observations in Chapter III, Chapter IV conducts a theoretical analysis of the status of universal jurisdiction under conventional and customary international law during respective periods in history. Under the classical jurisdictional regime, *primary permissive universal jurisdiction* over the crime of piracy was recognized. On the other hand, under the modern jurisdictional regime, *primary obligatory universal jurisdiction* has been expressly recognised in the provision of many treaties since the 1970s, but it is doubtful whether the same can be said within customary international law. It is observed that customary international law neither specifically recognizes nor prohibits it. This study concludes that universal jurisdiction in general is not prohibited under international law, and is thereby legal. Universal jurisdiction is not *per se* in breach of the principles of State sovereignty, the sovereign equality of States, or non-interference in the internal affairs of another State. In the absence of a specific rule prohibiting it and in accordance with the wide discretion given to States in choosing what kind of jurisdiction they provide in their domestic law, permissive universal jurisdiction, including that of universal jurisdiction *in absentia,* is therefore legal. However, the extent to which universal jurisdiction is obligatory may depend on the category of crimes in question, and thereby requires careful examination. In this regard, this study has submitted a new reasoning that may obligate States to exercise universal jurisdiction based on the principle of territorial sovereignty. Yet, such logic does not dispose of the need to prove with solid evidence that an obligation on the part of States has been established. It can be said that, at this moment, universal jurisdiction *in absentia* is not acknowledged as an obligation of every State constituting the international community.

How States gradually come to accept universal jurisdiction is well illustrated in their attitude toward universal jurisdiction over the crime of genocide. This study has conducted an in-depth examination of its legal status under different periods. At the time of the drafting and adoption of the Genocide Convention in the 1940s, the idea of universal jurisdiction was deliberately omitted from the convention, and, besides, there was no customary international law on universal jurisdiction over genocide. However, as time passed and as the political and legal environment of the international community changed, expectations concerning universal jurisdiction grew, and it was considered to be an ideal measure for prosecuting and punishing criminals more efficiently and thereby deterring the continued occurrence of acts alleged to amount to genocide. The Eichmann Trial in the 1960s had an encouraging effect for those who harboured such expectations, although the case itself did cast some doubt as a pure precedent for universal jurisdiction. In fact, this study maintains that it is very likely that permissive universal jurisdiction against genocide became customary international law much later than the Eichmann Trial. The appropriate time seems to be after the influence of the prescription of universal jurisdiction in many multilateral treaties in the 1970s. Although it is now frequently mentioned that universal jurisdiction against genocide is a norm under customary international law, this study has drawn attention to the existence of some ambiguity as to its nature. It is still to be proved with solid evidence that it is recognised as an obligation of, rather than a right of States. More dubious is universal jurisdiction *in absentia* since there is much resistance from States and the practices of States are too divergent to evidence its acceptance. It seems that the recognition of universal jurisdiction against genocide as an obligation is still in its infancy. However, this does not preclude new legal developments, therefore, *opinio juris* and State practice should be carefully followed for the purposes of any future re-evaluation.

Having made an analysis on the legality of jurisdiction, this study has proceeded to examine the appropriateness of exercising jurisdiction. Noting the danger of negative and positive conflicts of jurisdiction, Chapter V emphasises the need to clarify the rules in order to solve such jurisdictional conflicts so as to decide the venue of a trial. Therefore Chapter V attempts to compile some guiding rules that can be utilised in determining the appropriateness of jurisdiction, thus answering the question of 'Which jurisdiction should be exercised?'. In deciding the venue of a trial in the case of a jurisdictional conflict, after examining the legality of jurisdiction and rules prescribed in relevant treaties and conventions (if any), the appropriateness of jurisdictions should be assessed in accordance with the guiding rules.

Chapter VI then applies these guiding rules to non-territorial jurisdiction, namely universal jurisdiction. By examining the appropriateness of non-territorial jurisdiction with the guiding rules, this study dismisses the argument that jurisdictions other than territorial jurisdiction are improper and should not be exercised. This study concludes that, on the contrary, the exercise of non-territorial jurisdiction is considered desirable in certain situations, especially in order to prevent and solve negative conflicts of jurisdiction.

Chapter VI also particularly examined the situation in which universal jurisdiction should be exercised. This study concludes that, based on the rationales of universal jurisdiction, a State, in deciding to exercise universal jurisdiction, should consider some additional criteria. The observations deduced from the application of the guiding rules demonstrates, together with the analysis of the legality of universal jurisdiction in Chapter IV, the role of universal jurisdiction within the modern jurisdictional regime.

3 Propositions

3.1 Gross and serious human rights violations are strictly prohibited under any circumstance

The atrocities committed during the Second World War inspired the international community to acquire a strong commitment never to allow any recurrence of such tragedies in the future. At the same time an awareness of the importance of respecting human rights for establishing and maintaining peace prevailed. Consequently, the Charter of the UN incorporated the protection of human rights as one of its objectives, declaring its determination to 'reaffirm faith in fundamental human rights, in the dignity and worth of the human person'.[1] The prohibition and punishment of systematic or mass violations of fundamental human rights such as the right to life or to human dignity, with which this study is concerned, are no longer within the realm of the domestic affairs of a State, they are rather the concern of the international community as a whole.[2]

Such gross and serious human rights violations are prohibited under any circumstance by international law in various fields, namely, international humanitarian law, criminal law, and human rights law. As explained in Section 4.7 of Chapter I, this study is aware of the fact that the law in these different fields of international law has developed interrelatedly and this therefore prevents any restriction of the examination in this study to one field.

---

1 Preamble of the UN Charter.
2 See Section 2.3 of Chapter II.

For instance, the prohibition of gross and serious violations of human rights can be seen in international humanitarian law. *Jus in bello* which was referred to as the 'law of war' and constituted mainly the Hague law, of which the core concern was the preservation of the right to conduct warfare while restricting some methods of fighting, was given the name of 'international humanitarian law' after the Second World War. The change in name illustrates that more emphasis was given to the humanitarian perspective of protecting the victims of armed conflicts. The Geneva Conventions and their two Protocols provide that, as a minimum guarantee, the victims of armed conflict, especially civilians, women, and children, are to be given certain protection and must be treated humanely without discrimination. Gross and serious human rights violations committed during an armed conflict are likely to fall into the category of a war crime or crimes against humanity, which are strictly prohibited and cannot be justified as acts of war. As international humanitarian law has developed to regulate not only international armed conflicts, but non-international armed conflicts as well, the commission of such a crime during an armed conflict within the territory of a State may also constitute a grave violation of international humanitarian law.

Undoubtedly, gross human rights violations committed outside an armed conflict are also prohibited under international law. In this respect, international human rights law which has achieved a remarkable development after the Second World War clearly prohibits such acts. For instance, the Genocide Convention explicitly states that any act of genocide is prohibited irrespective of whether it is committed 'in time of peace or in time of war'.[3] In addition, considering that the treatment of one's own nationals was traditionally thought to be a domestic matter within a particular State, it is noteworthy that the Genocide Convention was elaborated with a distinct objective and effort to prevent and punish genocide irrespective of the nationality of the victims, therefore prohibiting the abuse of power by a State against its own nationals as well. Therefore, the prohibition of acts of genocide is irrespective of whether such acts are committed during a war or in peacetime, or against foreign nationals or one's own nationals. Similarly, international human rights law does not make the above distinction when prohibiting other gross human rights violations. The prohibition of gross human rights violations cannot be derogated from, even during a situation of emergency.

3.2 It is within the interest of the international community to end the impunity of individuals who are responsible for gross human rights violations

The strict prohibition of gross human rights violations under international law not only binds States, but individuals as well.[4] International humanitarian law, criminal law, and human rights law, all provide that those individuals responsible for such crimes should be held accountable. It is recognized that conducting a trial and establishing account-

3 Article 1 of the Genocide Convention.
4 See Section 2.3 and 2.4 of Chapter II.

ability is one of the means to uphold respect for fundamental human rights. In addition, prosecuting the commission of a heinous crime by means of a fair and impartial mechanism plays a vital role in reconciliation, the interest of the victims to see justice being done, and also the interest of the international community as a whole to deter such violence in the future. The importance of a deterrent effect is highlighted in the prominent example of Hitler proclaiming 'who, after all, is today speaking about the destruction of the Armenians?' as a prelude to his Holocaust policy.[5] It is recognized that the 'fair prosecution and trial of individual suspects can help significantly to build confidence and facilitate reconciliation in post-conflict societies, by removing collective attributions of guilt. Well-publicized prosecutions can deter crimes in current and future conflicts.'[6] Therefore, gross human rights violations should not be ignored or tolerated, and States should confront the criminality of such violations rather than remain acquiescent which may passively encourage others to commit similar crimes.

It is believed that the effective prosecution of individuals who commit gross human rights violations can serve the interest of the local, regional, and international community by contributing to establishing and maintaining peace and good order. The international community has reiterated this recognition especially after the heinous atrocities observed in the former Yugoslavia and Rwanda in the 1990s, and has elaborated new laws and mechanisms for pursuing individual responsibility.[7] Consequently, international humanitarian and criminal law has developed considerably in this respect. It is noted that the development of international humanitarian law, criminal law, and human rights law has been achieved through the mutual influence of these fields of law, and this is likely to continue in the future. For instance, one future objective of international criminal law is, in my opinion, to incorporate and establish international human rights standards within criminal proceedings at both the international and national level.[8] Therefore, the development of international humanitarian, criminal, and human rights law should be studied in correlation.

3.3 Notwithstanding the existence of various international criminal courts, the primary forum for prosecution is still the national courts

Recognizing the importance of ending impunity, this study concentrates on the prosecution and punishment of individuals at the national level. As explained in Section 4.4.2 of Chapter II, it must be reiterated that national courts will remain the main forum for prosecuting individuals. Notwithstanding the establishment of several international criminal courts, the main burden of prosecuting and punishing crimes rests

5 See M. Cherif Bassiouni and Christopher L. Blakesley 'The Need for an International Criminal Court in the New International World Order' 25 Vand. J. Transnational Law, p. 154.
6 'Report of the Secretary-General to the Security Council on the Protection of Civilians in Armed Conflict', UN Doc. S/2001/331, p.3.
7 See Section 4.4.1 of Chapter II, and Section 5.1 of Chapter III.
8 See, for example, Section 6.5 of Chapter V.

with States, hence with their respective national courts. Therefore, it must be recommended that States themselves should take an active role in ending impunity in addition to offering assistance to and cooperation with international criminal courts. To this end, it is important to ensure that national courts are able and willing to prosecute in order to end impunity.

3.4 The modern jurisdictional regime is formulated as a concurrency of various bases of jurisdiction, enhanced by the expansion of jurisdiction

After observing the history and composition of the jurisdictional regime in Chapter II, the following observations can be deduced. Compared to the classical jurisdictional regime, the modern jurisdictional regime underscores more strongly the concurrency of jurisdiction. Under the classical jurisdictional regime, the primary and dominant jurisdiction was undoubtedly territorial jurisdiction, and although *non-territorial jurisdictions* (e.g., nationality jurisdiction, passive personality jurisdiction, protective jurisdiction, and universal jurisdiction) were recognized to some extent, they never achieved a wide degree of acceptance and recognition in law and practice as they do now.[9] Contemporary treaties and conventions on crimes usually explicitly allow, or, moreover, obligate States to establish various bases of national jurisdiction.[10] This 'expansion' of jurisdiction observed since the 1970s in conventional international law resulted from the efforts to overcome the shortcomings of the classical jurisdictional regime dominated by territorial jurisdiction.[11] Thereafter, the recognition, acceptance, and application of non-territorial jurisdictions have been enhanced both at the theoretical and practical level, forming the extensive concurrent jurisdictional regime of the present day. Today, the exercise of non-territorial jurisdictions, including universal jurisdiction, is neither *per se* illegal nor inappropriate, and, on the contrary, is greatly encouraged in certain situations, namely where there is a negative jurisdictional conflict, and when territorial jurisdiction is unlikely to be exercised or it is unlikely that trials will be conducted in a fair, impartial manner, respecting human rights.

3.5 In discussing universal jurisdiction, the following distinctions should be made for the purpose of precision

3.5.1 Universal Jurisdiction and International Criminal Jurisdiction

This study uses the term 'universal jurisdiction' to envisage a jurisdiction exercised by States, distinguished from 'international criminal jurisdiction' exercised by various international criminal courts. The notions of universal jurisdiction and international

---

9 See Section 4.1 of Chapter II.
10 Section 4.3.2 of Chapter I.
11 See Section 4.3.1 of Chapter II.

criminal jurisdiction have been presented as being closely linked to each other since the proposals of each have been simultaneously discussed on a number of occasions. History shows that the idea of universal jurisdiction gained support when international criminal courts were unable to be established, resulting in the incorporation of universal jurisdiction within conventional international law.[12] Therefore, it is understandable that there are schools of thought that consider universal jurisdiction and international criminal jurisdiction to be theoretically identical. However, the similarities in the overall objective and the rationales do not automatically lead to the conclusion that the same law and rules apply and that they should be exercised in the same manner.[13] It should be reiterated that they are historically, theoretically, and practically different, as explained in Chapter IV.

3.5.2 Universal Jurisdiction and Universal Jurisdiction in Absentia

Categorisation within the notion of universal jurisdiction is also recommended for an accurate understanding. Universal jurisdiction is ordinarily based on the presence or custody of a suspect under its control. Therefore it should be distinguished from the jurisdiction asserted without such precondition since there are differences in their scope of acceptance.[14] Ordinary universal jurisdiction seems more solidly grounded in international law than the latter, which, in this study is referred to as 'universal jurisdiction *in absentia*'. While conventional international law provides for universal jurisdiction, universal jurisdiction *in absentia* is not a direct consequence of the expansion of national jurisdiction under conventional international law. It is observed that even the States that allow universal jurisdiction *in absentia* under their domestic law delimit its exercise by characterising it as a supplemental jurisdiction.[15]

3.5.3 Different Nature of Universal Jurisdiction (whether it is permissive or obligatory, and supplemental or primary)

We should also be aware whether universal jurisdiction discussed in a particular context is conceived as a right or as an obligation pertaining to States.[16] In addition, this study has introduced the distinction between the primary and supplemental nature of jurisdiction in order to illustrate how universal jurisdiction was and has been conceived in relation to other jurisdictions.[17] Accordingly, the combination of the above two

---

12 Section 2.5.1 of Chapter IV.

13 See Section 2.5.2.3 of Chapter IV.

14 See Section 3.2.4.2 of Chapter II, and Section 2.1 of Chapter IV.

15 Belgium decided to delimit its universal jurisdiction by amending its law. See Section 5.4.1 of Chapter III. Spain has limited its universal jurisdiction *in absentia* through court decisions. See 5.4.1 of Chapter III.

16 See Section 3.2.4.3 of Chapter II, and Sections 2.2, 3.1.1, and 3.2.3 and 3.2.4 of Chapter IV.

17 See Section 3.2.4.3 of Chapter II, and 2.2 of Chapter IV.

aspects deduces four categories of universal jurisdiction: (1) *supplemental permissive universal jurisdiction*, (2) *primary permissive universal jurisdiction*, (3) *supplemental obligatory universal jurisdiction*, and (4) *primary obligatory universal jurisdiction*.[18]

This study illustrates the development of the notion of universal jurisdiction from the classical jurisdictional regime to the modern jurisdictional regime, from a historical perspective in Chapter III and from a theoretical perspective in Chapter IV. Under the classical jurisdictional regime, universal jurisdiction in general was a right rather than an obligation, and was therefore permissive. Universal jurisdiction was construed as being supplemental to other bases of jurisdiction especially territorial jurisdiction, therefore it was only allowed after efforts to extradite suspects to other States had been exhausted. In short, under the classical jurisdictional regime, *primary permissive universal jurisdiction* was recognised for piracy through customary international law, whereas for other crimes, *supplemental permissive universal jurisdiction* was accepted by some States.[19] But universal jurisdiction began to be employed for different crimes of a serious nature as modern international law came of age, although somewhat slowly due to friction with traditional principles which had governed the classical jurisdictional regime. This change accelerated after the 1970s, when conventional international law instigated the expansion of national jurisdictions including universal jurisdiction.[20] Under the modern jurisdictional regime, universal jurisdiction in conventional international law has overcome its supplemental character also in fields other than piracy and has become a primary jurisdiction. Furthermore, because most contemporary conventions on specific crimes now incorporate the principle of *aut dedere aut judicare*, universal jurisdiction has become obligatory (when there is no extradition to other States) for States which are bound by these conventions. Therefore, today we can observe that *primary obligatory universal jurisdiction* is prescribed under conventional international law.[21]

3.6 National jurisdictions, even universal jurisdiction *in absentia*, are not prohibited under international law unless stated otherwise or unless their exercise would be in breach of other rules of international law

In analysing the status of a particular jurisdiction under international law, we must be aware of whether the exercise of jurisdiction is considered to be a *right* or an *obligation*. Generally speaking, international law does not prohibit any specific basis of national jurisdiction.[22] Unless a particular exercise of jurisdiction is in breach of other rules and principles under international law such as the rules on immunity, a State is not prohibited from exercising its jurisdiction. Therefore, even the most innovative and

18 See the explanation and figure in Section 3.2.4.3 of Chapter II.
19 See Section 2 of Chapter III.
20 See Section 4 of Chapter III.
21 See Section 3.1.1 of Chapter IV.
22 See Section 3.2.1 of Chapter IV.

disputed jurisdiction, such as universal jurisdiction *in absentia,* is not prohibited unless it clashes with other rules or principles under international law.[23] However, the fact that a certain jurisdiction is not prohibited does not signify that such jurisdiction has become part of customary international law. Whether or not a certain matter has become customary international law has to be examined individually for evidence of sufficient custom and *opinio juris* to form a customary norm.[24]

Considering the extraordinary position of universal jurisdiction under the classical jurisdictional regime (in which territorial jurisdiction had dominated) and the lack of a strong nexus between the exercising State and a crime, it is understandable that, even today, States still require explicit law which permits the exercise of universal jurisdiction.

3.7 It is possible that international law concerning obligatory universal jurisdiction may develop in the near future since law and practice relating to universal jurisdiction are still in transition

Although many people conclude without hesitation that universal jurisdiction is a customary norm, what they really mean is that *permissive* universal jurisdiction is a *right* pertaining to a State. There are disputes over whether universal jurisdiction has become a customary obligation, and, if so, over which category of crime, and in what circumstances.[25]

Finding something to be an *obligation* under international law requires a different approach from that of a *right*. It must be proved with due reference to explicit law which obligates States through a written provision under conventional international law or a well-established rule under customary law.[26] Moreover, in order to prove that an exercise of jurisdiction is obligatory, one must examine not only the particular basis of jurisdiction in question, but also the relation to the particular category of crime involved. Therefore, although there seems to be no opposition to making the prosecution and punishment of individuals who are responsible for gross human rights violations an obligation, the law is unclear as to which crimes, and which States, are subject to this obligation.

Evidence of *obligatory universal jurisdiction* is not evident in State practice, but the international community seems to be increasingly accepting and emphasising the idea of the interest of the international community as a whole in ending impunity, and universal jurisdiction as one measure to achieve this end. In this regard, this study observes the development and expansion of universal jurisdiction, and is aware of the fact that the law may change. It is remarkable how the idea of universal jurisdiction over the crime of genocide, which was excluded in the drafting of the Genocide

---

23 See Section 3.2.5 of Chapter IV.

24 See section 3.2.2.5 of Chapter IV.

25 See Section 3.2.2.5 of Chapter IV.

26 See Section 3.2.4.2 of Chapter IV.

Convention, has gained a large degree of support over the years.[27] Undoubtedly, the conceptual notion and practice of universal jurisdiction has expanded since the 1970s and also due to the development of the law triggered by the atrocities in the Former Yugoslavia and Rwanda in the 1990s which invited a renewed commitment on the part of the international community to end impunity. Therefore, although obligatory universal jurisdiction may not, as yet, be well established under customary international law at the time of writing, it may become so in the near future since the law concerning universal jurisdiction seems to be still in transition.

3.8 The principle of State sovereignty should prompt a State where a suspect is present to be under a moral and legal obligation to exercise its jurisdiction

If there is any jurisdiction that has become a customary obligation, it must be territorial jurisdiction. In my opinion, the stronger the nexus a State has over a case, the stronger is its responsibility toward the international community to pursue its accountability. Therefore, it is my belief that territorial States are obliged to respond to gross human rights violations.

In addition, the logic that deduces the responsibility of a territorial State may also raise the responsibility of a State where a suspect is present, that is, a State that is entitled to claim universal jurisdiction. I have put forward a theoretical reasoning employing the principle of territorial sovereignty to support the contention that a State in which a suspect is present is subject to a responsibility to apprehend that suspect and to ensure prosecution.[28] Under the principle of State sovereignty, a State has exclusive authority within its territory. Consequently, a State has the exclusive power to control who enters and stays in its territory, and to establish justice and the rule of law within its territory. In my view, this power entails not just a right, but the responsibility of the State as well. It is the responsibility of the State to secure a law-abiding environment within its territory, and the State can be criticized if it allows criminals to be present in its territory with no accountability without good reason. Therefore, a State where a suspect is present may resolve its failure to establish a law-abiding environment by extraditing him or her, or by exercising its jurisdiction over that person.

3.9 Jurisdictional conflicts should be resolved in a peaceful manner in accordance with the UN Charter and other rules under international law

One problem of maintaining concurrency of jurisdiction is the increased possibility of giving rise to jurisdictional conflicts. Although the objective of concurrency of jurisdiction is to prevent *negative conflicts* in which no State or entity exercises jurisdiction over a case, such a situation may still prevail due to the inherent reluctance on the part

---

27 See Section 4 of Chapter IV.
28 See Section 3.2.4.3 of Chapter IV.

of States.[29] On the other hand, when two or more States claim jurisdiction over a case, a *positive conflict* emerges.[30] Positive conflicts have a danger of evolving into aggressive disputes between States, as was evident in the Lockerbie Case.[31]

In reality, the power to decide the venue of a trial is virtually vested in the hands of a State having custody of a suspect, as explained in Chapter VI. This is because the custodial State generally has discretion in deciding to which State it will extradite a suspect when there are competing requests for extradition. As a result, the system of extradition may now function as a system to allocate cases between States.[32] In any situation, jurisdictional conflicts, just as any other conflicts between States, should be resolved in a peaceful manner and in accordance with the UN Charter and other rules under international law.

3.10 The venue of a trial may be decided by taking into consideration the legality of the particular jurisdictions in question as well as the appropriateness of exercising them

In deciding the venue of a trial in the case of a jurisdictional conflict, in addition to the legality of jurisdictions and rules prescribed in relevant treaties and conventions, the appropriateness of jurisdictions can be compared based on the following criteria examined in Chapter V: the nexus rule; weighing and comparing the interests involved; the gravity of the crime in question and of the charges; the date when proceedings have been instigated; and the capability of a court to ensure fairness, impartiality and the protection of human rights.

In addition to the above criteria, universal jurisdiction may have further criteria considering the rationales and history of universal jurisdiction. Historically, universal jurisdiction has developed with the aim being to prevent negative jurisdictional conflicts. Its rationales were the gravity of the crime and the absence or uncertainty of any jurisdiction that can be effectively exercised.[33] Therefore, universal jurisdiction was not construed as a jurisdiction that would compete with other jurisdictions. Accordingly, universal jurisdiction is most strongly desired when there is no other jurisdiction that can be effectively exercised over the same case.[34] In sum, a State, in deciding to exercise universal jurisdiction, should also consider the following: the seriousness of the crime, especially when basing itself on customary international law; the presence of the suspect within its territory; any other jurisdiction that can be exercised effectively and impartially, including that of other States; the possibility of extradition to

29 See Section 2.3.1 of Chapter V.
30 See Section 2.3.2 of Chapter V.
31 See Section 3 of Chapter V.
32 See Section 5.1 of Chapter VI.
33 See Sections 2.1 of Chapter III, and 2.3 of Chapter IV.
34 See Sections 3.1 and 3.3 of Chapter VI.

States having such jurisdiction; and the ability of its own institutions to conduct proceedings in a fair and impartial manner.[35]

3.11 The prosecution and punishment of individuals must take place in a fair and impartial trial

The interest of the international community in prosecuting and punishing the individuals responsible should be achieved through fair and impartial trials.[36] Fairness and impartiality are beginning to be emphasized, for instance, in the application of the principle of *ne bis in idem* – the principle of *ne bis in idem* will not protect a person from being subject to subsequent prosecution if the previous proceedings were a sham. In addition, suspects should be tried in proceedings which respect due process and the protection of human rights.[37]

As this study has illustrated, recent developments in international criminal law are underpinned by two major concerns. The first is the concern with respect to the lacuna of jurisdiction generating the prevalence of impunity. The second concern is the assurance of fairness, impartiality, and the protection of human rights in the exercise of jurisdiction. The second concern has drawn attention only recently compared to the former, and it thereby needs more careful contemplation as regards its actual content and consequences in the future development of the law.

3.12 States should fulfil their obligation under treaties and conventions on gross human rights violations that they have ratified

In order to end impunity, States should respect and adopt measures prescribed in various treaties and conventions which are related to the prohibition and prosecution of gross human rights violations. The effort to end impunity can more or less start with urging States to perform their obligations. States should prosecute as they are obliged to do so under the treaties they ratify. States should establish adequate national jurisdiction in accordance with their treaty obligations in order to enable their domestic authorities to exercise jurisdiction.[38]

3.13 Future conventions on gross human rights violations and other serious crimes should allow for multiple bases of jurisdiction (including universal jurisdiction) in order to dispense with safe havens for criminals

In order to strengthen the enforcement mechanism for the prohibition and punishment of crime, future conventions should have the objective to diminish possible obstacles

35 See Section 3.3.2 of Chapter VI.
36 See Section 6.5 of Chapter V.
37 See Section 5.2 of Chapter VI.
38 See Section 3.1.1 of Chapter IV.

to prosecution and punishment. First of all, it is better to allow various bases of jurisdiction since the concurrency of jurisdictions contributes to spreading the web of jurisdiction and thereby preventing negative jurisdictional conflicts and ensuring that safe havens for criminals will become a thing of the past.[39] Member States should be obliged to enact proper legislation for establishing jurisdiction, as well as to exercise jurisdiction over suspected cases. In addition, it is advisable and necessary to incorporate provisions on the principle of *aut dedere aut judicare*. Conventions should also incorporate extradition clauses (such as allowing extradition without bilateral extradition treaties), and any other measures to encourage, facilitate, and obligate States to cooperate with and offer assistance to other States for the purpose of prosecution and punishment.

3.14 The international community should assist States to accomplish a fair and impartial exercise of territorial jurisdiction

This study largely concentrates on non-territorial jurisdictions, especially universal jurisdiction. However, it is not my intention to underrate the importance of territorial jurisdiction. On the contrary, I believe that it should be recognized that territorial jurisdiction plays a significant role. It is very easy to criticise the standard of justice in a territorial State where gross human rights violations have been committed. However, rather than completely deny any possibility for trials in such territorial States, States, together with the international community as a whole, should assist territorial States in prosecuting and punishing such crimes in a fair and impartial manner. I will elucidate this last proposition in the next section.

4 Reappraisal of Territorial Jurisdiction

4.1 Status of Territorial Jurisdiction within the Modern Jurisdictional Regime

4.1.1 The Traditional Preference for and the Problems Involved in the Exercise of Territorial Jurisdiction

The prevalence of territorial jurisdiction which had ruled the classical jurisdictional regime is still relevant today. Even under the modern jurisdictional regime, territorial jurisdiction is considered to be the major and the most ordinarily practised jurisdiction, and there is a strong presumption in favour of territorial jurisdiction. However, while continuing to recognize the strong standing of territorial jurisdiction, it is acknowledged that such standing needs to be reconsidered especially in the case of gross human rights violations. As evidenced in the horrifying crisis in the Former Yugoslavia and Rwanda, gross human rights violations on a large scale often occur during a

39 See Section 4.3 of Chapter II.

violent armed conflict. In the event of a large-scale violation whose gravity draws international attention, local authorities are often found to be incapable of prosecuting and punishing the individuals who are responsible for these crimes due to a substantial or partial collapse of law and order in which national authorities lose control over certain regions before, during, or subsequent to such a violent conflict. The legal system thereby ceases to function properly and effectively and the rule of law disappears and is replaced by chaos. It can be speculated that the greater the damage resulting from a violation, the more difficult it is to expect the judicial authorities in the region where the crimes were committed to be able to react properly in response.

Furthermore, the capacity of national courts in the region to prosecute individuals in a fair and impartial manner in the midst or immediate aftermath of a conflict is often subject to serious doubt, and is vulnerable to accusations of arbitrary prosecutions. For instance, it is observed that Bosnian Serbs, Muslims, and Croats have each devoted most of their efforts towards bringing individuals from the other groups to justice for committing crimes during the Bosnian War rather than individuals belonging to their own group. Ellis has criticized the national courts in Bosnia-Herzegovina for not being able to guarantee a fair and politically unbiased judicial process.[40] Also he points out that judges are constrained by the political parties who elect them, noting this problem as the one which is inherent in the judicial system in Bosnia-Herzegovina.[41]

4.1.2 Reliance on Non-Territorial or International Jurisdiction

Deeply concerned by the fact that territorial jurisdiction may not be reliable, the international community responded by establishing *ad hoc* tribunals in order to end impunity and to establish accountability. The establishment of these tribunals signified the commitment on the part of the international community to ensure the prevalence of justice. It may be construed that such intervention by the international community was imperative in the situation described above. The ICTY and ICTR Chief Prosecutor Arbour commented that 'if it had been left to the parties in the former Yugoslavia to prosecute war criminals, you can be certain that none of these former belligerents would have prosecuted their own. They would have been on a campaign of trying to prosecute the alleged war criminals from the other side, and they would have denied that there were any of their side.'[42] Ultimately, she even suggests starting with the

40 See Mark S. Ellis 'Bringing Justice to an Embattled Region – Creating and Implementing the "Rules of the Road" for Bosnia-Herzegovina' *Berkeley Journal of International Law* Vol. 17 (1999), pp. 5-6.

41 See Mark S. Ellis, *ibid.*, p. 6. In addition, Ellis points to other factors which hamper the quality of the Bosnian judicial system such as the outside work which the judges have to do to earn their income, and their lack of training, in addition to the lack of qualified defence lawyers, resources and network systems.

42 See, Jennifer Llewellyn and Sandra Raponi '<Interview> The Protection of Human Rights Through International Criminal law: A Conversation with Madam Justice Louise Arbour, Chief Prosecutor for the International Criminal Tribunals for the Former Yugoslavia and Rwanda' *University of Toronto Faculty of Law Review* Vol. 57 (Winter 1999), p. 99.

presumption that 'the countries involved are normally either unwilling or unable to prosecute', rather than presuming that 'domestic prosecution will work fine'.[43]

Efforts to end impunity are vested in the actions of States as well. States are greatly encouraged to take action themselves in order to achieve this end. Consequently, States with non-territorial jurisdiction are also urged to take all necessary steps to promote justice. It may be reminded that, historically, the virtual lacuna of effective jurisdiction over serious crimes has promoted the 'expansion' of national jurisdiction, greatly enhancing the acceptance of non-territorial jurisdiction including universal jurisdiction. Indeed, international criminal and humanitarian law have developed making use of various bases of jurisdiction in order to overcome the shortcomings of relying on territorial jurisdiction to end impunity. This is how today's concurrent jurisdiction regime is formed.

4.2 The Role of Territorial Jurisdiction and the Importance of Assisting its Exercise

Being aware of the possibility of judicial incapacity and arbitrary trials in the exercise of territorial jurisdiction, and now that we have various bases of national jurisdiction together with international criminal jurisdictions being widely accepted under international law, the following question may be asked:'what is the role of territorial jurisdiction?'

Although history shows that international law has turned to and greatly relied on other bases of jurisdiction to end impunity, this study wishes to stress that the importance of territorial jurisdiction should not be ignored. It is very easy to criticise proceedings in a territorial State as not being up to international standards. To start with, gross human rights violations are often committed in a place where the rule of law is unstable. Moreover, after the devastating effects of such atrocities, a territorial State may not have the power or sufficient facilities to ensure the proper functioning of judicial authority. However, rather than criticising such a State as not living up to the international (or sometimes Western) standards of justice, it is important to help the State to establish an institution that can function correctly. The approach should not be to alienate the territorial State, but to establish or reconstruct peace and justice among the population in that region. The focus should be on eliminating the culture of impunity within the mentality of the population in that region, and to nourish the culture of accountability in order to deter any future occurrence of similar atrocities.

In response to a situation of gross violations of human rights such as the conflicts observed in the Former Yugoslavia and Rwanda, the international community should help the region not only in peacekeeping or humanitarian operations, but also in establishing justice. In ending impunity, the establishment of international criminal jurisdiction may not be enough. The international community should also support the

43 *Ibid.*

establishing or rebuilding of domestic legal structures that will systematise peace and justice in the future post-conflict period for the following reasons.

First of all, it is imperative for reconciliation and deterrence in that region. Without restoring an environment that can sustain law and order, lasting and stable peace for the region cannot be guaranteed or maintained. It is within the interest of the local community to establish or reconstruct institutions capable of guaranteeing and sustaining order based on the rule of law. The importance of establishing the rule of law for reconciling a society torn by conflict and for preventing future conflict was noted by Vieira de Mello, the High Commissioner on Human Rights, as he stated as follows:

> 'The best chance for preventing, limiting, solving and recovering from conflict and violence lies in the restoration and defence of the rule of law. Armed conflict stands as a bloody monument to the failure of the rule of law. We must break the cycle of violence. Where armed repression strips people of their right and dignity, let those responsible answer under the rule of law.'[44]

Also, the importance of national prosecution for a new government in a post-transitional situation is well explained by Roht-Arriaza as follows:

> 'Any transition from authoritarian rule to greater democracy necessarily involves efforts to establish and promote the rule of law. Societies in which massive human rights violations occur with impunity are by definition lawless societies. The lawlessness of the state itself serves to disempower ordinary citizens, making them fearful to think or speak out and breeding cynicism and passivity. As societies attempt to recover from these periods of lawlessness, one of the first opportunities to re-establish the primacy of law over individuals comes in the treatment of the former rulers, torturers, and jailers. If such people are treated summarily, extracting an eye for an eye, the transition to a society of laws is set back immeasurably.'[45]

Furthermore, it needs no mention that establishing regional peace contributes to international peace, and this is also thereby in the interest of the international community as a whole. The interests of the international community and those of the local community do not contradict one another. The interest of the international community in ending impunity for gross violations of human rights lies in establishing justice and deterring future crimes and not in denying territorial jurisdiction. Undoubtedly, the fact that a crime is of international concern does not compel it to be punished only by international criminal courts and to exclude national courts. In deciding the venue of a trial, as I mentioned in Chapter V, we should take the impact of justice into consideration. Conducting trials within the society that is most affected may contribute to making

44 'Message of the High Commissioner on Human Rights Day, 10 December 2002', UN Press Release on 6 December 2002.

45 Naomi Roht-Arriaza 'Introduction', in Naomi Roht-Arriaza ed., *Impunity and Human Rights in International Law and Practice* (Oxford University Press, 1995), pp. 3-4.

people confront the truth, to educate them concerning the suffering caused and to punishing subsequent acts, and thereby ending the cycle of violence and impunity in that region. Therefore, the impact of justice may be greater in conducting trials in a territorial State where the victims can see justice being done at first hand, thereby regenerating their faith in the judicial system, rather than conducting trials in a State which is distant from the victims and the society that were overwhelmed by the violence.

In addition, the historical prevalence of territorial jurisdiction within the classical jurisdictional regime and the continuous respect attributed to territorial jurisdiction within the current jurisdictional regime places the primary burden on a territorial State. It is a territorial State that is expected to take the most active role in establishing justice and peace in the region at first hand – although history proves that it tends not to do so and thereby the international community has pursued international criminal jurisdiction and non-territorial jurisdiction.

Placing some burden on a territorial State to take some action is also important because territorial jurisdiction should participate in handling the potential caseload of prosecuting and punishing persons who have committed gross violations of human rights. Even if an *ad hoc* international criminal tribunal is established to deal with crimes committed in a specific region/situation, or even if the ICC has jurisdiction over crimes, the number of cases that can be processed through these international criminal jurisdictions is very limited. This is so since many human rights violations are committed in a systematic and widespread manner comprising a great number of individual incidents. In addition, the exercise of various non-territorial jurisdictions such as universal jurisdiction may only process a part of the caseload which is unlikely to put an end to impunity when exercised alone. For these reasons, territorial jurisdiction is expected to play a major role in prosecuting and punishing criminals. For instance, the existence of the ICTR and the exercise of non-territorial jurisdiction by other States has not relieved Rwanda from the overwhelming caseload it must handle. The Special Representative of the Commission on Human Rights reported in 2000 that there were around 123,000 detainees still in detention six years into the transition, many without having been charged.[46] The overcrowding in Rwanda's prisons is caused by the stagnation of judicial proceedings, while the Rwandan judicial system is overwhelmed by the number of people in detention. As a solution for easing the overburdened justice system of the Rwandan national courts, the Gacaca system was reintroduced.[47] The Special Representative of the Commission on Human Rights stated:

46 See the Report of the Special Representative of the Commission on Human Rights on the Situation of Human Rights in Rwanda, UN Doc. A/55/269, 4 August 2000, paras. 97, 102.

47 Organic Law No. 40/2000 of 26 January 2001, for the creation of Gacaca Jurisdictions in Rwanda. Reprinted in H. Fischer and Avril McDonald eds., *Yearbook of International Humanitarian Law* Vol. 3: 2000 (T.M.C. Asser Instituut, 2002), p. 739. *See* also, the 1999 Report of the Situation of Human

> 'In an effort to ease overcrowding in jails, promote reconciliation at the community level and, importantly, ensure that justice is seen to be done, the Government plans to revive a system of traditional justice, known as Gacaca … there is no doubt that Gacaca does seem the only viable alternative and the Special Representative therefore supports this approach.'[48]

Another reason why assisting territorial jurisdiction is beneficial is that the exercise of territorial jurisdiction is most likely to be easier and less costly than that of other bases of jurisdiction. Suspects are most likely to be found within the territory of a State where the alleged crimes have been committed. The close proximity to the crime scene is advantageous in terms of access to evidence, victims and witnesses. The territorial State is likely to be able to respond promptly after the commission of a crime. On the other hand, the exercise of non-territorial jurisdiction may be time-consuming, sometimes after a considerable period of time has elapsed after the commission of the crime in question, after one of the victims comes into the territory of the State in question and files a complaint. Even then, more time is required since the State may have to send an investigation team overseas. In sum, a territorial State can investigate and prosecute with less costs due to its proximity to the crime scene, with no extra burden of translation costs or having to familiarise itself with the culture of the local community before the investigation. Considering the efficacy and facility of proceedings and the administration of justice, it is more practical to rely on territorial jurisdiction.

Ultimately, it is important to establish a judicial system free from political interference, capable of guaranteeing fairness, objectivity and impartiality in both substance and form, thereby capable of establishing credibility in law and order on the part of the local, regional, as well as the international community. Therefore, in my opinion, rather than totally dismissing the possibility of trials in a territorial State by criticizing it for not effectively achieving accountability, we should rather explore ways to enhance territorial jurisdiction.

For the above reasons, I think it is beneficial for the international community, with the cooperation of the authorities in the region, to assist in rebuilding a credible judicial system that can prosecute and punish gross human rights violations through fair proceedings. In search of ways to do so, some scholars propose the establishment of a comprehensive international system to provide technical legal assistance to States

Rights in Rwanda Prepared by the Special Representative of the Commission on Human Rights Pursuant to Economic and Social Council Decision 1999/288, *U.N. General Assembly Official Records*, 54th Session, U.N. Doc. A/54/359 (1999), paras. 146-64. Gacaca draws upon a customary system of community hearings to resolve local disputes. The new gacaca tribunals, however, merge customary practice with a formal court structure. The tribunals are judicial bodies and the judges can impose sentences as severe as life imprisonment.

48 Situation of Human Rights in Rwanda, prepared by the Special Representative of the Commission on Human Rights pursuant to Economic and Social Council decision 1999/288 of 30 July 1999, submitted on 17 September 1999.

emerging from domestic or international armed conflict,[49] but such a systematic international institution has not been established to date. I think that the international community can assist a State to develop a legal system which guarantees a fair and politically unbiased judicial process, thereby enabling it to undertake a prominent role in prosecuting violations and this is undoubtedly within its interest. By doing so, the international community can assist in establishing and maintaining peace and the rule of law in a particular region.

5 Is the Role of Non-Territorial Jurisdiction Auxiliary?

Hypothetically speaking, if territorial jurisdiction can be exercised in a fair and impartial manner, then there may be no need for other forms of jurisdictions including international criminal jurisdiction or universal jurisdiction to be exercised. In fact, to establish an environment in which territorial jurisdiction can be exercised in a proper manner serves the interest of the local community as well as the interest of the international community in ending impunity for gross violations of human rights. Although the importance of reconstructing or establishing a judicial system governed by the rule of law that can sustain fairness and impartiality is widely recognised, this is easier said than done. Considerable international efforts have been extended with this objective in mind, but there still remain many obstacles such as a lack of material and personnel resources, facilities, and financial support. Some criticise the lack of a master plan and an insufficient focus on the development of local capacity or on the viability of that system, and also the poor administration of the courts as the source of many of the shortcomings of the internationalised justice system.[50] Ratner and Abrams are of the opinion that a fair and effective judiciary requires four fundamental conditions: (1) a workable legal framework through well-crafted statutes of criminal law and procedure; (2) a trained cadre of judges, prosecutors, defenders, and investigators; (3) adequate infrastructure, such as courtroom facilities, investigative offices, record-keeping capabilities, and detention and prison facilities; and (4) a culture of respect for the fairness and impartiality of the process and the right of the accused.[51]

---

49 It is claimed that an international mechanism called 'International Legal Assistance Consortium (ILAC)' should be established to facilitate and coordinate NGO, government and UN efforts to this end. See "Facilitation of National and International Accountability Mechanisms: International Legal Assistance Consortium (ILAC)", annexed to 'Draft Guiding Principles for Combating Impunity for International Crimes (Revised October 30, 1997)', in Christopher C. Joyner and M. Cherif Bassiouni eds. (Association Internationale de Droit Pénal), *Reining in Impunity for International Crimes and Serious Violations of Fundamental Human Rights: Proceedings of the Siracusa Conference 17-21 September 1998* (Nouvelle Études Pénales, 1998), pp. 543-548.

50 See Suzannah Linton 'New Approaches to International Justice in Cambodia and East Timor' *IRRC* Vol. 84 No. 845 (March 2002), p. 109.

51 See Steven R. Ratner and Jason S. Abrams, *Accountability for Human Rights Atrocities in International Law: Beyond the Nuremberg Legacy*, 2nd ed. (Oxford University Press, 2001), p. 183.

If that which impedes the prosecution of crimes is a simple problem such as the lack of infrastructure, then the assistance given by the international community introduced in this chapter may be sufficient for achieving that end. However, if there are more complicated factors such as ethnic or other forms of group antagonism or there is political sensitivity among the local community, even with cooperation from the international community, it may still be better to conduct a trial in a foreign State or before an international criminal court, depending on the situation of each case. Therefore, the expectation placed on the role of international criminal courts and of non-territorial jurisdiction, including universal jurisdiction, still remains significant.

NEDERLANDSE SAMENVATTING

Het strikte verbod op grove schending van de mensenrechten in het internationale recht bindt niet alleen staten, maar ook individuen. Het humanitair oorlogsrecht, het strafrecht en de mensenrechten bepalen allen dat individuen die dergelijke misdrijven hebben begaan daarvoor verantwoordelijk moeten worden gehouden. Het is algemeen geaccepteerd dat het voeren van een proces en het vaststellen van verantwoordelijkheid een manier is om het respect voor fundamentele mensenrechten te handhaven. Daarnaast kan de vervolging van een gruwelijk misdrijf middels een eerlijk en onpartijdig mechanisme in het belang zijn van de lokale, regionale en internationale gemeenschap, omdat zij bijdraagt aan de totstandkoming en handhaving van de vrede en goede orde. In de erkenning dat een dergelijke vervolging een betere verwezenlijking van de mensenrechten en de voorkoming van toekomstige misdaden bevordert en tevens het recht tot een gevestigde instelling maakt, is dit onderzoek gewijd aan het internationaalrechtelijke rechtsmachtregime dat de vervolging van individuen voor grove en ernstige schendingen van de mensenrechten beheerst.

Het eigenlijke punt van zorg dat de aanleiding vormde voor dit onderzoek was de vraag hoe de straffeloosheid van individuen die verantwoordelijk zijn voor grove en ernstige schendingen van de mensenrechten moet worden opgeheven. In dit onderzoek worden dan ook de volgende centrale vragen gesteld: *Welke rechtsmacht kan en moet worden uitgeoefend teneinde de vervolging te bewerkstelligen van personen die verantwoordelijk zijn voor grove en ernstige schendingen van de mensenrechten? En meer in het bijzonder: wat is in dit opzicht de rol van universele rechtsmacht?*

De antwoorden op deze vragen weerspiegelen de algehele structuur van het hedendaagse jurisdictiestelsel. Hoewel het huidige jurisdictieregime in de internationale context wordt geformuleerd in termen van de samenloop van zowel nationale als internationale jurisdicties, concentreert dit onderzoek zich op de nationale rechtsmacht om zo de rol van de staat bij de handhaving van het internationale strafrecht, het humanitaire oorlogsrecht en de mensenrechten te definiëren. De reden hiervoor is dat ondanks de oprichting van verscheidene internationale strafhoven the grootste last van de vervolging en bestraffing van misdrijven toch neerkomt op de staten zelf, en daarmee op hun nationale rechters. Daarom wordt aanbevolen om staten zelf een actieve rol te laten spelen in het opheffen van de straffeloosheid, naast het bieden van hulp aan en de samenwerking met international strafhoven.

Teneinde een antwoord te formuleren op de twee hierboven geïntroduceerde centrale vragen, heb ik eerst in hoofdstuk II enige algemene feiten en aannames in de discussie toegelicht door de relevante beginselen in het internationale recht aan te geven, de verschillende grondslagen voor rechtsmacht uit te leggen en de ontwikkeling en structuur van het hedendaagse rechtsmachtstelsel te beschrijven. In de uiteenzetting van het hedendaagse rechtsmachtregime werpt dit onderzoek licht op het verschijnsel van wat ik noem de 'uitbreiding' van rechtsmacht – de theoretische and praktische toename van de erkenning, aanvaarding en toepassing van verschillende gronden voor rechtsmacht. Ik beschouw dit verschijnsel als de belangrijkste verandering die het hedendaagse rechtsmachtregime ertoe heeft aangezet om af te wijken van een aantal traditionele principes die het klassieke rechtsmachtregime beheersten. Om de overgang van het klassieke naar het moderne stelsel te illustreren en om de spanning tussen de verschillende gronden voor rechtsmacht voelbaar te maken wordt in dit onderzoek gebruik gemaakt van een speciale indeling in categorieën waarmee onderscheid wordt gemaakt tussen territoriale rechtsmacht en andere gronden voor nationale rechtsmacht. Deze laatste worden in dit onderzoek gronden voor 'niet-territoriale rechtsmacht' genoemd.

In vergelijking met het klassieke rechtsmachtregime, wordt in het moderne rechtsmachtregime de samenloop van rechtsmacht sterker onderstreept. Het lijdt geen twijfel dat op grond van het klassieke rechtsmachtregime de territoriale rechtsmacht de voornaamste en de overheersende vorm van rechtsmacht was en hoewel vormen van niet-territoriale rechtsmacht (bijvoorbeeld op grond van nationaliteit of passieve personaliteit, beschermende rechtsmacht en universele rechtsmacht) wel tot op zekere hoogte werden erkend, werden zij niet zo breed erkend en aanvaard in het recht en de praktijk als nu het geval is. Nu staan verdragen met betrekking tot misdrijven vaak expliciet toe dat staten verschillende gronden voor rechtsmacht vestigen of ze schrijven dit zelfs voor. Deze 'uitbreiding' van rechtsmacht die sinds de jaren zeventig wordt waargenomen in het internationale verdragsrecht was het resultaat van inspanningen om de tekortkomingen van het klassieke rechtsmachtregime, dat werd gedomineerd door territoriale rechtsmacht, te overwinnen. Sindsdien zijn de erkenning, aanvaarding en toepassing van niet-territoriale rechtsmacht zowel op theoretisch als praktisch niveau toegenomen en uitgemond in het uitgebreide stelsel van concurrerende rechtsmacht dat wij nu kennen.

Van de verschillende gronden voor nationale rechtsmacht belicht hoofdstuk III hoe de universele rechtsmacht zich in de loop van de geschiedenis heeft ontwikkeld, waarbij tevens de prominente en vernieuwende ontwikkelingen die het hedendaagse rechtsmachtregime kenmerken worden uitgediept. De universele rechtsmacht, die is ontstaan om jurisdictie te kunnen uitoefenen over het misdrijf piraterij, werd gaandeweg steeds vaker ingezet voor verschillende ernstige misdrijven, hoewel deze ontwikkeling zich door wrijving met de traditionele beginselen en regels, zoals die van de overheersende territoriale rechtsmacht, niet erg snel kon voltrekken. Het tempo van deze omwenteling begon echter te versnellen na de jaren zeventig toen in veel verdragen de uitbreiding van de nationale rechtsmacht, waaronder universele rechtsmacht, geleidelijk werd omarmd. Deze verschuiving in het internationale verdragsrecht kon plaatsvinden dankzij de vastberadenheid van staten om snel te komen tot preventie en bestraffing van gewelddadig terroristisch optreden. Daarnaast heeft de snelle ontwikkeling van het humanitair oorlogsrecht, die in gang werd gezet door de wreedheden in Joegoslavië en Ruanda in de jaren negentig, ook een grote invloed gehad op de praktijk en op het conceptuele begrip 'universele rechtsmacht'. Toch hebben de snelle veranderingen met betrekking tot universele rechtsmacht ook wel weerstand opgeroepen bij staten en de laatste tijd is een zekere aarzeling waarneembaar om deze rechtsmacht actief uit te oefenen.

Hierna leg ik in hoofdstuk III het theoretische begrip 'universele rechtsmacht' nader uit. De relatie met internationaal strafrechtelijke rechtsmacht en met de beginselen van *jus cogens* en *obligatio erga omnes* wordt uiteengezet om de wijdverbreide misvatting dat deze verschillende begrippen hetzelfde zijn als, of inbegrepen zijn in, het begrip universele rechtsmacht weg te nemen. In dit onderzoek wordt de term 'universele rechtsmacht' gebruikt om de rechtsmacht aan te duiden die wordt uitgeoefend door staten, hetgeen dient te worden onderscheiden van de 'internationaal strafrechtelijke rechtsmacht' die wordt uitgeoefend door de verscheidene internationale strafhoven. De begrippen universele rechtsmacht en internationaal strafrechtelijke rechtsmacht worden regelmatig gepresenteerd als onderling sterk verbonden concepten omdat hun eigenschappen vaak tegelijkertijd worden besproken. Toch leiden de gelijkenissen tussen de algemene doelstellingen en bestaansredenen van de beide begrippen niet automatisch tot de conclusie dat hetzelfde recht en dezelfde regels van toepassing zijn en dat deze vormen van rechtsmacht op dezelfde wijze moeten worden uitgeoefend. Het is nodig te herhalen dat de begrippen in historische, theoretische en praktische zin van elkaar verschillen.

In hoofdstuk IV worden de definitie, de bestaansredenen en de bronnen van universele rechtsmacht nader toegelicht. Binnen het begrip universele rechtsmacht wijst dit onderzoek ook op de noodzaak om universele rechtsmacht te onderscheiden van universele rechtsmacht *in absentia*. Universele rechtsmacht is gewoonlijk gebaseerd op de aanwezigheid of hechtenis van een verdachte en moet onderscheiden worden van rechtsmacht die wordt uitgeoefend zonder dat dit een voorwaarde is, omdat de mate van aanvaarding van beide verschilt. Gewone universele rechtsmacht lijkt steviger verankerd in het internationale recht dan die *in absentia*. Universele rechtsmacht stoelt op verdragsrecht, terwijl universele rechtsmacht *in absentia* geen direct gevolg is van de uitbreiding van nationale rechtsmacht onder het internationale verdragsrecht. Zelfs die staten die universele rechtsmacht *in absentia* toestaan op grond van hun nationale recht beperken de uitoefening ervan door deze rechtsmacht te kenmerken als een aanvullende vorm van rechtsmacht.

In dit onderzoek wordt de aard van universele rechtsmacht onderverdeeld in twee categorieën. Ten eerste wordt onderzocht of de rechtsmacht wordt *toegestaan* of *voorgeschreven* en ten tweede of hij *aanvullend* is of *primair*. Het aanbrengen van dit onderscheid helpt een beter inzicht te vergaren in de evolutie van het begrip universele rechtsmacht van het klassieke regime naar het huidige.

Op basis van de waarnemingen in hoofdstuk III, wordt in hoofdstuk IV een theoretische analyse gemaakt van de positie van de universele rechtsmacht in het internationale verdragsrecht en gewoonterecht gedurende verschillende periodes in de geschiedenis. Op grond van het klassieke rechtsmachtregime was universele rechtsmacht eerder een recht dan een verplichting en was dus *toegestaan*. Onder het klassieke rechtsmachtregime werd de *primaire toegestane universele rechtsmacht* over het misdrijf van de piraterij erkend. Voor andere misdrijven dan piraterij werd universele rechtsmacht geïnterpreteerd als een aanvullende grond naast andere gronden voor rechtsmacht, voornamelijk territoriale rechtsmacht, en werd daarom enkel toegestaan nadat alle pogingen om verdachten aan andere staten uit te leveren hadden gefaald. In tegenstelling hiermee wordt universele rechtsmacht onder het hedendaagse rechtsmachtregime juist vaak verplicht gesteld voor verdragspartijen, nu de meeste moderne verdragen over specifieke misdrijven het beginsel van *aut dedere aut judicare* bevatten. Nu zien we dus vaak dat *primaire verplichte universele rechtsmacht* wordt voorgeschreven op grond van internationaal verdragsrecht. Het valt echter te betwijfelen of hetzelfde geldt op grond van het internationale gewoonterecht. In het internationale gewoonterecht wordt universele rechtsmacht niet met name erkend, noch verboden. In dit onderzoek wordt dan ook geconcludeerd dat universele rechtsmacht in het algemeen niet verboden wordt door het internationale recht en dus rechtmatig is. Universele rechtsmacht betekent op zichzelf geen schending van het beginsel van de staatssoevereiniteit, het beginsel van de soevereine gelijkheid van staten of het beginsel dat staten zich niet mengen in de binnenlandse aangelegenheden van andere staten. Bij afwezigheid van een specifieke regel die universele rechtsmacht verbiedt en overeenkomstig de ruime keuzevrijheid die staten hebben om vast te stellen welke vorm van rechtsmacht zij wensen vast te leggen in hun nationale recht, is toegestane universele rechtsmacht, met inbegrip van universele rechtsmacht *in absentia*, dus rechtmatig. De mate waarin universele rechtsmacht verplicht is kan echter afhangen van de betreffende categorie misdrijven en dient daarom zorgvuldig te worden nagegaan.

In dit opzicht komt dit onderzoek met een nieuwe redenering die staten ertoe kan verplichten om universele rechtsmacht uit te oefenen op grond van het beginsel van de territoriale soevereiniteit. Dezelfde logica die gebruikt wordt om te concluderen tot de verantwoordelijkheid van de territoriale staat, kan ook leiden tot verantwoordelijkheid van de staat waar de verdachte verblijft, namelijk de staat die gerechtigd is universele rechtsmacht op te eisen. Volgens het beginsel van de staatssoevereiniteit hebben staten exclusieve zeggenschap binnen hun eigen grondgebied. Als gevolg daarvan hebben staten dus de exclusieve bevoegdheid om te bepalen wie het grondgebied mag betreden en verlaten, en om het recht en de handhaving daarvan binnen hun grondgebied te regelen. Ik ben van mening dat deze bevoegdheid niet slechts een recht inhoudt, maar ook een verantwoordelijkheid. De staat is ervoor verantwoordelijke een klimaat op zijn grondgebied te scheppen waarin het recht wordt nageleefd en staten kunnen terecht bekritiseerd worden als zij toestaan dat misdadigers zich op hun grondgebied ophouden zonder ter verantwoording te worden geroepen en als daarvoor geen legitiem excuus bestaat. De staat waar een verdachte verblijft kan het feit dat hij heeft nagelaten een dergelijk klimaat te scheppen goedmaken door deze verdachte ofwel uit te leveren, ofwel zijn rechtsmacht over de verdachte uit te oefenen.

Deze logica zet echter niet de noodzaak om door middel van solide bewijzen aan te tonen dat deze verplichting voor staten nu gevestigd is opzij. Op dit moment kan gezegd worden dat universele rechtsmacht *in absentia* niet erkend wordt als verplichting voor alle staten die samen de internationale gemeenschap vormen.

Hoe staten geleidelijk aan universele rechtsmacht begonnen te aanvaarden wordt duidelijk geïllustreerd door hun houding ten opzichte van universele rechtsmacht over genocide. In het onderzoek wordt een grondige analyse gegeven van de juridische status van genocide tijdens verschillende periodes in de geschiedenis. Ten tijde van de vervaardiging en vaststelling van het Genocideverdrag in de jaren veertig, werd het idee van de universele rechtsmacht opzettelijk uit de tekst van het verdrag gehouden en was er bovendien nog geen internationaal gewoonterecht inzake universele rechtsmacht voor genocide. Naarmate echter de tijd verstreek en het politieke en juridische klimaat in de internationale gemeenschap veranderde namen de verwachtingen ten aanzien van universele rechtsmacht toe en werd het gezien als een ideale maatregel voor een efficiëntere vervolging en bestraffing van misdadigers die zodoende ook afschrikwekkend zou werken tegen het verder plaatsvinden van handelingen waarvan men meent dat ze genocide opleveren. Het Eichmannproces in de jaren zestig moedigde degenen die deze verwachtingen koesterden nog verder aan, hoewel de zaak zelf enige twijfel opriep als zuiver precedent voor universele rechtsmacht. In dit onderzoek is zelfs het standpunt gekozen dat toegestane universele rechtsmacht voor genocide hoogstwaarschijnlijk pas lang na het Eichmannproces internationaal gewoonterecht werd. Het feitelijke tijdstip lijkt te zijn geweest ergens in de jaren zeventig toen de invloed van de voorgeschreven universele rechtsmacht in een groot aantal multilaterale verdragen voelbaar werd. Hoewel nu regelmatig wordt opgemerkt dat universele rechtsmacht over genocide een norm van internationaal gewoonterecht is, is deze rechtsmacht volgens dit onderzoek nog enigszins dubbelzinnig van aard. Nog steeds moet met solide bewijzen worden aangetoond dat deze rechtsmacht nu erkend is als een verplichting van staten, in plaats van als hun recht. Nog twijfelachtiger is universele rechtsmacht *in absentia* omdat er een behoorlijke weerstand tegen bestaat bij staten en het gedrag van staten op dit punt te ver uiteenloopt om het bewijs te kunnen leveren voor de aanvaarding ervan. Het lijkt erop dat de erkenning van universele rechtsmacht over genocide als verplichting nog in de kinderschoenen staat. Dit sluit echter nieuwe juridische ontwikkelingen niet uit en daarom moeten de *opinio juris* en de staatspraktijk nauwlettend worden gevolgd ten behoeve van een mogelijke herevaluatie in de toekomst.

Het gevaar van zowel negatieve als positieve rechtsmachtconflicten onderkennende, wordt in hoofdstuk V het belang benadrukt van opheldering over de toepasselijke regels die deze rechtsmachtconflicten kunnen oplossen, waarmee de plaats van berechting kan worden vastgesteld. In dit hoofdstuk wordt gepoogd een aantal richtsnoeren bijeen te brengen die kunnen worden gebruikt bij de beslissing over de juiste rechtsmacht, m.a.w. die de vraag kunnen beantwoorden: 'Welke rechtsmacht moet hier worden uitgeoefend?'. Bij de beslissing over de plaats van berechting in het geval van een conflict over de rechtsmacht kan, naast basering op de rechtmatigheid van de rechtsmacht en de regels uit de relevante verdragen, de juistheid van de verschillende soorten rechtsmacht worden getoetst aan de hand van de volgende criteria die in hoofdstuk V worden besproken: de nexusregel, het wegen en vergelijken van de betrokken belangen, de ernst van het misdrijf in kwestie en van de beschuldigingen, de datum waarop de gerechtelijke procedure aanving en de mate waarin een rechter in staat is om een eerlijk en onpartijdig proces en de bescherming van de mensenrechten te garanderen.

In hoofdstuk VI worden deze richtsnoeren vervolgens toegepast op niet-territoriale rechtsmacht, namelijk op universele rechtsmacht. Door de juistheid van niet-territoriale rechtsmacht aan de hand van de richtsnoeren te onderzoeken wordt het argument van tafel geveegd dat iedere andere dan territoriale rechtsmacht onjuist is en niet uitgeoefend zou moeten worden. Tegenwoordig is het uitoefenen van niet-territoriale rechtsmacht, inclusief universele rechtsmacht, op zichzelf noch onrechtmatig, noch ongeschikt, maar wordt in tegendeel juist toegejuicht in bepaalde situaties, namelijk in geval van een negatief rechtsmachtconflict en als territoriale rechtsmacht waarschijnlijk niet uitgeoefend zal worden of wanneer het niet waarschijnlijk is dat processen op eerlijke en onpartijdige wijze en met respect voor de mensenrechten zullen worden gevoerd.

Hoofdstuk VI onderzoekt met name situaties waarin universele rechtsmacht dient te worden uitgeoefend. Naast bovengenoemde criteria, gelden voor universele rechtsmacht ook andere criteria die de bestaansredenen en de geschiedenis van universele rechtsmacht betreffen. Historisch gezien heeft universele rechtsmacht zich ontwikkeld met het doel negatieve rechtsmachtconflicten te voorkomen. De beweegreden hiervoor was de ernst van het misdrijf en de afwezigheid van of onzekerheid omtrent rechtsmacht die in zo'n geval effectief kon worden uitgeoefend. Universele rechtsmacht is dus niet in het leven geroepen om te concurreren met andere vormen van rechtsmacht. Dienovereenkomstig is er een sterke behoefte aan universele rechtsmacht bij afwezigheid van een andere rechtsmachtvorm die over het betreffende geval kan worden uitgeoefend. Samengevat zou een staat bij zijn beslissing om universele rechtsmacht uit te oefenen tevens de volgende zaken moeten overwegen: de ernst van het misdrijf, met name wanneer de staat zich baseert op internationaal gewoonterecht, de aanwezigheid van de verdachte op zijn grondgebied, of er een andere rechtsmacht is, inclusief die van andere staten, die op effectieve en onpartijdige wijze kan worden uitgeoefend, de mogelijkheid van uitlevering aan staten die dergelijke rechtsmacht bezitten en de mate waartoe de eigen instanties van de staat in staat zijn om een eerlijk en onpartijdig proces te houden. De gevolgtrekkingen op grond van de toepassing van deze richtsnoeren en de analyse van de rechtmatigheid van universele rechtsmacht in hoofdstuk IV maken duidelijk welke rol universele rechtsmacht speelt binnen het huidige rechtsmachtregime.

Dit onderzoekt concentreert zich vooral op niet-territoriale rechtsmacht, met name universele rechtsmacht. Ik bedoel hier echter niet het belang van territoriale rechtsmacht mee te onderschatten. In tegendeel, het moet onderkend worden dat territoriale rechtsmacht een belangrijke rol speelt. Het is natuurlijk makkelijk om het niveau van de rechtspleging in een territoriale staat waar ernstige mensenrechtenschendingen hebben plaatsgevonden te bekritiseren. Toch zouden staten, in plaats van de mogelijkheid van berechting in zulke territoriale staten geheel uit te sluiten, samen met de internationale gemeenschap als geheel deze territoriale staten behulpzaam moeten zijn bij het op een eerlijke en onpartijdige wijze vervolgen en bestraffen van zulke misdrijven.

De hypothese is dat wanneer territoriale rechtsmacht op eerlijke en onpartijdige wijze kan worden uitgeoefend er geen behoefte meer bestaat aan de uitoefening van andere vormen van rechtsmacht, inclusief internationaal strafrechtelijke rechtsmacht of universele rechtsmacht. Het scheppen van een omgeving waarin territoriale rechtsmacht op de juiste wijze kan worden uitgeoefend dient de belangen van zowel de lokale gemeenschap als de internationale gemeenschap bij het beëindigen van straffeloosheid voor grove schendingen van de mensenrechten. Maar toch is dit gemakkelijker gezegd dan gedaan, zelfs al wordt het belang van het herstructureren of opbouwen van een systeem voor rechtspleging dat wordt beheerst door recht en dat blijvend eerlijkheid en onpartijdigheid kan bieden breed erkend. Aanzienlijke internationale inspanningen zijn al gepleegd met dit doel voor ogen, maar veel hindernissen blijven overeind, zoals een gebrek aan materiele en personele hulpmiddelen, aan geschikte voorzieningen en aan financiële ondersteuning.

Als wat aan de vervolging van misdrijven in de weg staat simpelweg het ontbreken van de juiste infrastructuur is, zou hulp van de internationale gemeenschap voldoende kunnen zijn om de problemen op te lossen. Wanneer echter complexere factoren in het geding zijn, zoals etnische of andere groepstegenstellingen, of wanneer de zaak politiek gevoelig ligt bij de lokale gemeenschap, zelfs na bemoeienis van de internationale gemeenschap, kan het toch beter zijn berechting in een andere staat of voor een internationaal straftribunaal te laten plaatsvinden, afhankelijk van de situatie per geval. Om deze reden blijven de verwachtingen van de rol die internationale strafhoven en niet-territoriale rechtsmacht, met inbegrip van universele rechtsmacht, kunnen spelen, hooggespannen.

SELECTED BIBLIOGRAPHY

Aceves, William J.
'Liberalism and International Legal Scholarship: The Pinochet Case and the Move Toward a Universal System of Transnational Law Litigation' *Harvard International Law Journal* Vol. 41 No. 1 (Winter 2000)

Africa Legal Aid (AFLA)
The Cairo-Arusha Principle on Universal Jurisdiction in Respect of Gross Human Rights Offences: An African Perspectives, adopted at the Follow-up Expert Meeting held at Arusha, 18-20 October 2002, http://www.afla.unimaas.nl/en/act/index.html

Akehurst, M
'Jurisdiction in International Law' *British Yearbook of International Law* Vol. 46 (1972-73)

Akhavan, Payam
'Beyond Impunity: Can International Criminal Justice Prevent Future Atrocities?' *American Journal of International Law* Vol. 95 No. 1 (January 2001)

American Law Institute
Restatement of the Law (Third), The Foreign Relations Law of the United States (1987)

Amnesty International
'Universal Jurisdiction: The duty of states to enact and implement legislation' (September 2001), AI Index: IOR 53/002/2001

Bantekas, Ilias, and Nash, Susan, and Mackarel, Mark (eds)
International Criminal Law (Cavendish Publishing, 2001)

Barboza, Julio
'International Criminal Law' *Recueil des Cours* Tome 278 (1999)

Bassiouni, M. Cherif
International Criminal Law Vol. II: Procedural and Enforcement Mechanisms, 2nd ed., (Transnational Publishers, 1999)

Bassiouni, M. Cherif
'Universal Jurisdiction for International Crimes: Historical Perspectives and Contemporary Practice' *Virginia Journal of International Law* Vol. 42 (2001)

Bassiouni, M. Cherif, and Wise, Edward M.
Aut Dedere Aut Judicare: The Duty to Extradite or Prosecute in International Law (Martinus Nijhoff Publishers, 1995)

Baxter, R.R.
'The Municipal and International Law Basis of Jurisdiction Over War Crimes' *British Yearbook of International Law* 28 (1951)

Benavides, Luis
'The Universal Jurisdiction Principle: Nature and Scope' *Annuario Mexicano de Derencho International* Vol. 1 (2001)
Bolton, John R.
'Universal Jurisdiction: Too Easily Sweeps Political Differences into Legal Arena' Legal Times (11 January 1999), at the home page of the American Enterprise Institute for Public Policy Research, *http://www.aei.org*
Bowett, D.W.
'Jurisdiction: Changing Patterns of Authority over Activities and Resources' *British Year Book of International Law* Vol. 53 (1982)
Broomhall, Bruce
'Towards the Development of an Effective System of Universal Jurisdiction for Crimes Under International Law' *New England Law Review* 35 (Winter 2001)
Broomhall, Bruce
International Justice and the International Criminal Court: Between Sovereignty and the Rule of Law (Oxford University Press, 2003)
Brown, Bartram S.
'The Evolving Concept of Universal Jurisdiction' *New England Law Review* Vol. 35 No. 2
Brown, Bartram S.
'Primacy or Complementarity: Reconciling the Jurisdiction of National Courts and International Criminal Tribunals' *Yale Journal of International Law* Vol. 23 (1998)
Carnegie, A.R.
'Jurisdiction over Violations of the Laws and Customs of War' *British Yearbook of International Law* Vol. 39 (1963)
Cassese, Antonio
'Is the Bell Tolling for Universality? A Plea for a Sensible Notion of Universal Jurisdiction' *Journal of International Criminal Justice* Vol. 1 No. 3 (December 2003)
Cassel, Douglass
'Empowering United States Courts to Hear Crimes Within the Jurisdiction of the International Criminal Court' *New England Law Review* 35 (Winter 2001)
Charney, Jonathan I.
'International Criminal Law and the Role of Domestic Courts' *American Journal of International Law* Vol. 95 (2001)
Cissé, Catherine
'The End of a Culture of Impunity in Rwanda? Prosecution of Genocide and War Crimes before Rwandan Courts and the International Criminal Tribunal for Rwanda' *Yearbook of International Humanitarian Law* Vol. 1 (1998)
Cottier, Michael
'What Relationship Between the Exercise of Universal and Territorial Jurisdiction? The Decision of 13 December 2000 of the Spanish National Court Shelving the Proceedings Against Guatemalan Nationals Accused of Genocide', in Horst Fischer, Claus Kreß, Sascha Rolf Lüder eds., *International and National Prosecution of Crimes Under International Law: Current Developments* (Berlin Verlag Arno Spitz GmbH, 2001)

Cowles, Willard B.
'Universality of Jurisdiction over War Crimes' *California Law Review* 33 (1945)
Cowles, Willard B.
'Trials of War Criminals (Non-Nuremberg)' *American Journal of International Law* Vol. 42 (1948)
Dinstein, Yoram, and Mala Tabory (eds)
War Crimes in International Law (Martinus Nijhoff Publishers, 1996)
Dugard, John
'Universal Jurisdiction for Crimes Against Humanity' *African Legal Aid Quarterly* January-March (2000)
Eser, Albin
'Common Goals and Different Ways in International Criminal Law: Reflections from a European Perspective' *Harvard International Law Journal* Vol. 31 No. 1 (Winter 1990)
Eser, Albin, and Lagodny, Otto, and Blakesley, Christopher L. (eds)
The Individual as Subject of International Cooperation in Criminal Matters: A Comparative Study (Nomos Verlagsgesellschaft, Baden-Baden, 2002)
Fawcett, J.E.S.
'The Eichmann Case' *British Year Book of International Law* Vol.38 (1962), p. 215
Griffin, Mary
'Ending the Impunity of Perpetrators of Human Rights Atrocities: A Major Challenge for International Law in the 21st Century' *International Review of the Red Cross* No. 838 (June 2000)
Hall, Christopher Keith
'Universal Jurisdiction: New Uses for an Old Tool', in Mark Lattimer and Philippe Sands QC eds., *Justice for Crimes Against Humanity* (Hart Publishing 2003)
Hasson, Adam Isaac
'Extraterritorial Jurisdiction and Sovereign Immunity on Trial: Noriega, Pinochet, and Milosevic – Trends in Political Accountability and Transnational Criminal Law' *Boston College International and Comparative Law Review* Vol. XXV No. 1 (Winter 2002)
Henzelin, M.
Le Principe De L'universalité en Droit Pénal International: Droit et obligation pour les États de poursuivre et juger selon le principe de l'universalité (Helbing & Lichtenhahn, 2000)
International Council on Human Rights Policy
Hard Cases: Bringing Human Rights Violators to Justice Abroad – A Guide to Universal Jurisdiction (International Council on Human Rights Policy, 1999)
International Law Association
'Final Report on the Exercise of Universal Jurisdiction in Respect of Gross Human Rights Offences', Committee on International Human Rights Law and Practice, London Conference, 2000
Jennings, R.Y.
'The Limits of State Jurisdiction' *Nordisk Tidsskrift for International ret og Jus Gentium* Vol. 32 (1962)

Joyner, Christopher C.
'Arresting Impunity: The Case for Universal Jurisdiction in Bringing War Criminals to Accountability' *Law and Contemporary Problems* Vol. 59 No. 4 (Autumn 1996)
Joyner, Christopher C.
'Redressing Impunity for Human Rights Violations: The Universal Declaration and the Search for Accountability' *Denver Journal of International Law and Policy* Vol. 26 (Summer, 1998)
Joyner, Christopher C., and Bassiouni, M. Cherif (eds)
'Reining in Impunity for International Crimes and Serious Violations of Fundamental Human Rights : Proceedings of the Siracusa Conference 17-21 September 1998', (Association Internationale de Droit Pénal), *Nouvelles Études Pénales* (1998)
Kamminga, Menno T.
'Lessons Learned from the Exercise of Universal Jurisdiction in Respect of Gross Human Rights Offenses' *Human Rights Quarterly* Vol. 23 No. 4 (November 2001)
Kissinger, Henry
'The Pitfalls of Universal Jurisdiction' *Foreign Affairs* 80 (July/August 2001)
Kittichaisaree, Kriangsak
International Criminal Law (Oxford University Press, 2001)
Köchler, Hans
Global Justice or Global Revenge? International Criminal Justice at the Crossroads (Springer-Verlag Wien, 2003)
Kritz, Neil J.
'Coming to Terms with Atrocities: A Review of Accountability Mechanisms for Mass Violations of Human Rights' *Law and Contemporary Problems* Vol. 59 No. 4 (Autumn 1996)
Macedo, Stephen
Universal Jurisdiction: National Courts and the Prosecution of Serious Crimes Under International Law (University of Pennsylvania Press, 2004)
Mann, F.A.
'The Doctrine of Jurisdiction in International Law' *Recueil des Cours* Tome 111 (1964-I)
McKay, Fiona
'Universal Jurisdiction in Europe: Criminal prosecutions in Europe since 1990 for war crimes, crimes against humanity, torture and genocide', obtainable at http://www.redress.org/unijeur.html
Meron, Theodor
'International Criminalization of Internal Atrocities' *American Journal of International Law* Vol. 89 (1995)
Meron, Theodor
'The Humanization of Humanitarian Law' *American Journal of International Law* Vol. 94 No. 2 (April, 2000)
Morris, Madeline H.
'International Guidelines Against Impunity: Facilitating Accountability' *Law and Contemporary Problems* Vol. 59 No. 4 (Autumn 1996)

Osofsky, Hary M.
'Domesticating International Criminal Law: Bringing Human Rights Violators to Justice' *Yale Law Journal* Vol.107 No.1 (Oct. 1997)
Pejic, Jelena
'Accountability for International Crimes: From conjecture to reality' *International Review of the Red Cross* Vol. 84 No. 845 (March 2002)
Princeton Project on Universal Jurisdiction
The Princeton Principles on Universal Jurisdiction (Program in Law and Public Affairs, Princeton University, 2001)
Randall, Kenneth C.
'Universal Jurisdiction Under International Law' *Texas Law Review* 66 (March 1998)
Ratner, Steven R., and Abrams, Jason S.
Accountability for Human Rights Atrocities in International Law: Beyond the Nuremberg Legacy (Oxford University Press, 2001)
Research in International Law (Under the Auspices of the Faculty of the Harvard Law School)
'Drafts of Conventions Prepared for the Codification of International Law: Draft Convention on Extradition', Supplement to the *American Journal of International Law* Vol. 29 No. 3 (1935)
Research in International Law (Under the Auspices of the Faculty of the Harvard Law School)
'Drafts of Conventions Prepared for the Codification of International Law: Jurisdiction with Respect to Crime' (hereinafter referred to as Harvard Research), Supplement to the *American Journal of International Law* Vol. 29 No.3 (1935)
Reydams, Luc
Universal Jurisdiction: International and Municipal Legal Perspectives (Oxford University Press, 2003)
Robertson, Geoffrey
Crimes Against Humanity: The struggle for Global Justice (London: Allen Lane 1999)
Roht-Arriaza, Naomi
'Pinochet Precedent and Universal Jurisdiction' *New England Law Review* 35 (Winter 2001)
Röling, B.V.A.
'The Law of War and the National Jurisdiction Since 1945' *Recueil des Cours* Tome 100 (1960-II)
Röling, B.V.A.
'Aspects of the Criminal Responsibility for Violations of the Laws of War' in Cassesse, *The New Humanitarian Law of Armed Conflict* (1979)
Sadat, Leila Nadya
'Redefining Universal Jurisdiction' *New England Law Review* Vol. 35 No. 2 (Winter 2001)
Schabas, William A.
Genocide in International Law (Cambridge University Press, 2000)

Schairer, Suzanne, and Eboe-Osuji, Chile
'The Jurisdiction to Prosecute Foreigners for Crimes Against Humanity Committed Abroad' *African Legal Aid Quarterly* January-March (2000)
Stern, Brigitte
'La compétence universelle in France: le cas des crimes commis en ex-Yougoslavie et au Rwanda' *German Yearbook of International Law* Vol. 40 (1997)
Steven, Lee A.
'Genocide and the Duty to Extradite or Prosecute: Why the United States is in Breach of Its International Obligations' *Virginia Journal of International Law* Vol. 39 (Winter 1999)
Strapatsas, Nicolaos
'Universal Jurisdiction and the International Criminal Court' *Manitoba Law Journal* Vol. 29 No. 1
Sunga, Lyal S.
Individual Responsibility in International Law for Serious Human Rights Violations (Martinus Nijhoff Publishers, 1992)
Sunga, Lyal S.
The Emerging System of International Criminal Law: Developments in Codification and Implementation (Kluwer Law International, 1997)
Tezcan, Durmus
Territorialité et Conflits de Juridictions en Droit Pénal International (L'Univesité D'Ankara, 1983)
van Boven, Theo
'Accountability for International Crimes: The Victim's Perspective' in 'Reining in Impunity for International Crimes and Serious Violations of Fundamental Human Rights' *Nouvelles Études Penales* Vol. 14 (1998)
van der Oije, Pita J.C. Schimmelpenninck
'A Surinam Crime Before a Dutch Court: Post-Colonial Injustice or Universal Jurisdiction?' *Leiden Journal of International Law* Vol. 14 No. 2 (2001)
van der Wilt, Harmen
'The Prosecution of Crimes Against Humanity: Some Reflections on the Dutch Approach' *African Legal Aid Quarterly*, January-March issue (2000)
van Elst, Richard
'Implementing Universal Jurisdiction Over Grave Breaches of the Geneva Conventions' *Leiden Journal of International Law* Vol. 13 No. 4 (2000)
Wilson, Richard J.
'Prosecuting Pinochet: International Crimes in Spanish Domestic Law' *Human Rights Quarterly* Vol. 21 No. 4 (November 1999)
Wolfrum, Rudiger
'The Decentralized Prosecution of International Offenses Through National Courts', in Yoram Dinstein and Mala Tabory eds., *War Crimes in International Law* (Martinus Nijhoff publisher, 1996)

ABOUT THE AUTHOR

Mitsue Inazumi (1971) studied criminal law and criminal justice at California State University at Long Beach (United States of America), from 1989 to 1991. She also studied at Nagoya University (Japan), from 1992 to 1994, and obtained Law Degree in 1994. She entered the graduate school at Nagoya University, majoring public international law. She received Master of Laws in 1996, and finished the doctorate course in 1999 at Nagoya University. She was a NGO delegate to the Rome Conference for the establishment of the International Criminal Court in July 1998.

Since 1999, she is Associate Professor of public international law at Kanazawa University, Japan. While working for Kanazawa University, she conducted her research at the Netherlands Institute of Human Rights at Utrecht University as a visiting scholar from September 2001 to August 2003.

Her research focuses on the national and international criminal jurisdiction for the prosecution of gross human rights violations, and she has published many articles on the Genocide Convention, universal jurisdiction, and the ICC. She is a member of the Japanese Society of International Law, Japanese Association of World Law, and International Human Rights Law Association in Japan, and International Criminal Law Network. She obtained her Doctoral degree from Utrecht University on 2004.

SCHOOL OF HUMAN RIGHTS RESEARCH SERIES

The School of Human Rights Research is a joint effort by human rights researchers in the Netherlands. Its central research theme is the nature and meaning of international standards in the field of human rights, their application and promotion in the national legal order, their interplay with national standards, and the international supervision of such application. The School of Human Rights Research Series only includes English titles that contribute to a better understanding of the different aspects of human rights.

Published titles within the Series:

1 Brigit C.A. Toebes, *The Right to Health as a Human Right in International Law*
ISBN 90-5095-057-4

2 Ineke Boerefijn, *The Reporting Procedure under the Covenant on Civil and Political Rights. Practice and Procedures of the Human Rights Committee*
ISBN 90-5095-074-4

3 Kitty Arambulo, *Strengthening the Supervision of the International Covenant on Economic, Social and Cultural Rights. Theoretical and Procedural Aspects*
ISBN 90-5095-058-2

4 Marlies Glasius, *Foreign Policy on Human Rights. Its Influence on Indonesia under Soeharto*
ISBN 90-5095-089-2

5 Cornelis D. de Jong, *The Freedom of Thought, Conscience and Religion or Belief in the United Nations (1946-1992)*
ISBN 90-5095-137-6

6 Heleen Bosma, *Freedom of Expression in England and under the ECHR: in Search of a Common Ground. A Foundation for the Application of the Human Rights Act 1998 in English Law*
ISBN 90-5095-136-8

7 Mielle Bulterman, *Human Rights in the External Relations of the European Union*
ISBN 90-5095-164-3

8 Esther M. van den Berg, *The Influence of Domestic NGOs on Dutch Human Rights Policy. Case Studies on South Africa,Namibia, Indonesia and East Timor*
ISBN 90-5095-159-7

9 Ian Seiderman, *Hierarchy in International Law: the Human Rights Dimension*
ISBN 90-5095-165-1

10 Anna Meijknecht, *Towards International Personality: the Position of Minorities and Indigenous Peoples in International Law*
ISBN 90-5095-166-X

11 Mohamed Eltayeb, *A Human Rights Approach to Combating Religious Persecution. Cases from Pakistan, Saudi Arabia and Sudan*
ISBN 90-5095-170-8

12 Machteld Boot, *Genocide, Crimes Against Humanity, War Crimes: Nullum Crimen Sine Lege and the Subject Matter Jurisdiction of the International Criminal Court*
ISBN 90-5095-216-X

13 Corinne Packer, *Using Human Rights to Change Tradition. Traditional Practices Harmful to Women's Reproductive Health in sub-Saharan Africa*
ISBN 90-5095-226-7

14 Theo R.G. van Banning, *The Human Right to Property*
ISBN 90-5095-203-8

15 Yvonne M. Donders, *Towards a Right to Cultural Identity?*
ISBN 90-5095-238-0

16 Göran K. Sluiter, *International Criminal Adjudication and the Collection of Evidence: Obligations of States*
ISBN 90-5095-227-5

17 Nicola Jägers, *Corporate Human Rights Obligations: in Search of Accountability*
ISBN 90-5095-240-2

18 Magdalena Sepúlveda, *The Nature of the Obligations under the International Covenant on Economic, Social and Cultural Rights*
ISBN 90-5095-260-7

19 Mitsue Inazumi, *Universal Jurisdiction in Modern International Law: Expansion of National Jurisdiction for Prosecuting Serious Crimes under International Law*
ISBN 90-5095-366-2

www.ingramcontent.com/pod-product-compliance
Ingram Content Group UK Ltd.
Pitfield, Milton Keynes, MK11 3LW, UK
UKHW051921100926
8556IPUK00021B/1305

9 789050 953665